KEN
SCHMIDT

MAKE SOME NOISE

The Unconventional Road to Dominance

SIMON & SCHUSTER

New York London Toronto Sydney New Delhi

Simon & Schuster
1230 Avenue of the Americas
New York, NY 10020

First Simon & Schuster hardcover edition November 2018

SIMON & SCHUSTER and colophon are registered
trademarks of Simon & Schuster, Inc.

For information about special discounts for bulk purchases,
please contact Simon & Schuster Special Sales at 1-866-506-1949
or business@simonandschuster.com.

The Simon & Schuster Speakers Bureau can bring authors to
your live event. For more information or to book an event
contact the Simon & Schuster Speakers Bureau at 1-866-248-3049
or visit our website at www.simonspeakers.com.

Interior design by Lewelin Polanco

Manufactured in the United States of America

1   3   5   7   9   10   8   6   4   2

Library of Congress Cataloging-in-Publication Data has been applied for.

ISBN 978-1-5011-5561-1
ISBN 978-1-5011-5563-5 (ebook)

Contents

Introduction

Don't you just love it when great lessons come from unexpected sources (he purposely asked somebody who just started reading a business book with a guy on a motorcycle on its cover)?

And that reminds me . . .

Back in the early 1990s, while I was still drawing paychecks as Harley-Davidson's communications director, I rode a brand-spanking-new, beautifully tricked-out Harley one hundred miles straight south from our headquarters in Milwaukee and directly into a Chicago luxury hotel's ballroom—talk about "making an entrance"—where a group of suit-wearing financial analysts presented me with an award. I smirked a bit when I read the plaque, which said something about "Excellence in Financial Communication," because I knew if they'd had more room, they'd have preferred it to reflect the real reason I was being feted and read, "Excellence in Turning Us On to Harley-Davidson Before Its Stock Price Quadrupled in Two Years" (helpful hint: everybody loves whatever it is you do when you're making them rich).

Man, what a time that was. We were basking in the glow of a cellar-to-penthouse, against-all-odds turnaround at Harley-Davidson that made us the unlikely darlings not just of the motorcycle and investment worlds, but the even more rarified worlds of culture, fashion, media, and—gulp—celebrity. Not too shabby for a company that, only a few years earlier, the world pretty much loathed. You think the doormen at that hotel would've let me blast through their main entrance back then? Hell no, they'd have called the cops. Your mom, trust me, disliked everything about Harley people.

Thing is, we weren't just hot, we were on fire, with long waiting lists of would-be riders willing to pay thousands of dollars more than our already high sticker prices to buy our sold-out bikes. We had politicians—up to and including the president—praising us and posing with our bikes for street cred, the biggest rock and country music stars touring our factories and hanging out with us, supermodels wearing our clothes, *People*-type magazine covers featuring A-listers and their bikes (I'm still shaking my head in disbelief over that), and reporters from around the world lighting up our phone lines, trying to figure out where Milwaukee is and what the heck we were doing there that was creating such a huge buzz.

All the while and as crass as it sounds, it was raining cash at Harley headquarters and on long-suffering Harley dealers. The glory and money were godsends after a decades-long drought marked by undesired products, horrendous image problems (see mom), brinkmanship survival, and near financial ruin in the fiercely competitive global motorcycle market. Suffice to say we were enjoying it.

When Elon Musk invents a time machine, I'm going to go back and re-live those glorious days and I'm sure everyone else involved in making this incredible success a reality will be booking passage, too. It'll be nice to see everyone thin, hairy, and giddy again.

But anyway.

As I stood there next to the bike, awkwardly holding the award and shaking the presenter's hand for the obligatory grip-and-grin photo op, an analyst asked me precisely the kind of obvious question one of his firm's clients, a professional investor—the kind who buys shares of stock in quantities needing two commas—would ask: "Who's the biggest threat to Harley's business?" Otherwise asked as "Who's Harley's toughest competitor?" A gift-wrapped, softball of a question if ever there was one.

No matter what you do for a living and how long you've been doing it, if you'd been in my shoes, black leather jacket, and (marginally cool) Harley tie that night, you probably could've answered that, right? Or at least taken a good-enough whack at it to sound convincing. A solid, one-word answer, name-checking a world-famous bike manufacturer would get you back to slurping your congratulatory cocktail and communicating like an award winner while analysts took turns posing on the bike and asking you if they look like *Easy Rider.*

Well, not so fast, friend. See, I never miss an opportunity to make some noise, the meaning of which you'll learn soon enough, in front of highly influential people. So obvious, lame answers to predictable questions just aren't in my repertoire. Investment recommendations issued by this guy's firm, and the others represented in the room, reached the eyes and ears of the world's biggest investors each week, all of whom could potentially become major Harley share owners. Because creating demand for said shares falls under my area of responsibility—and explains why I rode through Chicago rush-hour traffic in the first place—my mission that night was to increase the likelihood of these analysts making that happen. And at that moment, the window of opportunity couldn't be open much wider.

Now knowing the stakes, do you think you could answer that simple question in a way that would pique interest, be memorable and story-worthy enough to get repeated and thus achieve your goal of fueling more interest and demand for your employer's offerings? And at the same time, would your response build your employer's reputation for being staffed by likable, go-to people and great company ambassadors, worth spending more time with and listening to? And would it boost your personal reputation? Or would you just take the easy way out and answer the question the way the would-be Easy Riders (in Brooks Brothers and Ann Taylor) expected?

If you own, manage, or work for a business—of any size—you have opportunities like this every day to make some beautiful noise and stand out from your competitors. How you handle them says everything about your business and how you view your market and your place in it. It also says a lot about you, personally. The same goes for everybody working at your business, regardless of job title or responsibility. *Everybody.*

If you want to remove any doubts as to how you'd perform under such typical circumstances, I'm going to give you a chance to see how fast and thorough you are on your feet in the first chapter. I'll even put some pressure on you to make it more challenging and fun.

That little adventure will open your eyes a bit, but not nearly as wide as they'll get at the chapter's opening. (Okay, that's two obvious foreshadowing ploys in the last three sentences to encourage you to keep reading. I hope they work.)

So look. This is how I see it. All things considered, businesses are either dominators or also-rans. If you have to think about which yours is, I'm afraid it's the latter. But at least you've got plenty of company.

Also-rans—that's pretty much everybody—work hard and are good, perhaps even great, at whatever it is they do. Problem is, they go to war against competitors that do pretty much the same stuff they do, *if not the exact same stuff they do,* just as well. So their markets are predictable battlegrounds of look-alike, act-alike businesses that potential customers and other important publics see as equals.

In case you somehow missed them, the damning words in that last sentence are "predictable," "look-alike, act-alike," and "see as equals."

This means potential customers know they can buy from any of these businesses and that they'll be satisfied with their purchase. So, as anyone who's ever bought anything knows, they'll most likely opt to buy from whoever has the lowest price or is the most convenient, without giving it any thought. That's the punishment also-rans get for being also-rans.

Did I just describe your business and your market?

Also-rans haven't made "competing to dominate," let alone "improving competitiveness," the top priority of their businesses and rarely even consider or discuss what it means to compete, because they wrongly view "going to market" and "competing" as the same thing. That's weird, isn't it? I hope you find it as telling as I do that something as important as competitiveness is misunderstood or taken for granted in most businesses while everything else is studied, sliced, diced, measured, crunched, and manipulated out the wazoo.

Also-rans don't know why making a different noise than competitors is vital to their survival, so they just keep doing what they do: busting their butts to further streamline their processes while matching their competitors' moves tit-for-tat, chasing flavor-of-the-month business improvement trends, blending into the background, cutting prices to generate demand, and watching their margins shrink. Their frustration comes from knowing they're capable of better but—ahem—not knowing how to do that.

This helps explain some of the easiest ways to spot also-rans. They're the businesses that focus their collective energies on promoting their products and services using outmoded clichés like "quality" (you read that correctly) and "customer experience." As if that will make those products and services—and the people behind them—more attractive. As if that's all they have to offer. As if all of their competitors aren't saying that stuff, too. They then back up their predictable go-to-market approaches with indecipherable, nonmemorable product specs and jargony, secret-handshake language. Or data. You see this everywhere. Then look away.

Everything also-rans do looks, sounds, and feels just like what their competitors do. They use the same imagery and, hell, even the same colors in their go-to-market stuff. Their websites and brochures look interchange-able. Ditto their ads. They answer their phones or greet you the same way ("Can I help you?" How original.) You know what I'm talking about, right?

Also-rans live for sales and feel they have no option but to give in to market forces, swallow their pride, and make horrible sell-by-price deci-sions, far against their better judgment, to get them. You can practically hear them saying, "Our competitors are doing this, so we have to, too."

But oh, man, they pay for their complicit behavior. When also-rans are indistinguishable from their competitors and play the price game, they in turn have no choice but to become more efficient to lower their operating expenses and wring out some profit, right? As a consequence, they find themselves stuck in a fast-spinning, vicious cycle of sell low/reduce costs horrors that focuses all of their energies on the internal processes of their businesses when they should be focusing outward, where their customers, prospects, and other important publics are. Meanwhile, the nagging fear that those efficiencies will eventually max out keeps their leaders from sleeping well.

Can you think of any industry where this monkey-see, monkey-do, sell-on-price-then-improve-efficiencies-to-make-a-buck behavior isn't seen as business as usual?

As if all of this isn't horrendous enough for also-ran businesses, they're also plagued by difficulty in attracting and retaining employees, which cre-ates yet another vicious cycle of hiring/training/rehiring/training that's a major pain in the exhaust pipe, a huge drain on finances, and a fast-spreading cancer that weakens workplace cultures. It's tough to build a solid, commit-ted team when the players keep changing, isn't it? Or when there aren't enough talented candidates to fill the holes. This, too, is running unchecked across every industry, as is falsely vilifying millennials—"All they want to do is text, take selfies, and goof off!"—as the cause.

Ask owners or leaders of also-ran businesses how they feel about these problems and the impact they're having on every internal and external facet of their operations and their unanimous response is always "Well, it's just not good." And they're selling it short because it's a helluva lot worse than not good, which explains why they sighed so heavily and stared at their shoes while saying it. Then they shrug and ask, "Ah, but what can we do?" as if waiting for agreement that their hands are tied.

Well, I'm not in agreement with that and you shouldn't be, either. Not anymore.

See, also-rans don't have any acceptable excuses for being also-rans.

They can choose—because it's a choice—to become dominators. And they can count on me to show them how.

Dominators (cue blasting-trumpet salute) are the businesses making all the beautiful noise—the known, respected, sought-after, most liked, and highly successful champions of their industries and markets. The ones with fiercely loyal, tattoo-worthy supporters and customers who not only make repeat purchases from them, but advocate for them and bring them new customers and supporters. Even though they make, do, and/or sell the same stuff as those they compete against, dominators are noticeably and memorably different than they are. You can see it in the way they go to market and the things they do. You can hear it in the language they use. And you can feel it, because what they're doing pleases you.

Dominators crush also-rans and they do it on purpose. Whether they're small mom-and-pops or major conglomerates, B2C, B2B, or some oddball hybrid in between, and no matter what their businesses do—even if it's the dullest, nonsexiest, and even weirdest stuff you can possibly imagine—their leaders put "competing to dominate" above everything else in their business strategy. It's their top priority. It's why their businesses *exist*. And, not at all coincidentally, why they do so well.

Dominators have studied how their commoditized competitors go to market, said, "We're not going to be anything like them," and then brilliantly positioned, or repositioned, their businesses to be noticeably, meaningfully, and memorably different from them and to take advantage of their weaknesses. (And yes, I find it disconcerting that I just wrote a sentence lauding doing things so basic and vital that they should be viewed as givens. But there it is.)

The power source that drives dominators' businesses and keeps them from blending in with others in their market isn't awesome products and services (because they're typically similar to their competitors' offerings) or even great marketing. It's a unified, committed working culture that's hell-bent on supporting leadership and making their businesses more attractive by backing up their companies' positioning with specific actions, behaviors, and language that bring it to life. Even when employees are paid the same wages competitors are paying. You'll see what I mean and that this is very doable soon enough.

And I've saved the best for last. This one's so cool that I've pretty much built my career on it. It's my secret weapon that would-be dominators I work with say they'd never heard of until I enlightened them: Dominators know how to leverage basic drivers of human behavior for competitive advantage and do so in ways that attract and delight those they serve and hope to serve. That includes employees (see last paragraph). They know that delighted people tend to be loyal people and that delighted, loyal people tend to be very vocal people, so their important publics advocate for them, boost their reputations, and bring them new important publics. Anyone can do this.

Just as also-rans have chosen, intentionally or not, to run in place, acquiesce to their market's competitive pressure to conform, blend in, be predictable, and thus commoditize their businesses, dominators have chosen to make some noise, aggressively move into the passing lane, and blow past them. Why would anyone choose to be an underperformer? Who wouldn't want, at the very least, their customers to be loyal? And to bring them new customers? Are those you serve doing that for you? Are your employees bringing you new hires? Are your vendor/partners talking you up? How about your bankers or investors? Your local elected officials and other influentials? Media serving your industry and marketplace? I know you want them to.

How do your customers and other important publics—potential customers, employees, vendors, investors, partners, media, and people living in the communities where you operate—describe your business? Is your business doing anything for them that they feel is worthy of telling others about? Do they have any stories to tell about you? Look, there's not a business or industry on the planet that has customers who don't know and speak to potential customers. Not one.

Now let's talk about your favorite person for a sec. You. I'm a firm believer that all things business reflect all things human, so the same dynamics you've just read about are also present in our personal lives. People can choose to be dominators—the ones who make noise, are liked, get chosen to lead and do so extraordinarily well, the ones who get promoted over others who look better on paper, the ones who have the fattest wallets, and the ones others rely on and rally behind. Who'd choose to be a passed over, misunderstood, underachieving, face-in-the-crowd also-ran when they could have all of this?

I know you want your business to make noise and be a dominator, just as surely as I know you want the same for yourself. That's why we're here.

My job—and I take great pride in being damn good at it—is making businesses and people dominant. Well, actually, that's just a third of my job. The rest of it involves going on epic motorcycle adventures and telling stories about those adventures that make the first part of the job easier and way more effective. I'm guessing you didn't know that motorcycles and motorcyclists are the greatest teaching tools on the planet, right? If not, trust me, in a few minutes, you'll be convinced. Even if you, god forbid, don't like bikes.

I've been crazy busy for the last twenty-plus years since leaving Harley-Davidson and striking out on my own and, if my ever-expanding backlog of emails and voice mails is any indication, I'm going to stay that way. The engines powering me are the success I had at Harley, my extraordinary access to business leaders, my passion for having more fun than working people are supposed to have, and my ability to share what I've seen and learned in ways that get underperforming people and businesses moving forward. You'll see.

It was my job and pleasure at Harley-Davidson to reposition the nearly dead business, improve its blackened reputation, and attract customers, investors, and influential supporters like major media. Accomplishing that meant playing a highly visible role in one of the most celebrated, studied, and unlikely turnarounds in corporate history, which, even I have to admit, is pretty damn cool.

The Harley you've come to know by its now-ubiquitous presence and unmistakable roar—to say nothing of its winner-and-still-heavyweight-champion role in business school case studies—isn't just the most powerful player in the motorcycle industry, it's one of the most powerful players in *all industry*, with the most fiercely loyal customers in the universe. Quick: Name a company logo tattooed onto customer bodies other than Harley-Davidson's. As any of the now thousands of people who make their living in the Harley world say with pride, there's a little of my sweat mixed in that blood and ink. And a million great stories.

Success opens doors, but the kind of massive, against-all-odds success we created at Harley-Davidson blew them right off their hinges. Business leaders who hoped to capture some of that Harley black magic for themselves started inviting me in for show-and-tell. And my business life's second act was defined.

I've been extremely fortunate to have worked, as an advisor or meeting speaker, with over a thousand companies from nearly every industry imaginable: household-name brands, former Wall Street darlings, big- and small-time metal benders, software developers, clothing, food and consumer products manufacturers, health-care providers, mom-and-pop plumbing companies, financial services firms, and the people who made the cell phone in your pocket and the buttons on your shirt. In short, everybody doing everything. They brought me in because of my track record and my outspoken candor. And they gave me something more than money in return: an all-access pass behind all those executive doors.

This ever-deepening well of experience enables me to explain why products, services, and the businesses and (befuddled) workers behind them are underperforming, and I've learned to spot undiscovered competitive problems before they grow malignant. I know what bedevils businesses and what makes them outshine competitors because I can see how every new problem fits into a pattern of the ones I've helped solve before. Not to boast, but there aren't many people who can say that. (Okay. That was a boast. Sue me.)

My tales of on- and off-bike adventures, some of which you're about to read? They're not just a fun little bonus, they're a very important element of what I do and why it works. Learning while being entertained is the best learning—ask any preschool teacher—because it helps us personalize, visualize, and remember what we're being taught. You'll even *hear* it. If CEOs of some of the largest businesses in the world have benefited from my approach and had fun at the same time, so, too, shall you. I promise.

I know you're ready to climb on board and get to work. But we can't fire up our motors and take off down the road to dominance yet because, remember, we've got to get back to that award reception, where there's a roomful of people waiting and a question to be answered.

Know this: As a card-carrying dominator, I'd never allow myself to speak with anyone important to me or my business—and this room is packed with people matching that description—without first asking myself, "What do I want these people to remember and repeat?" (R&R. An important habit to develop that we'll dig into later.) My reason is simple: I may only get one shot at this and if I'm so predictable, confusing, jargony, or, God forbid, dull, that people I'm speaking with can't remember what I just told them, that means I didn't tell them anything. So they'll have nothing to repeat that will make noise on my employer's, or my, behalf.

There's no way I'm going to let that happen and blow this opportunity.

The safe answer to that financial guy's "Who's your biggest threat?" question would've been the one you—and they—were thinking: the largest company in the motorcycle industry, the eight-hundred-pound gorilla whose name rhymes with "Rhonda." Well, that kind of answer doesn't cut it with me and it won't with you by the time we finish up here. Which is why I kick-started a round of way more intensive questions and some powerfully differentiating, easily visualized, easily remembered, story-worthy answers when

I said, "The biggest threat to Harley's business isn't any of those famous, household-name companies [you'll see later why I avoid naming names whenever possible] from Japan and Europe that manufacture spectacular motorcycles and have much deeper pockets than Harley has."

The fuse was lit, so I dropped the bomb and made some noise: "Nope. Harley's toughest competitor is golf."

As they awaited the punch line for what they'd figured had to be a (lame) joke, I explained, "Look, we gladly go toe-to-toe with all bike manufacturers and enjoy poaching customers from them because we know them and their predictable, look-alike competitive approaches very well. But we have to look bigger picture to see where we fit—or don't fit—into the lives of people we serve and hope to serve because we compete against a helluva more than just the companies in our industry that are vying for their attention."

Then I explained that the golf industry and Harley-Davidson both want the same things: your weekend time, your weekend money, and that one thing you're so passionate about that you'll continue to invest and stay active in it over the course of your lifetime. Well, then as now, too many people choose golf—a hideous time dump that more often than not inspires disappointment and misery, requires years of expensive participation in order to be "average," and makes friends curse each other under their breath—as that outlet for their weekend time, money, and passion.

How can that possibly compare to the freedom of riding Harleys, an always glorious and rewarding lifestyle that never fails to inspire joy and is universally recognized as supercool? And that challenges, thrills, and relaxes you at the same time, makes you the envy of others, and fosters the kind of camaraderie everyone seeks but rarely finds? "Besides," I said, "I don't see waiting lists to buy golf clubs and I've yet to see a Pebble Beach tattoo." With all due respect, of course.

Look, these guys were in financial services, so golf was their second religion (after making gobs of money with other people's money, of course). Who doesn't know that? Suffice to say they were a bit startled by my lighthearted blasphemy, which was precisely my intent. But don't forget, they also spend their days talking to highly influential investment people and making recommendations. They're also the first people major media call when they need quotes about specific businesses. I needed these guys speaking well of us and recommending us, because Harley's just one of more than eight thousand publicly owned companies competing in securities markets. So I had to give them something new and memorable to talk about with others who'd also remember and talk about it.

They already had our numbers, charts, and graphs, so now they had a few story-worthy nuggets about our confidence, demand for our bikes, our approach, and the fierce loyalty of our customers, to add texture and meaning to them. They had a reason to make noise. And believe me, they did. I told them they should include photos of themselves on the bike in their reports and cover letters, if for no other reason than to prompt immediate reactions from people they sent them to, and before the night was over nearly every one of them had posed for pictures. (Am I good or what?)

These aren't little things, they're big things. Big things that keep building on each other and get people conditioned to the idea of standing out and acting like a dominator. But they're just the beginning.

In recent years, as financial services businesses have discovered their competitive shortcomings, they've become a rapidly growing part of my business. I've been called in to work with many of them and have spoken at dozens of their industry events. What's really great about this is the fact that I've been approached by people who were at that Chicago awards reception and every time this happens, they ask if I remember that night and if I remember telling the story about golf and the Pebble Beach tattoo. That was more than twenty-five years ago. And they haven't forgotten me, the story, the context, and the first time they ever sat on a Harley. Better, they say they've told that story countless times over the years. Some even own their own bikes now.

That's the power of noise. And it doesn't happen by accident.

And I can tell you this: If I'd been working for a company in the machine tools business, or floor tiles, dental equipment, real estate, copy machine repair, tax software, health care, asphalt, toilet paper, car parts, life insurance, or even embalming supplies, I'd have approached that Chicago meeting with the same mindset. So I'd be memorable. I'd tell them what they didn't expect to hear. I'd create demand for my business. And I'd give them something to talk about. Because I'd be upholding my employer's positioning, making noise, and kicking ass. That's. What. Dominators. Do.

If you're thinking you're ready to leave your frustrating, also-ran world in your rearview mirrors and start enjoying the view from the front of the pack, the unconventional road to dominance starts here. Trust me, it's going to be a helluva ride and you're going to love it.

Come on. Let's make some noise.

ONE

What Kind of Noise Are You Making?

Don't get too comfortable. Not yet. We've got places to go.

Before we can start discussing what it's going to take to make your business (and you) a dominator instead of an also-ran, you're going to need to get a quick, real-world read of where you stand right now and what you're up against. And I need to show you that the people most important to your professional life—like your customers, prospects, investors, fellow employees, everyone you need on your side—likely don't see you the way you hope or believe they do. So we're going to hit the road and take a short, virtual, eye-opening field trip.

The good news is, I promise this will be fun and way cooler than those god-awful excursions you remember from your school days, because—and this is the better news—rather than bouncing along in a yellow bus (see: grumpy driver, buzz-killing chaperones, irritating loudmouths, etc.) we'll be riding two-wheelers. As in motorcycles. As in see? I told you it'll be fun. And by the way, you won't be riding as my passenger; you'll be on your own bike.

Even if you've always sworn you'd never ride a motorcycle or believe yourself incapable of it, or you think your mother would kill you if she found out what we're up to, or even if you're the world's biggest wuss, please play along anyway and live a little. I guarantee nobody's going to get hurt and that you're going to get a huge kick out of your ride, remember it, and benefit from what it's about to teach you. The same goes for experienced riders. So come on. Let's go before someone chickens out.

The first part's supereasy. I want you to imagine, right now, that you're sitting on an awesome motorcycle. But there's a simple rule here: It can't be a Harley-Davidson. (I know. Bummer!) That shouldn't be a problem, though, because there are millions of great bikes out there. You're on one of them right now, so relax for a minute and soak it all in. See in your mind the wheels, fenders, gas tank, motor, handlebars, and all those shiny dials and gauges. Pretty cool, no? Now zip up your leather jacket, tighten down your helmet's chin-strap, and cinch up your gloves—we ride safe, even on imaginary bikes—because this is about to get good. By the way, that leather looks great on you. Seriously.

With your hands on the grips at the ends of the handlebars and both feet flat on the ground, lean your bike just a bit to the right and push back the kickstand with your left foot, as you would on a bicycle. There you go. It's way lighter than you thought it would be, isn't it? And supereasy to balance. Now, see that button next to your right hand grip—the throttle—that says START? That doesn't need an explanation. Push it. Woo-hoo! Listen to that engine sing! Twist the throttle a few times to savor that powerful, high-pitched howl blasting from your exhaust pipes. Woo-hoo again! Your heart's racing already and we haven't moved an inch! (Mine is, too. I love this stuff.)

Directly in front of your left foot peg (about where the pedal would be on a bicycle) is a lever; that's your gearshift. Push it down and you'll hear a satisfying "ka-chunk" as first gear engages. There it is! You're officially pregnant and there's no backing out now! Here. We. Go. Twist the throttle a bit to give her some gas, lift your feet onto your foot pegs, and . . . you're off! Hey, you're good at this! Now crank the throttle harder and feel that awesome rush of wind in your face as you accelerate, make some wide, looping turns, then race through the gears. This is what it's all about, baby! And it's about to get way better.

Follow me now. A quick turn onto this narrow back road will take us into the boonies a bit where we can take this ride up a few notches (and, remember, learn some things about your current competitive situation, in case you've already forgotten). Let's see: No traffic whatsoever? Check. Gorgeous canopy of tree limbs over the road? Check. Curvy twists in the road following a stream? Check. Beautiful horse farms and freshly cut hay you can smell as we blast past? Check and double check. I don't need to tell you how great this is because you already know.

There's not an intersection or stop sign in sight, so don't be afraid to open that throttle some more and enjoy the buzz. Go on, amigo, let it rip! That's the way! You're really moving now, laughing inside your helmet, feeling your heart working double-time in your chest; soaking in the sights, sounds, and smells; gliding through sweeping turns then onto this long, pool-table-smooth straightaway that's stretching out before us. It's gut-check time! Catch me if you can! Watch your speedometer climb as you go faster and faster and faster and

STOP!

Dream's over (for now). It's time to learn.

You have just one second to answer this question: What manufacturer's name was on the bike you just rode? One thousand one . . . Time's up. Oh, come on! You shouldn't have to think about this! But you don't know, do you? Which means you don't need to know.

Here's why: Your imaginary bike's brand name—and everything it represents—wasn't important to any part of your riding experience. So you didn't think it through that far. You just know you were riding a great bike that was doing exactly what it was supposed to be doing and having a blast. If I told you that the bike you just rode was a Kawasaki or a Honda, Suzuki, Triumph, Yamaha, or any other famous make, you'd be cool with that, because each of those companies is synonymous with fine motorcycles that nobody would be embarrassed to own.

Since you probably didn't assign your imaginary bike any differentiating visual or tonal cues, you couldn't tell the difference between what you were riding and the gazillions of other equally great bikes you've seen over your lifetime. Anyone who happened to look up from the sidewalk or heard you zoom past likely didn't know who built the bike you were on, either, because just like you, they can't tell the difference, even at a short distance (trust me, even people who make their living selling motorcycles often can't tell them apart if they can't see the logos on the fuel tanks). And they all sound identical don't they? That high-pitched engine whine— "RHEEEEEEEEE!"—that's a pleasure to the ears announces clearly, in every language on earth, "Motorcycle!" It just doesn't announce who built it.

Okay. Time for some more fun. Only this time, we're going to turn the tables a bit and take a quick virtual ride on a Harley (black T-shirt optional).

Let's see if anything changes. Again, throw your leg over, grab the bars, lower yourself into the seat, and check out the accents, gauges, and gadgets. Everything is right where it should be and familiar to you now. So zip up your jacket, lock down that helmet, and cinch those gloves because it's time to burn some gas. Stand her up, flick the kickstand back, and notice that it's just as easy to balance between your legs as your prior ride (you thought it would be a lot heavier, didn't you?). Grab your right hand grip, thumb the start button, and—whoa! Listen to that deep rumbling engine thumping to life! Ba-BOOM-Boom! Ba-BOOM-Boom! Ba-BOOM-Boom! What a completely different sound! She means business, so it's time to let her loose. *Vámonos, muchacho!* Follow me!

Kick her into gear, give her some gas, and see what she can do. The combination of that deep, throaty-sounding engine and the wind in your face is completely intoxicating, no? It's making you feel powerful—like you've become a different person. Don't deny that!

I know another great road that's as amazing as the last one, so let's get to it. Go ahead, rev that engine and let it roar, just to make sure the folks on the sidewalk know what's coming (as if they don't know). Look at them looking at you. Feels good to be noticed, doesn't it? Now imagine your mother's stunned face—oh, dear God!—if she happened to look over from her car just now and recognize you. We've got places to go, so hammer that throttle and smile as you blast past them and leave them in your dust. Don't be shy, man! See if you can catch me. Bury that throttle, watch your speedometer climb higher and higher, and

STOP! (Sorry.)

Those people on the sidewalk, still-shocked Mom and, likely, anyone else within hearing distance of you and your bike, knew precisely who built your machine without having to think about it. Or even see it. That deep, rumbling noise blasting from those exhaust pipes has been Harley's calling card around the world for well over one hundred years. But unlike the noise from all other bike makes that screams, "Motorcycle!" your bike's noise has a name attached to it. Everyone recognizes it immediately. It's distinct, powerful, memorable, and commands attention. It's a noise that makes pictures appear in your mind. It's a noise that says, "This is different than everything else."

It's the noise of a dominator.

And it metaphorically just taught you my greatest lesson about competition. Your business is like one of the bikes you just rode; it makes noise.

(The same lesson applies to you personally: You make noise, too.) What kind of noise are you making?

Of course, I'm not talking about engine noise or any mechanical sounds your company makes while doing whatever it does. Nor am I referring to any sound your business uses, like your ad jingles or any background music that plays on your website or when callers are on hold.

I'm talking about your real, bankable noise, which is made up in large part by your reputation and everything that word implies. Your noise is what the people most important to you or your business—customers, potential customers, employees, suppliers, investors, media, and people in the communities where you operate, your boss—say about you. It's what precedes you and stays behind after you've left.

Your noise is also every association, thought, and feeling your important publics have about you and everything they see and hear that reminds them of you and only you. And it's the pictures that form in their minds when they think about you or hear or see your name mentioned.

Your noise is what makes you different from businesses—and people—you're competing against who do the same things you do. It's what attracts people to you and makes them prefer you over others. Or not. It's what pads your bank account or leaves you nervous at the end of the month when the bills come due.

Your noise is either instantly identifiable, memorable, and meaningfully differentiating or it's the same buzzing drone your competitors are making, leaving you indistinguishable and one of many in a crowd, as with the first bike you rode today that nobody could identify. RHEEEEEEEEE! The bottom line is, your noise determines whether you're a dominator or a struggling also-ran. You with me so far?

Quick experiment to further prove my point: If you were to tell some friends that you just took a ride on a Honda, they'd probably light up and say, "Hey! Way to go!" But if you told the same friends that you just rode a Harley-Davidson, they'd react way differently, wouldn't they? As in, "Whoa! You?!" Or, "When you getting tattooed?" Because Harley-Davidson means something to everyone, everywhere.

Think about it: despite the obvious fact that Harley-Davidson and its competitors are all manufacturing and selling the same thing and it's very hard for nonowners, otherwise known as potential customers, to tell one company's products apart from the others (especially when their engines aren't running), everyone—you, me, and your mom included—believes

Harley-Davidson is night-and-day different than everyone else in the market. And we all believe that, even if we've had no actual experience with motorcycles, based on what we've heard others say about the company, its products, its dealers, its customers, and its approach to business. Period. You know this despite the fact that you can't recall the last time, if ever, that you saw a Harley ad or some other paid promotional tool. You just *know* this.

So let's connect the dots here: do you know how a potential customer views the players in your industry or market, your business included? I do. The same way those people on the street saw you on the non-Harley bike. They know—*everyone knows, without even having to think about it*—that just as the bike industry is full of great businesses that make, distribute, and sell great but indistinguishable products and/or services, your industry or market is, too. All they know is what they see, hear, expect, and experience from businesses just like yours that go to market and promote themselves and their look-alike products and services the same way their competitors do. You're one of many, lost in the crowd. RHEEEEEEE!

When look-alike competitors are all saying and doing the same things, potential customers—and even current ones—can't tell the players apart *and assume they don't need to.* You can think of a million examples of this (and if you can't you've never chosen a plumber . . . Realtor . . . gas station . . .). Meaning those potential customers would be content to buy from any of them. Which means nondistinguishable competitors typically struggle and, worse, resort to "low price" to generate attention. And we all know that ain't good.

So I'll ask again, now that we're on the same page: What kind of noise do you make? Is it attractive and instantly recognized as yours? Or is it a static, droning hum, indistinguishable from sound-alike competitors? What are the most important people in your life saying about you right now? What are they saying about your competitors? Is one of your current customers making beautiful noise for you by telling someone who doesn't know you yet that she should be doing business with you and telling him why? Or are you simply meeting that customer's base-level expectations, leaving her with nothing to remember and discuss?

As you're thinking about your competitive environment—the businesses and people you're competing against—you're coming to the realization that you're all pretty much interchangeable, aren't you? Just imagine how much that dynamic would change if one player in your industry or market (that'd be you, Sherlock) changed its game to make itself noticeably dissimilar from its competitors, made vocal advocates out of its important publics, and started making a different noise than the others. That competitor would clearly stand out, wouldn't it? And be more successful. And worry less.

You see—he said, stepping up onto his soapbox while patriotic-sounding music rises in the background—here's the thing about all of this that's so frustrating: These days, it's safe to generalize and say that all businesses, yours of course included, are really quite good at what they do. It takes an amazing amount of talent, creativity, and entrepreneurial drive, to say nothing of Herculean courage and saintlike patience, to run any business anywhere. It's not easy! The things we invent, design, create, manufacture, make, bake, sell, construct, service, install, and everything else we do— while running at one hundred miles per hour at all times—in the name of commerce? It's astounding what businesspeople are doing, how well they're doing it, and how much better they're doing it this year than last. We've all enjoyed the benefits of this and have learned to expect nothing less.

And look at the backbone of the business world, small businesses. When you see statistics showing that there are twenty-eight million small businesses in the United States alone, that means there are at least that number of leaders possessed of those rare gifts in the last paragraph helming them. And millions more like-minded and talented lieutenants on their leadership teams. Combined, these people are keenly focused on busting their butts to build the kind of work cultures that enable them to do that thing they do well so they can keep their doors open and their phones ringing.

With all of these tremendous positives going for these millions of businesses, though, there's one hugely uncomfortable nugget of truth that's working against the lion's share of them (music abruptly stops): They flatout don't know how to compete. I'm talking about damn near all of them, from brain surgeons to tree surgeons. From carpenters to accountants to restaurants and to farmers. From booking agents to bookstores. From machine shops to car dealers to repair shops to junkyards.

How else does one explain the utter lack of marketable differentiation between players within industries and markets? Or the fact that pretty much every time we come in contact with a business, we're satisfied with what we get but remember nothing positive about it? Or can't even remember who we did business with last week and last month? Or the simple U.S. Bureau of Labor Statistics stats that tell us that roughly half of the businesses that start this year will be dead within five years and nearly two-thirds will be gone within ten? Or that so many businesses are struggling to survive? And worried about their future? And unable to invest in new growth opportunities?

I've learned—and have yet to meet anyone who can disprove it—that what separates dominators from also-rans in every facet of every industry in the business world isn't what competitors are producing, providing, and/or selling. Or the methods used to produce, provide, and/or sell them. Or "the people" (quotes intentional) behind making that happen. No matter how great any of these might be nor how frequently this stuff gets promoted. Nor is it where business gets transacted or the prices being charged.

Dominators crush also-rans because they make the most noise in their market. Which means dominators know how to compete. Which means they:

Make it a business-wide, leadership-driven priority to ensure that they are noticeably different from their competitors—*even if they're all doing the same thing or selling an identical product or service*—in ways that customers and other important publics find attractive;

Make it a business-wide, leadership-driven priority to ensure that they are placing more visible emphasis on the human side of their business—by overtly pleasing the people upon whom they're dependent—than the product or service they sell;

Make it a business-wide, leadership-driven priority to ensure that they have more vocal advocates recommending them than their competitors do;

Make it a business-wide, leadership-driven priority to ensure that everyone working in their organization knows what to say and how to say it consistently—in all interactions with important publics and through all channels—to maximize the effectiveness of their competitive messaging, inspire advocacy, and maintain positive marketplace narrative; and

Make it a business-wide, leadership-driven priority to ensure that everyone working in their organization knows what kind of behavior to exhibit in all interactions with important publics to bring their narrative to life.

I'm sure you noticed the intentional repetition of "business-wide, leadership-driven priority." Get used to it, because the solution to becoming a dominator resides at the source of nearly all competitive problems: The top of the organization. Noise is business strategy, not some sort of function or "program" that gets delegated to staff. You'll see.

If your first instinct is to be protective of your business and say, "We're already doing a lot of those things to stand out," or "Our marketing people have this covered," or, "We're already doing a great job of explaining ourselves and our products/services to our market," or "Our products/services are great and sell themselves," or (gulp!) "Our market only cares about low price," you're far from alone. I hear this all the time. Ditto that if you're personally protective and say, "Hey, I know what to say and how to be memorable to differentiate my company . . . it's the other people working here who don't." I'm no Sigmund Freud, but I know denial when I hear it.

Here. Wanna see something cool? (Remember that question because it's the best opener in the world. No human being has ever answered it with a "no.") It's very easy for me to tell when a business of any size, whether it's a one-man shop or a ten-thousand-person global enterprise, has or hasn't made dominance a top-to-bottom, company-wide priority. Anyone can do this.

All you have to do is enter a business, or call it, or visit its website, or talk to one of its reps at a trade show, conference, or at your workplace to see if that business is making an obvious effort to dominate the also-rans in its market space. Or not. You just need to know where to look and keep your eyes and ears open.

Here's a quick illustration to show you some obvious "tells" that instantly let you know—denial be damned—you're not in the presence of a dominator or even a would-be dominator. Instead, you're in the presence of someone merely going through the motions, doing what's expected.

I go to a lot of trade shows and conferences, more than seventy a year, in every industry imaginable, so I get to see lots of businesses self-inflicting serious wounds and effectively killing any chance they have of ever making great noise and becoming dominators. You're about to pop into a trade show with me and see what this looks like. And what to look for. And, of course, what we'll be working to avoid at your business as we move forward.

I hope the sad irony won't be lost on you that the business-killing behavior you're about to witness is happening in the very place where the exact opposite is supposed to be happening. Making it even more sadly ironic is the fact that the businesses gathered here have paid a ton of money to participate in an event where most of them are actually working against themselves.

By the way, I guess it's only fair to mention now that you, personally, will serve as Exhibit A in this illustration. So you're not just at the show, you're working it from a booth, promoting your business and yourself. Look at you, all large, in charge, and trade-show-like in your khakis, comfy shoes, and a polo shirt bearing your company name. And a name tag of course.

You've got one and only one mission today: You're here to attract new customers to your business from the sea of prospects walking the floor. Naturally, your competitors are here, too, tucked into their booths, hoping to do the same thing. (You're not worried, right? Especially if you just said you've got this stuff covered.)

Look who's approaching your booth: a very important somebody who knows nothing about you or your business. Game on! We're watching you! Let's see if we can spot any competitive problems we can fix (and, perhaps, some of your personal awesomeness).

She's here! Uh-oh. Her facial expression reads noncommittal from the get-go—the typical "trade show face." (That's your first tell.) Upon recognizing that she's not immediately impressed by your "How ya' doin'?" opener and whatever she's seeing in your booth, nor making eye contact with you (tell), what should be a great opportunity for you is already slipping away. And she's only been here a few seconds. (Step it up, amigo! There's still time! We're counting on you!)

So you ask a few more obvious questions while she's looking over your display like, "Can I help you find something?" or "How familiar are you with . . . ?" (whatever it is you sell or represent) that she responds to with no conviction whatsoever (two big tells). Now you're struggling a bit and rubbing your hands together because you know the stakes are high, you want to make a powerful impression, and you don't want this person to think your business is predictable, an also-ran, or, God forbid, boring. And because you want her to like you and want to spend more time with you before sliding your brochures into her bag and moving on to meet your competitors, each of whom wants the same thing: to be the one she prefers.

Mostly, though, you're struggling because you don't have some great, supercool things to say—even though, dammit, you *know* you're supposed to and thought you did—that would make her feel supercomfortable in your presence and glide off your tongue to confidently say who you are, what you do, who you do it for, and why people should choose you over everyone else.

You know, stuff she's *never heard in a business conversation before* that would pull her toward you, engage and delight her, make her curious to hear more, and spark a deeper conversation. Stuff she'd remember and repeat.

So you do what most people in this situation do and fire off a quick, "Okay. Here's what we do" elevator-type speech (tell) that, for the umpteenth time, feels okay to you, but fails to trigger much of a reaction because it's devoid of anything distinctive and sounds like something she's heard many times before. (This is a trade show, remember? She's heard those same "What we do is . . . " lines *minutes* ago from someone else. And another person before that.) And that's when things take a turn for the worse. You realize you're about out of fuel . . . and the silent pause is *killing* you . . . your important somebody isn't saying a word (still a tell) . . . so your mind starts racing and . . . that's when you deliver your most dangerous blow.

Now you're thinking and talking at the same time, an uber-risky maneuver everyone knows is a pileup waiting to happen, but you feel emboldened by your ability to keep your lips moving. Your flailing arms shake loose a torrent of buzzwords, business-speak, and industry jargon (tell times three) that sound impressive to you but disappear into the ether when they fail to spark a reaction (because, *again*, she's heard this same gobbledygook from others today). The silent pause returns.

Realizing it's now or never, you go for broke, put on your imaginary Evel Knievel cape, gun the engine on your stunt bike, and start blasting toward the launch ramp into glory by describing who you aren't (tell)—and name-checking competitors (tell)—rather than who you are, to distance yourself from the pack. Because you're different than they are, right?

You're also roadkill. And it took less than a minute to lose control, skid, flop over the end of your launch ramp, and finish your Knievel show in a mangled heap. Your unimpressed important somebody witnessed the whole thing, won't forget it, and is starting to shuffle about uncomfortably (tell) while looking over your shoulder for an escape route. Even though you're essentially lifeless now, you somehow manage to cough up a few lines about your "commitment to quality" (tell) and your "unique customer-first philosophy" (tell). Those are death rattles! And all they earned you was a polite nod and a "see ya later" (tell). She didn't even drop her business card in your fish bowl (tell), hoping to win the free dinner at Texas Roadhouse (love those fried pickles!) you're raffling.

Off she goes just in time for the next prospect to waltz in. The show begins anew.

Oh come on, man! What just happened here?! And how many more times today is this going to happen? You know who you are, what you do, who you do it for, and why people should prefer you over others inside out and backward. You live and breathe this stuff every day; it's in your DNA. You're not just good at it, you're very good at it and you love it. But she doesn't know that, does she?

Somehow the right words—and the supporting visible emotions and actions that would convey them and trigger positive reactions—didn't seem to come when you needed them the most. So you played it safe for a while. Then when you noticed you weren't getting anywhere, you tried way too hard, went places you shouldn't have and crash-landed. Without even being aware you were doing it!

Just about everybody handles the situation you just lived through the same way, so don't feel bad. And I'm sure it was familiar to you because you've been on the receiving end of blown attempts like this many times over the course of your life at trade shows, places of business, or even at your kitchen table (ever sit across from a window salesperson?). But I hope you see how easy it is—it's practically standard operating procedure in the corporate world—to kill any chance of building preference and demand for who you are and what you do. And to connect the dots to larger competitive issues.

The exposed tells raise some serious (I might say obvious) questions about your competitiveness, like:

> Why did everything about your booth or display area—and your presence therein—look familiar and predictable to your visitor, as evidenced by her "trade show face"?

> How did you not realize the danger of putting yourself in front of people your business needs to impress when you're ill-prepared, unrehearsed, and not primed to kick some major ass?

> Why did your business permit that to happen?

> "How ya' doin'?" Seriously? That's your opener to the person who could potentially become the biggest customer you've ever had? That's as bad as "Can I help you?" (I already threw you a bone: "Wanna see something cool?" works 100 percent of the time).

How can you describe your business with words that instantly engage listeners, are memorably different, distance you from competitors who do the same things you do, and make those listeners want to hear and learn more?

How can you do that if your business is among the millions out there that are "dull," "unsexy," or "not cool"? And if you sell or do things that are "invisible" and/or only appeal to a very small, highly specialized market segment?

How can you describe your passion for what you do in ways that are sincere and believable—and use it as a contagious, powerful differentiation tool—when passion's such an intangible, personal thing that even Shakespeare and the Beatles struggled to connect with it?

What, in the name of every god in the universe, are you doing mentioning—and, thus endorsing—your competitors when the conversation is supposed to be about you?

If *you're* having trouble impressing that important somebody you just met, what are your fellow employees—sales staff, customer service reps, field people, the other studs working the booth, the person answering your phone, new hires—saying and doing when they're in that situation every day, in front of the people your business most needs to turn on? Do the math! That's a lot of potential crash-landings!

What do the other vehicles that carry your go-to-market messages when they can't be delivered personally—stuff like your website, ads, show booth signage, go-to-market materials, and social media posts—say? The math just got a lot harder!

That's a lot of big, important stuff to think about (and please tell me you're thinking about them), but I'm not done yet, because there are even bigger questions that best all of those, some of which you've already been tipped to and were perhaps top of mind as you read the last few pages:

What must your organization do to develop and implement a dominance strategy to maximize the probability that every facet of your go-to-market approach, and every interaction with important publics, are instantly recognized as different from competitors who are essentially selling the same thing you're selling?;

What must your organization do to develop the language needed to communicate your strategic differences and distance your business from your competitors in ways that customers, potential customers, and all other important publics find appealing and—equally important—will repeat?;

What must your leadership do to ensure this language becomes embedded in your entire organization's DNA and gets routinely and consistently used in all critical communications? And;

What must your leadership do to ensure your entire organization "lives" this language and your dominance strategy by exhibiting behavior that brings it to life in ways that important publics notice immediately, find attractive, and remember?

I know, I know. That's a lot of stuff to process. But get this: the most crucial question of all from our trade show adventure couldn't be more obvious, yet you probably overlooked it, even though you've been tipped to it several times already. It's the one that ultimately determines your competitiveness, makes or breaks your business, and takes us straight back to that important somebody you just flopped in front of:

What is she going to say about you?

Boom! That's your noise! Remember what I said earlier: Contrary to what most of us have been led to believe, competitive advantage doesn't come from what you make, do, or sell, how well you do those things and the people and processes involved in doing them. It can't. **Competitive advantage lies in what the people who are most important to your business say about your business. Period.** There is no industry on earth where this doesn't apply. That's why making noise is so important!

Let's say that very important somebody at the trade show today is a potential customer (because she is, right?) and a group of other potential customers she'll meet at the show's cocktail party tonight asks her about you or if she met anyone (and/or any business) today who impressed her—a conversation that happens multiple times at *every* show. This should have been a slam dunk for you, but I'd bet the odds of her being a passionate advocate for you and sending these people your way are slim to none, wouldn't you? She has to say *something*, doesn't she? What's it going to be? (Hint: She won't mention your "commitment to quality" statement.)

Or what if she's a reporter writing a big story for the main publication your target market reads and was simply looking for something or someone noteworthy to write about and provide some great sound bites? Since you didn't make it past, "How ya' doin?" by saying anything worthwhile, she'll end up writing about one of your competitors. So without even realizing it, you just blew a golden opportunity to tell your story to a huge audience of prospects. (I've been that reporter so I know of what I speak.)

Or what if she's one of those people who seem to know everyone important in your industry? Or in the local marketplace you serve? Like your potential partners, suppliers, bankers, bloggers, social media mavens (like those trade show tweeters who can't stop tweeting and if you don't know what I'm talking about, you haven't been to a show recently #relentless), recruiters . . . you name it? Every industry has lots of influential people like this you need to have on your side.

Now you see why I said competitive advantage lies in what the people who are most important to your business say about your business. So, obviously, that means it's vital that they're saying the right things. Which means it's *more vital that you're saying the right things.* That gal at the trade show was a live, in-the-flesh, honest-to-God "gimme." You were in a rare and valuable position to have tremendous influence on what she'll remember about your business (and you), what she'll say about it to others, and how she'll say it. She gave you every chance in the world. If you'd played your cards right, she'd be making noise for you by repeating what you told her, building your reputation the way you want it built, and referring you to others. Pretty simple, no?

It doesn't take much reflecting to realize how easy and common it is to overlook opportunities like this. Or to think back on how many of these your business has failed to capitalize on.

The bottom line is you can't be a dominator if your customers and other important publics can't tell you apart from your competitors, aren't advocating for you, and aren't bringing you new customers. Tattoo that onto your brain so you don't forget it.

I'll ask this question of you again and again to ensure that it's always on your mind: What kind of noise are you making?

I learned about the competitive power of noise—and how to harness it and the destruction caused by lack thereof—in the same place where I learned many of my most profound lessons about life, business, and how the world works: the global motorcycle market. You're going to do the same, because you'll see direct parallels to your own market. And your own life.

Here. I'll show you. Were you to take a quick look into it, you'd see that the bike market isn't just fiercely competitive, it's also commoditized, just like yours. That's right: even with their mind-blowing innovation, technical brilliance, and cool factor, motorcycles are commodities. Meaning, the marketplace—prospective first-time customers, in particular—can't tell the difference between manufacturers (even with household names) and their amazing, but look-alike products. All I have to do is park a black Harley Sportster next to a black Yamaha Bolt and cover their name plates to instantly confuse people. Even people who've been riding a long time will do double takes and say those bikes are practically identical twins. So how does someone choose?

When prospective customers believe all players, products, and services within an industry are interchangeable, they tend to use lowest price (and/or convenience) as their primary purchasing criteria. So companies that aren't interested in competing, or don't know how, take the path of least resistance and "compete" with price. Sounds like your industry or market, doesn't it? Everyone who competes on price—with the very real exception of the Walmarts of the world that are specifically designed to do so and have the scale to pull it off—regrets it. It's a death trap.

Harley-Davidson, with its *fiercely* loyal and *passionately* vocal customer base attracting new customers into its ever-expanding family, stopped playing the product and price game years ago and doesn't play it now. They intentionally make a different noise and stand for things that not only resonate positively among their important publics, but *transcend* the hardware they make and sell. The company dominates its segment of the overall market and its dealers dominate their local markets because they're specifically positioned and managed to do so. Everyone you know who owns a Harley bought it because he (or, increasingly, gods be praised, she) was talked into it by friends, coworkers, or other trustworthy people. That's the power of noise and that's where you want to be. And by the time we wrap up here, you'll be well on your way there.

Teaching businesspeople the lesson that competitive dominance is powered by distinctive differentiation and vocal advocacy—noise—and sharing what's required to make that happen is the premium fuel powering every facet of a wonderful career that's taken me around the world and given me access, as you read a few minutes ago, to leaders of more than one thousand businesses, serving every conceivable industry. So it's not only taken me on a long, mind-expanding road trip that I selfishly hope will keep me up on two wheels until I'm so old I'll need three, it's rewarded me with up-close, current, first-person perspectives on how and why businesses struggle to compete when they could be dominant. It's amazing what I learn just by sitting across from big kahunas and hammering them with (often uncomfortable) questions. More so when we're out riding bikes together.

And speaking of riding together, now that you've got your first rides with me out of the way and have proven yourself road-worthy, you're officially riding along with me. That you've stayed with me this far tells me you're tired of playing the same games your competitors play and busting your butt day after day only to find the payback for all of that effort comes in shorter than you think it should. And that you want to learn how to take advantage of skills and talents you and your coworkers currently possess so you can dominate those competitors and leave them in your dust.

It also tells me you're ready to do what it takes to move forward, rather than simply talking about it and waiting for someone else to create a miracle (rebranding, anybody?) that will likely never come.

Even more positively, it tells me you're about to have a good time, because I insist on making everything I do fun. Otherwise, what's the point? And who deserves a good time more than you? There's plenty of work involved, but don't worry. I always make it priority number one to ensure that business trips with me are as educational as they are pleasurable, so it's safe to assume you're going to learn a lot and enjoy yourself as we roll along.

And while I'm on the subject, the fact that you've joined me on a business trip means that you should feel free to write off the cost of this book and any food and beverages consumed while reading it, so by all means, do as I do and go for the good stuff. If you're reading this on a plane, write off the airfare, then upgrade to first class for your next leg and write that off, too. If you're sitting poolside at a hotel, wave that waiter over, order up appropriate refreshments, and write everything off, including the room. Don't sell yourself short! If you don't treat yourself, who will? Anyway, what's the worst that could happen?

The best thing about riding with me, though (tax code know-how notwithstanding), is you'll be pleasantly surprised as I share stories you've never heard and lessons that, I promise, will change your view of how the business world works. And how you fit into it. And how you can use that knowledge for competitive advantage. Unlike the stories and descriptions you've read in, shall we say, more traditional business books that stick to the nuts and bolts of, well, business, mine take a decidedly different path. My business stories and lessons are typically disguised as motorcycle-related tales. And I've got lots of them. You already read one. And you were in it!

There's a deliberate method to such madness: My motorcycle tales are used as easy-to-visualize, easy-to-understand, and easy-to-repeat (so you can share them with others) launch points for lessons on differentiating your business, making beautiful noise, and becoming dominant. My motorcycle stories will even show you how to leverage basic drivers of human behavior for competitive advantage in ways that, I guarantee, you'll never forget and will use often. Nobody—and I mean *nobody*—ever sees this coming.

To whet your appetite, my human behavior lessons will show you how to understand and leverage basic human needs to attract people and turn them on (you've seen your last "trade show face" and uttered your last, "Can I help you?"), improve business and personal relationships, and make loyal, vocal advocates out of those you depend on. They'll also help you determine which behaviors you and your fellow employees will need to exhibit in front of your important publics to bring your differentiation to life. You'll see what I mean. And dig the hell out of it.

With motorcycle themes recurring throughout *Make Some Noise* and because Harley-Davidson is the driving passion behind my effort, I can see why you might be inclined to think this is going to be a Harley-Davidson book. Two words: It's not.

Publishers not as astute, sophisticated, and brilliant as Simon & Schuster have asked me for years to write the kind of "Harley" (quotes intentional) book that would go heavy on drama, include lots of photos of tattooed, bikini-clad women and assorted Hell's Angels types, and be devoid of any words with more than three syllables. Their false assumption being that's what it takes to sell "Harley" books. (Any quick scan of a bookstore's Discount section will yield all the evidence necessary to back me up on that. Emphasis on *"Discount section."*) Writing a book that perpetuates ridiculous stereotypes, offends good people, and sells zero copies has never interested me.

Other publishers have asked me about writing a Harley-themed "branding" book, since the company is largely recognized as a great "brand" success story. One word: ugh. I'd rather do one of those discounted tattoo/bikini books than go that route. Or be waterboarded. I'd much prefer to tell you how to make your business successful than share the intricacies of how another one, that you can't possibly replicate, did. And as you'll learn, I'm not a fan of branding in the sense most people know of it. That's putting it lightly.

With *Make Some Noise* I'm going to teach you how to become a dominant competitor in both your business and personal lives by sharing *actionable* lessons I learned helping revitalize what today is the one of the most successful market dominators in the universe—that motorcycle company mentioned five times in the last three paragraphs—as well as those gleaned from the thousand-plus businesses I've worked with or spoken to in my lifetime. And to do so in a way that anyone, from the CEO of a multinational behemoth to the owner of a one-person cake decorating business, can understand and apply.

See, the operative word here is "actionable." Some people get scared by that word, but business owners know what I'm talking about. This isn't the *Harvard Business Review* (with all due respect). You're not Intel, Amazon, or Google (ditto that respect) and you're not going to be because they beat you to it. And your customers probably aren't going to tattoo your logo onto their bodies like Harley's do. So telling you specifically how these companies do what they do wouldn't help you much, would it? You don't work in a dream world. Nor do you have bottomless bank accounts to play with like these behemoths do (but call me if you do!).

Based on the conversations I have every day with business owners, leaders, and aspiring leaders who are hungry to learn how to improve their businesses and their personal performance—and sincerely want to take action to do that—I know what *you're* hungry for. You want to:

Stop working harder than you ever have just to be an also-ran, when you'd much prefer to be a dominator.

Learn how to set your business, and yourself, apart from competitors who do the exact same things you do, sell the same products and/or services you do, and present themselves the same way you do.

Bust out of the commodity mindset that's invaded your work culture and led everyone involved to believe that low price (or convenience) is the only competitive lever in your arsenal and the only thing customers expect.

Discover how to inspire loyalty among those you serve and make them vocal advocates for your business (and you).

See what behaviors you and your fellow leaders and employees exhibit every day that turn people off and what turns them on. And even if you're like most businesspeople who've never given this a second of thought, you want to learn what every human being on the planet needs but only few find. And you want to be richly rewarded for helping them find it.

Uncover how and why "a great quality product" (or service) fails to offer you or anyone else competitive advantage and spearhead your business's evolution away from one that lives and dies on "product" (or service) to a humanized, people-first business that customers seek out, want to buy from and recommend to others, no matter what business you're in or how "boring" it is. (And for those doubters who passionately cling to a "product trumps all" philosophy, I'm going to prove you wrong and you're going to thank me for it.)

Learn how to get people to like you, follow you and want to spend more time with you;

Get to the bottom of why social media likely isn't working at your business (Hey! You just gave me a thumbs up! #Disappointed), learn how the collective failure of the business world has fueled its sad rise, and how to uncover the opportunity hidden behind it.

Find out what's required to improve your personal visibility and value, and, if you're like every other underappreciated and passed-over worker in the universe, shorten your path to promotion and higher pay.

As if all of that weren't enough, you also want to have some fun and enjoy some good stories while learning these invaluable lessons that you can put to work immediately.

Well, that's what I'm here for and what *Make Some Noise* is all about. I'm guessing you can see how hard it would be—to say nothing of bizarre—to shoehorn bikini babes and outlaw bikers into this.

But while I'm (sort of) on the subject, allow me to address the noisy, two-wheeled elephant in the room. Look, I get it that not everybody on the planet loves bikes as much as I do. Lots of folks obviously do, but way more can take them or leave them. Some, of course, don't like them at all and have nothing good to say about them. I understand and respect everyone's point of view on this.

I'll tell you straight up, though, that no matter where I am in the world, whether I'm working with household-name behemoths or mom-and-pops, CEOs or CSRs and everyone in between, I don't talk about business without talking about motorcycling, because in my world they're inseparable in ways you probably wouldn't expect and quite understandably wouldn't presume to learn from.

You'll soon see, as millions of others I've shared my passion with have, how their profound visual, aural, and emotional attributes make motorcycles powerfully potent, memorable, and fun learning tools. And why my email inbox and voice mail have been jammed for years with business leaders inviting me over for some show-and-tell. Or, when I'm having a lucky day, inviting me over for some show-and-tell followed by a long ride (those calls and emails tend to get returned first).

Uh-oh. I heard that. Do I detect a little bike-related discomfort and skepticism here? That's okay, I'm cool with it. Lots of people question whether they'll be able to see any immediate connections between motorcycling and business learning and/or believe that, because their business isn't "sexy" and "cool" like motorcycles, my lessons might not apply to them. This is most prevalent, naturally, among people who've never ridden before (which, tragically, is most people), nor spent any time with me. It doesn't last long, though.

In fact, I've seen the toughest skeptics on earth—from actuarial software developers to heart surgeons to elderly nuns who run managed care facilities—whoop with glee when I've taken them on the journey we're about to share. *They made the connection.* And so will you. I kid you not. Now picture those nuns in your mind, with leather jackets over their habits, sitting on bikes, with lit Marlboros dangling from their lips, revving their motors and looking tough. See what I mean about profound and memorable visual attributes? Now picture a balance sheet or Net Promoter Score report. I rest my case.

Even if (you think) you're not a bike person, I promise you this: You *will* learn from motorcycles, you *will remember* what you've learned from them, and you *will* use motorcycles when you teach what you've learned to others. You'll also (think of the nuns!) enjoy yourself.

There's a helpful adage I love to invoke anytime I'm discussing the whys of motorcycling—as a sport, lifestyle, and teaching aid—with those who've not experienced it. It likely goes back over a hundred years, has been inked across a gazillion black biker T-shirts, and concisely answers just about every question motorcycle people get from nonriders, including:

"Why do you ride motorcycles?"

"Aren't motorcycles dangerous?"

"Why did you spend so much money on something you can't use every day?"

"What are you doing here?"

"What the heck took you so long?"

"What makes you think I'd want to do that?" and, of course,

"What would possess a person to get a Harley logo tattoo on his forehead?"

The answer to all these is simple: "If I have to explain, you wouldn't understand."

What it means, simply, is "How can I describe how great something you've never personally experienced feels?" Any person who's ever navigated high school should see an easy parallel there.

Rather than trying to rely on words alone to describe the unexplainable—and to set the stage for everything we'll experience together here and how we'll learn from it—let me paint some pictures for you that will trigger your imagination, bring motorcycling to life for you, and ramp up your comfort level.

See (he said, arms on his lap, sitting sidesaddle on a beautiful black-and-chrome motorcycle), all of us have things in our nonwork lives that we're passionate about—sports, hobbies, literature, the arts—and our world is full of exciting, challenging, engrossing, and fun ways to enjoy them. But, unlike, say, golfers or trombonists who can handily describe their passions, motorcyclists know that every time we're up on two wheels, we're in an impossible-to-describe universe that transcends *everything*. So there just aren't any handy words we can use to describe how, when we're riding, we're intensely exhilarated yet relaxed at the same time, a paradox that shouldn't be possible. When's the last time you felt that way? And when's the last time every one of your senses was simultaneously assaulted so pleasurably that you couldn't stop grinning?

If you were to ride the same road on a motorcycle that you've just driven in your car, you'd begin to know what motorcyclists know. From behind your car's wheel, fully enclosed and temperature-controlled, you statically observe scenery (while texting, talking on the phone, and doing other stuff you have no business doing). Sure, that's okay and you're getting from Point A to B, but you're completely separated from the world and sense only what you can see. And because your mind easily drifts and you lose focus (see texting, talking, etc.) you miss a great deal of what you really should be seeing. If that isn't a great metaphor for a tragic life, well, what is?

But on a bike, you're *in* the scenery. You're not just soaking in the beauty around you, you're feeling it in the sun's heat and the cooling breeze. You're hearing the wind over the roar of your engine. And you're inhaling—even tasting—the richness of your environment, like pine trees, salty sea air, or the freshly cut hay you smelled on our virtual ride. All at the same time! Your brain synapses are firing like machine guns, keeping you hyperalert and focused on everything around you *and* in the distance, while you're fluidly shifting your body in concert with every twist and turn in the road. But here's the best part: In the midst of all of this, somehow, incredibly, your mind is completely clear. This is freedom. Beautiful, euphoric freedom. Hence the grin.

See what I mean, though, about "If I have to explain . . . "?

Luckily for everyone, riding offers a sublime gift that anyone can understand: Motorcycles, hands-down, are the world's greatest social lubricants. They always—*always*—start conversations. Which is why a CEO who's guarded in his office will spill his guts about the problems he's battling when we climb off our bikes at a scenic overpass. We simply communicate more and better when we're enjoying and challenging ourselves and sharing the experience (instead of competing with each other like, say, on a golf course or at a Battle of the Bones trombone throwdown, or sitting through long training sessions). How great is that? Watch what happens anytime two or more riders—complete strangers—share the same place, because I promise you there's going to be storytelling and laughter. And ain't that a beautiful thing?

The last time strangers at a gas station introduced themselves to you while you topped off your minivan and shared stories about what lies ahead on the road you're traveling was exactly when? Never, right? Well, that's an everyday occurrence in the riding world. Take a seat on a plane next to somebody reading a motorcycle magazine, ask, "What do you ride?" and settle in as she delights you with stories (and cell phone photos) of her adventures until the plane lands. You know how vegans and CrossFitters can't shut up? Motorcyclists are worse! Wouldn't it be awesome if your important publics were that vocal?

Motorcyclists, you'll come to appreciate on our journey together, know what everyone else hasn't figured out yet. We see and experience the world from a spectacularly different point of view. We challenge ourselves while discovering incredible beauty in places most people haven't bothered to look. But it doesn't stop there, because we share what we've found with others so they can discover it, love it, and share it, too. There are two underlying truths at play here: The pleasure of discovery never grows old and passion grows when it's shared. So discover and share we do. It's why we're here!

And speaking again of passion, I've loved motorcycles nearly all of my life, since long before they housed, clothed, and fed me (and completely overtook my garage). From imitating Evel Knievel on my twisted and bent Schwinn Typhoon bicycle to my first ride on a minibike to the disastrous teenage blunder of buying a fixer-upper Honda with an older brother (let's just say we didn't communicate well when it came to schedules and expenses; I think he still owes me some gas money), their ability to spark my imagination wouldn't let go. If you swoon at the sight of old minibikes, step-through lightweights, dirt bikes, or any other vintage bikes that make that glorious ring-ding-ding-ding sound (if you know it, you're hearing it right now), you know of what I speak. If that isn't you, there's somebody within earshot of you right now who matches this description. I was lucky enough to be alive in motorcycling's boom years of the 1960s and '70s and to fall in love with something that's never failed to love me back. Who grows tired of passion?

So imagine my glee, way back in the fall of 1985, at having hustled my way into a meeting at Harley-Davidson, the most storied motorcycle company in the universe, to discuss PR strategy. I remember striding through the massive old door at the company's red-brick headquarters building in Milwaukee, Wisconsin, as clearly as I recall seeing the diamond at my first major-league ballgame as a kid. If I have to explain . . .

Just standing in the ancient lobby, looking at the company's first motorcycle from 1903 on its (to me much-justified) pedestal, then walking well-worn halls that smelled of decades of gasoline and cigarette smoke—while seeing motorcycles or parts thereof scattered everywhere—was intoxicating. I entered the company's marketing department, which then was shoehorned into the basement of the company's ancient parts warehouse, to find it was physically so small it would fit into *my* basement. It had a dull linoleum floor, wires hanging overhead, mismatched desks, and furnishings from decades before the *Mad Men* era (in other words, the place was a shithole, which I hope I'm allowed to say here). In the bonus column, though, it was staffed by a crew so passionate and dedicated that they each did the work of at least two people. Tellingly, they laughed at their obscene workloads and the fact that they had next to no budget to work with. Great and lovable folks, all. Who cares what a place looks like when it's inhabited by wonderful people?

My buzz went from sky-high to intergalactic when I was introduced to one of the bike industry's all-time legends, Willie G. Davidson, grandson of one of the company's founders, bike designer without peer, bearded face of the company, and owner of a well-earned reputation for being impossibly cool. Upon shaking his hand, I spied a photo behind his desk of him with Evel Knievel and, well, I guess you know how I felt about that. To this day,

Harley enthusiasts from all over the globe make the pilgrimage to Harley headquarters with hopes of being able to say, "I met Willie G." Google his image some time and you'll find thousands of such personal encounters. I know of no other leader in the corporate world who's given as much of his time and his heart to customers as Willie G. And I feel sorry for any business leader who doesn't see the lesson in that.

Oddly enough, my strongest memory of that first day was how freaked out I was to see that Harley employees wore ties to work. What da?! That said a great deal about how painfully anchored the company was at that time to outdated traditions that were draining the life from it. Ties on Harley people? Unthinkable! Even those nuns would've winced. (Willie G. didn't wear one, though. God bless him.) I couldn't help but wonder why employees lacked the nerve to speak up and say, "Let us wear the clothes we sell in our dealerships so we look like we love our stuff!" And which leader would argue against it. But since then I've learned time and again that fear is never in short supply in rigid, old-school, command-and-control working environments.

I knew the company was near broke and on borrowed time, largely due, I'd eventually see, to the same self-inflicted wounds that I've watched bleed life from much of today's business world, in every industry (we'll get into that a little later). I also knew I'd have the rare chance to throw my energy into something that I loved and to work with others who felt the same way—the greatest thing anyone working for a living could ever hope for. I figured that if we, the perfectly average people flying the Harley-Davidson flag, could make this business attractive and competitive again, I'd be part of an extraordinary resurgence. The odds were less than favorable, but at that early point in my life, and in sharp contrast to many of the company's longtime employees, I had nothing to lose. I did, however, have a motorcycle license and a rack full of ties.

What I couldn't have known driving home after that first day, with overly charged nerves and a bag full of Harley swag, was that I was about to start a journey that would ultimately teach me things far more valuable and important than the business of motorcycles. I'd eventually see and discover for myself that the most valuable lessons a person can acquire are precisely what they don't teach you in college (because they'd rather stick to predictable, time-honored curriculum with supporting charts and graphs). It's also the stuff that's never discussed in the business world because it's hidden—as the truth often is—under layers of "just shut up and do your job" tradition, hierarchy, needless complexity, and excuse-making.

I'm talking about seeing how the world, once you've stripped away all the folklore, technology, consultant-speak, buzzwords, and business-book acumen, *actually works*. I'm talking about what instinctively turns people on and what turns them off. And the simple, yet counterintuitive reasons why businesses that compete against each other *actually imitate each other* rather than creating distance between themselves. And understanding basic human needs—which couldn't be easier—and leveraging that simple knowledge into improving business and personal competitiveness. And you'd better believe I'm talking about the amazing competitive advantage a loyal, vocal customer base can bring any business. *Any business. Your business.*

These rich, personal discoveries came to me not as the result of implementing brilliant business strategies—like you, I've not seen many of those—but by simply observing, as new improvement tactics were attempted, what worked, what didn't and, most important and typically well after the fact, figuring out the *why* behind each. It's those *whys* that give me golden access into CEO offices and keep me crisscrossing the globe to share what I've learned. Great leaders (emphasis on *great*) don't just want to learn methods to make things better; they want to know why, and be able to explain why, the stuff works. And so do you, if you ever want to see the view from the corner office.

I hope you're like me. I was the kid who took apart his transistor radio, bicycle, and family lawn mower to see how they operate (disclosure: I'm not claiming there weren't parts left over after reassembly). I'm one of those guys who habitually attempt repair of virtually anything before calling in experts, if only to gain know-how of what they're working with (and, of course, the possibility of enjoying that great buzz that comes with solving tough problems themselves). Curiosity is a gift I wish we all opened more often because it encourages us to look deeper into what's happening right in front of us, rather than just accepting things at face value.

Most business leaders I talk to don't even know answers to simple, basic questions like why their customers buy, or don't, from them or why they can't retain great employees—because they've never asked! If you're not asking questions like this, who is?

My curiosity has served me well as I've had the rare opportunity to work with businesses of every size and scope imaginable since leaving Harley-Davidson—and question *everyone* with my hunger for learning how and why things work or don't work. If you've ever met me, you know this: I'm going to hammer you with questions and keep on hammering until I understand you, how you do things, why you do them, and how you know they're working. You can't tell me too much.

To my great joy, I've learned that curiosity—especially asking, "How do you know this?" and "Can you prove it to me?"—doesn't just uncover a lot of what's hiding in plain sight; it also pays really well, something new hires and those just starting their careers should take to heart.

I recall with immense satisfaction the day the CEO of one of the world's largest tech companies—I promise some of their gear is in your workspace right now—asked me to fly all over the country, sit across from his most senior lieutenants, plus a few board members, and "clobber the hell out of them with the same questions you just asked me. And don't let anyone off the hook." Yes, sir!

Not only was the payday as epic as the opportunity to learn from some of the biggest names in technology, but I got to relearn, for the umpteenth time, the sad truth that not even the most senior execs in some of the world's biggest companies are immune to the disease of telling the boss what they believe he or she wants to hear rather than what needs to be heard. And in every case where I've witnessed this sorry phenomenon, CEOs and other top leaders believe or suspect it's happening and speak ill of it. While tolerating it. That says something, doesn't it?

Given the extraordinary access I've had with such a vast number of businesses (many of which you've been buying from your entire life, some of which are one-person operations) and the intimacy I've enjoyed with their leaders and their people, I'm always asked what I've seen and learned and if I've discovered any common threads that run through the working world, regardless of business size. So I'll answer that here, quickly.

I've seen time and again just how painfully easy it is for companies of any size to unknowingly mimic competitors, commoditize themselves, and become struggling also-rans (or worse) in the markets they serve.

Whether I'm talking about large corporations or small family operations, I've met very few business leaders who've included any element of "competition" in their overall business process, let alone made it the first priority of that process. They're driven by the notion of competing yet they don't formalize it, preferring to believe that if they do what they do well, their business will prosper at the expense of competitors.

I've listened too many times as disgruntled workers at underperforming companies described how uninvolved, invisible, or dispirited leadership limited their desire to work and improve. Or destroyed it altogether. And

I've heard leadership in these same businesses lament that they can't retain employees, while saying their employees are way more eager to complain then to "speak up and tell the truth." (We just saw this, didn't we?)

I've rarely seen a struggling business where two employees, including executive leadership, can answer very basic "Who are you? What do you do? Who do you do it for? And why should I do business with you?" questions the same way. How can they possibly expect prospective customers to know who they are when they don't even know themselves? (Sounds like your workplace, doesn't it?) Man, that's crazy!

But you want to know what's *more* crazy? Most of these leaders answer those basic questions using the exact same, trite descriptions ("Quality!" "It's an experience!" "Our people make the difference!") that their competitors use and was spewed earlier in our trade show visit. Uh, in what universe would anyone in business want to be described the same way as a competitor? The craziest part of all, though, is the fact that few business leaders even think about something as simple as this, let alone make it a priority to address it. Talk about a real and present danger!

(Go ahead and google the term "People Make the Difference" and see how many hits you get. Would you want to be buried in that mess? Are you?)

By far the most common thread that runs through most of the businesses I've met with over the years—in every corner of the world and among people of all ranks and ages—is the defensive belief (hope?) that "somebody, somewhere, is going to do something that's somehow going to make my life easier and my job better. So until that happens, I'm just going to keep on doing what I'm doing."

Know what I mean? You probably hear it (and say it) all the time: Once that new website comes online . . . or once those new products get approved for sale . . . or the management shakeup or reorg happens . . . or our social media strategy gets implemented . . . or our trade association pressures new legislation . . . or raw materials prices recede . . . or interest rates go down . . . or we get that new truck . . . or our merger is completed . . . or our rebranding is introduced . . . or . . . You get the picture. Somewhere along the line, leaders stopped telling their charges that the people most impacted by problems are the ones who stand to gain the most from solving them. So. Together. They. Wait.

(Quick question: Do you think that dominant businesses—and people— wait for someone, somewhere, to somehow solve their real and imaginary problems?)

All the news isn't bad, of course. Far from it. Very positively, I've learned that anyone, and any company—even in the dullest industry imaginable—can transform to become visibly and meaningfully different from competitors in ways that drive success and make them dominators. Anyone.

I've seen many times that perfectly ordinary people—given constant, enthusiastic encouragement, and a say in what they do—are capable of doing extraordinary things to the delight of their marketplace. That goes double in businesses where those perfectly ordinary people understand the concept of "accountability," a word that, in a business managed to be a dominator, has positive connotations. Tellingly, it's seen as a negative in also-rans. You've experienced this, haven't you?

And I've taken great pleasure in seeing that every business that makes it their daily mission to make vocal advocates out of the people they depend upon for their livelihood defeats those that don't. The same goes for everyone who works for a living.

I've learned time and again that Visible Passion (you'll see later why the *V* and *P* are capitalized) is the key ingredient to building and sustaining not just great work cultures, but customer and employee loyalty—two very much endangered species. Is it not the common denominator with every business and person you admire?

I've joyously found that what I've believed my entire professional career is undeniably true: The best way to teach, foster curiosity, and inspire change is to share stories and lessons that are applicable to everyone, easy to visualize, and, above all, trip emotional triggers. That way we don't just remember and use what we've learned, we also remember how to best *describe* what we've learned when we're sharing it with others. And no organization can be successful, let alone hope to be dominant, if its people aren't modeling the positive behavior of their leaders and sharing their knowledge with each other.

But my greatest delight? That's simple: As soon as I start talking about motorcycling and the conversation turns to "being a dominant competitor," nobody ever says, "Count me out." Everyone wants to join in and hear more.

So let's get rolling.

TWO

Objects in Mirror Are Closer Than They Appear

I have a theory about competition: The desire to lead rather than follow isn't something we're born with, it's something that rises within us as we master something difficult and push ourselves to exceed other people's mastery of that same thing.

For example, legend has it that the first motorcycle race was held the day the second motorcycle was built—somewhere back in the late 1800s—and I believe that. Imagine what an astounding sight that was, given that anything motorized was beyond nearly everyone's imagination back then and the roads of that time were, essentially, dirt paths carved by the hooves of horses and oxen and wheel ruts made by the carriages they pulled. It *almost* goes without saying that the roads were also heavily speckled with the "exhaust" from those beasts. What fun.

Early written reports and illustrations indicate that those first contending motorcycle/contraptions had steam engines and wooden wheels, if you can wrap your brain around that. What's certain, though, was the courage of those first two racers. Man, you'd have to be *very* sure of yourself and your newfangled machine to sit atop a primitive, cobbled-together, late-nineteenth-century boiler and make it hot enough to push out more steam than your competitor's similar mount. Picture yourself with that boiler at full steam between your legs, powering your wooden two-wheeler through the ruts and poop, running neck-and-neck with another equally unproven challenger. What could possibly go wrong? (And imagine the stunned look on your mother's face if she happened to peer out from under her parasol and spied you doing *that*.)

That's what competition does to people. If you're running a business (or a function within one), that desire to outperform your industry or market peers and keep them in your rearview mirrors is what gets you out of bed in the morning. Nobody's immune to it.

I can say with complete assurance that I've never possessed anything close to the kind of courage required to do what those early racers did, but I always wanted to race high-performance motorcycles grand prix or super-bike style. Picture insane speeds on beautiful, twisty tracks where racers turn their bikes so sharply their knees actually drag on the pavement and you'll get a feel for what I speak of. My ego allowed me to believe I possessed the skill to do it (albeit at a *very amateur* level or whatever level exists below that) so I desperately wanted to try it, see what it felt like to move crazy fast and push myself to my absolute limit. If I'm being honest, I mostly wanted to see what my "limit" looked like and, of course, where I stood against others. Plus there's just something about motorcycle racing— the skill, courage, hardware, and, of course, the great sights and sounds— that makes it beautiful and magnetic to people like me.

As is often the case with such lofty (and it must be said, dangerous) pursuits, some of my riding friends had this same itch in need of scratching. Curiosity—in liquid form, if you know what I mean—got the best of us and in the "I will if you will" school of reasoning that you're supposed to have outgrown by adulthood, challenges were made and accepted.

(Now that you're starting to know me and my methods, see how many "tells" and business metaphor/lessons you can spot as this story progresses.)

Soon thereafter, big checks were written and my pals and I found ourselves trackside at racing school, squeezing into head-to-toe leather suits and nervously eyeballing each other and the other students who, like us, were trying to shield their uneasiness by talking cocky. After a lot of intense classroom talk about the technical know-how needed to safely negotiate a track that has very sharp turns after long straightaways (as if guys like me needed such talk . . .) the instructors put us on racing bikes.

Oh my God! What a rush! Just knowing that there was zero chance of seeing any vehicles coming toward us from the opposite direction—the beauty of riding on a closed track—meant we could push ourselves and our bikes further than we'd ever dream on an actual road somewhere. We ran dozens of practice laps, single file, following professional racers, with huge buffers of space between riders. There were instructors stationed trackside, pointing at exactly where we needed to lean and hold our lines through each turn before we hammered the throttle back onto the straightaways. With each lap, everyone's wobbles and goof-ups decreased, turns became smoother, and we collectively gained speed and confidence. I'd never moved so fast in my life. Hey! I'm good at this! (That's what your high school English teacher referred to as "foreshadowing.")

Then the racing started, with no pros to follow nor trackside instructors pointing at targets. Everything was fine in the first long straightaway, but it was in the turns where things went apewire for me and I instantly became very religious (as in, "OhGodOhPleaseOhGodOhPlease"). Because now we were jammed together and there were screaming bikes—with, I'll remind you, amateur pilots—just inches away from me in every direction. I started to obsess about how precarious things had become and lost focus, which, I believe goes without saying, you don't want to do at high speed.

Job one in racing, as it is in all motorcycling (and metaphorically, business and life), is to always "look where you want to go," meaning don't focus on the road directly in front of you, focus *way up the road*. In turns, this means focus past your exit point. The reason for this is simple: A bike always goes where its operator is looking. So it's next to impossible to maintain a safe path through congestion if you're looking in the wrong place instead of your exit point, while moving at high speed. That, of course, is exactly what I was doing.

I kept losing my lines as my head wavered from side to side. To create more space around me, I'd try to reroute myself on the fly and would end up teetering off the edge of the track when I'd run out of room (prompting more talking to God). To stave off my horror and hyperventilating, I'd dial back on my throttle. Naturally, what little confidence I had left collapsed further as I slid back in the pack, where I'd remain alongside some other crushed souls.

Lucky for me and everyone else, I didn't cause any pileups. Unlucky for me, they don't give trophies to losers. And friends are quick to point stuff like that out, aren't they?

After a thorough assessment of my shortcomings and determining that beginner's jitters had gotten the best of me, I did the only responsible thing I could think of and signed up for a second class (see: disgruntled wife). And wrote another big check (see: hugely disgruntled wife). Different track. Same instructors. Same fast bikes. Same problems in the turns. Same back of the pack slumped shoulders. The long and short of it is, I'm just not as good at this racing stuff as I thought I was. Oh, who am I kidding? I stink at racing.

Instead of focusing on what I should be doing and executing on that, I was looking where I shouldn't have been and overreacting to what my competitors were doing. And because I didn't know precisely where I needed to be—because there was nobody to follow and nobody standing trackside and pointing the way—I made a lot of decisions on my own. All of them bad. Taking big risks couldn't compensate for the fact that I'd single-handedly taken myself out of the race.

In the plus column, at least I tried, right? I got to see how it felt to move at warp speed. I can also truthfully say I've raced and can tell stories about it. And that I found my (current) limit and didn't hurt myself. There's even an unexpected bonus: I discovered why racehorses wear blinders.

(Well, how'd you do? Did you spot the tells and business lessons?)

No matter what we do or what business we're in, we all have the same challenges to overcome if we want improve our competitiveness, let alone become dominant. Like the hard lessons in my racing story, this means we have to start looking in the right place and worry less about what our competitors are doing. And the less proficient among us (think of your fellow employees or team members or unskilled racers) need someone to follow and to admit that we need someone to follow.

Now would be a good time to start doing that. But there are some major potholes in the road if front of us that we need to identify if we're going to get around them.

The first of them, as we discovered on our trade show trip and I learned twice on the track, is the fact that we're human. So we're big on denial and wishful thinking. Leaders believe—or want to believe, as you read earlier— what underlings tell them, thus perpetuating workplace chatter that says our businesses are better, faster, smarter, and more valuable than they really are. We also assume that, because we're good at what we do, our customers and other important publics also believe we're good at what we do, like us, are loyal to us, and recommend us to others. It just feels better than facing the possibility that this isn't so.

The second, equally big pothole is this: When it comes to assessing our present situation, solving problems, or taking advantage of opportunities, we have a tendency to do what I did on the racetrack and look the wrong way—and hastily jump toward quick fixes or change our long-term priorities when a short-term threat surfaces.

Combine both of those potholes and we create a third, supernasty one: We take unnecessary risks that often fail and, in turn, create fear and keep us from venturing beyond our comfort zones again, so we never make it to the front of the pack.

You see evidence of this stuff all the time, like, say, when a manufacturer rushes a product to market to stave off a competitive threat before it's ready and embarrassing, expensive recalls ensue. ("I thought you said our Galaxy 7 phones were ready!" Samsung leaders presumably yelled when some of their Galaxy 7s caught fire, the news went viral, and they were banned from all commercial aircraft. Ka-ching!) Or when a business determines the best way to confront the shrinking margins in a commoditized marketplace is to focus all of its efforts on improving internal efficiencies. Or when a small business bets its savings on an expensive "rebranding" that fails to create miracles. Or that time you had to make a presentation but didn't practice enough and fell on your face in front of your boss, customers, and the (backstabbing) coworkers you were hoping to impress. (Like me on the racetrack or you, earlier, in the trade show booth: *We're never as good as we think we are!*)

We can't fix the fact that we're human, at least until robots replace us all. But we can absolutely start looking where we need to be looking, point ourselves that way, and give the employees and team members riding behind us someone to follow. And we can absolutely identify our shortcomings.

Let's be really clear about something. As you now know, it's not what your business makes or sells that's holding you back, nor is it competitors that make or sell the same stuff you do and use low price as combat weapons. It's also not your branding or your social media shortcomings, China, economic headwinds, or your regulatory environment. Nor aging baby boomers, hard-to-reach millennials, tough-to-penetrate minority markets, unpredictable weather, or any other flavor-of-the-month excuse.

As for your personal competitiveness, it's not your lack of an advanced degree, lagging technology know-how, short tenure, that ugly bowling shirt you wore at the company picnic, or even nepotism that's holding you back.

See, most of us have learned through experience to place blame for our competitive problems on what we hope or believe to be true, what our bosses say is true (based on what they hope or believe), whatever our inner-office reports reveal as true, what consultants are paid to say is true, or media and trend watchers claim is true. But we don't often enough look at what really *is* true.

It's time to do that.

I can see what's holding you—and just about everyone else—back because I'm wearing my "Reality Goggles" that allow me to see truth in perfect clarity. I've got a pair for you, too. They're really cool and look just like those old aviator goggles fighter pilots wore before they were adopted by motorcyclists after World War II. They're going to give you the benefit of a too-close-for-comfort view of the obstacle that's blocking your path to competitive dominance. Then, together we're going to reroute our way around it to where the views and rewards are life-changing.

I've just set our Reality Goggles' lenses to wide angle, to prove that the business world is chock-full of very well-intentioned people, working harder than they ever have, utilizing the most advanced tools and technology ever available . . . and blowing their most obvious opportunities for success. We've not traveled far together yet, but I'm hoping you can spot at least some of the problems here based on what we've witnessed together so far, without needing me to point them out. That's a hint to look for them! Strap on your Goggles with me and watch as—excuses be damned—the ordinary becomes even more ordinary.

See what I see? It's a small town financial advisor leaving the home of a prospective first-time life insurance buyer: A bright, fortyish professional guy with a wife and young kids. The smiling advisor just finished explaining, with the help of colorful, digitally presented charts, graphs, and tables, the various features and benefits of three different, but nearly indistinguishable, policies from well-known firms. She also left printed versions behind, in a nice folder, for the new parents to mull over. Meaning, our advisor did precisely what she was trained to do and what she does every day.

Pretty harmless so far, right? Wrong! Way wrong!

Her employer and the millions of other people in the industry they represent will wonder why so many life insurance prospects, like that eager young dad—*people who've made the call and expressed their intent to buy what these folks are selling!*—aren't pulling the trigger and actually buying policies. They'll continue to assume the product is the problem (and the opportunity). Or blame the Internet. Or assume they're losing business to low-fee discounters. Probably a combination of all of the above.

That advisor and her firm? They're in the game and they'll tell you that. They're putting in long hours, getting trained, licensed, and retrained, chasing down leads, building thorough proposals, dressing sharp, showing up for appointments on weekends and weeknights, and flat-out hustling. It's hard work! They're collectively representing companies who not only have superb products, but have also spent billions of dollars on advertising to make you familiar with who they are.

What none of them are doing, though, is competing to dominate. Because if they were, there's simply no way they'd be playing the exact same game the rest of their industry is playing by pushing product as they've done for eons. And there's no way that young dad wouldn't have pulled out his checkbook.

No, like just about everything else that gets bought and sold every day, life insurance isn't exciting and sexy—it's just a bunch of paper covered with indecipherable data and legalese. It's not something people purchase frequently (maybe only once in a lifetime) and think about a lot, let alone brag about. Policy owners frequently can't quickly recall who their insurer is (and I'm one of them!). Yet everyone knows life insurance is an absolute necessity and intends to buy it if they don't already own it.

So wait a minute. Wasn't that advisor just sitting across from a live human being? Isn't that the holiest of Holy Grails for salespeople, the companies that employ them, and the companies that provide what they're selling?

If you're thinking, "This is a sales problem," you're looking in the wrong direction and I'll prove it to you. Remember: We need to look *way down the road*, not at what's immediately in front of us!

Let me hit the fast-forward buttons on our Goggles and show you that the worst of the competitive damage in this story hasn't even been done yet. That comes later today—"through the turn"—after that young prospective insurance buyer meets three friends for their weekly round of golf. Can you guess what it is?

Let's watch: There they are in the locker room at the country club, putting on their golf shoes, making fun of each other, and having some laughs. Each of these friends is in roughly the same life stage, with a young family at home (and a wife who hates golf). Do you know what our hero's going to say about what happened over his kitchen table this morning—as in *just a few hours ago*—with the financial advisor? I do. And I hope you do, too! It's not going to be pleasant, is it? What's he going to do, say how much he enjoyed his visit and explain why he's buying a specific life insurance policy by citing its product specs from actuarial tables? Then sing its sponsor's ad jingles? You know better than that, of course.

Look through the turn! With this morning's event still fresh in his mind, that young prospect should be serving that advisor—and, by proxy, her employer—up on a platter to his three friends who will take his recommendation seriously because *they need life insurance, too! And quite possibly a financial advisor!* So what in God's name was she doing pushing product?! And why was she trained to do that?! That's no way to compete!

That was horrifying to watch, wasn't it? That young prospect didn't have a thing to say about that salesperson, the experience they shared together, what she was selling, or whose products they were. As in, "Hey, you'll never guess what I did this morning." Which means nothing happened that's worth discussing. Nothing. Which means that no new demand for her or her employer's services, nor the products they sell, nor the companies that supply them with those products, has been built. Which means everyone involved in this story—most notably the prospective customer—gained absolutely nothing.

Remember, I said this isn't a "sales problem." It's way bigger than that. This is systemic, top-to-bottom, bottom-to-top failure. It's taught and modeled behavior, meaning it's what's expected and even demanded by leadership in this industry. It's what we see every day. And precisely what all of us, as human beings on the receiving end of it, find uncomfortable and unattractive. It's why we think we can just go to the Internet, attempt to educate ourselves on these products, and make informed purchase decisions without the help of an advisor or salesperson. But this doesn't work for us because the products are complicated and we can't understand them or see any differences. So we abandon our research and avoid purchase. Or, worse, buy something cheap—that we'll regret later—from God-knows-who. See? The good guys aren't winning!

This is fixable!

But what's that you say? You're not in the financial services industry and you don't sell insurance? And you didn't see parallels to your own business? Well, then, let's tighten up the view in our Reality Goggles a little more because . . .

In that same town, a maintenance engineer for a midsize manufacturing firm that makes metal clothes hangers for the dry-cleaning industry has a problem. He's flipping through parts catalogs and checking look-alike websites, searching for roller bearings needed to replace broken ones on a machine that's vital to the firm's existence. Downtime is expensive.

He knows of at least three companies who could take his call and solve his problem, but instead he's losing time looking up parts numbers and comparing prices. He'll eventually call the company with the lowest price for the bearings he needs, hear "Can I help you?" and be put on hold (cue tinny-sounding music that sounds like it's coming from a worn-out eight-track) while a customer service rep tracks down the parts. Ah! She has good news: They're in-house and will be overnighted for arrival the next day.

Our maintenance guy will tear that shipping box open the minute it hits the receiving desk, pull those roller bearings out, and whistle a Creedence tune as he bolts them onto the machine and breathes life back into it. Big deal, right? Hooray for everybody involved!

No, not even close! Look way down the road, not at what's in front of you! It's just another day in the plant for him—he's just doing his job! There are thirty other machines on the shop floor cranking out hangers 24/7. This guy buys so many parts that two weeks later, he'll not be able to recall which company he bought those bearings from. He'll not bother to share today's repair success story with any of his fellow maintenance engineers, who do much the same thing he does every day, because what's there to talk about? A year from now, after he's retired and fishing in Florida, his replacement will run into the same problem on that machine, wonder who to call, and, you guessed it: Shop around for price, just like he did. That's more wasted time. Lather. Rinse. Repeat.

Those machine parts manufacturers? They're out there hustling like crazy. They're working with OEMs (original equipment manufacturers) to stay current on what's happening in their markets and stocking up on frequently demanded items. They're cranking out catalogs and constantly updating their mailing lists and websites. Their social media people are tweeting God-knows-what about God-knows-what to God-knows-who every day. Their sales guys are driving hundreds of miles a week, shaking hands, knocking on doors to drum up more business, and leaving behind stress balls and water bottles emblazoned with their corporate logos and 800 numbers. Everyone's running as fast as they can. Yet they're still relying on "lowest price" to win business. And watching their margins shrink.

But wait. Let's hit the rewind button on our Goggles for a minute. Our maintenance hero has spent time on that parts company's website, met personally with its salespeople over the years, and just spoke over the phone with one of its people. Yet he can't remember who he did business with and had no reason to discuss them? And didn't recommend them over all others when he handed the job over to his replacement? Why the hell not?

It doesn't matter if you're in the business of making sandwiches, removing tonsils, selling eyewear, or manufacturing boat engines, I trust you saw a pattern starting to take shape among these two imaginary scenarios. At bare minimum, you saw people working very hard but not getting very far.

But did you also notice that it wouldn't require a tectonic shifting of the earth's plates to create different outcomes? And that—contrary to what many business leaders believe—the competitive shortcomings you just witnessed aren't problems for sales or marketing departments to solve? And I bet you can imagine hearing legions of people in industries like these (like yours) saying, "This is just the way it is and we can't change it," or "Our customers only want low prices."

Lord, have mercy on the excuse makers.

It's easy, of course, to point out other businesses' competitive problems like we just did. But now it's your turn. Let's zoom in further with our Reality Goggles and look directly at your business life, to see if we can spot any land mines and obvious opportunities to improve your competitiveness. Spoiler alert: We can.

There you are! Look at you, pounding away on the job, eating at your desk (sigh), sitting through meeting after meeting on performance improvement initiatives, listening to coworkers spout tired business truisms ("Skate to the puck!" "The only thing constant is change!"), and poring over sales and marketing challenges, budgeting shortfalls, pricing issues, and (God forbid) branding and social media strategies. Just another day in paradise.

But out there in the market you serve, something completely ordinary is happening that's way more important than all of that. Only you're not there to witness it. So let's fine-tune our Goggles even more and eavesdrop.

See what I see? It's one of your company's customers, taking her seat on a plane and checking emails on her phone as, completely unexpected, an old friend she hasn't seen since college nabs the seat next to her. After quick catching up (and, of course, stifled giggles about who got fat and who didn't), their conversation turns to business. Your customer's friend complains to her about a nagging problem he's having at his business, which happens to be not only the largest and best known in your market, but the dream account your company has been unsuccessfully trying to get a meeting with for years. The challenge frustrating him is similar to one you've helped your customer's company tackle for years. He's about to ask if she's familiar with a firm he's thinking of hiring to take this monkey off his back. Uh-oh! It's one of your competitors!

Your company's name—and, yours, too, if you're the client contact—is about to come up. It sure as hell *better* come up, right? Would you bet on it?

Just think: If she tells him, "Wait, I've got a better idea for you," and serves your company up glowingly, the dollars and prestige involved could be life-altering. If there was ever a time in your life you wanted somebody to talk you up, man, this is it.

So. What's she going to say about your business? About you? About how your firm is different and better than the firm her friend is considering—a firm that just happens to do essentially the same things yours does but charges less than you do? Is she going to describe you using the same language and excitement you'd use to describe yourself to such an important and influential person? And not only say how much she likes you but even offer to introduce him to you?

The stakes couldn't possibly be higher. What. Is. She. Going. To. Say? If thinking about this makes your stomach muscles tighten, trust me, you're not alone.

See? No matter *what business you're in*, the people most important to you are going to talk about you to others who either don't know you at all or don't know you the way you wish to be known. Conversations like the one you just witnessed happen all the time on planes, in meetings (isn't "networking" why people come to seminars and conventions in the first place?), grocery stores, on the sidelines watching kids' sporting events, golf course bars, in back rooms, elevators, email exchanges, and social media posts. Given those high stakes, it should be safe to assume that you could predict, with some confidence, what a customer or other person important to your success would say about your business and you.

Except, of course, you probably can't. Because you've never thought about it. Hardly anyone does. Because hardly anyone looks at competition through the Reality Goggles we just peeked through. Meaning most of us blindly assume that, of course, our customers like us and what we sell and would recommend us to others if asked.

But think hard: When was the last time you recommended a business to somebody? You probably can't remember. Yet somehow you want to believe that your business's customers would do that for you. Ego! Denial! Get thee behind me!

If you're not regularly looking through the turns and thinking about what your business's customers are going to say to their friends and associates—as in the scenarios we just watched—and what it's going to take to *make sure* they say what you want them to say, who is? Your marketing department? Your social media staffer? Give me a break, man. These aren't marketing problems, these are business strategy problems. They get addressed and solved at the top, with their corrective actions developed and implemented as company-wide priorities. Or they don't get solved.

We'll be working on this.

But before we move on, I want to share one final scenario with you. This one isn't about business, per se. It is, however, going to be close to your heart because it stars your favorite person in the world: you. In all of your magnificent glory. This time, it's completely personal.

Gaze one more time into the Reality Goggles and crank the zoom lens down all the way: Look, there you are again, only this time you're in comfy clothes (saggy waistband and all). It's well past quitting time, you're at home digging into a plate of tuna casserole at the family dinner table, and your kids are giving you the same mumbled responses to your "So, what did you do today?" questions that they give you every night. And that's perfectly fine. Everyone's smiling (which, considering the bland casserole, is saying something), you're completely relaxed, and a restful, quiet evening with your feet up is coming your way.

But, back at your workplace, in the small conference room next to the top guy's office, things aren't at all fine. Company brass are slumped in their seats with their sleeves rolled up, eating takeout sandwiches and looking miserable. It's been a tougher than expected year; that's no secret. But what's happening in that room certainly is. Management's prepping to do something they've stalled on for months and will soon hate themselves for: a major workforce reduction. Fuses are short and nerves are fried.

Department by department, they're projecting the employee roster up on a screen and going down the list, name by name, discussing who's vital to the business and, thus, safe. Questionable employees get highlighted in yellow for later debate while "expendable" ones get crossed out with painful winces, but nary a word of discussion.

Uh-oh. They're doing your department right now. The human resources chief just read your name and your boss is drawing breath to speak. . . .

Come on. You should be safe, right? You've been with the company a long time. You know you've always been a solid contributor and one of the first people to arrive every day, so that's got to count for something. You're loyal, bust your butt, uphold the company's values, keep your nose clean, and have never had a bad performance review.

But remember, you're looking through Reality Goggles. Who at your level at your company—*people you're now competing against for your survival*—can't also describe themselves the same way you just did? Aren't those things the very least a boss should expect from someone on his team?

As with the earlier tale, if you ever wanted someone to talk you up, this is it. So, then: What. Is. He. Going. To. Say?

Here's the deal: While businesses (presumably like yours) are focused on the daily functions and processes needed to do whatever it is you do to hit financial goals, improve efficiencies, and everything else needed to survive, the world isn't paying any attention. And very likely won't. Unless what you're doing is so utterly spectacular that it provides recognized and sought-after advantage to you—which, in the small-business world in particular, is rarer than rare—your internal knitting and the effort you plow into doing what you do simply doesn't register outside your doors.

Just like you busting your butt every day in that last scenario, nobody notices when they're getting what they expect. Think of salespeople who push product because that's what they're trained, retrained, and rewarded to do; they're driven by the transaction that's dangled in front of them, and the metrics and goals behind it. The would-be customers you just saw in the life insurance and roller bearings scenarios didn't exactly appreciate and reward that effort, did they? Why would they?

The moral of the story is this: Nondominant businesses are focusing too much attention on the wrong things! Ditto nondominant people!

To become a dominant business, you need to start looking further down the road instead of at what's immediately in front of you. You need to start looking at what it's going to take to make your important publics prefer you over your competitors, seek you out, and advocate for you. And then you need to reconfigure your business process and culture around making that happen. The same goes for you, personally.

I know what you're thinking and the answer is "no." Unlike branding and rebranding, marketplace dominance doesn't require massive capital investment. What it requires is a top-to-bottom, bottom-to-top, side-to-side radical change in perspective and attitude. And better utilization of the time you're already spending doing wasteful things. I'm here to help you *make* money, not spend it. And put you out in front of the pack.

What do you say we saddle up, kick this thing into gear, look way down the road and through the turns and start competing like our lives depended on it?

NOISE CUBED

You've got work to do—your first official assignment—but it's only going to take you a minute. I want you to type out, word for word, what you see in the box below. Then print it out and display it in the most visible area of your workspace so you and people working with you can see it.

> **Noise Cubed**
> 1. What are people saying?
> 2. What do we want them to say?
> 3. What are we doing to make them say it?

(Personalize this by replacing the "we" with "I" if you want.)

I promise you that this little crib sheet I invented in my first job out of college is going to be as helpful to you and the others you share it with as it's always been for me. It's going to sit at the top of your business processes as the driving force of your competitive strategy and constantly remind you and everyone working with you what you're working toward.

It's also going to make you a smarter, sharper communicator because, by the time our journey together winds down, you'll be much more thoughtful and consistent with the words and messages you share with your important publics. Equally important, you'll find it to be a bulletproof touchstone for decision making, as in "Will this action, new product, or statement we're considering make people say about us what we want said?"

I still have the faded and tattered 8½" x 2" sheet I first taped to the top of my typewriter(!) at Harley-Davidson (only it didn't have the "Noise Cubed" title on it because I didn't have a name for it then). It served me and the company very well, as it will you.

You see, back then I was tasked, broadly speaking, with improving the company's reputation and making it more attractive to prospective motorcycle owners and investors at a very low point in its then-eight-decade history. At that time, Harley's noise—and corresponding bank balance—were deep in the danger zone, the results of a particularly nasty (and, in retrospect, totally preventable) one-two punch: Preposterous "outlaw biker gang" stereotypes hovered over the company's customer base and everyone associated with it (bike dealers and, of course, the company as a whole), while grossly exaggerated product reliability issues were taken as gospel in the marketplace.

Naturally, Harley's competitors weren't dumb, so they took full advantage of this. Honda, in particular, launched a brilliant offensive to take advantage of those negative stereotypes and gained worldwide acclaim for one of the most successful marketing campaigns of all time, "You Meet the Nicest People on a Honda." They implied directly and successfully that the folks riding Harleys weren't so nice while Hondas were for *everybody* and in very little time took claim to the top of the worldwide bike market. Meanwhile media outlets seemed to relish saying that the Harley-Davidson—the sole remaining U.S.-based motorcycle manufacturer—had outlived its usefulness and was writing its own obituary. Probably because it was.

What would you have been thinking about, if you were me?

There were lots of very well-intentioned voices and ideas from various areas of the company offering suggestions on how to approach this. Which is precisely why Noise Cubed is so valuable. There'd be few if any second chances, so I needed to get focused immediately on what was most important and get strategic on the double. If we couldn't figure out a way to get the people most important to Harley-Davidson to talk about us the way we wanted to be talked about, we were screwed. Period. It's well worth saying, too, that being essentially broke meant there was very little money to play with, so there was no way Harley was going to promote or buy its way out of this mess.

Those gang stereotypes I just mentioned were spawned and perpetuated by Hollywood and the media world, highly influential voices who found in riders of large, loud, attention-grabbing motorcycles (spelled Harleys) something they could use to instill fear into the hearts of non-Harley riders (spelled the majority of the human race) everywhere. The huge, often ridiculous falsehoods used to "substantiate" these stereotypes (chain-swinging violence, murder, drugs, kidnapped teenaged girls, etc.) spread like wildfire and were, to say the least, a very strong purchase deterrent.

At least two full generations of children were raised in a world where they were told that guys who rode and sold Harleys were thugs. I grew up liking every bike manufacturer *except* Harley. I nearly passed out once as a teenager when my Honda broke down and I pulled to the side of the road just in time for a group of Harley riders to pull up. I was scared to death that they were going to light me on fire, something I'd heard they regularly did to riders of Japanese motorcycles in those days (I'll not say here how they reputedly "extinguished" those burning riders). Forty-some years later I'm still embarrassed to say they actually helped get me on my way.

You can find on my website stories about how and why this "outlaw biker" phenomenon came to be. It's great campfire storytelling (if I say so myself).

You don't need me to tell you that misinformation creates all sorts of obvious problems and that it's just plain wrong to stereotype and judge people by their appearance (and that the world would be an infinitely better place if we'd all just stop doing that). But here's something important we can learn from these negatives that most people don't think about and that's relevant to all businesses: When what we see and experience in real life doesn't match what we've been led to believe, there's an instant disconnect. So the legions of Harley riders who didn't look like "outlaw bikers"—picture your mailman or everyone's grandpa riding past your house on his bike—didn't blip on anyone's radar because they didn't look the way everyone expected Harley riders to look. Meaning they were invisible and, thus didn't exist and certainly weren't talked about.

The opposite of that equation is equally problematic: When what we see and experience in real life matches what we've been lead to believe, we then believe even stronger. Which explains why I freaked when those Harley riders approached my broken-down Honda or why, when you saw some biker-looking dudes rolling through town, you assumed—because they looked just like the guys in the B-movies and that Mom warned you about—they were Hell's Angels–types on a drunken killing spree. Oh, the humanity. (They were probably heading to a picnic. With badminton.)

A reporter at the *New York Times* inadvertently set me straight on this and gave me one of those radical perspective changes I mentioned earlier. Very early in my reputation repair work, when I was telling her about the "real" riders who made up the vast majority of the Harley-riding family, she cut me off and told me she was having none of it. "All I know is what I see," she complained. "And what I see are rough-looking bikers. Case closed." (Me: "But . . . but . . . but . . .") Little wonder, then, that Harley's defensive, "Look at us for who we really are," messages hadn't yet resonated with the masses. (That reporter has *no* idea how many times I've invoked her in discussions with business leaders over the years, especially those running businesses that make promises and claims they don't deliver on. And I'd bet you can name a lot of those. All we know is what we see.)

So suffice to say that pretty much everyone in the non-bike-riding world harbored very negative perceptions about Harley-Davidson. That'd make it a *little tough* to attract new customers, wouldn't you say? Would you have bet your retirement funds on a company with such a black cloud over its head? (By the way, I was kidding about the badminton a minute ago.)

As destructive as Harley's "outlaw biker" image was, though, it wasn't the company's biggest problem. The second blow of that nasty one-two punch was much more destructive and is certainly one that any business owner can sympathize with: The most important people in the company's selling dynamic—millions of motorcycle owners riding competing brands (aka "the bike market")—would tell anyone who'd listen that Harley's products were hugely unreliable (I'm being polite here; their language was much more colorful).

Like a lot of old-line manufacturing companies, Harley was guilty of producing some less-than-great products in the 1970s and early 1980s. The company's quality had indeed declined and in many ways paled when compared to the stuff rolling off assembly lines in Japan and Germany, the then-perceived world heavyweight champions of quality. But Harley's quality wasn't anywhere near as bad as these folks, most of whom had exactly zero experience with Harleys, were saying. Nobody's could be! But who cares? Paraphrasing the late, masterful comic Rodney Dangerfield, who once argued, "When a kid says you're fat, you're fat." When the most important people in your market say you stink, you stink.

Harley stunk.

Who were riders telling their "Harleys stink" stories to? Anyone shopping for a bike or even considering it. Harley's protests to the contrary, naturally and tellingly, fell on deaf ears. Who'd be crazy enough to buy a Harley against this backdrop?

Two platinum-clad lessons can be taken from this:

First, if the market (or any people important to you) owns your narrative, you're totally out of control and in big trouble.

Second, everybody turns a skeptical ear to what businesses and people say about themselves, but we attach a ton of belief to, act on, and repeat what we hear from others. Negative voices and inaccurate stories can create a lot of damage quickly, right? (See: 2016 U.S. presidential election.) It's sad and telling that businesses spend and spend and spend hoping to reverse this and make you believe what they say about themselves. God, what a waste.

Both of these lessons validate Noise Cubed and the need to make vocal advocates—saying what we want said and how we want it said—out of those we depend on.

Lots of times when I'm telling stories like this about Harley's struggles, people ask, "Is that when Harley rebranded?" and it always makes me cringe. Uh. No. That term hadn't even entered business vernacular yet and, to put it bluntly, I often wish it never had. I've seen way too many businesses—especially small ones—waste way too much time, effort, and money chasing something—"branding" or "rebranding"—that ultimately didn't generate a single measurable improvement. I bet you have, too.

I much prefer to focus on something way more important than that. Like taking advantage of what we already have—talented people, great products and services, courage, and passion—and better deploying it to stake our claim in our market, distance ourselves from our competitors, and force them to chase us.

FONZIE KNOWS: POSITIONING IS COOLER THAN BRANDING

I've spent the lion's share of my teaching time with businesses that serve viable markets, make, sell, or distribute great products, service their customers well, and employ great people with vast knowledge and experience. Which, if you're catching on to what I've been saying, doesn't mean much because that pretty much describes all businesses.

In almost every introductory phone call or discussion with folks at these businesses, I don't even bother taking notes when they recite the litany of problems that they're facing, because the song's so familiar to me now: Our margins are decreasing, our workplace morale is in the dumps, our once-loyal customers are turning to Internet suppliers and low-priced upstarts, and nobody's returning our calls like they used to. Sometimes I get the B-side: "Things are going pretty well right now, but we're seeing warning signs."

When businesspeople get nervous and frustrated (see above), they mutter false assertions like "Our markets have changed" (you'll see later why I believe *markets can't change*) or nonsense like "We need a social media strategy." They'll spit out buzzwords in an effort to sound on top of things while at the same time disparaging something they don't understand, like

"We need more relevance to gain traction with impossible-to-reach millennials." Eventually, the excuse makers reach for the classic, it's-got-nothing-to-do-with-me-but-we've-gotta-blame-somebody chestnuts, "Our marketing stinks" or, worse, "We don't have any leadership."

Honk if this sounds like anybody you know.

I always try to start my business fact-finding discussions at the very top, talking with company leadership (the people frequently blamed for everything, see above). I can usually tell in just a few seconds if the business they lead is in *real* danger and it's not because they sing one of those familiar, sad songs. It's deeper than that. Other than when they come right out and say, "We're screwed," (which I've heard a lot), it's when their top dog can't answer my three simple Noise Cubed questions about their competitiveness—you know them: What are people saying? What do we want them to say? What are we doing to make them say it?—or when no two people in company leadership can answer them the same way. That points directly to every major competitive problem they're facing and answers why they're having them.

When asking the Noise Cubed questions, I'm asking about their narrative and their *positioning*; the noise they're currently making in the market and the noise they want to make.

When company leadership tells me what they (claim to) believe their customers are saying and I hear the same tired, knee-jerk, God-bless-America answers I hear everywhere else, like "They say we stand for quality," or "Our people make the difference," or "They consider us to be trusted advisors," I know where our work together needs to start.

Come on, man! Could you ever imagine yourself describing and recommending a business you just bought from using language like that? In your entire life, have you ever used language like that in a conversation? This is the kind of thoughtless prattle businesspeople say because they think they're supposed to, because everyone else is, and because they just flat-out don't know what else to say. I call this stuff the dull, predictable, lifeless, meaningless, nonmemorable, nondifferentiating, profit-killing, job-destroying language of a dying business. It's awful and it's got to stop. If you wouldn't say it to your grandmother at your Thanksgiving dinner table, don't say it to anyone else!

So I'll typically counter their nonsense by groaning, then asking, "So if I lined up one hundred of your customers right now and asked them what they say about your business or why they do business with you, you're convinced this is what they'd tell me?"

That one's always greeted with silence. That's okay because it means they *heard* me all the way to their souls. It feels bad to suddenly realize that something you blindly believed in, even if it didn't seem entirely plausible, is exposed as fraud. Like when you discovered the truth about Santa.

Taking it further down the boulevard of painful truth, I then ask, "If I lined up one hundred of your *main competitor*'s customers and asked them to describe your competitor, wouldn't you expect to hear pretty much the same lifeless good products/good people language you believe your customers would use to describe you? And are you okay with that?"

This is big stuff, people, and we have to be realistic. I've already told you that being described the same way as a competitor—in predictable, lifeless language, no less—is a problem, especially if your business is stalling, you're using low price as a competitive weapon, and your industry is filled with look-alike businesses (and name one that isn't).

Think for just a moment about the last five companies you spent money with. What were your reasons to choose them? Other than "They have the best price," or "They're closest to my house," most of us have to scratch our heads and dig really deep to discover why we buy from specific businesses, don't we?

But think of how you describe businesses you enjoy and are loyal to. "They're cool." "I really like them." "They're always good to me." Note how you didn't immediately rely on knee-jerk comments about those businesses' products, services, and/or price, but rather you personalized your language and *humanized* their business. That's where we want your business to be. (We'll soon talk more about the "humanization" of business.)

It gets really fun when I ask company leadership the second Noise Cubed question: If one of your customers were talking about you to an important prospective customer, like in the life insurance, roller bearing, and couple on the plane scenarios we looked at through Reality Goggles earlier, what would you *want* him or her to say?

At this, almost everyone sends me a signal that I'm about to make some serious money, by leaning back, folding their hands atop their heads, gazing to the heavens, taking a deep breath, and uttering three ugly—and very telling—words: "Well, I guess . . ."

Because that's when I rudely interrupt. Game over.

Come on, man! You *guess*?! This is the holiest of Holy Grail conversations! This is your reputation! The most valuable asset you have! *You guess?!* If you don't know *exactly* how you want your customers to describe you, you're beyond out of control and ceding a ton of ground to your competitors.

Why make it easier for them? For now, memorize this (the reason will become apparent shortly): **A business's reputation is a mirror reflection of its culture.** If business leadership doesn't know how to answer the second Noise Cubed question, how can the people working under them—the entire organization—know what they're striving toward? No wonder so many companies have a hard time engaging and retaining their people.

At bare minimum, every employee in your business needs to know precisely how to answer the second Noise Cubed question. And everyone in your organization needs to use and hear these words so constantly that they become engrained in your business culture's DNA. If we want our customers—and everyone else we're dependent upon—to describe our business in language that's going to create demand for us, then we first need to know how to do it ourselves! Makes sense, right? We'll be working on this.

See, this is why I say making noise isn't the sole responsibility of the marketing department. In the commoditized, look-alike, me-too, price-is-king markets we serve, noise is business strategy. And if improving your business's reputation to make that distinct, powerful, attractive (Harley-like, if you will) noise and become market dominant isn't at the very top of your business process, what in God's name is? Your business is either positioned and managed to succeed where competitors fall short or it's not positioned at all. The same can be said for you personally.

In my view, everything we do—*everything*—is positioning. In your personal life, the whole kit and caboodle from the way you comb your hair, to your clothing choices, the car you drive, the decorations in your home and office, your attitude, the people you hang with, and the words you use: That's all positioning. That's how you hope to be seen, remembered, and described. And even if it's completely routine to you, you work pretty hard to project your positioning because it's how you say, "This is who I am."

Unfortunately, unintentional negative forces also apply here. The things you do repetitively that are predictable, colorless, lame, dull, careless, selfish, etc.—to say nothing of that ill-fitting shirt you sometimes wear—are also positioning and say, "This is who I am." In business as in life, of course.

You know who understood positioning really well and teaches it even better? Milwaukee's most famous motorcyclist, our old pal Fonzie, from my favorite 1970s TV show, *Happy Days*.

What's the first thing you remember about the Fonz? He was cool. Why do you remember that? Because he *was* cool. He said he was cool, constantly. Everything he did was cool. He snapped his fingers and hot chicks draped themselves all over him (happens to me all the time after I give a speech somewhere). He hit the jukebox in just the right spot and records played. He rode a cool bike (which everyone's memory says was a Harley even though it wasn't, a careless oversight given that the show was centered in Milwaukee!). He always looked cool—his hair was perfectly greased and he was never without his signature leather jacket.

The Fonz *was* cool. He never wavered. So everyone said he was cool. The coolest. He carved out a distinct niche to separate himself from everyone else and was consistent with the words he used to describe himself. Equally important, he very intentionally lived in a way that accurately reflected his desired positioning. When other characters on the show talked about the Fonz, they described him as he described himself and colored their stories about him with the cool stuff they—or others—saw him doing. Damn, man. Who didn't like the Fonz? And want to be like him? Or be with him?

As simple as it sounds, that's what I'm talking about here. It's identifying the things we do and say that our competitors can't or won't and leveraging the real (not phony), noticeable values, attributes, or positive associations people have with us that separate us from everyone else. It's pinpointing and communicating the things that make us us. And like the Fonz's, our positioning has to be backed by our unwavering behavior (because bad—really bad—things can happen when it doesn't, as we'll see).

You want to see how positioning looks when it's done well? Just pop into a Trader Joe's and notice the off-kilter beach-themed décor, the handwritten signs, and the disarmingly friendly Hawaiian-shirt-wearing staff. When did a floor employee in a supermarket ever speak to you unprompted before? And they're everywhere! But wait—it looks like every product is the store brand. Uh-oh. That's a deal breaker, right? Who'd ever come back to this festival of weirdness and oddball products? Apparently, everybody.

Somehow, in the notoriously cutthroat, low-margin, me-too food industry, Trader Joe's is stealing share from its old-line competitors and attracting virtually all demographics (their parking lots have as many luxury sedans as minivans; take that, Whole Foods!). Once you've checked out at TJ's—the fastest checkout line you'll ever see in a grocery store—their success and sky-high customer loyalty won't surprise you. And you'll know why the dull, predictable, stodgy, robotic supermarkets you've grown up with are so scared a TJ's will open near them.

TJ's promise of great food—even sans famous brand names, which highlights just how remarkable their success is—plus great values and superfriendly people is the real deal. Their people clearly uphold the company's superfriendly positioning because *that's exactly what their leadership demands of them*. And the world notices and rewards them for it. TJ's are springing up everywhere.

On the other hand . . .

Remember that *Happy Days* episode when straight-laced, nerdy Richie Cunningham tried to reposition himself by imitating Fonzie? He wanted to be cool and attract girls, but we all knew he'd bomb. Even with his leather jacket, shades, slicked-back hair, and tough-guy affectations, everyone knew it was the same old freckle-faced Richie Cunningham, saw right through the ruse, and called him on it. Rebranders beware! You just can't claim to be something you're not. At least not for long. (Remember my gal at the *New York Times:* "It's not what I see!")

There's nothing easier to spot than businesses that pull a Richie Cunningham. I bet you can name several off the top of your head. I know I can. Like, remember when American Airlines wanted you to describe them as the most passionate flyer and spent God knows how many hundreds of millions promoting that with "We love to fly and it shows"? Or how about United's "friendly skies" and their promises of friendliness? Come on, man. I'm a gazillion-miler and I've never seen either of them do anything to match their promises. Why claim to own the market for passion or friendliness if you don't mean it, don't even try to live up to it, and don't treat *every* passenger like a valuable, awesome human being?

Just look at United's home page: It looks like an order form accompanied by an irritating credit card ad and basically says, "We're just doing the minimum to get by." You, I, and everyone we know can see no difference between the major me-too airline players and use low price as our default purchase criteria when "choosing" carriers. Every time. We deserve better and they know that. They just won't give it to us because our options are so limited. For now. (PS: Here's a quick tip for airline management: For the love of God will you stop forcing your flight attendants to interfere with my flight by hawking your credit cards? They always looked pained when they're doing this. Doesn't that say something?)

It's telling that a massively successful industry was spawned by major airlines failing to distance themselves from one another and actually compete. Every time you check or book flights on Expedia, Travelocity, Kayak, or any other booking site after clicking the "sort by price" button, you're seeing evidence of this. (Quick. Think of parallels in other industries. I know you can.) Kudos go to any airlines—Southwest comes to mind—that don't play this "shop by price" game. Maybe Trader Joe's should buy some jets?

On the other hand, here's an easy, positive example everyone can identify with. Think of Apple. You probably can't remember the marketing language they used early on, back in the 1980s, to support their positioning as a low-cost alternative to Microsoft's dominant PCs, but I can: "Apple does more—costs less." They wanted you to think of them as cheap! Man, those days are long gone (my iPhone cost me almost nine hundred bucks!). What would they look like today if they'd stuck to that approach? Would they even be here?

Apple evolved to the much sharper, story-worthy "Think Different," and backed it up by ensuring that everything they did, from their totally uncommon work culture to their brilliantly designed products, to their advertising, website, and retail experiences, reflected that new and more desired positioning. Most Apple staffers would rather cut off an arm than copy a competitor, and that's true from top to bottom. Soon "different" was the first word that came to mind for Apple across their entire target market. Bingo. And that was more than twenty years ago. It's just continued to get better since then.

Remember: Your reputation—your noise—is a mirror reflection of your culture.

Apple is not the only successful company to figure this out, of course. Here's another A-list example everyone can learn from: Call the investor relations department at Disney and tell them your investment club would like some hard copies of their investor kits to analyze. No sooner do you notice the obvious eager-to-please attitude of the person you're speaking to than she's offering to overnight everything to you—at Disney's expense—so you won't have to wait. She's not working in a theme park where you'd expect smiles and sunshine; she's a backroom support person. And she's exhibiting precisely the exceed-all-expectations, uber-friendly behavior you'd want and expect from a company like Disney. It's not part of the job for someone representing the happiest company on earth, *it is the job*. You won't forget her, and you'll tell others about the call ("Why can't everybody do that?"). Like I just did. Jackpot, baby!

I know what you're thinking: It's easy for huge business leaders like Trader Joe's, Apple, and Disney, with enormous budgets and tons of talent (geez, I wonder how they got that way), but my business is nothing like that. I know. I know. I wanted to offer you something I knew you could immediately identify with. So now let's look at a small mom-and-pop operation where the exact same rules apply and the results are just as brag-worthy.

In the tiny hamlet of Johnsburg, Illinois (population 6,000), you'll find the extremely well positioned and highly successful Huemann Water Conditioning. Unless you happen to live in the far northern suburbs of Chicago, you've never heard of them; they're just another of the twenty-eight million–plus small businesses in America, operating far from the main drag and blending into the scenery. A family-run water softener business? Sexy they aren't (unless you happen to dig that sort of thing, in which case they're sexy as hell). But Huemann is worth knowing about because they play in the big leagues and they've been competing spectacularly for decades.

In addition to every Chicagoland plumbing company for one hundred miles, Huemann battles Home Depot, Lowe's, Sears, national hardware and farm supply chains, and a specialized household-name behemoth ("Hey Culligan Man!"), each boasting the kind of huge footprints, low prices, and advertising budgets that have driven most of the industry's smaller, family-run players out of the market. Huemann knows they'd lose if they tried to compete on price alone; in fact, the high-end equipment they sell costs more than the stuff at the big-box stores. And they rarely spend a penny to advertise. Yet they have legions of loyal customers who'd be happy to tell you about them and recommend them.

So how do they pull this off and why are they so successful? Because they're positioned to. Huemann has built and communicated an exceptionally friendly, people- and community-first "small-town" culture that reflects and upholds the attitudes of its leadership. While the industry gorillas throw their all-things-to-all-people weight around, Huemann plays small ball. And they do it on purpose, with superb execution. Their employees aren't just extra nice when inside customer homes, they're flat-out neighborly. Management tolerates nothing less than overt eagerness to please in the presence of customers. Employees schedule evening and weekend appointments to work around customer's schedules and spend extra time in seniors' homes because, as founder Tom Huemann and his son, Joe, have been telling employees for over fifty years, "Seniors always need something heavy carried up from the basement, and we're the people who will do it for them. They could be you or your parents one day."

Huemann crew members serve on volunteer fire departments—and their customers know it. They're active in their churches and in local government. Ditto. They're reserve members of the military. Ditto. And if customers don't know this stuff, crew members will make sure they do. I've actually seen people wave at Huemann trucks when they drive by. Their reputation for being consistently decent and refreshingly polite is no accident—Huemann recruits a certain type of employee (outgoing, involved, and personable) and proactively manages its staff to ensure they live up to the company's positioning.

Check this out: Every February, Huemann employees unload semi-truck loads of Girl Scout cookies for distribution from their company garage. What nice people! And what local paper wouldn't run that photo? A testimonial on their website sums Huemann up nicely: "This is how every American company should be run." Customer comments on the company's Facebook page are so flattering it's almost criminal. Go ahead and look. It's that small town thing, writ large. Who's not attracted to that? And who'd want to compete against that?

I once heard a college football coach say something that's long stayed in my memory because I believe it has a direct parallel to business. He said, "What you're seeing when you're watching a game is either what's being coached or what's being tolerated." I'd say Huemann leadership is doing some mighty fine coaching, wouldn't you? Folks, just being "good enough" won't win against the big boys.

Well then. Let's see. A small business benefiting from delighted customers telling positive stories to neighbors—even though it's selling something most folks don't fully understand and buy only once or twice in a lifetime? (Hey life insurance people, real estate agencies, financial advisors, community banks, credit unions, and home builders, are you feeling me?) Huemann's success very clearly isn't about advertising, promotion, digital wizardry, and price discounting. It's about creating *and living* strategic positioning and making beautiful noise in their market.

It's also what you're going to be doing. But it's not like you can just flip a switch and do this. There are some hurdles to clear.

Most businesses I work with fall into one of two categories: The first includes companies of the sort I mentioned earlier that ignore positioning altogether and focus on meeting internal goals like "We're going to be the leanest, low-cost, ISO-certified manufacturer in our industry by 2020." There's nothing wrong with that goal, per se. But there's plenty wrong with assuming anybody outside the company's doors cares enough about that company's internal knitting to use it as purchasing criteria.

They don't. And neither do you nor I.

From a potential customer's standpoint, your internal processes and efficiency—as undeniably important as they are to you—are simply the processes that get you in the game. Now you've got to sell against a ton of competitors who are also lean, efficient, ISO-certified, licensed, bonded, non-GMO, organic, grass-fed, etc. What else have you got? Can you imagine a corporate purchasing person, anywhere on the planet, saying to herself, "If only I could find a lean, low-cost, ISO-certified, high-quality drill press replacement parts manufacturer"?

The real crime in these internally focused companies, which exist in all industries but tends to skew more toward the B2B space, is that employees who get hammered day after day to focus on "inside" issues (quality and manufacturing metrics, sales quotas, etc.) have a hard time viewing their business as a customer would and thus don't get overly excited about competitiveness initiatives.

I ask a lot of nonsales people at B2B companies, "What do your customers look like?" Most of the time, they shrug their shoulders. "Do they work in an office, a desk on a shop floor, or a service counter?" Again with the shrug. "Are they young and tech-savvy or old-school and prefer the phone?" Now they stare at their shoes. Yikes! I simply can't imagine going to work every day and not knowing everything about who's paying the bills that make my life possible. What do you think: coached or tolerated?

The second equally large category I see is companies that take a hard swing at differentiating themselves by updating their websites and advertising but don't take their positioning far enough because they gloss over the cultural, behavioral elements required to bring it to life. So they miss how staffers at Trader Joe's, Disney, Apple, or Huemann set those companies apart.

That's a formula for failure, because when customers tell stories about a business, they're describing their key associations—*what they see, hear, and experience and how they feel about it.* When your behavior doesn't bring your positioning to life, Richie Cunningham, people notice that immediately. We see you for who you are.

And hold on to your hats, folks, because that's the best possible segue I can think of to briefly discuss the fiery, money-eating death pit known as "branding." (I know, I know. Be strong. Bear with me.)

Countless business owners apparently believe they can throw a fresh coat of paint on the building and say they're new, different, improved, and—wait for it—branded (or rebranded). Those initiatives generally culminate with lots of pomp and exciting unveilings of new logos, slogans, color schemes, signage, and website graphics. Often, it's well-intentioned marketing people, or overly compensated marketing agencies, who've led them to think this will fix everything. You've seen plenty of this, so what do you think? Does it?

I've spoken at well over a thousand industry meetings in the years since I cashed in my chips (well, stock options) at Harley to take on the world, and I seriously doubt anyone has seen as many "rebrandings" rolled out as I have. The new visual treatments and verbiage are almost always presented as a silver bullet, as in "The barrier that's been limiting our success is about to be lifted!"

Picture this (and sorry if it causes a painful flashback): The big moment, tirelessly promoted internally for the last few years, is about to happen. The lights are dimmed and (whisper this as you read it) the auditorium goes silent as a company honcho walks across the stage to the spotlit podium, where she reads a brief speech about the necessity for a rebranding, the incredible amounts of work by an incredible team that made it all happen, and how excited everyone should be. The future starts now!

A spectacular, lavishly produced, multiscreen video begins as music lifts. Just look at those fast cuts and cool visual effects, interspersed with faces of smiling employees (Hey! It's Sheila from Receiving!), close-ups of products being developed (3-D CAD screens that rival a NASA setting!), and images of company facilities and events as they've evolved over the years (Aww, the company picnic from 2004!), culminating in the grand finale—the current logo and company tagline *morphing* into the new, highly anticipated logo and tagline.

Wow! It looks incredible! Cue the thunderous applause! The lights come up, followed by new logo caps (possibly lapel pins, T-shirts, or—yep, rub-on tattoos) tossed to everyone while balloons drop from the ceiling. "Eye of the Tiger" (or, failing that, "Don't Stop Believing") blasts at maximum volume while everyone moves to the hallway for a slice of logo-iced cake and some good times. The cake gets inhaled and then . . . well . . . what? The CFO, who never got a straight answer to her "How do we measure ROI on this?" question, is the only one looking glum right now. And she has every reason to be: She's seen the math on replacing all corporate signage, the decals on the company's trucks, packaging, letterhead—*everything bearing the old logo*—with the new look.

The last time you spent money at a company and talked them up because you liked their new logo was when? New artwork, slogans, and website redesigns are fun and might even momentarily rally your troops and convince some prospective customers to take a second look, but they most certainly don't make phones and cash and registers ring over the long haul no matter how "relevant," "forward-looking," or "emotionally powerful" they are. Here's a conversation that will never happen: "Honey, let's switch banks to the one across the street that just changed its logo."

Am I against new logos and slogans? Heck no! I love them! But they don't change a business's fundamentals, philosophy, employee culture, or reputation, do they? Nor do they inspire advocacy.

It's simple: Why waste time and money on a new hairstyle when what you really need is a heart transplant?

Before we start to dig in to how your business should be positioned, I want to share the three big takeaways I learned through trial and a ton of error while working to reposition Harley-Davidson and the trunkload of other companies I've worked with since. Each of these relates directly to you:

First, if you want to position your business—or yourself—as new and different, you need to ensure that people *notice* you're factually new and different in ways they value.

Look no further for proof than the U.S. automotive industry and their seeming inability to change their approach. Their products certainly change for the better and they advertise relentlessly (Other than ad agency people and TV networks, who isn't sick of car commercials? When did annoying the hell out of people become good marketing strategy?), yet their culture hasn't noticeably changed, and most of us still loathe going to a dealership. Meanwhile, relative upstarts like Hyundai and Kia are taking larger pieces of the pie each year. How much louder can warning bells ring? And how much longer can they be ignored?

Second: Culture, everyone who's ever worked for a living will concur, reflects a business's leadership. Which is why I'm so adamant that positioning must be a visible, leadership-driven, company-wide priority, not merely a marketing tactic. Repeat that last sentence if it didn't stick the first time. Or swing by Huemann's on the first Saturday of every month for their Salt Sale Saturday—look for the long line of cars—and see it for yourself. (That's right, long line of cars. To buy water softener salt. Sexy!)

Third, as important as oxygen and new to most people: When you discuss a business—when you're describing it to someone new, relating an experience you had, or simply telling a story about it—you use or imply the pronoun "they." ("Huemann? They're awesome.") As hinted earlier, *you humanize every business you talk about.* You're very likely not describing their products, taglines, slogans, or some faceless entity; you're describing the business as a collection of people, and the stories you tell will depend on the experiences you had with *them*. You're not mad about the electronic widgets in your cable TV box—you're mad at the people *behind* your cable TV box who keep jacking up your bills and leaving you on hold when service issues ruin your movie night. "They stink!" You can think of lots of other businesses you'd describe that way, can't you?

It's amazing how many business leaders never stop to consider that damn "they." I've seen scads of them go silent when I explain this to them and I know it's because they're trying to imagine how their customers are describing them and hoping (perhaps praying) it's positive. I often ask leaders, "Do your customers and prospects see your business as an 'it' or a 'they'?" Meaning, are their first associations with you the things you sell ("its" like ball bearings, pizza, insurance, office machine repair, hotel rooms) or your people?

If all your business is known for is a product (or products), it's extremely difficult to build customer loyalty. That goes double if you're only known for the low price of those products. We're humans, remember? *We're infinitely more loyal to other humans than we are to easily replaceable products.* Quick! Name some products you're loyal to. Not so easy, is it? Which is why your business needs to be a "they" instead of an "it."

I wasn't taught this—I don't believe anyone's being taught this—but discovered it simply by listening when I ask people to describe their relationships with businesses. I hear a lot more "they" when people spoke glowingly (or negatively!) and lots of "it" when they immediately default to discussing products and prices. When the only thing you're known for is what you sell, you're leaving yourself defenseless against competitors who sell that same thing; they'll just undercut you on price.

These takeaways seem obvious once you think about them. What's not obvious is what to do about them, right? It's not like your employees—whether there are two of them or two thousand—are begging you to change what's expected of them. Leaders bemoan all the time the difficulty in introducing improvement initiatives of any kind to their charges.

The most frequently heard—and completely understandable—laments I hear from them are "My employees all listen as we explain what we'd like our business to become, then they say, 'Great. What's any of this got to do with me?'" Or "I don't ever talk to customers, so I don't have to be involved in this." Or worse, "Yeah, here we go again. Let me know how it all works out."

From what I've witnessed, there are three primary reasons employees at nearly all levels don't believe they need to participate in positioning initiatives or do anything differently. You've likely witnessed all of these, even if you're still wet behind the ears in the working world.

The first and biggest obstacle to success is poor communication from the get-go. When a business is working to alter its approach to its marketplace to improve competitiveness, employees are often treated as an afterthought when in reality, they'll determine how successful those efforts will be. They're not part of the process, they *are the process*! They're the "they" that customers and other important publics will or won't be talking about!

Second, regardless of the job, environment, or tenure, people who work for a living mimic the behavior of their superiors. You probably didn't know this, but just look around and prove it to yourself. This can be really good. Or horribly bad. If company leaders (execs, managers, supervisors, shop stewards, team directors, etc.) bad-mouth the business (its products, customers, suppliers, other leaders, etc.) and groan at initiatives to improve competitiveness, everyone working under them acts the same way and repeats the negative garbage they're hearing. It's human nature. Seriously, is there a business in the world that doesn't have "Oh, No. Here We Go Again," as the opening cut in its greatest-hits collection? This aversion people who've witnessed less-than-successful attempts to improve their companies have to seeing "another $&*# program" being shoved down their throats by leaders who also happen to be singing the "Oh, No. Here We Go Again," song is *learned behavior*. (And, by the way, "bad morale" isn't an employee issue; it's a leadership issue. Employees are simply modeling what they're seeing and repeating what they're hearing from their leaders. Case closed.)

It goes without saying but I'll say it anyway: When leaders speak and act positively, are visibly passionate and involved, encourage their charges, and connect with them (instead of "communicate at" them), that behavior is also modeled.

The third common stumbling block is that ugly truth that work cultures don't change simply because leadership or, God forbid, the marketing or human resources department says they have to. No company ever became "customer driven" or "people friendly" or "community minded" simply by saying so. But you wouldn't believe how many times I've heard top execs say things from the podium to their employees like "Starting now, we'll be creating great experiences for our customers," as if they just waved some sort of magic wand. "Now go make it happen! (And let me know how it works out.)"

The lessons to take from this are, again, threefold. Cultures evolve for competitive advantage: 1) when executive leadership makes it their organization's top priority; 2) when all employees are involved from early ideation to implementation and understand, appreciate, and can explain what's required of them—and what's in it for them; and 3) when full, enthusiastic participation from all people holding leadership positions is demanded and monitored from above (remember: dominators *love* accountability).

I know I've hit you with a lot of concepts in a short amount of time. If your head is spinning, that's good—it means you're considering new strategies and wondering if you and your organization have the fortitude to position or reposition yourselves and kick some serious ass in your market.

Know this: You do. So, then, back to Noise Cubed.

1. What are people saying about you?
2. What do you want them to say?
3. What are you doing to get them to say it?

CHAPTER

THREE

Truth in Packaging, Italian-Style: Managing Position and Narrative to Dominate

It's high time to start thinking about not only how to make sure you're properly positioned and living your positioning in ways that get noticed and reacted to, but also how to create your positioning language and manage your narrative to improve the chances that they're talking about you and saying what you want said.

To get in the proper frame of mind and prepped for what lies ahead, let's start where I always start: with a bike story. Ride with me in spirit and I'll give you the main course (that's a little more foreshadowing; food will be a recurring theme throughout this chapter). Here goes.

We're lost. Again (a recurring theme throughout my life). Somewhere at the southern base of the Alps in northern Italy. But what do we care? We're in heaven. And it only took us three days to get here. I'm not worried and you'd better not be either.

We kinda-sorta knew where we were at sunrise, as we loaded our bikes beside our tiny cottagelike *pension* hotel (picture weathered wood exterior, geranium-stuffed window boxes, a beautifully simple white-cross-on-red-background Swiss flag, and lazy cat curled by the door) in the small burb of Horgen, Switzerland, on Lake Zurich, maybe a half hour outside the city it was named for. With bellies still full from the incredible stew and spaetzle dinner the innkeeper prepared for us after our late arrival from the Alsace region in France last night—as always, we took the scenic route— we reluctantly pulled our raingear on to combat the light mist as we sipped our morning joe.

I'm riding a Wide Glide on this venture, a classic Harley cruiser strongly reminiscent of 1950s and '60s era choppers, only much more refined, with full suspension and brakes that actually work (anyone who's ever ridden a true chopper will tell you that "brakes" were more a polite suggestion to slow the rear wheel than actually bring you to a quick halt, and "suspension" was your backbone). Because I opted to go bare-bones on this trip—the better to appreciate the incredible twisty mountain roads we've been feasting on—there's no windshield, so I'm riding with a full-face helmet to block the wind and, if needed, rain. Other than a headlamp and turn signals, there's nothing but a speedometer mounted to the handlebars, meaning there's no stereo, GPS, temperature gauge, or even clock. I'm also riding "bagless," so there are no built-in places to store gear, which explains the week's worth of necessities stuffed into a thick, waterproof duffel and bungeed onto my backseat. Talk about packing light!

In fact, all five of us on this venture are riding cruisers, which are sadly becoming things of the past as more and more riders around the world are opting for the creature comforts of gadget-laden, long-distance touring machines. Hard to argue, of course (I own touring bikes myself), but the pure essence of motorcycling—nothing more than two wheels, a loping motor, a seat, some handlebars, and the rush of the wind—is something everyone should experience and savor. On a journey like this one, with equal measures of incredible beauty and challenging roads, riding a cruiser only intensifies the glory.

Wheels pointed south toward the mountains and rolling against the morning rush of city-bound commuters in their expensive-looking German sedans, our spirits are lifting with the misty lake-effect fog. As the road narrows, oncoming traffic disappears, and the villages give way to countryside, we take full advantage of the opportunity to get more aggressive with our throttles and let fly. Within minutes of starting our gradual Alpine ascent, we can only laugh with surprise as we get hit with short swirls of wet snow. All this means is that the ever-cooler temperatures as we climb will require more café stops than we'd usually need. And, naturally, the most pastries we'll consume in one morning in our lives. Nobody on earth makes pastries like Europeans. And surely nobody would argue that.

As our ascent becomes seriously steeper, it becomes increasingly challenging to keep our eyes on the road versus the spectacular scenery of rolling green pastures, tiny postcard-worthy villages, and mountain farms made better by the occasional clanging of bells hanging from the necks of dairy cows. Looks great. Smells great. Sounds great. Talk about sensory overload! This isn't awesome in the overused way that word's used today, it's awesome in the dictionary sense of the word.

Concentration can't waver here, though, because the road is chock-full of ridiculously tight hairpin curves and double-S twisties (think of the letter *S* with another *S* on top of it—or think of squiggles, the most unmanly word you'll read today). Over and over, clouds build then throw brief sputters of cold rain mixed with snow, giving us just a little more to think about as we share those turns with Euro truckers coming the opposite direction at insane speeds. How these guys can barrel through these turns and hold their lines is an incredible testament to their skill. Or bravery. Either way, it's nuts. This passage is more goat path than roadway. Which, of course, is why we're loving every second of it.

As we ascend above the tree line and even above the clouds, the drizzles disappear and the alpine scenery becomes lunar-like—brown and barren in some spots, snow covered in others. We're well layered for the cold, but I'll admit my fingers are pretty getting stiff (next time, electric heated gloves—yes, they exist). In patches of bright blue skies, the scenery extends as far as we can see. France to the east, Germany to the north, Lichtenstein to the west, and to the south, Italy. Safe areas to pull over and enjoy the views, though, are very few and far between. There's little automotive traffic, save those occasional trucks, but we're seeing plenty of motorcycles coming the opposite direction, which is always a good sign. We'll follow some of them into the parking lot of a very tiny, chalet-like roadside café with a waterfall running down the sheer rock face behind it. Who wouldn't stop here?! Added bonus: The only vehicles in the lot are bikes, their license plates a European geography lesson.

Lots of hellos, laughs, and broken English "Where're you going?" and "Please to take our peek-sure?" ensue as we shimmy shoulder to shoulder with each other in the tiny place, then squeeze back outside to see the falls and take those peek-sures. Great stuff—as warming for the soul as the massive fireplace and espressos were for the body. Superb news comes when riders rolling from the opposite direction tell us they've ridden through nothing but sunny, beautiful conditions.

Rested and warm, we begin the final climb before what we know will be a long, magnificent ride down the other side. Gooey with excitement, we're getting heavier on the throttle and soon we know we've reached the top because the only road we can see stretching out in the valleys before us is going downhill. So we're whooping and fist pumping as we start attacking the curves with intensity.

My Harley's thundering beneath me, its throaty exhaust echoing off the sheer rock wall that's been toeing the road's edge and blocking light from a landscape that, for miles, has been barren and lifeless. Or so I think. Flying through a blind curve, my heart bursts as I reflexively panic-skid to an abrupt halt. My feet firmly on the ground, I'm now simultaneously gasping for breath, grinning, and staring directly into something I've never seen from up close before, just inches from my Wide Glide's front fender: a Swiss cow's ass. Interesting, but not exactly the view I had in mind.

This is crazy! Anyone unlucky enough to go over the edge here and fall to the bottom wouldn't just see his life flash before his eyes, he'd have enough time for the full-length director's cut including the deleted scenes.

My pals to my right and left, having panic-stomped and squeezed their brakes in time with mine, are shaking their heads in confused relief and enjoying the same views with their own cows, as the small herd's tender frantically swats his charges with a stick, encouraging them to make way for us noisy intruders. At that exact moment, it's safe to say that all of us—five nearly frozen Harley riders, the tender, and his dozen or so unimpressed cows—were thinking the exact same thing: "What the hell are they doing up here?"

And that's precisely why I ride motorcycles. Well, that and the fact it was a business trip.

Aren't you glad you got to see that?

After several more hours of the greatest roads, riding, and scenery anyone could hope to experience, we find ourselves on much flatter terrain. The unblocked sun means we've been gradually shedding and storing our extra layers, raingear, and gloves in the autumn-like temps and the bone-dry pavement has given us the green light to go heavy on the gas and revel in our already off-the-charts spirits. Sweeping, scenic roads through gorgeous lakeside towns beckon and we dutifully follow. This is the essence of motorcycling in rural Europe, on mountain passes and minor roads laid down centuries before the notion of highways, let alone pavement, even existed. They pull us in, thrill us to our bones, bring us face-to-face with quaint, traditional lifestyles and gorgeous architecture, then spit us out. And we do it over and over. Right up until we realize we're lost.

But what do we care? We're in heaven. We know we'll eventually find our way to Italy's Lake Garda, where the Southern European Harley Owners Group (H.O.G.) rally is set to open tomorrow. It strikes none of us as unusual that it took three very long days to get this far from our departure point in Frankfurt, Germany, a distance we could easily have covered in seven hours, were we the freeway-riding type. Plus we'd stopped along the way to visit Harley dealerships and enjoy lingering meals with their owners. (The food and hospitality were exceptional. Local *fois gras et vin? Oui et absolument!*)

I'm not remotely proud of what I did to help get us back on track. As we found ourselves rolling into the shopping district of a very small village near Lake Maggiore, we eyeballed the sidewalks looking for someone who might be able to guide us where we needed to go. I coasted up next to the first person I saw, a rather elderly woman (expression on her face exactly what you're imagining right now) and broke into my best idiotic American-style Italian—which is to say, five or six mispronounced Italian words sprinkled with English, hollered loud and slow. The poor old gal was having none of it. So naturally I started speaking louder, flailing my arms, and, to better help her understand the gravity of the situation, waving a map.

Maybe it was our road stubble, our dirty, menacing-looking bikes, or, more likely, me making a complete moron of myself that frightened her, but she turned and started to hastily make tracks. Instinctively and stupidly, I rolled slowly alongside her and continued my very offensive charm offensive. This attracted the attention of a few men up the sidewalk who threw down their cigarettes, jogged over, and made it very clear that this was someone's precious Nonna I was chasing down the street. At that point, the obviousness of my blunder registered immediately and I thought of my own Italian grandmother and how I would have reacted if I'd seen her waddling away from five leathered-up men on frightening Harleys. I spit out a guilty-as-charged "*Scusi, scusi,*" which was the wrong term for that situation, but the only one I could think of. I felt as stupid as I'm sure I looked.

We backed our bikes up to the curb and wandered into a small market where we found someone behind the counter who was able to show us our exact location on a map. Perfect! We charted a course to get (somewhat) pointed in the right direction and were none the worse for the wear. So, naturally, it was time for some celebratory snacks and cappuccinos. While the other guys inhaled gelato (always a good call), I noticed the store was selling half-moon-shaped fruit pastries that reminded me of the Hostess fruit pies of my youth, so I had to try them. I couldn't tell from the package illustration what fruit it was, but I was too hungry to care. Besides, everybody knows there's no such thing as a bad Italian snack. Washing it down with cappuccino confirms it.

By the time I'd finished happily stuffing the third unusual-tasting treat down my throat, I figured out that the fruit on the package was a fig. Uh-oh.

I will tell you this as a friend: You don't ever, ever want to eat three fig pies when you're on a long motorcycle trip in an area that doesn't have plentiful rest stops. *Capisce?* Anyway . . .

As we drew closer to the Lake Garda area, our already epic ride reached quantum levels as the roads gradually became choked with Harleys. I wish there was a way to describe how magical it feels to be completely surrounded by Harleys—hundreds, eventually thousands of them—all headed in the same direction to the same place, en masse. The mechanical roar, the friendly waves, the country flags flying from rear fenders, Scottish riders in kilts (swear to God), the smiles coming from every car window, horns bleating . . . it's intoxicating. Even the world's biggest motorcycle hater couldn't deny the joyous beauty in this.

We hit the rally in time for its opening ceremony, had a few frosty Morettis, then met up with friends from Harley's European team, slapped a lot of backs, stuffed ourselves with olives, cheese, cured meat, and pasta, then walked from our hotel to a small bar where we and a few hundred more Harley riders acted foolish and told stories until closing time.

All in a day's work.

To this day, though, I can't shake knowing that I should have played things differently with the old gal on the sidewalk. I have to believe that she relayed our story—and her fear—to her friends (and maybe still is), thus only furthering lingering negative stereotypes about Harley riders. Or starting new ones. The same goes for the nicotine-fueled guardian angels who'd rushed to her aid. Because that's what people do. Clearly I know better and clearly I blew it. I was careless while wearing the team uniform, an ill-will ambassador. This little episode so easily could have had an infinitely more positive result.

So. As I've asked before and will continue to ask: What are the people your business served or spoke with yesterday saying about your business right now? If your business has multiple employees who interact with customers, potential customers, and other important publics in the flesh, over the phone, or online—some companies have *thousands* of people matching this description—you can see how many opportunities exist to bring your positioning to life, spread your most important differentiating messages, and make consistently powerful noise. Or, as I inadvertently did in the above story, do exactly the opposite.

Remember when I told you about Harley's problems when the market controlled everything being said about the business and everyone associated with it? And how much harm that caused? A great lesson we can take from that is, you're either working to manage your narrative—the strategically chosen, easily memorable, differentiating words you use to support and validate your desired positioning that your important publics associate uniquely with you and repeat in their conversations with others—or you're not in control. There's no in-between on this! Living your positioning and managing your narrative have to exist hand in glove. You've seen it—and spoken of it—when it works. And when it doesn't. Let's break them both down.

Think of a recent positive thing you've heard or said about a business. You may have to scratch your head a bit to recall such an instance (I'll wait). And here's the thing: The instant that memory crystallizes in your mind, you'll know whether or not that business is intentionally living its desired positioning and if its narrative is under control.

If you're having trouble thinking of a current personal experience, you're probably thinking too big. Focus your thoughts on small, local businesses that you're apt to regularly frequent. Restaurants are an easy pick and offer great lessons because they're easy to visualize. Plus, it's easy to draw parallels between them and your own business, as you'll soon see.

My wife and I had two very recent experiences with high-end restaurants in Washington, DC, that perfectly showcased the power of one organization working together to make great noise and one that, apparently, believed its product did all the talking. (Remember: When we describe a business, we use or imply the pronoun "they." Even great products can't speak for themselves.)

Remember how I pointed out "tells" in our trade show visit to show you obvious mistakes? Be alert and see if you can spot the positive and negative tells in these two examples. I'm betting you can. (Actually, by the time we're done here, you'll find yourself habitually identifying tells with every business you encounter. That means you're thinking like a dominator!)

The first, Marcel's, was exceptional from the get-go, something I've rarely said about a restaurant. The gentleman taking my phone reservation was very polite and conversational, asking if we were attending the theater or another event that night and informing me that they provide complementary black-car service to local shows—a surprise and a great touch, especially in a city where traffic and parking on a weekend night is hell. He also asked if the staff could help us celebrate something special like a birthday, graduation, or anniversary to make for a more memorable evening, something we've all heard before, but he went further, saying that no request was too big and that their chefs and crew loved to be challenged. His eagerness to please and boast about his coworkers was most definitely noticed and appreciated. All in all, a brief but very pleasant conversation with some memorable wows. Free limo service?! Uh, hell yes!

When we arrived, the parking valet announced us to the maître d', who greeted us enthusiastically by name—as if he knew us—then ushered us to our table. The setting was quiet, comfortable, and beautiful. Our waiter was so polite, conversational, attentive, knowledgeable, and helpful (offering multiple recommendations and samples of wine, for example) that my wife and I joked that we wished he'd move in next door to us. He said it was his job to make our evening exceptional and he obviously meant it. Every seat at every table was occupied so they were obviously running at full steam, which, as we've all experienced, easily leads to problems. Not so here.

The food was as spectacular as it was creative, miles beyond our expectations, even given the high prices. Yet, believe it or not, I can't recall, only a few weeks later, what I ate (suffice to say it wasn't steak and potatoes). And the best part of that is, it's not important. My wife and I each felt, from start to finish, that we were being doted upon, catered to, and made to feel important and special. That, as we all know, is a rare and delightful feeling. I'm convinced that no one else in the dining room that night was receiving better treatment than we were. I would have seen it if they were.

Marcel's? They're exceptional. I'm just repeating what the waiter said (See? *That's how it's done!*). I can't say enough positive things about them. What a memorable evening we had. And what a well-run operation.

And isn't that precisely what one should expect from a pricey establishment? And isn't that the very least they should be able to deliver on? Would that such was always the case (heavy sigh).

Not far from Marcel's is an equally pricey place I'll spare from embarrassment by changing their name to John's. Suffice to say it's a very popular eatery, which, at the time of this writing, is experiencing buzz as a "place to see and been seen." I love a good buzz (you can quote me on that), so I wanted to find out if it was justified.

Let's start with my first impression, a phone call with a harried person who seemed interested only in ending the call as quickly as possible. Look, I get it. You're busy. That's your problem. Strike one. On arriving a few nights later, the maître d', after eyeballing us and determining we weren't fat cats (what does he know?), hurriedly walked us to what had to be one of the worst tables in the house. Guess I was supposed to tip him to get a better table? Not in this lifetime, buddy. Strike two. We then got a great look at the entire operation as we sat . . . and sat . . . and sat . . . at least fifteen minutes, waiting to be acknowledged. My wife has the patience of an itchy squirrel and started fidgeting and looking for someone to offer assistance. The first two people we flagged over were support staff with zero mastery of the English language and an uncanny ability to disappear without a trace. Strike three. One out.

Finally, someone comes to take drink orders. Our cocktails, with their steep prices, were quite good and, in other circumstances, would have been worthy of conversation, but they weren't good enough to erase the ten minutes we'd waited for them to appear. Strike one. While soaking up the atmosphere, we spied our waiter and other staff members waiting hand and foot on some apparent big shot/heavy tipper (I'll not comment on his "date," who looked forty years his junior—but hey, it's DC and she's got bills to pay like everybody else, if you know what I mean). Huge strike two. Waiter comes to take dinner order and is clearly in such a hurry that he doesn't want to answer questions without simply barking out his recommendations (not surprisingly, some of the most expensive stuff on the menu). Strike three. Second batter's out. Our patience is about shot.

The food arrives and oh my God! Stop the presses! It's very, very good and I'm wallowing in the kind of food-induced ecstasy that makes my eyes roll. It's so good I can't wipe the silly grin from my face. My compliments to the kitchen crew for bringing their A game and making John's uber-steep prices a bit easier to swallow. Once again, I can't recall exactly what I ate (I travel constantly and eat out all the time) but I know I loved it.

The waiter asks if we'd like dessert, which we decline, only to have him plop our bill on the table immediately. As in, "We've got customers waiting. Please move along." Strike one. Quick trips to the restroom require us to squeeze, literally and uncomfortably, between tables, making it a journey of desperation and, frankly, embarrassment. Strike two. The waiter—without asking a single question about our experience and without offering anything remotely sincere in the form of thanks—scoops up the bill, never to be seen again. Strike three. The side is out. And so are we.

While the differences here are obvious (they are, aren't they?), the reasons behind them likely aren't. Both places did a great job of providing a "high quality" (quotes are there for a reason I'll explain later) product and, thereby, meeting the most obvious and attainable of our expectations, especially given the high price points. Remember, even though it was spectacular, I can't recall precisely what I ate at either place.

But what would you say about the overall strategies of each establishment? The working cultures of each? And what's expected and demanded of employees by their leaders? What's being coached versus what's being tolerated?

I'm sure the owners of John's would be quick to apologize and equally quick to say our waiting team had an off night. You know, a rare misstep. And that could easily be true; nobody bats a thousand. But what would they say of every other turnoff we'd experienced from the very beginning? Why were we made to feel like second-class citizens—and worse when we saw others being fawned over? Why did no person working there make an effort to connect with us? I'm hard-pressed to imagine that my wife and I are the only people who've ever felt shortchanged by their staff.

I've long been convinced that most businesspeople view their business the way they wish it to be seen and would be rather disheartened if they peered through Reality Goggles that show how it looks in real life from a customer's point of view. Because John's product is great and gets positive mentions in write-ups, perhaps their management assumes they're golden. But "product" isn't what my wife (a frequent Yelp contributor) and I are talking about when we describe a restaurant, is it? How quickly would you make a reservation at John's based on what you just read?

When John's management and employees sit down together at staff meetings, do they ask, "What do we want people to say about us?" and "What do we have to do make them say it?" Then bust their butts to make sure it happens? Well, what do you think? And do you think it's coincidence that both the waiter at Marcel's and I used the same word to describe them? He said "exceptional" more than once and so have I.

If you think of every negative thing you've ever heard or said about a business, you can likely track it back to its sources: The belief that products speak for themselves, unmanaged positioning, and sleepwalking leadership. Remember the third leg of Noise Cubed! A business's strategy and market presence has to reflect its desired positioning—meaning we have to be who we say we are and do what we say we do. Always. And it's the responsibility of leadership to create a work culture that ensures it.

Back during Harley's tough times, its dealers could have held cures for infectious diseases on their sales floors and *still* nobody would have come in. There was an invisible force field around these dealerships that essentially said, "Unless you're already one of us, keep out." Sure, they and their staffs were working their butts off, but when it came to positioning, controlling narrative, and making noise in the local markets they'd served, they were sleepwalking and waiting for someone else—say, "corporate"— to solve their competitive issues.

Imagine the power each of these dealers had to overcome at least some of the company's issues in the markets they served. They didn't need to save the world and solve all of Harley's competitive issues; they just needed to be the best, most talked about bike dealerships *in their local markets.* Had these small, family-owned businesses known then what most of them know now, they could have overcome many of those obstacles under their own roofs without waiting for someone else to tackle the larger problems. It would have made a huge difference in their individual bottom lines.

A more recent example I'm sure you're familiar with comes courtesy of the folks at Chipotle, who took a royal beating when serious food integrity issues—fueled by E. coli and the instant fear it breeds—surfaced in a few of their restaurants in late 2015. The former darling of the quick service restaurant industry has yet to recover to its stellar performance levels and quite possibly never will.

Would their situation be different if the chain were widely known for anything other than its products? Did we ever get the sense from the people working in their locations that they were making any real effort to delight us, other than simply taking our orders and giving us what we asked for— great-tasting food? Do you feel a personal connection to them or recall any times when they made you feel special? Or made any kind of overt effort to treat you as anything more than the next person in line?

(Here's a hint for everyone in a customer-facing business: If the first and only things a customer sees are the tops of your employee's heads? You're playing with fire.)

A quick study in contrast would be Chick-fil-A, who suffered a substantial crisis of their own back in 2012 (do you even remember what caused it?), resulting in reams of negative press, organized boycotts, countless social media rants, and even televised removals of some of their locations from college campuses. Yet they recovered any lost ground very quickly and not just because their product (it's a chicken sandwich, people!) tastes great.

If you can find a quick service restaurant chain whose staff is as routinely courteous, overtly friendly, and delightful to be around as Chick-fil-A's, I'd like to know about it. They're very good at this. They demand of their employees—and the managers they mimic—nothing less than complete dedication to delighting customers. And it shows. (Plus, I'm sure their corporate leaders have since learned what not to say when publicly discussing hypersensitive social issues and likely won't make that mistake again.)

I don't have access to the data, but I'm pretty sure both of these quick serve restaurant giants pay their counter people similar, if not identical, wages, so you can't blame any positioning missteps on the quality of their hires (which leadership people do all the time, as in "What do you expect from people at the bottom of the pay scale?"). Yet one thrives while the other struggles.

I'm firmly of the belief that Chipotle learned a valuable lesson that eventually punishes all who ignore it: When you live by product, sooner or later you die by it. (You hear that, car companies? What happened to Pontiac?) I'm guessing they're now focusing as much on how to positively harness the collective energies and passions of their people, to create a more inviting customer atmosphere, as they are on ensuring product integrity. For the sake of their employees, I sure hope they are.

Another thing to consider: Every business makes mistakes. But who are we quick to forgive? People we feel we know and are attached to—or faceless corporate entities? "They" or "it"?

Remember what I said earlier, "The people most impacted by problems are the ones who stand to gain the most from solving them." Meaning: Although the issues facing Chipotle, Chick-fil-A, and Harley, back in the day, played out nationally (even internationally), each organization's franchisees ultimately held the most power to confront and defeat them. Because they're the "faces" and "voices" of the business.

In fact, I always tell companies with multiple locations that the largest single responsibility of those running these locations—think retail outlets, distribution warehouses, hospitals, banks, franchises, service centers—is managing what the people in the local marketplace they serve feel about and say about the *local* business. Because that's all they can control! And narrative must be both strategic and managed or it's out of control!

Just like a Chick-fil-A franchise manager, the person running the Grainger Industrial Supply facility in Harrisburg, Pennsylvania, is 100 percent responsible for what maintenance and repair people in Harrisburg feel and say about Grainger in Harrisburg. What customers experience Grainger employees saying and doing under Grainger Harrisburg's roof or when Grainger employees are on customer shop floors determines how competitive this location will be against the other industrial equipment firms fighting for those Harrisburg dollars. National advertising and promotions can shape perceptions and expectations and drive traffic into individual locations, but generating loyal, vocal, repeat customers is a local responsibility.

Positive narrative is gold. But you have to earn it.

If you think about everything you've read up to this point, and the various scenarios and business situations we've reviewed, you'll see that there's a common denominator among the successful businesses and people: They're worth talking about. In other words, they're story-worthy. They've positioned themselves, lived up to that positioning, and said and done things that others find compelling enough to share with others. (The opposite, of course, defines the nonsuccessful.)

Speaking of being story-worthy and how and why it's important for you and your business, I have a quick question for you to fire up your brain: What world-famous travel destination positioned itself so spectacularly, after a high profile rebranding failure destroyed its "cool factor" and dampened demand, that its positioning slogan has become a catchphrase you typically use while telling stories about it? I'll give you a hint: Its positioning is so powerful that, no matter where you live or what language you speak, all I have to do is hint at its name for that slogan, the incredible mental imagery that accompanies it, and a story or two to instantly come to mind?

Did you figure it out? If not, just finish this sentence, because I know you can: "What happens in Vegas . . ."

See if you can remember this: Back in the 1990s, the powers that be out in Vegas took a long look at improving their competitive situation and determined that Vegas would have to be more attractive to families if it was going to stop losing business to the travel industry's 800-pound gorilla, Disney. So Vegas rebranded itself as a family destination and invested heavily in a massive indoor amusement park, water slides on the Strip, and other kid-friendly attractions and activities to lure families in.

Bad idea. Bad, bad idea. Among the many problems that come to mind with this rebranding was: The taboo, risqué, and very "adult" stuff that

Vegas is most known for continued unabated while the "family" stuff was in operation. Good Lord, what a train wreck.

So now in Vegas you had kids and their families spilling out of the water parks just in time for rolling billboards to cruise down the strip featuring nearly nude young women under a header saying "Cheerleaders Will Come to Your Room" while nearly every taxi passing by toted a sign with similarly unclad women promoting a strip joint. Disney had nothing on this kind of good, old-fashioned family fun! Imagine the uncomfortable conversations this caused between parents and their kids. And how uncomfortable the presence of kids made adult visitors feel when they were trying to live out their Sin City dreams. Bottom line: Is there a less appropriate place for kids on the planet? The disconnect was as stunning as I'm sure it was bad for business.

So Vegas looked where they should have looked earlier—way further down the road instead of at the distractions right in front of them—to determine where they needed to be. And determined that they had to play to their strengths, rather than trying to be something they clearly couldn't be, if they were going to create the kind of storytelling that brings new visitors and keeps cash registers ringing.

And what's Vegas most known for? And what's it have that no other destination has that people find powerfully attractive? It's not just the obvious givens of gambling in spectacular casinos and great shows. But combine those with taboo, risqué stuff, elements of danger, adult freedom, and opportunities for misbehavior, and, well, that makes for one helluva potent cocktail, doesn't it? So Vegas repositioned itself to play to its strengths and prompt countless stories. And for nearly two decades, has been packing them in and smashing records.

There's not a CEO or marketing person alive—yours truly included—who wouldn't love to claim credit for something as once-in-a-generation great as "What happens in Vegas stays in Vegas." How's this for brilliant? You only had that to hear that slogan once to remember it, it's absolutely unique to Vegas (another travel destination couldn't copy it without looking pathetic), it mentions the product twice(!), and it's so fun to repeat that you've used it as a punch line or storytelling device any time you or somebody you know has returned from there.

Equally awesome is that fact that every time you hear "What happens in Vegas," images appear in your mind. And those images tend to be, well . . . let's say . . . filthy! Isn't that great? Vegas's positioning is sinful and taboo without being overtly so, because that's exactly where your mind wants to go. And of course that's exactly where Vegas wants it to go. They don't have to show you tawdry imagery because you apply your own after seeing or hearing just those seven words! It's dynamite in a bottle and I love it.

What I love most about it, though, is the valuable lesson it teaches us. A lesson that's very easy to share with your coworkers.

See, the greatest thing about "What happens in Vegas stays in Vegas," perhaps the most spectacularly executed positioning platform of all time, is that's it's a big, fat lie. There's not one element of truth to it! The people behind Las Vegas know this, of course; the irony's not lost on them.

Just think: If what happened in Vegas actually stayed in Vegas, there'd be no Vegas! If Vegas visitors never talked about it, nobody who hadn't been there before would know anything about it, would they? So why would anybody go there?

I don't know anyone who took his or her first trip to Vegas after seeing an ad for it or stumbling upon it while doing an Internet search for vacation destinations. Do you? We take our first trip there because we've heard stories about it from everyone we know who's been there. And those stories painted pictures in our minds and made us curious enough to say, "I'm gonna have to go see this myself one day." And off you went. (And just think how damaging the "I went to Vegas and there were kids everywhere!" stories were.)

If you came home from a trip to Las Vegas and didn't tell stories about the wonderfully over-the-top hotel you stayed at, by name, of course, the amazing shows you saw, the crazy story your cabdriver told you about all the wackiness that went down last weekend, the fantastic restaurants you enjoyed, the money you almost won playing blackjack, the perfect bodies tanning by the hotel's ridiculously decadent pool (Spoiler alert: the hottest of those bodies are paid to be there for your viewing pleasure and story sharing with cell phone photo visual aids—I'm sorry, but that's just so brilliantly simple I have to salute it), and the sinful, raunchy, taboo stuff being promoted everywhere, Vegas would be in big trouble. And they know that. They know only too well what happens when the storytelling turns negative. Or stops altogether.

Put simply, the livelihood of hundreds of thousands of people, including every property owner, blackjack dealer, housekeeping staffer, waiter, entertainer, pole dancer, bar back, cabdriver, or money counter out there, is dependent on everyone who visits—that's you—raving about it to your friends and coworkers back home and telling them *everything* that happened when you were in Vegas. And, best of all, telling them that they have to go and see it themselves.

The most important thing to learn from is this is directly applicable to you and your business: If, as a Vegas visitor, you keep what happened in Vegas in Vegas when you get home, you're not creating any new demand for Vegas—your lack of storytelling means you're not bringing them a single new visitor—which puts all of those jobs in jeopardy. This also dumps the onus of new visitor acquisition squarely on the shoulders of marketing people. And as everyone knows, "marketing" is an expensive way to attract new blood!

There's a very simple cause-and-effect formula at work here. So repeat after me: "No story means no demand."

If customers of *any* business (like, say, yours) don't have something positive to say about it—without being asked—that business is at a very strong competitive disadvantage. Dominant businesses know that vocal customers bring them new customers and work to make that happen.

What do the people you depend on say about you? What stories to they tell? Do they tell stories at all? (Again, think back on the scenarios we viewed through our Reality Goggles earlier and how storytelling would have made a huge difference for all parties involved.)

If you're going to be a dominant competitor, you absolutely need the people you serve and are dependent upon—the people who know you best—to value what you do and have at least one good story or anecdote to tell about you. And you need these stories to be the stories you want told, using the same language you'd use to describe yourself. When people are telling your story for you and using your preferred language, it means your positioning is working and that people understand you, like you, and want others to know about you. So your reputation is being built one delighted person at a time.

Which means, in a nutshell, you need to do things for people that exceed what you're doing now. We—that's all of us—have to change our game.

Let's take this Vegas study further and uncover the greatest lesson I can share from it. If, after returning from a trip to Vegas, you kept what happened in Vegas in Vegas and told nobody about your experiences there, it would mean just one thing: Las Vegas met your expectations. And *that,* friends, is where the competitive wheels of nearly every nondominant business (and person) in the world fall off.

I'd happily bet my eyesight that no human being in the history of the world ever told someone a story about a time when his or her expectations were met—no matter how high those expectations may have been—or when someone gave him or her what they'd paid for. And the reason for this is simple: It would be the most mind-numbingly boring story ever told!

(Examples: "Guess what? When I dropped my shirts off at the cleaners, they said they'd be done by five on Thursday. And, wow! They were!" Or, "I checked in at the hotel, went up to my room, and the bathroom was clean!" See? Yawn.)

And just who or whom created this problem? We did. In a commoditized world, meeting expectations is a total no-brainer. The tragic dividend of our global economy and the ever-increasing digitalization of everything in our lives is a business world that's gotten so painfully good at giving us what we want, when we want it, and how we want it, at prices we're comfortable with, that we've grown to believe that every business in existence is "good enough" to take care of us. We've learned this through personal experience—I mean, is there anyone among us who doesn't order things online from businesses we've never heard of? Our expectations are met by everybody, every time, right? We're as accustomed to this as we are to breathing, so, naturally, we don't talk about it.

When the lightbulbs you ordered online from Light Bulb Planet on Monday—after comparing prices and finding theirs the lowest—arrive at your door on Wednesday, do you tell anybody about what you bought and who you bought it from while strongly recommending lightbulbplanet.com? Of course not. Did you even remember their name as you tore open the brown box by your front door that they'd sent? Of course not. (We buy lots of things from lots of businesses and the brown boxes *always* show up!) Worse still, will you even remember their name the next time you need bulbs?

Did Lightbulb Planet do anything you'd notice or say anything you'd remember? Was there something delightfully unexpected on their website that made you take pause? A surprise in the box? A personal note? A touch of wit? A quick follow-up phone call to say thanks for the business? Something—*anything*—that would compel you to do business with them again or tell a story about them? Or enthusiastically offer them up if somebody asked for a recommendation? Not likely!

What you experienced with Lightbulb Planet was just one of the thousands of faceless, baseless, nameless, emotionless, totally nonmemorable, and never discussed transactions you'll have over the course of a year. After chowing down at a massive all-you-can-eat buffet, can you remember everything that you ate the next day? Let alone a few months from now? Can anybody?

Your customers are just like us. They've been to lots of buffets. They shop around, too. Brown boxes show up at their doors all the time. They're completely comfortable doing business with strangers—if those strangers are willing to sell at the lowest price or are more convenient. And totally used to getting exactly what they needed and what they paid for. This stuff's even scarier in the B2B world; can you imagine how many of these "just-as-expected" transactions professional buyers have in a year?

So ask yourself:

Are you behind some of those faceless, baseless, nameless, emotionless, totally nonmemorable, and never discussed transactions? (Remember the roller bearings scenario. A sale was made. But so what?)

Are you just another player in a market full of look-alike, me-too competitors that do what you do very well, but always meet expectations?

How can you keep customers loyal, when they've got so many other good options?

No matter how hard you're working—and we're all working very hard—are you simply doing what's expected of you? And giving your customers what they're paying for?

You know the answer to every one of those questions.

Remembering your glimpse through the Reality Goggles on tuna casserole night, when company leadership is looking into the future, do they see you as somebody they definitely want on the team? Or do they see you as somebody who works hard, but is simply meeting expectations and getting by?

Repeat after me: No story means no demand.

So maybe you don't have the world's sexiest products, jaw-dropping technology, or incredible services. Or billion-dollar marketing budgets. Well boo-hoo. That doesn't put you at a disadvantage if the businesses you're competing against have the same challenges. And guess what? They do! We may not be able to change what we're selling (plastic pipe is plastic pipe) and we certainly can't change our market (pipefitters are pipefitters). But we certainly can change our positioning and our behavior to become more story-worthy.

And that's just what you're going to do.

Now think about all those Vegas dependents again, and what they represent and uphold. They're so good at delighting us and blowing our minds with spectacles and surprises that we don't meet many people who come home from there without telling at least one good story—typically, without being asked. And when you're there, having fun, gambling, going to shows, and partying, you're seeing lots of evidence of the sinful, taboo, and raunchy stuff that Vegas is known for. Even if you don't, ahem, participate in any of that yourself or ever intend to (I'm guessing most people don't), you know it's there. Meaning Vegas is living up to its positioning!

But here's how it all comes together: As incredible as Vegas spectacles are—and they're extraordinary by any measure—much if not most of what you will say about Vegas will be heavily influenced by the city's dependents—ordinary people (just like you and your coworkers) doing extraordinary things: the hotel reception employee who upgraded you and your spouse to a suite when he learned it was your anniversary; the limo driver who not only told you about the hottest new restaurant on the strip but actually called to get you a reservation there; the sexy barmaids by the pool who sprayed sunscreen on your back and acted like they'd known you your whole life (gentlemen, I defy you to not tell that story—ditto ladies, when it comes to the chiseled Adonis-types bringing drinks to your cabana); the disarmingly pleasant engineer who showed up in your room five minutes after you called the front desk to say the air conditioner was on the fritz; the chatty blackjack dealer who whispered that maybe it's not so smart to stand with a soft 17 when she's got a face card up (you should've listened) while you sipped your third free cocktail of the hour delivered by an angel with perfect legs. See what I mean?

What would our Vegas stories be like if these folks simply processed transactions, went through the motions, and did only what they were expected and paid to do?

Here's another very important—and "betcha didn't know"—lesson we can take from this. It's actually as much a life lesson as a business lesson. Nearly every story we ever tell about *anything* contains three elements: people, experiences, and how those people and/or experiences made us feel. You can recall how this played out in my Marcel's story and easily imagine it in every Vegas story. As in, "Thank God that friendly blackjack dealer at the Aria helped me out. She totally saved my night!" (Where do you think my friends went to play blackjack after hearing that story?) And of course, any negative stories we tell go heavy on how they made us feel, don't they?

So. Then. Noise Cubed: What's being said about you? What do want said about you? And what are you willing to do to make that happen?

This is your reputation and your story-worthy stuff. It's the essence of positioning, it's everybody's job, and it's precisely what you—and your team—should be thinking and talking about. But there's a dangerous obstacle you'll want to confront and steer clear of. You see, most businesspeople don't look way down the road *like you're starting to do* and many don't want to do the work necessary to create strategic positioning and lead the cultural evolution required to bring it to life. Instead, they think the fastest path to delighting important publics, prompting storytelling, and driving demand is the digital path (check your inbox or spam folder for proof). And that's a huge, debilitating problem. It's not a shortcut!

Let's look at this. Everyone knows of incredibly "unsexy" businesses like local accounting firms, specialized equipment manufacturers, and pay-roll software consultants out there who are absolutely *killing it* while competitors flounder, right? Well, these aren't just businesses that understand positioning and know the massive value a vocal customer base can have on attracting new customers. They also recognize what most business leaders don't: that our world has grown tired of being relentlessly marketed to, sold to, and underserved. So they're taking advantage of this! And rising above it! And where are their competitors? Meeting expectations and trying to win the battle in the fake, digital world and in your mailbox.

Think of your customers and other important publics out there, wherever they are. The explosive growth of our digitally powered, always-on, 24/7-connected world means more business-sponsored messages will cross their eyeballs today than yesterday. Way more. And this won't abate any time soon. It's obscene. Yankelovich research says anywhere from 3,000 to 20,000 corporate-sponsored messages reach every one of us every day through every channel of media, print, packaging, and, especially, on every electronic device we own. That's insane! You can't watch a video from any source online now without a commercial preceding it. It's irritating as hell and you know exactly what I'm talking about.

The numbers will change (for the worse) and be open to dispute and that's okay, because what's important isn't precisely how many umpteen thousand messages we get shoved in our faces, but how many we remember and act upon. Because that's a number you can count on less than one hand.

Do you want to know what's even more insane? It's marketing folks who, hoping to cut through all this digital fog, deal with this problem by simply *increasing* the frequency of their messaging. Which just makes it even worse. Just imagine: Right now, some genius is saying, "Hey! I've got a great idea! Let's take something that's not working too well and irritates people, and increase our investment to do even more of it!" Then other geniuses will agree and approve the budget to do it! This happens every day at businesses all over the world and helps explain all of that noncreative, nonactionable, and nonmemorable stuff landing in your mailbox or inbox every day. And why it's so easy to ignore it.

It's not just digital, of course, that causes all this undue grief. Do you think that if you were to suddenly stop receiving mailed newsletters from, say, hospitals in your area, you'd care? Heck, would you even notice? Just asking. Know this: They want to send you more. Can you recall a single memorable story or message from any of those newsletters? Or any time you deliberately chose to go to one of their facilities because of something you saw in one of those mailings? I know I can't. Health care's as competitive as any other industry. Yet the competitors simply watch, react to, and copy what each other are doing instead of looking further up the road.

Why do so many businesses think they need to bury us under their constant messaging, other than the fact that the digital stuff's inexpensive? Did we ask them to do this? Why does every cashier on the planet suddenly need our email address? How can this not get even worse over time? And worst of all, why would anyone risk their reputation by sending us things we don't want that clearly show they've run out of ideas and have nothing worthwhile to say? What does this say about them? It tells me they're desperate, they've run out of ideas, and they're grasping at straws.

I smell opportunity, don't you?

I'm convinced that, as a result of this continuous crush of messaging, we've become a world of, at best, professional ignorers and at worst, committed disbelievers. Thus, marketing averse. Under a crush of me-too messaging, we've come to strongly doubt what businesses say about themselves and the products or services they sell (if we ever believed them in the first place). And we've learned to turn blind eyes and deaf ears to obvious puffery (like how every car dealership in the world is number one).

All of which means we're now way more likely to remember and act upon things we hear others say about businesses we've yet to experience ourselves.

When somebody tells you about a great movie she saw—even if you don't know her well—or another tells of the great experience he had switching his entire business from one software platform to another, how can that not influence you?

When I tell new-to-the-sport fishermen that I'm fiercely loyal to the people at St. Croix Rods because their family-owned business takes great care of their customers and still makes their rods in America, guess what I see them carrying the next time they board my boat? (And how do I know that about

St. Croix? Somebody on a dock told me! And I eventually got to meet the family behind the company—as have thousands of other fishing enthusiasts who also enjoy telling stories about it). And when I tell them they'll be able to see into the water better wearing Costa sunglasses than the trendy, household name brand they're currently wearing because Costas are designed specifically for fishing plus look supercool? Ditto. Ad and email copywriters, to say nothing of corporate social media posters, know they can't come close to matching that power no matter how many times they reach out to us.

If I had a dollar for every Harley someone bought as a result of hearing my stories, I could buy my own island. (Ditto stories about St. Croix, Costa, Craftsman tools, Stihl chain saws, Filson hunting clothing, I could go on all day.) I bet you've got a few favorites you talk up, too.

I'm sure it goes without saying that we of course recognize the flip side of this, too: that hearing someone telling stories about a dreadful experience he or she had with a business essentially kills any chance of our ever choosing it. Noise goes both ways.

By now I know what you're thinking, because it's exactly what I'd be thinking if I were you: "Okay. I get it. So what do I need to do to develop my desired positioning and narrative? And what do I need to do to be story-worthy to make some killer noise?"

Well, the first thing we're going to do is take a few more steps back, rather than blasting ahead into the "how-to" stuff and getting creative. It's superimportant to get comfortable with a few basics so we won't wander off track later. The last thing we want to be accused of is firing before aiming, because that's just not smart. And we needn't look any further than the social media world to see how horrible that can look.

Which is a perfect cue to say that I've got a Brontosaurus-sized bone to pick with social media. We need to talk about this.

Somehow and some way, a lot of businesses—quite possibly yours—have been led to believe that one of the fastest, most cost-effective means of connecting with important publics, bringing positioning to life, controlling narrative, and attracting customers is through social media. Given how much attention it gets, it's understandable that people might see it as an easy, affordable "Must Do" and a game-changer. Because this is true only in rare circumstances, though, I very much beg to differ. Look way down the road!

Quite honestly—and I know this upsets a lot of people (especially young professional people who scowl at me when I say what I'm about to say)—I can think of no larger scam that's been foisted upon the business world than the false hope of social media. That goes double for the small business world. Face it. For most businesses, it's snake oil.

No offense intended, but, please, just look how it's played out. Every business wanted in, because it sounds so exciting and promising. And every business heard about other businesses that were (allegedly) doing it superbly and feared they'd be left behind or forgotten if they didn't start doing it superbly as well. So darn near every business got enthused, developed some semblance of a "social media strategy" (or at least appointed someone as "social media coordinator"—those scowlers I just mentioned), and dove headfirst into the pool. Or, more likely, apprehensively dipped a toe into the pool's shallow end, hoping to figure out how to stay on top as they went deeper.

And darn near every one of these businesses wonders what they're doing wrong since they've yet to see the positive results they'd believed would come their way. Those businesses that didn't dive or tiptoe into the social media pool? They're worried that the world is passing them by. I hear this every day.

Ladies and gentlemen of the jury, I ask you: What's crazier than a business with a social media strategy (or some semblance of one) that doesn't first have a social strategy? As in, what—*exactly*—should we be saying to people and what—*exactly*—do we want them to do?

Way too many businesses just throw stuff out into the digital ether to "build relationships" because they believe they're supposed to. And they do it frequently because they believe they're supposed to. And the reasons they believe they're supposed to stem from the same source: Someone in their organization went to a seminar and heard about the billions of people who've opened Facebook, Instagram, and LinkedIn accounts over the last several years. The takeaways everyone knows by heart: "Those people are waiting to connect with you!" "Your customers expect you to have a strong social media presence!" "Don't miss the boat!" That's when foreheads bead with sweat. I bet you've witnessed this yourself.

It's just wrong, folks. While there's certainly an impressive list of businesses who've mastered the art and science of social media and successfully used it to their advantage—typically because they *already had legions of loyal fans* or their businesses were specifically created *to seamlessly mesh with digital devotees*—the list of social media success stories, especially among small businesses, is a short one. It's absolutely minuscule in the B2B world.

What social media success stories can you recall? Any? Closer to home, do you follow tweets from the store where you bought your mattress? Are you Facebook friends with your dry cleaner? Your utility company? You've seen—and ignored—the signs on their doors asking you to follow them. How about the people who supply your office supplies or copy machine toner? You've ignored their requests footnoted on the bottom of their invoices and emails, too. It's not that you don't like these businesses and the people behind them, of course. You just don't feel the need to share your life with them and it seems unnatural to you. I find it very telling that so many car dealerships—among the first businesses to aggressively dive into the social media pool—are throwing in the towel and admitting defeat: "It didn't work for us."

Believe it or not, I don't hate social media. Not even close. I'm just not a fan of it for business and I especially dislike that too many people think they can use it as a quick, cheap end-around to building a loyal constituency instead of properly positioning themselves and being story-worthy.

I believe strongly that what social media (Facebook, in particular) does extraordinarily well is providing a simple tool for friends—actual, honest-to-God friends—and family members to stay present in each other's lives. That's a brilliant, amazing, and, for many, life-improving thing. What it doesn't do well is allow businesses to build relationships, attract new customers, and improve their sales. Regardless of what's being taught at seminars. (Boy, do the folks who get paid to present social media "how-tos" at said seminars dislike me.)

Going a little deeper, I strongly believe that social media is a great place for friends who wish to *maintain friendships and continue stories and personal conversations that have already started*, but it's a hellishly hard place to start stories and conversations with people you barely know or don't know at all. No disrespect to the folks at my bank, but you have nothing to share with me that I want or need to know when I'm enjoying what little personal time I have. If you did, you'd have told me during the times when I've stood in front of your people or when I was online with you. Masonry supply companies and manufacturing lubricant distributors with Facebook pages? Good luck. May the force be with you.

My social media message to business leaders: Adjust your expectations and slow down. Unless your business is beloved and already has lots of fascinated followers who want frequent contact and opportunities to share their stories and passion—Disney, professional sports teams, popular nightspots, and hobbyists come to mind—don't sweat social media. It's a Trojan horse that will likely frustrate you and your staff. If you fear that your business's Facebook posts look strangely out of place among your customers' posts of family vacations, smiling children, adorable puppies, and last night's dinner, you're right to feel that way. You're raining on their parade.

Just ask yourself: Would I, as a customer or other important public, (honestly) see benefits to being Facebook friends with my business? If the answer is yes and your coworkers and customers concur, then we're going to work together to do it right so it improves your competitiveness. If the answer is no, we'll just pretend it doesn't exist and be no worse for the wear. Or at least table it for later discussion.

I hope you'll give that some serious consideration and maybe even draw some relief from it. I feel better just getting that off my chest.

And while we're at it, I have a few more items and ground rules to cover before we move ahead. Getting comfortable with these now will help corral the random ideas and concerns swimming around in your brain while you read this and help you avoid some costly, very frequently made mistakes later. Man, I just hate rework, don't you? I always say the only thing worse than rework is having to explain why you're doing rework. And the only thing worse than *that* is explaining why you're doing rework to the people who are paying for it.

As words and ideas bounce around in your head about how you'd like your important publics to describe you—and what you'll need to say to and do for them to influence that—here are a few basic "Schmidt-isms" about communication that will hopefully stay with you forever and help you to think more strategically.

I can't stress this one enough: If I can't *remember and repeat* what you just told me, you didn't tell me anything. You shouldn't have to read over that again to memorize it. You'll be amazed by how often such a simple rule gets overlooked and how much time, money, and effort have been wasted as a result (see: social media posts and "I hate rework," above).

I promise you'll recognize this example of what violating this rule looks like: I get a kick out of Super Bowl commercials that feature chimps. I'm guessing you do, too (which probably says more about us than we'd like to admit). But the next day after seeing one, I can't recall what they were about or what their message was and I have to scratch my head to recall who paid millions of dollars to put it in front of me. See rule above, "If I can't remember and repeat . . ."

That's an obvious case of waste on a grand scale, but what about much further down the food chain? Well, you know how easily you get confused when doctors describe what's ailing you and what they're going to do about it? Because they're using language you're completely unfamiliar with and can't understand? You see this same situation nearly every day in the business world. Here's an easy target: Look at the language tech and electronics businesses use to "help" you select products and services. I defy anyone without a degree—or at the very least, an expert-level mastery—in electronics engineering to understand the terminology being used on product specification sheets and even in ads in displays.

How about cell phone companies that tout 5G of data per month in their plans? That's awesome, right? The ones with only 4G don't stand a chance! Or do they? What, *exactly,* does 5G of data mean? How can I describe it? Other than it's one more G than the 4G guys? How does it help me? And make your offering better? Why? Why? Why would you tell me things (and pay many millions of dollars to do it) I can't understand and repeat when you're trying to sell me something? And why, for the love of all that's beautiful in the world, would you expect me to do my own research to educate myself and learn what this stuff means before I buy?

Quick: What's your modem speed? What's a great modem speed versus a poor one? Quick: Which type of gas should you put in your car—E10, with 10 percent ethanol, E15 with 15 percent, or E85, which, uh, means, what, exactly? Quick: How many BTUs (allow me to help: that's British Thermal Units) would you need a new window air conditioner for your spoiled kid's dorm room to produce? A lot or a little?

Don't you think stuff like this should be easier to understand? And that any of the businesses in these industries could easily change the game and present themselves and their products differently and more memorably to drive demand their way? The more obvious question that leads to, of course, is "Why isn't it?" You'll see why—and why this nonsense happens in the first place and, of course, how to avoid it—a little later. For now, I simply want to plant the notion that your eventual challenge will be describing what you do and why others should want to do business with you in language that's understandable, repeatable, and, best, yours and yours alone.

In addition to the obvious problems and challenges presented when terminology isn't understood, there's an important bottom line: When the only thing you've told me that I can understand is your price—and it's not the lowest—you've probably just lost any chance of selling to me and there's no way I'll be an advocate for you. How would I know what to say?

Here's another Schmidt-ism I teach that dominators use beautifully to their advantage: "There's no such thing as subtlety when you're competing." Meaning, tell me what you want me to know! Spell it out for me! We can't and shouldn't rely on important publics to "read between the lines," or "get the gist of what we're implying," because nobody's going to take the time to do that.

For instance, no matter how obvious you might think it is, don't wait for me to notice that you "really care about me," that you're "looking out for me," and that you "want me to do more business with you"; show me with your effort and tell me—in language others aren't using. That way I'll know what to say when I'm talking about you.

To those business leaders—and they're legion—who say, "We're humble. We let our actions (or, God forbid) our products do our talking," I say two words: Good luck. How can I help you build your reputation by repeating what you've told me if you haven't told me anything? In the time it takes me to figure out what you're all about, I've lost interest or have been won over by one of your competitors. There's no such thing as subtlety, right? Tell me what you want me to know!

My final Schmidt-ism for this chapter, and intentionally saved for last, is one that's frequently greeted with disbelief, controversy, and even shock: "Please. Right now. Wipe 'quality' from your go-to-market vocabulary." I don't want you to use the Q-word while describing your business, your products, your services, and your approach to *anyone who doesn't work with you and for you*. Ever again.

Whoa. That's a tough one, right? I must be out of my mind—at least that's what I've been told countless times when people first hear me say it.

I know it clashes hard with what most businesspeople have been taught, led to believe, and teach to others. Trust me, I know all about how deeply entrenched, bowed to, and worshipped quality is—especially in product, manufacturing, health care, and construction industries. But please. Hear me out.

Picture this: You're in a grocery store, in front of the dairy case and about to reach in for a gallon of milk when an employee from one of the represented dairies approaches you, holding a milk carton in his hand, and says, "Before you choose, I hope you'll consider ours, because it's white." You recoil a bit, scoff, and say, "Duh! Of course it's white!" Then he says, "And it's cold, fresh, healthy, and delicious." You scoff again (hoping someone from security will show up and toss this guy out) and say, "Yeah, I know!" Then he says, "And it meets or exceeds all sanitary and safety standards." To which you say, "I certainly hope so!" And he closes with, "Brought to you by highly trained people who care."

That dairy guy's ridiculous, isn't he? Well, put on your Reality Goggles, because he's no different than you telling a potential customer about your quality.

If you've got just a few seconds—live and in person, online, on the phone, on your website, in an email, direct mail, ad, or brochure—to connect with important publics, set yourself apart and build preference for yourself, your business, your approach, and your products and/or services, why on earth would you waste that opportunity by telling them what they already know, take for granted, and have heard from every other business in the universe? It's just not smart. And—assuming you want to dominate your competitors—it has to stop.

Remember, in our commoditized world, everyone in your marketplace has fully come to expect that everything you sell or do (unless it's intentionally super cheap) has good—if not great—quality. Because it does. And that it fully meets or exceeds all standards and requirements. Because it does. Otherwise, there's no way you'd be in business. Yet everyone talks about quality like they've just invented it and like customers are thrilled by it.

As absolutely vital as the Q-word was to competition a few decades ago, we—that's all of us—take it as a given today. It's the lowest rung on our expectations ladder. Is it widely known that all of your competitors have shoddy quality? Doubtful.

Apparently, most business leaders didn't get the message or are stuck in a 1980s time warp (wondering why *The Dukes of Hazzard* no longer rules the airwaves), which is why so many businesses continue to hang their hats on the Q-word and why it's now, from my view, the most overused and (I dare say) useless word in competition and demand creation.

Skeptical? The next time you're at a trade show for *anything,* look around the booths and displays and grab a bunch of handouts, sell sheets, and brochures. The Q-word will be everywhere. Or pick up a trade publication and look at the ads. Ditto. Look at your competitors' home pages. Or read the product packaging in any store. You just can't escape it. And oh, baby. When everybody you're competing against is saying the same thing and losing themselves in their self-made fog, your heart should start racing a bit because it means they're handing you a golden opportunity.

To be clear, I'm not saying for one second that quality isn't important. It's absolutely vital to the success of any business and must remain a key *internal* focus and priority. It's as important as oxygen. But it's highly unlikely that it's giving you competitive advantage in a world where it's always expected.

Yet I know for absolute certain that people—company leaders and quality zealots, in particular—remain skeptical even after my (brilliant) opening arguments. So allow me a closing argument, to nail the quality coffin shut once and for all.

I can be anywhere in the world talking about competition and, of course, motorcycles, and I constantly hear the same thing from bright, highly educated people like CEOs of household-name companies and Ivy League PhDs. They say something like "I know what makes Harley such a strong competitor in a fiercely competitive global marketplace." (I brace because I know what's coming.) "Harley's got amazing products and great quality."

Look, I realize that's high praise and said with good intentions, but I always have to stand back, lock eyes with these folks, and say, "Uh, that just ain't so. And it can't be." As they recoil with surprise, I continue by sharing a simple if/then equation that's applicable to every business in the universe. "Obviously, Harley's products and quality are first-rate. But if the company were to use them as its main competitive levers, what would that require?" Nobody has *ever* spoken up when I ask this, by the way. The answer's incredibly simple! It would require the companies Harley competes against to have products and quality that take a back seat to Harley's. And oh man, they don't. Just look at current motorcycle offerings from Honda, BMW, Ducati, or any other major make for all the proof you need. Their products and quality aren't good or even great; they're phenomenally great! Their fit, finish, engineering, technology, and innovation are absolutely outstanding, because no market would tolerate anything less than that, let alone from famous name companies.

So why would anyone want to contribute Harley's or anyone else's success and market dominance to the Q-word? That's an easy one to answer: *They feel like they're supposed to because they believe "product is king,"* *so "quality" is their knee-jerk, above-all answer to everything.* And probably because they—or the leadership they're mimicking—cut their business teeth during the quality era toward the end of the last century, when it was all the rage.

Look, you'll have plenty of time to share your quality philosophy and stories of your internal processes with your key external publics later—if they want to learn more about it—after they've gotten to know you and understand your key positioning language. Leading with the Q-word and making it the thrust of your competitive strategy makes you look like you don't understand your market and how to separate yourself from the pack. It also makes you an "it" instead of a "they." I know you don't want that.

You know you need to stand for things in the marketplace that transcend the products and/or services you sell, distance you from competitors, and make you noise-worthy, from the get-go. Otherwise, potential customers will turn away from you faster than you turned away from that sad sack with the milk jug. And faster than you delete spam messages. And toss the junk mail into the can. And faster than that repulsed Italian grandmother toddled away from me and used her Italian grandmother karma to make me eat those fig pies.

FOUR

Your Market Didn't Change and Neither Did You. But We Sure Did.

Remember when being really good at something was enough to keep phones ringing and bank deposits swelling? I don't. I've been told many times, though, that such a world once existed, by well-meaning folks who very much believe it to be true. Or at least want it to be.

There's a sign posted in a beautifully restored, ancient theater where I've enjoyed many a movie that makes tidy work of describing the inaccurate overglorification of our collective pasts: "If you'd like us to make this even more like the good old days, we'll turn off the air-conditioning." Meaning: As great as those long ago days seem to have been, they probably weren't as good as we've chosen to remember or been told they were. Meaning behind the meaning: Life was never a cake walk and running a business was never easy.

But you sure wouldn't know that to talk to leaders of nondominant businesses who'd willingly sacrifice a limb (or, failing that, a lazy employee or two) to bring back the good old days. You've probably experienced this: higher-ups who longingly speak of those wondrous days of yore, when things were so much easier, customers were not only simple to attract, but were predictable and loyal. Back when it damn near rained cash. You know, those days before business got tougher because their market changed. Those days their businesses need to, somehow, rally the troops to bring back.

Well, attention Kmart shoppers and wistful backward glancers, I've got news for you: The gig is up. Markets—yours very much included—can't change. And your business will never become a dominator, or even a major player, until you refresh your perspective and accept that reality.

But go ahead and admit that you think I'm wrong, believe markets can change, and that yours has. It's okay, I'm used to being told I'm wrong. I hear it every week. But believe me when I say I'm going to change your mind and that this will make you a better competitor. You might as well say it a few times now so it sticks: Markets. Can't. Change. Because I can promise you'll be saying it later.

To help you come to grips with something that flies directly into the face of conventional wisdom, please join me as I relive a memorable, yet sadly common discussion with a titan of the business world where this issue was front and center. You're with me in his office and, as you'll see in a little while, you're not there as window dressing.

There I was, sitting across from the top dog of a global hotel empire—you've likely warmed his company's beds a time or two—when I experienced a painful moment I liken to when a doctor must inform a patient complaining of an unsightly rash that what he or she actually has is a serious disease. Of course, nobody ever wants to hear and confront such an awful prognosis, especially when they have no idea they're sick in the first place. Being the bearer of such news is only slightly better.

(I'll be a gentleman here and keep our hotel giant's name confidential to avoid embarrassing anyone. As I've met with leadership teams of several major hotel chains, it's fun for me to imagine them trying to guess whose boss I'm referring to here.)

Mr. Hotel had just finished describing, with equal measures of pride and concern, the enormous nine-figure investments his business was about to make to refresh and upgrade the best known of its hotel chains, one that's a household name and typically on the short lists of business travelers. Many of the chain's properties, he'd said, had started to look a bit worn around the edges—that rash I spoke of—and needed some major cosmetic surgery to return their youthful glow. It sounded like a mammoth undertaking with nerve-racking timelines and lots of moving parts. Nobody drops that kind of money casually.

The initiative was being launched, he said, to improve the power of his company's brand at a time of great consolidation and upheaval in his industry and at a time when, in his words, his market was changing. More than once he said he wanted his people to regain their old swagger, a song familiar to business leaders the world over.

So—dramatically removing the stethoscope from my ears like a TV doctor—I started to give him some hard news. Something along the lines of "Look, man. You're talking to your market right now. It's me. I'm in hotels, often yours, over one hundred nights a year, every year, for business and pleasure, and you know what? I don't recall having banded together with every other hotel customer, putting it to a vote, and making it known that we will only spend more nights in your hotel chain if you make expensive improvements *because we've changed.*"

> *(If you're trying to imagine his facial expression as I'm telling him this, just recall the look on your parents' faces when you said you should be trusted with the family car and allowed to stay out past curfew because you're "sixteen now." See that same, sarcastic "Oh, really?" face.)*

The truth is, I explained, no matter how nice those refreshed lobbies, new mattresses, carpets, and updated bathrooms were sure to be, they wouldn't be enough to change my or, likely, anyone else's view of his business. The only way those upgrades would make a huge difference would be if his company's hotels were largely known as outdated eyesores. Of course, they weren't. His competitors' weren't, either.

The prognosis I shared is one you've heard me use before: "You're giving your properties haircuts when what they need are heart transplants. Sprucing up the facilities is not going to make your chain more attractive to me nor increase the odds of my staying with you more frequently. The most you'll see from these investments, if anything, is a one-time blip from corporate meeting planners."

I'm bluntly honest when my meter's running and have found that it puts me in good stead with leaders who appreciate such. Well, not today. Mr. Hotel was clearly agitated. His facial expression had switched from bemused disbelief to that of someone who's just been told he's got a life-threatening illness from someone who's not a doctor and who had the audacity to say something repugnant to the man atop a global empire.

"You don't know the back-office side of the hotel business," he huffed, which couldn't be more true. He also said, correctly, that I wasn't privy to the tons of market research the chain had completed that said potential guests would view these improvements favorably. So I sipped some more coffee and asked who, in history, ever checked the "No" option when asked a loaded question like if improving a property would make it more desirable for future visits. This resulted in more huffing and puffing, his face gaining a crimson hue that might make an actual doctor take pause.

(It must be said here that he, like many other business leaders, appears to have grown quite comfortable receiving rousing support for major initiatives from the "yes" people whose offices surround his. Those same people, tellingly, never spoke of or to him by his first name, and instead always called him, "Mister Hotel." I've seen a lot of that "Mister" stuff at big, older companies, by the way, and I find it repulsive.

Leaders: If your employees, *adults you're paying to be on your team,* aren't comfortable enough, let alone permitted, to refer to you by your first name—you know, the way human beings do when they speak of or to each other—do they even know you? Do you think they enjoy being made to act inferior to you through their forced "respect"? Do you think they've ever answered tough questions from you honestly? Are you running a business or a kingdom? I flat-out refuse to call any businessperson by anything other than his or her first name and hope everyone will join me. Let's put an end to this "I'm superior to you" culture killer.)

I like to think I'm a nice guy who takes no pleasure from sharing painful news. I do, however, much enjoy getting pushback and hearing people defend their positions after I drop a bomb, because this almost always sparks great conversations where both sides can learn something new and feel like they've won something. To me, that's how consultancy and teaching are supposed to work. But I don't do so well with "I'm right so that means you're wrong" condescension. Shoot the messenger if you must, but keep it civil. I'm only here to help, but I'll admit that on this day I took a lot of bullets and had to work to calm Mr. Hotel down before things went beyond control. I knew we were reaching a breaking point when his executive assistant popped her head in, pulled the door shut to mute his voice, and looked at me with the universally understood facial expression that says, "Sucks for you!"

So, while bracing myself for more of his ire, I help up my right palm in the time-honored, "Come on, we're all friends here; let's just please be cool" gesture, licked my lips and . . .

Oh, man. Wait a sec. This is getting pretty heavy, isn't it? Borderline depressing, even. Part of you is taking Mr. Hotel's side and meanwhile, some bigwig in Detroit who's always insisted on being called Mister is picturing his hands around my neck. What do you say we lighten things up a bit and see if we can't take this story in a different direction then the current "he said/I said" and learn the important lessons that were shared that day in a more pleasant and memorable environment? You know me pretty well by now, so you know what that means. When I want you to remember and repeat something, I need to show it to you and tell you about it in ways that make that easier for you. The best place for that, we all know, is on two-wheelers.

So leather up, then, and join me in spirit as I relive an uber-cool ride from last autumn that will bring some very potent and important lessons to life. As with all rides and many learning experiences, it's the stuff we don't expect to see that can upend our way of thinking and help us to commit those discoveries to memory. And don't worry about Mr. Hotel; we'll see him again soon enough. As a matter of fact, we're taking this ride today to bring us face-to-face with what he's up against. One way or another, you're up against many of the same challenges he's battling, so keep your eyes open and be on the lookout for potential problems, causes, and opportunities. You'll see them and, when you do, think about how you'll discuss them with others. Because you will.

Let's ditch the corporate environment, burn some gas, and live a little.

Look. It's me. I'm up and out on the road with the sunrise—which is the ideal time to get away from high-traffic areas and something that fast becomes a habit with urban-based riders—heading away from the Washington, DC, area toward, eventually (maybe?) Columbus, Ohio. I'm free to roam, Lord knows I will, and all signs indicate it's going to be a great day. What signs, you ask? It's a workday and I'm on a motorcycle. Enough said.

What do you think: Should I roll the dice and jump on the (always over-crowded, rage-inducing, stop-and-go) DC Beltway to see if I can make some time? Not on your life, *mi amigo,* even without the stuff in parentheses and even at this early hour. I'll not see a single freeway today, yet another sign of a great day. It might take me a little longer to get away from busy urban congestion using only minor roads, but so what? I'm not on the clock. And besides, everyone knows there's nothing worth seeing on the freeway. Any freeway. Ever.

Riding through and away from congested urban areas is the least sexy part of a ride to me, and usually the only time when I have my stereo cranked. I'm superalert, yet oddly relaxed (that paradox again), pounding through the gears, enjoying the rush of the warm wind, and slurping hot coffee from my handlebar-mounted mug at red lights. The Allman Brothers are busy keeping me company and, per usual, doing a mighty fine job of it.

Please pay close attention here and, no matter the length of the ride, always do as I do without fail: I'm checking the eyes of every motorist within range, making sure they meet mine and acknowledge my presence during that brief second when they look up from their cell phones. If I can't see their eyes, which, it pains me to say, is fast becoming the new normal, I assume stupidity on their part and move away from them on the double. Why invite trouble? It's like improving your competitiveness; you can't get ahead if you're blending in or invisible.

I also study the front tires of vehicles coming toward me, the better to notice anything indicating they're about to make a jackass move, like, say, an abrupt left-hand turn across my lane without the courtesy of a turn signal warning. And because the drivers behind me are no different than those in front, I'm checking my rearview mirrors constantly and swiveling my head from side to side to ensure that we're pinging on each other's radar.

Motorcyclists need to exercise this extra sense—the one that says *you have to expect every other person on the road to do precisely what they're not supposed to do*—remain vigilant and separate yourself from threats. Count on drivers to see you and maintain a safe distance? Don't make me laugh. Count on them to use turn signals? Dear God, no. Count on them to do moronic things? Always. These are great habits for *any* motorist to develop.

Within just a few short miles, I'm already rural and in farm country, where traffic is a foreign concept. I'm still vigilant about safety, but enjoying the tranquility, which means the Allmans are on mute. They're bike people so they understand. It's hard to believe I'm minutes from one of the busiest eight-lane freeways in the world, yet I'm on smooth, narrow roads seeing colorful fall foliage, rolling hills, one-lane bridges over rambling streams, plus orchards and pastures crowned with rising, knee-high fog. If scenery like this, golden hued by breaking early morning light, doesn't make rising from bed at zero dark thirty seem worthwhile, I have to wonder what would.

Something amazing happens when you're riding a bike along gentle curving roads that are steeped in college-level physics and hard to describe ("if I have to explain . . ."), but all motorcyclists know of what I speak and find great pleasure in it. You don't "steer" a motorcycle as you intuitively would a bicycle, whereupon, to turn right, you pull the right handlebar back while pushing the left hand forward. Nope. Not only will that not work here, it will work against you.

Rather, to turn right, you turn your head and focus your eyes directly on where you want to go, then *push your right-handlebar grip forward and away from you* and gently lean with your bike to the right, never losing your visual focus. Pushing the handgrip forward while leaning eases the tires off their flat center strips onto their sidewalls and carries you through the turns (do the opposite for turning left, of course). It's neither intuitive nor magic; it's science. When you're locked in on a smooth, curvy road, simultaneously nudging the bars and leaning through curves, it's a perfect dance of rider, machine, inertia, and gyroscopics working together. The one-hundredth time you experience this in a day's ride feels no less amazing than the first. Physics can be cool.

As if things aren't already superb, I'm moving the buzz meter even further past the red line by making an impromptu detour off a tiny two-laner in the middle of nowhere toward an antiquated ferry I'll use to cross the Potomac River from Maryland into Virginia. After a quick lesson about how Confederate soldiers used the ferry during the Civil War, gleaned from a historic marker near the loading ramp, I'll ride aboard with a dozen cars and enjoy a pleasant river crossing, watching ducks and sipping coffee atop machinery that's changed little since the ferry's 1817 start-up. I think it's safe to say we all could benefit from more antique ferry boat rides in our lives.

Admit it. You're starting to like this. And just think about all those people a few miles away on the freeway, stuck in traffic, worrying about being late for work, swearing at their windshields, and risking lives by pecking at their cell phones. Who'd want that?

(You've already forgotten Mr. Hotel, haven't you? No worries, we'll bring him back in soon enough. And here's a heads-up: When we next see him, you'll be doing a lot of the talking. Anybody who attends a meeting with me and doesn't speak up will never get an invite again, because who'd want you back? Another heads-up: If you want someone to remember and repeat what you're saying, think about ways to help him/her visualize it. Practice this and, I promise, it will become automatic and you'll get more invites to meetings with important people. Making noise gets rewarded.)

Nearing Leesburg, Virginia, and its famous Civil War sites, the skies are turning darker and moving fast. Oh boy. So much for the sidewalk café breakfast and battlefield stroll I was loosely considering. I opt to keep rolling and take on the odds that I can reach the other side of those approaching clouds before they drop their payload. But the first gentle raindrops to hit my windshield, less than fifty miles of farm road later, tell me that's not going to happen, hint of what's about to be unleashed, and prompt a quick scan to find a place to seek cover and pull on my raingear.

I know what you're thinking: Riding a motorcycle in the rain? No thanks. I know, I know. But dig: There's rain you can ride safely and comfortably in—specifically the soft, drizzling kind—if you have the proper gear. Heavy, blinding rain, on the other hand, is the stuff you'll want to avoid, or get out from under, pronto. Both kinds are on the menu today.

Seeking shelter, I'm heading into the commercial part of town and, what do you know? There are multiple gas stations at the same intersection. Like everyone else with a pulse, I recognize all of them by name. Less surprising, their signage says all of their gas prices are identical today. Which one should I pull into? Which would you choose? Does it even matter? If you're thinking like a dominator, you see the huge competitive issues of commoditization at play here. You see them, right? If you owned one of those gas stations, would you be happy with this situation?

I'll forgo the luxury of choice and simply pull into the one that has the most room under its awning.

The rain's intensity is building fast, so pulling under that awning proves a good move. This allows me to top off my gas—which smart riders do *every* time we're near a gas pump—and my coffee cup, chat up the cashier while studying the wall map, inhale some Krispy Kremes, then decide if I'll need to head back out to pull on my raingear. My rain gear of waterproof jacket, pants, booties, and gloves rolls into a bundle that's smaller than a loaf of bread, yet is built for the toughest conditions imaginable and would keep me bone-dry in a monsoon. But should I deploy it? Murphy's law says donning rain gear has the same effect as washing your car in that it guarantees rain. So for now, I'll opt to wait it out and enjoy my healthy breakfast.

The cashier opines that I must be crazy to be out riding a motorcycle on a rainy day, but when I inform her, "It beats the hell out of working," she quickly changes her mind and jokes that she's quitting so she can ride along. Sweet old gal. We had a few laughs as she imagined how she'd explain her disappearance to her family. I swear to you that the *only* reason I can recall that all of this happened at a Sheetz convenience store is that she was so friendly and chatty. I can still picture her. How could this not impact my purchase behavior any time I roll up to an intersection needing gas and see a Sheetz as one of my options? I mean, really. Who remembers where they buy gas on road trips?

Minutes later, Murphy weighs in and the rain tapers to intermittent sputters. I'm off again, rolling west through farm and timber country and, soon enough, into West Virginia. The raingear stayed stowed.

Here's one nobody ever sees coming: West Virginia is far and away my favorite state for riding. In a country overloaded with exquisite beauty and spectacular riding opportunities, there's something about West Virginia—and not just the surprised looks I get when I say it—that always makes it my first choice when asked to pick.

See, unlike most states where you have to put on a ton of highway miles through traffic and alongside texting idiots to reach "the good stuff," in West Virginia, it's always right in front of you, if not just a few minutes away. And what's not to love? It's got vistas that stretch forever comple-ments of the Shenandoah, Allegheny, and Appalachian Mountains and the vast valleys between them, twelve million acres of forest land, plus rivers and streams galore. Best to me, though, are its countless miles of amazing, smooth "lumber" roads with one incredibly tight turn after another, gor-geous scenery and forest smells to die for, where the only other vehicles present for miles at a time are occasional lumber trucks. West Virginia's so overlooked, it's criminal. Please don't tell anybody.

My goal today is to get to Route 50 and use it as my east-to-west GPS—with spur-of-the-moment side jaunts, of course, to answer, "I wonder where that skinny road goes" questions—across the state and into rural eastern Ohio, where, incidentally, the riding is also glorious. Pull out a West Vir-ginia map some time and search for 50; you'll probably need to squint a bit. Look how snaky the thin red line is, then multiply those snakes a hun-dredfold and you'll see why it's one of my all-time favorite riding roads. It's nonstop twists and turns through some of Mother Nature's best work, the stuff two-wheelers were made for.

Cruising Route 50 in sunshine is a religious experience. Double that when it's raining, which, of course, it is now. But just barely. The raingear's on now and I'm comfortably dry inside it. This road demands my full at-tention, but because its ridiculous layout keeps speeds low, I'm still seeing and enjoying everything around me. The humid steam rising from fresh-cut hay in farm fields smells pungent and delicious. There are long stretches where tree limbs enshroud the road and block the sky overhead. Creeks are running fast and brown with the fallen rain. But what's most pleasing to me are the number of "S curve ahead," "hard right-hand turn ahead," and 10 mph speed limit signs. When's the last time you saw a 10 mph sign? They're constantly warning me that the upcoming curves are wicked tight and twist and turn in unexpected directions (razor-sharp uphill right turns after equally sharp left turns at the bottom of steep drops). It's incredible, counterintuitive, and a complete disaster for anyone in a hurry.

Who's crazy enough to be out on a road like this on a day like this? Motorcyclists, of course. While acknowledging each other with time-honored, two-finger waves (meaning: I see you, friend, and acknowledge your immense coolness), our exaggerated, wide-eyed expressions and huge grins tell each other exactly what we're feeling: This is awesome!

Motorcycling has few hard-and-fast rules, but I need to expand on one we learned on the racetrack: Whatever your eyes are looking at, that's where you bike is going. Stare at a dead squirrel on the roadway—commonly referred to as "target fixation"—and you're going hit that squirrel. That poor little guy's suffered enough. Stare at massive boulders by the roadside or the back of a Mack truck and you'll be the one suffering. This is why we need to remember that, before entering any turn, it's vital to look all the way through its exit point, to what lies beyond. When you're looking through your exit point, the bike will carry you there. It takes only tiny fractions of a second to make note of all the squirrels, boulders, and other potential problem starters jostling for your attention. Just don't stare at stuff you don't want to hit!

(Did you catch the business parallel in the last paragraph? You can't move forward if you're looking the wrong way. Just ask Sears. Whatever you're looking at, that's where you're going.)

This safe riding review is extra important today, not just because the curves are insane but because the road surface is often blanketed in wet leaves, which can be as slippery as ice. This is why we're keeping our speeds under control, looking through the curves ahead—not at those leaves—and minimizing chances for sudden surprises to make us panic-squeeze our brakes and risk a skid. Yes, it's intense and requires sharp concentration. And yes, the added challenge and blasts of adrenaline ramp up the fun factor. If this feeling of intensity and joy could be bottled, I'd be a billionaire.

Suddenly—in barely a second—it's Armageddon as the rain switches from slow drip to fire hose and is pounding down harder than I've ever experienced on a bike. I know I've got to seek shelter because it's nearly impossible to see. Man, this is crazy. I must be, too, because I'm giggling nervously under my helmet. The road is turning into a river right before my eyes and the roadsides are completely flooded. There's no place to pull over so I put my flashers on and plod along at a barely rolling pace until I spot a ramshackle backcountry church, pull in, and race under the leaky but effective awning by its front door. Spotting me, three other motorcyclists also pull in and, within minutes, storytelling, laughter, and route comparisons ensue. I bust out my trusty stash of Mike and Ike candy, which my fellow refugees eye suspiciously before digging in and rediscovering just how great it is to eat kid food. Eventually the rain slows to here-and-there sprinkles, allowing us to stroll back over to the parking lot, ask questions about each other's bikes, towel-dry our seats, and prepare to mount up and go our separate ways.

And that's when I see something that, on a day where I've already had way more than my fair share of fantastic visuals, has me shaking my head in bewilderment. Remember how the early morning ferry ride took me back in time to those good old days (of war, disease, and unimaginable suffering)? Well, what I'm seeing now is blasting me forward into the future: One of the riders attached a cord from his helmet-mounted camera into a small video screen that he'd permanently mounted within chrome trim atop the fuel tank of his bike. Yes, believe it or not, a TV on a motorcycle.

As he began replaying some of the riding he and his friends experienced today—with supersharp clarity, I might add—we were all transfixed and laughing, but I couldn't stop obsessing about seeing a TV on a bike. This wasn't an entirely new feeling for me, because it's the same way I felt the first time I saw AM/FM stereos, then CB radios, then cassette decks and CD changers, followed by cellular technology, GPS, and Bluetooth technology, and, now, touch-screen entertainment systems that incorporate *all of that* into one unit, on some bikes. But a TV screen? Whoa. That's straight out of *The Jetsons*. (Next up, air-conditioning. On a motorcycle. I'm serious. I've yet to see it, but I know it's already available.)

Almost every time I've shared this TV-on-a-bike story with businesspeople, they've been quick to smile, shake their heads, and conclude that this is just another example of how markets change with time and how hard it is to keep up with that change, let alone get ahead of it. Things *had* to have been simpler in the good old days when the only things a motorcyclist needed were two wheels, a motor, a seat, and some handlebars, right?

So here's something for you to think about: Isn't it amazing how much *your* market has changed over the years? And how those changes have made it tougher to compete now versus the good old days?

Ha! Gotcha! Those were trick questions. Guess you weren't thinking and forgot already that markets can't change. Huge points for you, though, if you weren't duped.

If you didn't pick up on my tomfoolery and answered both of those questions with a defeated and reflexive yes, well, I'll give you a pass. But just this once. None of us has to look far to find business leaders (Mr. Hotel, take a bow) who sigh and shake their heads while whining about those cursed market changes that have bedeviled their businesses and made them less competitive than they once were—real or imagined—or as they'd like them to be. There's also a betting chance that you and/or others at your business are guilty of such whining.

Who among us doesn't hear this "market change" demonization all the time? It's so widespread now that most of us take it as a given. Need proof of how common and accepted it is? Just look at how books are sold and read these days. It's obviously different than it was ten years ago, when bookstores were everywhere and there were no downloadable, digital books you could read as you do now on your phone, tablet, e-reader, or computer. So, all together now: The market has changed!

Look how people are eating healthy today, opting for organic, locally farmed, and gluten-free while drinking "milk" from almonds and soy beans: The market has changed!

Now look at the auto industry and how everyone in America seems to be driving big gas guzzlers: The market has changed!

Or, wait, now we're driving smaller, fuel-efficient cars: The market has changed!

Or wait, we're not buying as many cars as before because of Uber: The market has changed! Or wait, how about those electric cars? Or (gulp!) driverless cars?

Or look at *any* business in any industry where whatever was being sold for years through a live and in-person sales force, or in a brick-and-mortar setting, or over the phone, is now being sold on the Internet: The market has changed!

As little as I enjoy being the bearer of bad news, I have to bluntly cut to the chase here: Regardless of your business or industry, even if you're the owner of a two centuries-old river ferry, your market hasn't changed one bit because—as I already told you—markets *can't* change. Which means offering up "Our market has changed" as an excuse for softened demand and/ or diminished competitiveness makes about as much sense as blaming John

Wilkes Booth for the demise of the Lincoln Town Car. You'll never hear a market dominator complaining of market changes, but you'll sure hear it from everyone else.

While many are quick to write these "market changes" off as harmless, perhaps nostalgic, pining for past glory days, I'm just as quick to cry foul. You need to start doing this, too. Business leaders who rely on blame-shifting and buck-passing like this, even when it seems everyone else is doing it, are keeping their businesses from confronting reality, looking through the turns, and moving forward. This is a huge problem and I hear it at way more than half the businesses I visit.

It's vital to realize that no matter the job, the employer, or seniority in the workplace, people who work for a living model the behavior of their leaders (more on this later). If you're blaming your performance and competitiveness issues on market changes that are out of your control, your employees and coworkers are, too. So you're not moving forward and neither are they. You're all looking in the wrong direction.

Mulling it over for a few seconds is all it takes to connect some obvious dots and realize how daft it all sounds. It's the *market*'s fault that you're not as competitive as you'd like to be? See what I mean? It's like saying, "Those damn customers! What's wrong with them? How can they not see how awesome we are?" Or like doing a 180 on the classic failed relationship line and saying, "It's not me. It's you."

See, when we blame our competitive shortcomings on invisible phantoms—like changing markets—we're absolving ourselves from any responsibility for those shortcomings. This, naturally, explains why so many businesses think they can maintain status quo, focus on doing what they do, and "wait it out until the market comes back" or invest heavily to "lure the market back." (Rebranding, anyone?)

So here's the deal: If you or others in your business are blaming changing markets for your problems, you need to confront cold, hard reality. The problem isn't "Your market has changed," the problem is "Your business *hasn't* changed."

Just look around at your own industry and you'll see plenty of examples to back me up. No matter what's being sold or how it's being sold, the needs and expectations of your customers and prospects have naturally evolved and increased over time. When businesses are stuck in a time warp, saying and doing things the same way they did them twenty or even five years ago, but catering to an audience that's living in the present and being courted by forward-thinking (versus backward-facing) competitors, the disconnects get expensive. For these unchanged businesses to keep existing customers in the fold or lure former customers back, the knee-jerk move is to use low price as a competitive weapon. We all know what follows: Backward-facing, me-too competitors lower their prices in response and the proverbial race to the bottom is on.

That surely isn't the market's fault.

I know this goes against the grain of what most people choose to believe, so let me be superclear. Markets can't change and we can't, without spending a ton of money that we don't have, change markets. But we *can* change how we view markets. And that new, accurate perspective can enable us to improve our competitiveness as a result.

Let's put our Reality Goggles back on for a minute, zoom in, and take a real-world look at what I'm talking about here. See, in and of themselves, markets are not human. Not. Human. Which at the very least means markets don't make decisions. It also means markets are neither persuadable nor immovable, logical nor illogical, loyal nor disloyal, price-conscious nor price-oblivious. Because they have no emotion, feelings, expectations, nor attitudes, markets aren't "knowable."

Markets are, in a word, people. You've heard the expression "You can't see the forest for the trees." Well, replace forest with "market" and trees with "people." And because markets are people, markets are just like you. Those are five very important words: Markets are just like you. Because they *are* you. Which is why I told Mr. Hotel, "I'm your market."

Look at yourself through your Goggles. No matter what you're buying, your first inclination is to do business with people you know and like—the way I now have a soft spot for Sheetz versus famous-name gas stations and convenience markets. Or you choose based on what people you trust have said, or recommendations they've made. Barring any personal past experiences or recommendations from others, and when you see no differences between suppliers, you do business with whoever offers the lowest price or the most convenience for whatever you're after.

You have neither preference for, nor powerful, positive associations with any businesses that have met your expectations, processed your transaction, and given you what you paid for. You ignore or don't return calls from people you once did business with because you've found faster, easier, and cheaper alternatives. You like to self-educate by digging around on the Internet to help you make decisions. You like what's cool, hot, and popular.

You don't like being pestered with spam and junk mail. You don't like getting surveys from companies asking "How did we do?" You have no qualms about bad-mouthing companies that have disappointed you and take pleasure in telling others of any great discoveries you've made or story-worthy moments you've experienced.

Those people who make up your market? They do the same things you do because—say it—they *are* you. Your market is just like you. Isn't it ironic that we hate it when people we serve or wish to serve exhibit behavior—like shopping for low price, not taking our calls, being disloyal—that's identical to our own? Expecting them to be any different than we ourselves would be, what's the word? Crazy.

Did the ferry boat operator's market change from two hundred years ago? A dozen or so pages ago it would be easy to knee-jerk and say it has, but you're wiser than that now. Horses and carriages have long been replaced, women no longer wear bonnets, men aren't in top hats, and there aren't nearly as many farmers or blacksmiths as back then, but we still need to get across the river and don't want to drive miles out of our way to reach a bridge. And did those 1800s travelers enjoy looking at the ducks any more or less than we do now? The ride isn't free now and it wasn't then, either. We're still paying an agreeable price for a desirable service (the nostalgia comes free of charge). See? No change.

You and everyone working with you and for you need to know this: Whether you're selling hotel rooms or hamburgers, machined parts or shoelaces, when it comes to competitive shortcomings, the market isn't your problem; you are your problem. Blaming competitiveness and performance shortfalls on your market is self-defeating and keeps you from focusing on what's possible and, more important, fixable. The only one who can fix you is you. And who knows better how to please someone with a story-worthy experience better than someone who enjoys being pleased and telling stories?

Let's get back to Mr. Hotel for a few minutes and pick up the conversation where we left off: with him asking, "Why the hell not?" when I told him his big investments in property upgrades, in response to market changes, wouldn't be enough to turn me on.

I said something to the tune of "Let's break your world down to two very important groups of people. The first group is guests who've stayed in your hotels who you're hopeful will prefer you, choose you over your competitors for their future travel and recommend you to others. The second is people you'd like to attract for their first-ever stay with you." In other words, customers and prospects.

I told him, "I'm very much in the first group and while I can't recall any horror stories that would preclude me from staying with you again, I also can't recall any positive 'they' stories that would sway me your way versus the also-famous-name hotels with similar features and prices on the other side of the street, either. But here's the most important part of that sentence: I've stayed at your properties, meaning I breathed the same air and shared the same space as multiple hundreds of your employees over the years. And nobody did anything I can recall positively *nor* negatively. I can't think of one meaningfully differentiating thing or experience that's common to all of your properties, resonates with me, and is story-worthy. So I don't have what you want most: preference for you." This was the first time I noticed that he was getting what I was saying instead of just being defensive.

"But that doesn't mean you're out of the game," I explained. "Not by a long shot. Because I don't have positive 'they' stories for any of your competitors, either" (like the gas stations when I rolled up to that intersection earlier).

I painted a picture for him and said, "I imagine I'm like all guests at your properties in that I've always been greeted by a smiling face on arrival and the front desk staff has always welcomed me warmly and processed my check-in. 'How was your trip in?' (yawn) seems the de facto front desk icebreaker and begs for—and almost always gets—a monosyllabic answer: Fine. It's followed by 'Is this your first stay with us?' If yes, the reflexive response is, 'Welcome.' If no, it's, 'Welcome back.' Because I won't likely check out in person when it's time to leave, I'll give my email address when asked so I can get a copy of my room charges sent to me. 'Do you need assistance with your luggage today?' always gets a two-syllable answer: 'No, thanks.' "

If all of that seems familiar it's because it's the same conversation, if you can call it one, that happens at nearly every hotel you've visited, other than the cheapo, bottom-feeder variety, the kind where the desk clerk sits behind bulletproof glass. (And nothing says "Relax and get comfortable" quite like bulletproof glass, with the possible exception of cigarette burns on the bedspread and hairs in the bathtub. But I digress.)

Based on that check-in experience, market dominators would be quick to detect problem areas and would want to ask Mr. Hotel (remember, you're supposed to be talking at this meeting, too), "Given that it's your hotel's first big chance to impress people, why would your check-in process be indistinguishable from all others? Is this how you want it?" And "What, if anything, will guests recall about these conversations with your desk clerk that you'd like them to fondly recall and repeat?"

What happens after check-in? Here's how I explained it: I'm up the elevator, then down the hall to my room, which, as expected and as usual, is clean, comfortable, and appropriately equipped. The bathroom's tidy and well stocked, with a placard giving me the option to "join us in being good environmental stewards by reusing your towels." We can all see this stuff in our mind's eyes, can't we? The room's windows are a crapshoot in that they face either something pleasant, like a beach, pool, or gardens, or something repugnant like a parking lot or rooftop. There's a small, empty fridge (minibars, alas, are fast disappearing) that I'll reflexively open, even though I'm sure it'll be empty, and a coffeemaker on the counter. If I'm lucky, there will be two free bottles of water by the coffeemaker. More likely, there will be two grotesquely expensive bottles of water bearing tags reading "For your enjoyment." Plug in your own punch line here, unless you find enjoyment in paying eight bucks for a quart of warm water.

There will often be a greeting letter from the hotel manager on the desk, which I'll not read. Who would? If there is something important I need to know, the front desk person would have said as much. Sitting on the bed is a breakfast room service menu to hang outside the door and, on the nightstand, a "call us if you need anything" envelope signed by a member of the housekeeping staff (for gratuities) and a "How'd we do?" survey card to fill in at the end of my stay.

Room-wise, there's nothing offensive here, so far, other than that ridiculous water. Nothing heart-stopping to complain about, nor rave about. It's like nearly every stay in a hotel at this price point, right? I'll sleep well on my comfy mattress (not giving one thought to the hundreds, if not thousands, of others who did God-knows-what upon it; just imagine where those pillows have been).

I'll probably use the hotel's gym and have at least one in-house restaurant or room service meal. Both will be "decent."

It's when my stay is through that the hotel chain's major competitive problems will come into stark focus. You'll probably see them before I point them out. I'll use express checkout and, thus, bypass the front desk—and the obligatory "How was your stay?" query from the desk staffer. Think of the timing behind this hackneyed question for just a moment and its absurdity becomes obvious: Hmmm. Do busy travelers want to offer up suggestions for improvement and identify problems we experienced during our stay that are too late to rectify, while slowing down the line for the busy people behind us? Or do we just want to be on our way? And do hotels really want the last thing bouncing around in our minds as we exit to be the things that disappointed us? Timing, people!

(Quick sidebar: "How was your stay?" has the same impact as a similarly ridiculous and ill-timed question we've all been asked a million times by checkout cashiers in retail environments, "Find everything you're looking for?" This isn't good business. What would happen if you said no instead of your usual yep? Would that cashier be prepared to shut down the line, page an associate, wait for said associate to call, then tell him what you need and have everyone behind you in line wait until the product is found—assuming it's findable—and brought up to you? Would that cashier even have a clue of what to do? Again, think of the timing. They're asking you this question at the worst possible time of your visit, when you're leaving. Your last taste of that business on exiting is going to stay with you for a long time: You couldn't find something you wanted, problems ensued, and you felt bad for "causing" them. That's just dumb. Good-bye time should be happy, memorable experience time, right? People pleasing people. Come on!)

Later that day, I'll receive an email of my room charges, which is very helpful for filing expense reports. The next day I'll get an emailed request for a few minutes of my time to fill out a survey about my stay, which, I learned years ago, will contain way too many damn questions. This request, to me, is a ridiculous waste of my time and will be deleted unopened for the same reasons I ignored the "How'd we do?" survey card.

Think about this survey stuff for just a minute and you'll see more obvious wrongs in these attempts to do right, or, more accurately, be *perceived* as doing right.

Here's one of those little quirks about the human species I love to share. Once upon a time, while volunteering with Harley's demo ride program, I developed a theory that I think would stand up to the highest levels of scientific scrutiny. As demo participants completed their rides, Harley volunteers would ask, "What would we need to change on the motorcycle you just rode to make it more to your liking?" And guess what? Every single person answered the question. My theory, then, goes like this: In a captive environment, 100 percent of us will answer a simple question asked by someone standing right in front of us. One hundred percent. Every time.

Now it's time to swing for the fences. "So, Mr. Hotel," I said, "with all due respect, I was *there* on your property, which means *your market* was on your property (and is, right now), rubbing shoulders with your people. I passed members of your staff in the elevator or in the lobby, who had every opportunity to make me feel welcome and appreciated, take my temperature, and address any problems I might be experiencing. Or to make good things even better. But you're asking me now, *after I'm gone*, how you did and what you could have done better? How can you possibly react to anything I say at this point? How could this possibly benefit me? Knowing that, why would I want to tell you?"

He was actually smiling now. He'd been in my shoes as a hotel guest before, too. He just never connected these dots. If everyone answers a face-to-face question when asked, when should his hotels ask guests questions? It couldn't be more obvious.

I told him, "Once upon a time, I filled out your surveys, probably driven by guilt only a marketing person can understand. I stopped when I noticed the communication was one-way: I'd tell you what you did wrong and hear nothing back, nor see that my comments had any impact or were in any way even acknowledged. For my time and effort I got back in return the same thing you'll get from me now, a whole lot of nothing.

"But think like a dominator for a minute. If just one (one!) of your employees stopped me in the hall—because it was demanded of him and all other employees—and said, 'Hey, I sure hope you're finding everything to your liking. Is there anything I can do to improve your stay or make your room more comfortable?' everything would change. After having a mild coronary from the shock and shouting, 'Finally!' I'd be able to say, 'Yes. The batteries in my TV remote control are dead. Could you please get some fresh ones?' (This is a common problem. I don't want to mess with it so I just ignore it, just like the person in the room before me did. And the one before her.) I'd be able to say, 'Wow, your Wi-Fi sucks. It's really weak, slow, and worth nowhere near the fifteen bucks you're charging for it.' Or (and this one always ticks me off when I discover it at five a.m.), 'There's only decaf by the coffee machine.' Or, 'Can someone pick up those disgusting room service leftovers that have been sitting on the floor outside my door since when I checked in three hours ago?'"

The point isn't that these problems I'm identifying are supereasy to remedy, which nobody would deny. The point is, Mr. Hotel, why didn't your people ask me when I was *right there in front of them*, when they could have fixed my problem and I could have seen them enjoying the opportunity to please me? When they could have, at the very least, exceeded my low expectations with minimal effort? When I could have a personal experience that would likely prompt a conversation or some semblance of one that I'd find pleasant, remember, and, quite possibly, talk about at some point in the future when someone asked for a hotel recommendation in Indianapolis?

We all know now what would have happened if one of your people had asked me a question: I would have answered it. I promise. Even if all I said was "Nope, everything's great," I'd have noticed and remembered being asked. And if I was asked that question or one like it on every visit in any of your hotels around the country or around the world, I'd notice how eager to please your staff is.

Mr. Hotel's mood had changed dramatically from sour to enthused because he could see opportunity that didn't have a large price tag attached to it. Thinking like a dominator means you see how easy it would be to turn all of my problems of a few paragraphs ago into memorable, winning moments, right? Like, "Hi. I'm here to change the batteries in your TV remote. And for bringing it to our attention, please enjoy an on-demand movie, or free Wi-Fi, on us." Or "Here's a gift card for a free cup of coffee in our lobby Starbucks or a cocktail from the bar." I bet you can think of a few more right now without breaking a sweat.

Why shouldn't it be that way? If you, dear reader, were the manager of this hotel, wouldn't you insist upon your employees being 100 percent focused on delighting your guests? Of course you would. And wouldn't you find it disheartening to know that a few days after guests leave your property, your business is asking them to fill out a survey? As in please take time out of your overloaded schedule . . . to do us . . . a favor that will give you no benefit whatsoever?

When I'm in your city again and choose a different hotel than yours, please don't say it's because I've changed and fallen for the charms of the hotel across the street that tweets like crazy and has fifty-inch flatscreens while yours only has forty-inchers and your social media is haphazard. And that it's hard for you to charge a premium for your rooms when the hotels across the street are matching you almost to the penny on price (and, of course, vice versa).

The bottom line, then, for Mr. Hotel: "You just didn't do enough to earn my preference, so I don't have any positive 'they' stories to tell. And that's precisely why I view your hotels the same way I view any commodity. All in all, you're consistently good at what you do. But I've got so many other consistently good choices now. And there are likely *millions* of people—the trees, not the forest—who've stayed with you who match my description." Is there any doubt that what he's selling is a commodity, a gas station of sorts?

If you're going to bust out of that destructive commodity mind-set and dominate your competitors, Mr. Hotel, you're going to have to ask the Noise Cubed questions: What are people saying about us? What do we want them to say about us? And what do we have to do to make that happen? Then you're going to unleash the unlimited power of an awesome weapon you already have at your disposal: Your people, most of whom have numerous opportunities every day to create story-worthy experiences for your guests. Or at least impress them with their proactive efforts to be attentive, hospitable, and delightful.

Your people are going to lift your reputation and bring life and resonance to your soon-to-be-updated facilities. Because, you know, those new marble floors, plush mattresses, and high-tech toilets, nice as they'll be, can't speak for themselves. And people need only see the new stuff once before they take it for granted—what do we care how much you paid to upgrade and refresh when we already expect it to be nice? That money and whatever it's paying for aren't putting you in the lead, they're merely keeping you in the game.

To draw parallels to your business, let's widen our perspective to the bigger picture of the overall hotel marketplace. How does the market— that's you, I, and everybody else with a pulse—view the competitive landscape? Well, we're all quite aware of the household-name, midlevel hotel chains that are competing for our presence and preference. But which do you prefer and which would you recommend? Hilton? Marriott? Hyatt? Sheraton? Embassy Suites? Wyndham? DoubleTree? You've surely stayed at at least a few of these, if not all of them. They all seem to be pretty much everywhere you'd ever need a hotel, they all have point systems to reward frequent travelers, and they're all priced similarly. So? Which one is it? I'm confident you'd say, as I would, "I'd be happy with any one of them and, if they're all pretty close together, I'd shop with my wallet and choose the cheapest of equals." Who wouldn't?

(Another quick sidebar: I used a dangerous word in that last paragraph. My shoulders slump anytime business leaders or marketers say they're working to build "awareness" of something. Marketers even put "awareness" in their strategies and brag as awareness data trends

upward as a result of their amazing awareness-building tactics. Well, I've got three words for the awareness crowd: Cut. The. Crap.

Awareness, from a competitive standpoint, is the lowest and least meaningful rung on the competitiveness ladder. This is business, dammit, so I want to dominate my competitors. I don't just want potential customers to be aware of me; I want them to prefer me and do business with me! Otherwise, what's the point? Is it a victory for the Women's National Basketball Association that I'm aware of them and what they do? I sure as hell hope not, since I've never been to a WNBA game, nor watched one on TV. They've not earned one penny from me and likely never will. Aware? Yes. Prefer? No. No offense intended to WNBA, but it's just not my thing and, at least as it exists now, it won't be. I've yet to cross the threshold at a Carl's Jr., but I'm certainly aware of them. A bazillion parents are aware of fishing but have never taken their kids to try it. I could go on, but you get the point.

Leaders: When your marketing people are showing you data to prove how your business's awareness has gone up, ask them to convert that awareness into something you can use to pay bills or you'll find someone who will. Please.)

Let's take a quick look at that second group Mr. Hotel wants to attract, new blood. And let's say that someone in that group is looking to book an overnight stay in Indianapolis. New blood here means folks who've not visited any one of his chain's hotels yet as well as those who have, but have yet to visit the chain's location in Indy. How do these folks (aka "the market") choose a hotel when they're planning a trip? The same way you and I would.

Sometime when you have a minute or two, go to a travel site like Trip-Advisor, have it search for hotels in Indy or any random city, and look at what people have to say in their reviews. You'll find reviews at travel-booking sites like Travelocity and Expedia, too, to name just a few. While yes, you may see some comments, good and bad, about properties and room furnishings, the most frequent and powerful comments you'll read will be about the hotels' staffs. Some reviewers come to bury, others to praise. Either way, they can be very convincing.

I hope you find it telling, as I do, that when you're reading a review and reach negative comments about staff, you tend to stop reading, eliminate that property from your list, and move on to the next one. That's what bad noise does. Fair or not, just one sour review turns you off, doesn't it? Who wants to stay somewhere where you know someone just like you has been slighted, regardless of how new and improved the property is? You're much more inclined to read long reviews when someone's raving about a hotel's staff, and the reason's simple: You'd like to experience the rare pleasure of being treated as the reviewer was (in an attractive, comfortable environment).

As you know about noise, when someone's telling a positive "they" story, we listen. Their preference for that business puts it on our short list of options, if not at the top of that list. If, as a result of our experience with that referred business, we, too, have a positive "they" story to tell, the cycle starts again; a new customer will be drawn to that business based on our story. The snowball just gets bigger and bigger until, eventually, that business outshines its competitors. That's dominance.

I'm not sorry if that sounds overly simple and is so heavily rooted in common sense. I know people, and so do you, who prefer to hear complex solutions to business challenges, because they believe anything simple isn't worth doing. That doesn't register with me. The simple notion that it takes next to no effort to flowchart the actions and reactions in the last three paragraphs is all it takes to turn those who prefer complexity into doubters. Let them doubt and make things so complex that they can't be easily solved. Not only will they never be dominators, but they will always be at risk of extinction.

Let's do a Fonzie and think about positioning for a minute. Let's look at the competitive weaponry the physical properties—otherwise known as "the product," the stuff we see and touch—these hotels offer. We won't have to look far to reach some obvious conclusions. I wake up in hotel rooms nearly as often as in my own bedroom and typically don't know whose property I'm in when I crawl out of bed. How about you?

Why, I've long wondered, hasn't one of these chains taken it upon themselves to be clearly, meaningfully, visually different than the others? Remember, I'm not even talking about harnessing their work cultures for competitive advantage here. I'm also not talking about major architectural values. I'm just wondering why simple positioning is overlooked. Why are there no recognizable trademark features like consistent touchpoints, a memento, a monogram on the damned pillow, an inspiring quote on my room door to send me on my way in the morning attached to any of these? Why is everything so sterile? What's the point of being in business if you're going to be so glaringly indistinguishable from your competitors? It makes no sense!

(If by chance you're reading this on a plane, look up. Quickly find something inside your jet that tells you what airline you're on. There are probably no signs or logos of any kind and no familiar color schemes, so you'll have to look at the in-flight magazine—finally, a use for those things!—to find something that identifies the airline. This is absurd. In an effort to control costs, leadership chose to not put their name on anything, thus sending a clear message that says, "We could be anybody." WTF?)

Between minimal efforts to position themselves positively and equally minimal efforts to create memorable experiences for guests, it's no wonder there's so much consolidation in the hotel industry. Because travelers don't seem to care whose name is on the roof as long as their expectations were met, which, of course doesn't take much, that's a competitive disaster that can only be mitigated through volume. So whichever chain controls the most rooms is going to "win" by default. What happens when there's no room left for consolidation because the smaller chains have all been acquired? Everyone involved loses.

But let's say just one of the household-name players or, perhaps even a new entry, positions itself to dominate and builds a reputation for being noticeably and pleasingly different from competitors. And makes visible, consistent efforts to make guests feel good about themselves and the people making them feel that way. And becomes story-worthy as the reward for their effort. I'd bet on their success and you would, too, no matter what the rooms cost.

You're seeing parallels here to your own business and your competitors, aren't you? And continuously thinking about all the ways that you and your competitors resemble each other and make similar noise, no? And how your people smile, act friendly, and say much the same things as they do. And how your positioning mirrors theirs. And how, if your business and the people who work there aren't giving customers positive, memorable, unexpected experiences, they have nothing to say and thus don't create any new demand for you. And why at many businesses the perceived only routes to growth are through new products, acquisition of competitors, or "rebranding." Or the new fun buzzwords, "innovation" and "disruption."

Do you think if you accompanied me back to Mr. Hotel's office, you'd have enough ammo to contribute to the conversation? Or even carry it? I think you do. Once you know what to look for, it gets easy to spot fixable competitive issues. The simple fact that you're *looking* means you're starting to think like a dominator.

Before we snuggle up to him again, or you gather your fellow employees for a serious heart-to-heart talk about improving your noise, let me load you up with some more ammunition so you can completely blow them away with your expertise. You'll want to be able to tell people not only what's happening right now in their competitive environment, but why it's happening and what the future holds.

Remember that motorcycle-mounted TV we encountered earlier? It has one helluva story to tell. It's a story you need to know and repeat. And it's coming up next.

FIVE

Beware Brain Pain and the Coal Mine Canaries of Commoditization

You know I love to say the best lessons come from the least-expected places. Well, my new riding partner, the best lesson I know of for how to suck the competitive life from a business—and the telltale signs that it's in big danger—can be taken from a simple household appliance. Like the one I was just talking about. Trust me, you'll remember what you're about to read here and you'll repeat it to your coworkers. I'm counting on that.

Remember back when you had a big, heavy, traditional box-full-of-tubes TV in your living room and how the cool factor and out-of-reach price tags on the first amazing new flatscreens you ever saw just blew your mind? And how much you wished you had one? And how anytime you were in a consumer electronics or big-box department store you'd linger, just staring and wondering how all that mind-blowing technology got jammed into something so thin? Sure you do. I can't think of any product in my lifetime, computers included, that generated such intense desire. They were just so damn cool and their benefits were so obvious and simple to understand. You were in love at first sight. Oh man, we all were.

TV salespeople were even more excited by the new stuff than we were, and rightly so, because they were riding a wave of flatscreen-generated cash that would soon become tsunami-like, flooding their bank accounts. Almost overnight, flatscreens were everywhere, and everyone was talking about them. When their out-of-reach prices inevitably crept down a bit, you took the bait and did some serious research because, even at lower price points, they were still four-figure-plus purchases—even the smaller models. So you did your homework, dropped that bundle of cash, brought one home, and somehow let news of your new purchase slip into conversations with friends. Just like the rest of us. And hearing us talk about our flatscreens compelled our friends to take the plunge and buy one, too.

And if this seems like only yesterday it's because, well, it was.

Should you ever need a great, easy-to-grasp lesson in what's scarily wrong with just about every industry in the world today—why it's so easy to be lured into low price as a (likely nonsustainable) competitive weapon, so vital to harness the power of Noise Cubed by getting strategic with your positioning, and so mightily important to maintain a work culture that's in synch with the real world and brings your positioning to life—let flatscreens be your coal mine canaries. They'll tell you precisely what to avoid with your positioning and go-to-market tactics. Flatscreens not only changed how you view television, they're about to change how you view the business world.

Take a little field trip to a consumer electronics store—a small local one or a household name chain—or any big-box retailer with a consumer electronics department, make a beeline straight to that long wall where the flatscreens are displayed, and watch as a painful and avoidable horror story plays out right before your eyes.

For the sake of our field trip experiment, you're not here just to look, you're here to buy a flatscreen. Right now. You've got money in your pocket and you're not interested in driving all over town. And you're not after some ninety-inch, NASA-worthy, 3-D heart-stopper of a TV that was named "New Product of the Year" at the Consumer Electronics Show, you're just after a nice forty-incher for your office or your spoiled kid's bedroom. You're not here for a luxury item, you're here for an appliance that, at the time of this writing, is going to set you back about $250. Few if any people reading this would call that price point a bank breaker or one that warrants a lot of pre-purchase research. And never mind that $250 is less than a quarter of what you'd have spent for the same-size product a dozen or so years ago.

I'll bet my eyesight that you don't have a particular brand name, let alone a list of specific product features, in mind before starting your search. Do you? That's fine and makes you just like everybody else.

Now go hit that sales floor, pick one out, and spend your money. Just look at that massive display of flatscreens up on the wall, aglow with technological wizardry that's light-years ahead of the first one you bought, yet superaffordable. They're all waiting for folks like you to give them good homes. Each one's beaming the same beautiful, superhigh-def images of dew dripping from lush foliage in a rain forest and bright green frogs sucking bugs out of the air with their lightning-fast tongues. The colors are spectacular. Man, they look great, don't they? But you're not buying all of them; you just want one. But which one?

As you're looking up at that display wall, plastered end to end with forty inchers, notice that you're standing flat-footed, slowly shifting your eyes from side to side, letting it all soak in. What you're doing is completely natural to our species. In fact, it's how we hunt. As in, with weapons. For food. You're looking for something different—anything—about any of the flatscreens that jumps out at you and catches your eye, breaks the display pattern (like a deer's brown fur against snow), separates that product from the landscape, and pulls you in for a closer look. But the products you're now eyeballing resemble each other so closely that they're indistinguishable. They're identical black rectangles beaming identical images. No one item pulls you toward it, so you remain frozen in place for a few more seconds. And that's a big problem. But not so much for you, as you'll soon see.

Today, midsize flatscreens generate about as much excitement as canned peaches. As every player in the consumer electronics industry jumped into the early feeding frenzy of the flatscreen world and new start-ups appeared, negative competitive forces took hold. This didn't take long. Manufacturing efficiencies and massive inventories of copycat products pushed prices so low, so fast that distinction left the industry. Despite their amazing technology, flatscreen value and corresponding prices dropped so much that some stores started *giving* them away as premiums ("Buy a recliner—we'll throw in a flatscreen!").

Because every industry player was mimicking its competitors, adding every conceivable buzzwordable feature you can imagine (or, more realistically, can't imagine), the resulting me-too environment of look-alike stuff and nondifferentiating noise killed any chance of single players claiming any real, desirable, memorable, repeatable, story-worthy marketplace advantage.

Now get closer to the goods and begin the slow end-to-end walk in front of the product display that I call the "march of death," that plodding, mindless march that essentially leads to nowhere. Start at the right side of the wall and move left. Everybody does.

In about the time it takes to blink, your eyes pick up on the fact that each set has a price tag in the upper right-hand corner, while your brain instantly deduces that each of these prices, for similarly sized products, are all close to one another. Yep. As expected, they're all roughly in the $250 range, give or take a few bucks. None is priced low enough to break the pattern and gain your immediate attention, because you're just not that cheap. (But here's a hint: You're going to be.) Besides, the only remarkably lower prices hang on the sets of questionable origin, from companies no human has ever heard of. Most of us lack the courage, if that's the right word, to roll the dice on no-name stuff, which is probably why we don't see as much of it as we did a few years ago.

After that quick price-checking scan, your eyes will shoot to the lower, center bar of each TV to where the brand name resides. That name, of course, is where the story gets told and demand gets built, right? It's where familiarity, appeal, reputation, and preference reside. But uh-oh. This little exercise isn't helping you at all because you instantly recognize every name you see and, rather than helping you, the names and logos melt into a meaningless blur. I'll bet you can name more than a dozen big-name TV brands off the top of your head—Pioneer, Philips, Magnavox, Panasonic, Vizio, LG, Samsung, Mitsubishi, Toshiba, Sanyo, Siemens, Sharp, Sony. And that's just for starters. You know they're all reputable and you wouldn't be embarrassed to own any of them. But quick! Can you name one advantage that any of those brand names would give you? Just one? Or can you recall a positive story or anecdote about any of these manufacturers that might sway you? *Anything?*

More to the point: Is there any brand name represented that you could describe positively using or implying "they," which would mean you've humanized that business in a positive way that makes you prefer "them" over the others? ("I like Toshiba because they . . ."). It's safe to assume you don't—I've yet to meet anyone who does—so you can't tell the difference between the players and assume they're all the same. In other words, you know they're all good. Or more accurate, good enough for you.

It's crazy, but what was recently a prized "want" is now a commodity, like printer paper and motor oil. You could swap the names on the bottoms of the TVs and nobody would notice.

Like most people, you don't feel comfortable opting for the set that's on sale today for just a few bucks less than the next cheapest. Not yet. You need some help to make your decision. So you're about to do something that no business should ever want a potential customer to do: You're going to engage your brain.

This just got ugly and one of the most important lessons not only in competing to dominate, but simply *survival,* is about to reveal itself.

Do yourself a huge favor and tattoo these three words onto your forehead so you'll never forget them: "Brains. Cause. Pain." Visualize how this tattoo would look on your noggin so you won't forget those words.

See, we humans don't like to use our brains unnecessarily and we very much don't like being forced to. God forbid, we don't ever want to have to do math unless we absolutely have to. The bottom line lesson here is that if your prospective customer has to *think,* process data, and crunch information in order to choose between you and your look-alike competitors, you've greatly decreased, if not destroyed, any probability of that person buying from you. (The same goes for any prospective employee, partner, or other important public you're attempting to make prefer you.) "Brains. Cause. Pain."

Here's how this plays out: Because you couldn't tell which TV to take home just by looking at them and found no meaningful resonance or advantage in any of the brand names, you felt the need to do some self-educating. You know, so you could make an informed, *logical* purchase decision. And what better place to seek that education than on the product spec tags accompanying each product?

These product specs are obviously meant to help you decide which product is right for you. And they're not just giving you fine-print stuff, they're putting their main selling points in large, bold type up at the top. You know, the important stuff that's going to help you make that decision. The stuff that's going to strike some chords of familiarity with you. The stuff you're going to remember and repeat when somebody asks, "Why'd you pick that one?"

Say it with me: Remember and repeat. Remember and repeat. Remember and repeat. If I can't remember it, I can't repeat it. R&R, baby. Don't forget it.

So the plan is, you'll work your way from flatscreen to flatscreen, checking the spec tags to vacuum up the memorable benefits and messages that will aid you in your decision making. Simple enough, right? Well, watch how fast things go to hell.

Let's say the first setup is the Samsung. Just flip that tag over and say to yourself, "Samsung, what do you want me to know, remember, and repeat?"

Well, lo and behold, Samsung, in large bold letters, boasts as its first major selling point, under its brand name and product number, "120CMR (Clear Motion Rate)." Hmmm. What do you make of that?

Have you ever used or heard the term "Clear Motion Rate" in a discussion or do you have even a ballpark idea of what it means? Answer both with a no. And what about that data point in front of it? Is 120 the best Clear Motion Rate number to have? Is that high, low, average? You couldn't possibly know. So why is it there?

Do you know what we do anytime we're confronted with terminology and data we don't understand? You should, because it's exactly what you did when you last bought insurance, a computer, or a lawn mower: We compare the terminology and data we don't understand to other companies' terminology and data hoping to find something we *do* understand, so we can make an important discovery.

Things don't get any better, though, when you flip over the tag on the next set, a Vizio, which lists as its first major selling point "240 Effective Refresh Rate." Which do you suppose is preferable, Effective Refresh or Clear Motion? Do you suppose you're the only one who doesn't know the difference? The Vizio's number is twice as big, but are we comparing apples to oranges? Is 240 twice as good? Twice as bad? Or the same, because clear motion means only half as fast as effective refresh? This is beyond crazy.

Let's complicate things more. Next up is a unit from Sanyo, which boasts first and foremost of its 60Hz refresh rate. Hertz? That's three different TV manufacturers, right out of the gate, each using different terminology to describe something—"refresh"—that none of us can interpret, with data points that are meaningless to the human race. *And leading with it.* Not at all helpfully, the Sanyo also offers as a key selling point the fact that it has both "Compos" and "Compon" inputs. That's helpful. Not.

Next up comes the Toshiba offering with its "120 BF Rate" (groan) and "brushed thin bezel." BF? Anybody? Here's a conversation that will never happen: "Hey, man. Nice TV. Why'd you go with the Toshiba?" "Are you kidding? Check out that 120 BF rate and that brushed thin bezel."

I'm not picking on anybody here, I'm simply reporting the facts. All of the product information I just shared was lifted verbatim from spec tags in Sam's Club in Gaithersburg, Maryland, taken in order from the first four sets on display.

I could list the top selling points of the comparable forty-inchers of at least fifteen top brands, and every one would lead with a different, indecipherable spin on "refresh" with an equally indecipherable data point in front of it, along with a lot of other fancy-sounding words that nobody is familiar with.

This is, in a word, stupid. I hope you can come up with a better word.

Now you see what I mean about "Brains Cause Pain." This stuff's not helpful at all, is it? But here's the thing that brings us back to earth. In the midst of all that indecipherable data and confusion, there's one nugget of information we *do* understand: the price, of course. That's a problem. A massive one at that.

So now you're about to do something that the younger you would never have considered: You're about to spend a few hundred dollars (not bank-breaking, but still . . .) on a product having given little if any thought to the company that built it and, equally remarkable, the business you're buying it from. Because you just don't care. Because you know you'll likely be satisfied with whatever you buy before you even buy it, since you know it's coming from a reputable manufacturer and you're buying it from a reputable business. You're going to take it home, plug it in, and see that it works, well, just like a flatscreen should. It will serve you well and meet your expectations, which, you're learning, is another massive problem.

But we're not done.

You've not pulled a flatscreen off the shelf and shoved it into your cart yet. You've walked end to end down the row of products, confusing yourself with those crazy specs, when something, finally, grabs your attention and piques your interest. It's a price tag—a whopper—and it's hanging on a Sony. This unit costs $150 more than the products hanging next to it so, naturally, you're curious to know why.

Of course you remember a time when Sony televisions, fueled by the company's impeccable brand halo, massive advertising budget, and just a handful of worthy competitors, could command that price premium. When you saw a Sony in your friend's house, you wanted one, too, because you believed it was the best stuff out there. That envy, coupled with the (imagined) owner prestige, was the lifeblood of the brand and the reason the company could command premium prices.

But for lots of reasons—not least of which is that impressive wall of products to your right—you don't feel so strong about Sony anymore, so you're trying to figure out why it costs so much more. Your head is now swiveling back and forth between the Sony and the Philips or Toshiba hanging to its right, like you're watching a tennis match, looking for differences.

That head swiveling is like a ringing dinner bell for the hungry salesperson, who, finally taking an interest in you despite knowing you've been on the floor for ten minutes, comes striding in, fired up and ready to close a deal.

At this point, corporate suicide is about to happen right in front of you. We've all borne witness to this.

(Quick time-out: What do we know about our salesperson? You see his diplomas on the wall boasting logos of all the major electronics manufacturers, his employer, and various electronics industry trade associations you've never heard of, so you know he's been trained up-side down and backward on anything and everything to do with selling TVs. He knows his stuff in microscopic detail just like, I imagine, you (and your salespeople) know pretty much everything about everything your company sells. This guy lives and breathes flatscreens.

He has two missions today: He wants to sell you the high-margin Sony, then talk you into an expensive extended warranty. He got a big pep talk about doing just that at this morning's sales meeting. He role-played with another associate, under the watchful eye of the sales manager, on how to turn your no into a yes—especially on the ex-tended warranty. He knows he can earn points toward dinner for two at Texas Roadhouse if he's successful. And he really wants to treat his wife to a free steak and those fried pickles they do.

All that training and encouragement is about to be put to the test. Back to the action!)

Wanting you to fill your cart with that premium-priced Sony, our highly trained salesman ramps into high gear, all smiles, cozies up next to you, and asks what I believe to be the very worst question in all of retail, the same question you've heard a million times in your life and only rarely ever responded to positively: "Can I help you?" (You know how much I hate pre-dictable, ubiquitous opening lines in business-related conversations.) Before you can ask about the Sony, he leaps into the breach.

"I really like this Sony," he announces. Combined with a lot of palpable enthusiasm, that could've been a supereffective opener for him, but instead he follows it up by treating you to what he's confident will be a dazzling dis-play of the bottomless depth of his product know-how: "It's got a Trilumi-nous display with 8 million individual pixels—versus an industry standard of 7 million—that will deliver near-perfect visual quality out to a distance of forty feet, an intelligent picture optimizer with Motionflow XR960 for ultraclear motion—which is awesome—five-channel S-Force 3-D surround sound that delivers optimal tonal quality to a distance exceeding forty feet, a 16-to-9 aspect ratio . . ."

Uh-oh. Instead of turning you on, this stuff is as confusing as the nonsense data on the tags, if not more. (Motionflow XR960? Anybody?) You didn't attend any of those training seminars that he sat through, nor do you have a Ph.D. in electronic engineering or anything close to it. As these "selling points" and "features and benefits" bang off your eardrums, the gears inside your body begin to seize up. Virtually every thought and feeling you're experiencing right now is negative and deep in the black:

"What in God's name is he talking about?"

"Why is he doing this to me?"

"Oh no! He's about to ramp up the pressure and I'm so nonconfrontational, he'll end up talking me into buying this!"

"I must really be dumb."

"He must think I'm really dumb."

"I knew I should've done some homework."

"I don't like this guy! I've got to get away from him."

"This sucks."

It's obvious our well-intentioned salesperson failed to tattoo "Brains. Cause. Pain." onto his forehead and God knows, you're feeling it. He's somehow under the assumption that we humans are rational, logical, and data-driven when nothing could be further from the truth. He doesn't realize that every important "thing" you've ever bought in your life, every business decision you've made, heck, every decision you've made *period,* was driven way more by your gut—your emotions—than your brain. So he's aiming at the wrong organ.

Somebody needs to tell him this: The only decision a person makes using his or her brain exclusively is life or death. Everything else comes from the heart. "I like this." "I trust you." "That's so cool." "I believe you." "Dude, that's awesome." "That feels right." "My friends will like this." None of that is brain-driven. Our salesperson's recitation of numbers and indecipherable jabber has done nothing but confuse you, render you uncomfortable, and made you dislike him. Can't you just see life insurance salespeople and financial planners—the world heavyweight champions of nonmemorable language and data—squirming in their seats as they read this?

So why do you suppose our salesperson is dumping this half ton of useless technical-sounding gobbledygook into your lap? Do you think it was his idea? I'd wager he's doing this because some much higher-up at his company decided this is the best direction to go to generate sales, then someone else trained him to do what you just witnessed and it's what's demanded of him as an employee. This has been happening for generations and you can see the damage it's caused in the form of indistinguishable products at giveaway prices.

Can we agree that this is flat-out nuts? And if push ever comes to shove, can we always remind ourselves of the Schmidt-ism that says if a customer can't remember and repeat what he or she has just been told after hearing it just once ("What happens in Vegas . . .") then it's useless?

Our salesman's one-act play is going to end badly and with more pain because, as he's prattling on, you're now starting to do exactly what he shouldn't want you doing—math in your brain. You didn't have to drill too deep today and break a sweat, though, because a second-grade level is all that's needed. But it's still math (in the last place you expected to need it). You say to yourself, "Hmmm. I know I can afford to buy that Sony for four hundred bucks. Looks like a nice TV. Might even impress my in-laws. But . . . for two hundred fifty bucks, I can grab any of these other TVs. They look just like the Sony, so who's going to care? Who'd even notice? Maybe some of the parts in the other TVs aren't quite as good as Sony's, but who'd know? It's just a TV. I'll save a hundred and fifty bucks and that's a hundred and fifty bucks *I can spend on something else, somewhere else.*"

And at that precise moment, flush with the satisfaction that you correctly ran the numbers, you will reach up and pull down the TV from the name-brand manufacturer that, on that particular day, was on sale and had the lowest price. Maybe it's just one dollar less than its closest competitor. You'll plunk it into your cart, avoid making eye contact with the slump-shouldered salesperson, and bolt for the checkout counter. Mission accomplished.

Well, what do you know? You *were* that cheap after all. Your selection criteria for your flatscreen came down to the product that was a measly buck cheaper than its closest competitor. And see, now your sales rep's in pain. But he's not alone.

At the precise moment you plunked that lower-priced option into your cart, Sony, that retailer, that sales rep's fellow well-intentioned employees, and every look-alike brand you passed over today each moved one step closer to extinction. These are self-inflicted wounds, aren't they? If you follow business media, you know that consumer electronics retailers are presently rebuilding their business models and seeking investment capital to evolve from pure-play brick-and-mortar resellers to hybrid brick-and-mortar/online resellers. They're doing this, they'll say, because their "market has changed and migrated to low-price-Internet businesses."

While we can likely agree that the hybrid model might make sense, I trust that "market change/migration" nonsense triggered screaming alarms in your ears. You can likely name at least one of the biggies that are in trouble or—remember Circuit City?—gone. In any of these scenarios, former employees of these businesses are going hungry and that's just so wrong and avoidable. Look at the other products these businesses sell—computers, printers, home entertainment stuff, car stereos (remember those?)—and you'll see the same downward death spiral you just saw with the flatscreens. When will it stop? And who will lead the charge?

If you're still having trouble coming to terms with my argument that markets can't change (and/or migrate), here's something I know you'll get right away: You, I, and everyone we know have been in these electronics stores, most of us countless times over the years. Not only did we buy major products there, we scooped up tons of ancillary stuff, too—like ink cartridges and paper for our printers, computer memory upgrades, cords, chargers, games, cameras, CDs, and DVDs. We've all spent a lot of money in these places.

Think about it for just a second and you'll likely agree that what I've just described is a business leader's golden dream come true. What else would you call a situation wherein you have potential customers in your building, many of whom have been there before, intending to buy your desirable products, standing alongside your salespeople and staff? Your products, your people, and customers—all in the same place at the same time. It just doesn't get any better than that.

So what did those retailers do to take advantage of these amazing opportunities when we were on their turf, standing toe-to-toe with their people? (Hint: If you're thinking like a dominator instead of an also-ran, the question almost answers itself.) Did they make an obvious effort to separate their business from their competitors while also delighting us and making us feel good about ourselves? And them? What did they do and say to be story-worthy so we'd advocate not only for them, but for the products they represent? What did they do to ensure we remember them and their people as amazing, committed, passionate friends? To instill inside us any sense of loyalty? To create any semblance of a meaningful, memorable experience?

Did they ever even try to do any of those things, or did they simply take our money and give us what we came in for during the years when they were our *least inconvenient* choice or when we had nowhere else to go?

You know the answer without having to think.

These businesses, it's worth recognizing, sell really cool things that a lot of us enjoy and may even be passionate about, yet all of those faceless, baseless, nameless, emotionless, totally nonmemorable transactions eventually came back to bite them and the indistinguishable products they sell where it hurt.

Everyone involved in this story needs to confront the truth that we didn't change and we didn't migrate. No way, José. These businesses gave us no reason to stay and be loyal. They just sold us stuff that, we'd all eventually learn, we could get from someone else for less money. In other words, by doing nothing for us, they pushed us away. Repeat that if it didn't sink in the first time.

You know cold reality dictates that in a commodity-like environment where we can't tell the difference between products and players, we will always take the default action of buying the lowest-priced product we can get—especially if we recognize the brand name—from the most convenient source. We have no reason to distrust the product, so who we buy it from matters little at this point, does it? How did Jeff Bezos build Amazon.com and his personal fortune? This is how. Contrary to what you may have heard or read somewhere else, he's not eating retailers' lunches; they're feeding them to him. He knows that if we're not loyal to his competitors, he's got us where he wants us. By our wallets.

Look how many businesses and people in the flatscreen story, in addition to the folks already named, suffer real pain as a result of businesses that have chosen to compete for transactions rather than compete to dominate. Remember, it's not just the manufacturers of the stuff being sold, but all the players in their so-called value chain, including their suppliers, distributors, transportation companies, and the respective employees of all these businesses. Go deeper and you'll even see the local communities that benefit from jobs and taxes generated by every business involved with this. A lot is at stake here and much is lost.

That's the past and present situation, but we can't ignore the future. How many businesses, do you suppose, would like to get into selling flatscreen

TVs, now that so much profit margin has been knocked out of them? Would you want to sell them? That's a yes-or-no question.

Perhaps you're like others who've answered that question with a maybe, saying, "Sure, lower-end flatscreens have become loss leaders, but don't forget those electronics retailers have oodles of high-end, supersized flatscreens plus lots of audiophile-worthy gadgets and gizmos that may make up for any lost revenue from their smaller flatscreens."

Would you like to bet your bank account, otherwise known as your life, on that?

I'll caution that the same behavior that sucked life and money from flatscreens will do the same with the higher-end stuff (see: Sony) and everything else being sold alongside them. Remember, these competitive problems we're looking at don't lie with the products being sold, they lie with the behavior of the businesses manufacturing and/or selling them. Forty-inch flatscreens *were* high-end stuff, remember?

Also cautionary—and this, surprisingly enough, is news to most people—is the reality that anytime the majority of revenue and/or income for a particular product segment is coming from high-end products, it means demand for low- and mid-priced products has deteriorated. When that happens, most marketing and product development initiatives get pointed toward building demand for the high-end stuff, while prospective customers in the lower segments get ignored or shortchanged. These lower segments are where future business is supposed to come from, right? When everything below the head dies, the Grim Reaper stubs out his Marlboro and starts honing his scythe.

Yes, fat-walleted audiophiles will still splurge on theater-worthy flatscreens, just as they will on outrageously expensive hi-fi equipment, to ensure they have the very best, but this isn't what I'd call good news for electronics manufacturers or resellers. Think about it: When's the last time you bought stereo components? Do you think your kids will want them one day? Will this stuff even be around? When I was in college, a great stereo was every guy's most prized possession or want. College kids now are happy watching movies on their damned *phones* and listening to music with fifteen-dollar earbuds.

Please don't be fooled into thinking these problems reside only in the consumer products sphere. Perhaps you're like many who, while reading this chapter, are disagreeing and saying to yourself, "Not so fast, biker boy. The products my business makes and/or sells are technical and very precise (pharmaceuticals and business software come to mind) and my customers are very much processing information and making well-thought-out, rational choices."

If that sounds like you, I simply ask, is what you make and/or sell an absolute necessity with no available substitute? Do you have no competition whatsoever? Are your customers repeating your technical language and data in their discussions with your prospective customers in ways that separate it from your competitors' technical language? Just look around, man! No business is bulletproof. There's no such thing as unique. You *will* be copied. Stop thinking like a monopoly.

And there's something I want everyone, believers and doubters alike, to take from our electronics store field trip and accompanying discussion, in the event you didn't connect all the dots and personalize it. It's this: It doesn't matter what you make and/or sell, be it construction equipment or women's clothing or cheddar cheese or lawn maintenance, your business and industry mirrors what you just saw with those flatscreens, doesn't it? No matter how special you believe it to be, I'll remind you again that you're selling a commodity. Everyone is. The question is, will you heed the lesson of those coal mine canaries that are gasping for breath and dying or will you be the dominant-minded business that takes advantages of your competitors' mistakes?

Or perhaps you're like many business leaders who, even after I've shared stories with them about Noise Cubed, service industries like hotels, products like flatscreens, and the perils of commoditization, say, "Yeah, I get what you're saying. And I get why this noise stuff works for companies like Harley that have cool stuff to sell and rabid fans. But [look out, here it comes] our products and services are really boring and aren't sexy. So our challenges to improve competitiveness are way steeper because no matter how you look at our market, it's always going to be driven by price."

My response to this is always the same, and if you've heard me speak, you've heard me say this: Boo-hoo, methinks you've not been paying attention. Because if you were, you'd have noticed that what I'm talking about here has nothing to do with the products being sold and instead has everything to do with the people involved in selling and buying them. At the end of the day, regardless of what's being sold, there are sellers and buyers. People. People are going to choose which people they're going to buy from. It's when they don't have preference for a particular supplier—a "they"—that price becomes their purchase criteria.

Anytime I hear self-defeating comments like these, they're always accompanied by a "what's the use?" attitude that tells me pretty much everything I need to know about the work culture the complaining person wallows in. And as soon as I hear stuff like this, I immediately spin the tables by forcing the excuse maker to defend their workplace. Like this: "Oh, I see. I guess nobody wants or needs your stuff and there's really no reason for you to even exist, right? And nobody in your business ever actually speaks with customers or prospects, so you're completely invisible to the world, which makes you valueless." They never agree with that, of course. Then I say, "See, the problem is obvious. You're selling the wrong stuff," and tell them this short story.

I was at a major gathering of executive leaders from many of the largest, household-name life insurance companies in the world. It was a plush, let's say miles-above-average, event. Stone crab claws and filet mignon tend to go down easier after a few well-blended martinis, don't you think? Anyway, I was going to be speaking to the group and leading a discussion on positioning, so I sat in on their morning presentations to gain more insight into the—for me and, I suppose, most people—mysterious, yet gloriously profitable world of life insurance. Plus it always helps to just sit and listen at industry meetings, regardless of the group, to help learn more about their business, get comfortable with their language, and to gain a better feel for the group's collective mood.

One of the big insurance kahunas got up to discuss the "state of the industry" and projected a slide onto the screen that everyone stared at like it was something they'd all seen a gazillion times. As a newcomer, though, I was wide-eyed by what it showed and his explanation. He said that, in over fifty years of surveying their core markets, the industry had never experienced higher levels of purchase intent (that is, the stated desire by target customers to purchase insurance). I thought, "Fantastic! Good for you!"

Then he dropped the first of two bombs: His next slide showed actual purchases of life insurance, year to year, by their core market and he said, with obvious pain but to no one's surprise, "However, the percentage of those saying they intend to buy and then *do* actually buy, has never been lower."

(Quick time-out: Okay, at this point, I'm flat-out stoked, because what he's describing as a problem is, from my purview, a market domination-minded person's dream come true. But I'm pretty sure I'm the only person in the room who feels this way.

Are you seeing what I'm seeing? Meaning, are you seeing an opportunity to dominate a market where all players are bemoaning their collective difficulty? Look closely and you'll see the target customer understands the need for the product being sold—in this case, insurance—and fully intends to buy it, but doesn't. Ooo-la-la! That's not a problem! It's spectacular knowledge because it's pointing out a massive, exploitable opportunity: There's obviously a barrier to purchase, so whoever removes it first will pave the road to dominating their market. And man, that's what we live for, isn't it? I love this.)

Our man released a second, even more deadly bomb when he concluded his remarks saying something along the lines of, "So it's never been more of an imperative for us to add more features and value into our products to make them more attractive and turn these prospects into buyers." Nods all around.

And that's when I needed to be defibbed. Remember when I said what happens if you look at the squirrel on the road when you're entering a turn instead of looking through the turn? An entire roomful of executives was looking in the wrong direction!

I couldn't believe what I was hearing and that I seemed to be the only one not nodding in agreement. So at the first break, I raced up to my room (well, suite, sue me) and hastily reworked my presentation.

I was surprised that I got a little nervous before I took the floor, which typically doesn't happen with me, because I knew I was about to risk offending my hosts and didn't have adequate time to rehearse, meaning my risk was double.

So I opened my presentation by saying something along the lines of, "Okay. Let's be clear. People *want* to buy life insurance, which is something they'll do maybe just once or twice in their lives. While they don't understand the definitions and nuances involved, they know they need insurance to provide security for their families when they're gone. But they're not pulling the trigger, right?" Nods all around. Then it was my turn to drop a bomb: "*So the collective belief in this room is that the best way to convert these hesitant prospects into customers is to add more features to your products? Haven't you been doing that exact thing for years? If that was a plausible solution, your charts would tell a much better story, wouldn't they?*" Cue the sound of crickets and butts shifting in chairs.

I told them I'm in no way unique. I'm just another head of household who owns life insurance. Two policies, in fact. But to be perfectly honest, I don't even know what companies my policies are with, because the premiums are auto-paid annually and I don't read and remember what little paperwork comes my way among all the other mail I receive. What would I learn from it anyhow? I know I'm heavily insured, pay steep premiums for that privilege, and that my agent and his employer are making good money off of me every year. Perhaps I should be embarrassed to admit I don't know who insures me, right? Nah. That's not my problem. I can easily pull my policies from my file cabinet if needed.

I then told them about my personal experience buying insurance just two years before the meeting and challenged them (as I'm now challenging you) to identify opportunities in my story to make a different noise in the marketplace and dominate competitors. In other words, stop thinking like someone who has difficult-to-differentiate products to sell. (Stop looking at the damn squirrel!)

The *Reader's Digest* version of my story went like this: Lovely wife sees me not getting any younger, yet still doing a lot of potentially dangerous stuff like riding dirt bikes, snowboarding, climbing trees to hunt deer, etc., and announces with wifelike conviction that I need to take out more life insurance. A lot, in fact. I agree—as if I had another option—and call my insurance agent. By the time I finished telling him I wanted to buy more life insurance, he was already sitting at my desk across from me (a joke that always gets a laugh from insurance salespeople but missed you by a mile).

The agent then did what agents have seemingly done since caveman days: He starts sliding documents in front of me and describing the details and options available to me. It's very obvious to me that he fully understands the intricacies and minute details of what he's speaking. What should be obvious to him, but isn't, is that I *don't*. (Remember and repeat. Remember and repeat. Remember and repeat.)

We're looking at thick policies for term, variable, and even some pseudo-hybrid stuff. Lots of numbers and details. Charts and tables galore. All numerical. Look, I'm not stupid. My favorite Fortune 500 motorcycle company trusted me with running its investor relations functions and talking to Wall Street every day, so you'd think I'd be able to understand personal life insurance policy language and data. But this is only the second-ever life insurance conversation I've had with a provider. This is language and calculus with which I have no comfort whatsoever.

I'm sure I asked a few questions and I'm confident in saying he asked,

"Do you have any more?" before we wrapped up. But I guess I was too embarrassed to ask any more. ("Brains. Cause. Pain.") As he began packing up
his things, my agent said I should discuss the options with my wife and that
he and I could reconnect at the end of the week to act on whichever policy
the missus and I selected.

*(By the way, this probably seems familiar. Do you remember that fi-
nancial advisor we watched through our Reality Goggles earlier? This
was the inspiration for that.)*

When he called on Friday and asked if I'd had a conversation with my
wife, I said, "Well, I tried, but I felt like a complete idiot and embarrassed
myself." Then I just told him straight up that I didn't really understand the
options and which of the three policies would be the best choice. He responded with, "Well, with the first option you can hedge against this . . ."
and "the second allows you to hedge against that . . . " etc. Then he said, "So
which do you want?" And I said, again, "I still don't know."

More than once I simply told the guy, "Look, please just tell me what
I need and that's what I'll go with. I trust you." But rather than do that—
which, I suppose, might violate some law or industry standard—he kept
further trying to make the unexplainable differences between the three
complex (to me) plans understood.

Is this or is this not ridiculous? Judging by those fifty years of data that
show prospects not buying, I know I'm not the only person in the country
who's been through an experience like this. You've been there yourself,
haven't you? (There's a great closing line in Woody Allen's *Love and Death*
where Woody says, "There are worse things in life than death. If you've
ever spent an evening with an insurance salesman, you know what I mean.")

So bearing in mind that none of this was my idea in the first place and
that the missus wasn't going to tolerate any delays, here's what I did: I told
my advisor, "I'm taking this first option, just to get it over with," and he
quickly agreed it was a solid choice (you don't say!). I pulled the trigger
and ink hit paper. So I'm further insured. But I'm also confused. Who's
my carrier again? What am I paying for? What will my heirs get when the
Reaper calls my name? Were it not for my wife's insistence, it's a safe bet
I'd be among those data points on the chart showing prospects who intend
to purchase yet don't go through with it.

But come on! The key players in the conference room—all, mind you,
intelligent, powerful people—believe the way to fix this problem and get

people like me to sign on the dotted line is to *add more features to the products*? Do you think that will solve their problem? Is it any wonder that more and more people feel their best option is to do their own research and purchase life insurance online? (Talk about confusing—the language and comparisons are even tougher in digital format.) Think like a dominator and think about the view through those Reality Goggles.

I machine-gunned the group with the kinds of questions that prompt silence: "What do you suppose I said about my whole insurance-buying experience to my friends? If I was the kind of person who hung out at a country club, is this the kind of stuff you'd want a barroom full of well-off prospects to hear? Do you think anyone in the history of the world ever had a discussion with friends about the various features and benefits of a life insurance policy?"

But then I asked the most important questions: What, specifically, would you have wanted me to say to my friends? What would you want me to tell the gang at the country club? *This, friends, is a gift-wrapped opportunity for you to become a "they" instead of an "it."*

It's my strong opinion—and, hopefully, now yours as well—that the life insurance industry is pushing the wrong thing. They're trying to promote and sell a product. And while they rightly use emotional drivers like "security" and "comfort" to create demand for their products, they overpower that human connection with gobbledygook that for many of us kills the sale. If we, as consumers, bought these products several times a year, over the course of a lifetime, of course we'd understand them. But most of us will buy life insurance just once or twice. How can we be expected to know and remember the minutiae, let alone the general stuff? I also can't sit down with a brain surgeon and instantly understand what she does and how she does it. Or a nuclear physicist. Or somebody who sells IT consulting. Or market-integrated auto-feed systems for container-making machinery.

So, no, life insurance policies aren't sexy. They're invisible. Look how they're sold and you'll see much of what you saw in the flatscreen exercise. The competitiveness question is, "Do you want customers and prospects to understand and discuss the ins and outs of your product? Or do you want them to speak fondly of the awesome people behind it and the surprisingly great ownership experience, while having one or two *memorable and repeatable* messages to share about the product?"

Which carrier will be the first to say enough's enough, reposition themselves, and smash through that purchase barrier by harnessing the power of Noise Cubed? Which has the courage to make people, instead of products, their primary competitive lever? Which flatscreen manufacturer will do the same?

Who's going to be first in your industry or market to make a different noise?

Up next, we'll briefly explore how and why commoditized behavior happens and how all nondominant businesses unwittingly stepped into the trap that's ensnared them. By the time you finish reading that, you'll be well prepared to explain to Mr. Hotel, along with consumer electronics execs, those life insurance honchos, and every business leader you know, what they're up against, how it happened, and how they can take advantage of their sleepwalking competitors before it's too late.

You've caught on.

SIX

Why and How Businesses Lose Their Competitiveness

Here's a fun idea: Let's commoditize ourselves. Come on, it's easy. Let's make ourselves indistinguishable, do and say nothing more than what's expected of us, minimize our value, become a marginally competitive also-ran, and then lose sleep over it while others eat our lunch.

Okay, that has to be the worst idea of all time, New Coke notwithstanding, and nobody would ever choose to do something so dumb. So, given that, why and how does commoditization take hold so easily? And why do so many people and businesses become aware of it only when it's dangerously late, then do nothing to stop it? I've yet to find an industry where commoditization hasn't forced the weak to sell on price and made everyone else run in place faster. Have you?

While we've already learned how we, as people (thus consumers, thus markets), have come to see competing businesses as equals and have become very comfortable shopping for lowest price and highest convenience when we see no difference among players, we haven't yet looked into what happens inside businesses that led us to see the world this way. There's a definite cause-and-effect thing happening here, as you'll soon see. And you'd damn sure better believe it's avoidable. And fixable.

Here's a quick experiment you can do—and teach others to do—from where you're sitting right now, to see how businesses inadvertently, yet also deliberately, position themselves to be also-rans. I say inadvertently because nobody intends to commoditize their business, and deliberately because, as you'll see, the actions that cause their problems are self-directed. We'll get to why this happens in a few minutes.

Let's get into it. I'd like you to pretend for a second that you're about to move to a new city or town for a job change, or something way more fun like retirement or to be closer to family. If that's not your thing, pretend that you've finally bitten the bullet and bought a second home in a dream location to reward yourself for a lifetime of hard work all the BS that comes with it. Key among basic necessities, buying a new residence means you're going to need to select a nearby place to do your banking. Since your new location doesn't have a branch for your current bank, you're going to need to find a new one and you're going to find it, most likely, the way you find most basic necessities in your life, online.

So here's where we get scientific. Just as you'd do in real life, fire up your Internet browser, then open Google or, if you happen to work for Microsoft, Bing. In the search bar, type in that new city or town, followed by "bank," and let it rip. Then start at the top of your search findings and open the first website, give it a cursory once-over, then move on to the next one. Do about ten of these. Or until your will to live dies. This is similar to when you were first looking at flatscreens. You're hunting, remember, looking for something different that jumps out and breaks the pattern.

What did you notice about those bank websites, having seen each for just a few seconds? I can tell you without having looked over your shoulder that most of them were blue (ooh! the color of "trustworthiness"). I can tell you that the nationally recognized banks' pages seemed to operate on the notion that you already know who and how great they are and that you're simply seeking direction to their local branches. I can also tell you that you probably can't remember a single headline, message, slogan, visual, or banner that you saw on any site, nor correctly recall the bank that posted that nonmemorable item. You could randomly swap bank names and insert them onto other banks' home pages and nothing would look out of place. Most if not all of the imagery looked completely predictable (construction job site with hardhat-wearing guy talking to well-dressed female banker with an open notebook that's there to imply, "We listen!"), or a hugging young couple in front of a house where a "Sold!" banner is plastered across its for-sale sign ("home ownership!"), or a group of serious-looking business execs—one holding his glasses—sitting at a board table looking like they're having a superimportant meeting ("strategy!").

Each home page has multiple icons to click for more information about loans and savings rates and even a plug to "Like us on Facebook," on the odd chance you're the kind of person who wants to have a social media friendship with your new bank. Or "Follow us on Twitter." Imagine the fun.

Now here's the best part: I'm no Amazing Kreskin (go ahead—google/ Bing him if you don't know the name), but if your move was an actual event rather than make-believe, I'm certain which bank you'd end up choosing in your new locale. And here's a hint: Your choice will have absolutely nothing to do with the quick search you just performed. The bank you'll ultimately select, after scanning their attempts to lure you in, will be . . . drumroll, please . . . the one closest to your new home.

Ugh. What a letdown, right? Especially after the work you put in. But the reason for this isn't as obvious as the convenience would indicate. No way. It's because none of these banks, in your research, presented themselves in a way that was noticeably different or in any way intriguing to you. None made you want to dig deeper into their site or say, "Ah, that's cool," or "That's the one for me." They presented themselves as the old-line, same as they always were, predictable, interchangeable commodities that they've allowed themselves to become. Since they're all the same, none of them would be worth driving an extra half block—which would take less than thirty seconds—to visit, would they? As for the name on the door of your new bank, you couldn't possibly care less. It's got a vault. It's got tellers. It's a bank. It'll do the trick.

Let's all agree, shall we, that this most assuredly is not competition. It's senseless, self-destructive behavior. And look out—it's highly contagious.

There are few guarantees in life and this, as you know, is one of them: When all things are perceived as equal, potential customers will always choose the most convenient and/or cheapest option.

Before we go further, please do yourself a huge favor and avoid jumping to the same false conclusion many business leaders I've led through this experiment have jumped to and say that the festival of blandness these banks presented online reflects "marketing problems." Come on, man. Give me a break. The Web pages, hence marketing, you just saw, were accurate representations of how the leaders (thus, their employees who model them) of these banks view their individual businesses and their competitive environments. Which is to say they see nothing about their bank that's in any way interesting or special and aren't outwardly interested in competing, let alone dominating. You can almost hear them saying, "We're just another boring bank. What do you want?" I mean, you do realize these bank leaders have seen their competitors' websites, right? So they know where they stand and what they're up against. And what they did—or, more accurately, didn't do—about it.

It only gets worse from here. Without having set foot in your new bank, you already know what it looks, sounds, and feels like, don't you? It's quiet as a chapel and there are a few tables, with pens chained to them, for filling out forms. Maroon velvet ropes will steer you into line and lead you toward the counter, where semi-smiling tellers are presently working with other clients. When it's your turn, a teller will look your way, nod, and say, "Next!" You'll approach and he or she will say, "How can I help you today?" You'll say you want to open an account and the teller will ask you to please take a seat until a manager can assist you.

Can you think of any business in the world that would benefit more from changing its positioning to move away from predictability and blandness toward instantly noticed difference than a bank, given the fact that we all need one and are familiar with their routines? Wouldn't the black cloud that's hovered over the entire banking industry since the mortgage scandals and economic implosion of 2007 prompt at least some of the banks leaders to say, "Let's change the game here—for our benefit"? Bluntly, the opportunity to kick some serious ass and stand out from the dull pack couldn't be more obvious. Banks, like all other for-profit ventures, surely want to grow at the expense of their competitors and attract new blood. So what's everybody waiting for?

For more bank positioning disasters, look at the first section of your Sunday newspaper this weekend. Notice—because I'm telling you to look for them—all of the local bank ads. What do you remember about any of them after you've set the paper down? Anything? Do you think it was worth it for them to buy expensive ad space when they're not saying anything in their ads that makes them stand out? Or anything that makes them even remotely interesting? I bet you noticed that almost all of them are promoting a rate of some sort. Do you think it's worth it for them to pay to advertise CD rates of less than 2 percent? Oh boy! Who's that going to attract? *That's what you paid a bundle of cash to tell me?*

I know why these ads, some of them filling entire pages, are here. Do you? It's simple. And sinful. It's because that's the way it's always been done in the banking industry. Sunday papers apparently mean bank ads, so many banks are afraid to not buy that expensive space, because they know their competitors did and they're certain that somebody—I've no idea who—would notice their absence. And since they have nothing interesting to say, they promote their rates, on the odd chance that you happen to be shopping around and that one-hundredth of a point here or there makes you sit up and take notice. Are you going to do the math? "Brains. Cause. Pain."

It's as if the leaders of these banks are saying, "Why bother to compete when we can offer the illusion that we are by buying bigger ads than everyone else?" Or, equally frightening, "Let's take something that doesn't work very well, if at all, and costs us a lot of money, and just keep doing it." Not what I'd call brilliant strategy. (Picture newspaper publishers greedily rubbing their hands together and snickering.)

Please don't think I'm telling you this because I enjoy picking on banks, because I surely don't. Banks aren't the only businesses that are making things hard for themselves by choosing to not openly compete. Far from it. To prove it, replace "bank" in your search bar with virtually any other business you might need at your new house (painters, auto repair, dry cleaner, business machine repair, landscaping, you get the picture). Or type in the name of the industry you currently work in or are interested in, regardless of what it is. The results will mirror what you saw with banks—only they won't be so reliant on blue. You'll see a lot of the same words and imagery used over and over by businesses competing for your attention (quality, customer satisfaction, certified) and look-alike visual treatments. Could the opportunity to up the game be more obvious?

Let's stop the make-believe now and look at your current business to see how it stacks up against your competitors. Here's an experiment I created that forces us to face reality. I've opened *a lot* of skeptical business leaders' eyes with this. I call it my "Go-to-Market Smack-Down."

To play along, have an assistant gather as much go-to-market stuff as he or she possibly can—think print ads, yellow page ads, brochures, sell sheets, printed screenshots of website home pages, stationery, premiums, the kitchen sink—that you and your competitors use to promote your businesses. Then have them cover with masking tape or Wite-Out all company names, logos, and obvious visual identifiers (recognized 800 numbers, etc.) and scatter all of the materials faceup on a conference table.

Now the fun starts: Invite key coworkers in one at a time and give them fifteen seconds to pull your company's go-to-market stuff out of the mess. With the tape over the obvious visual identifiers, they'll see that it can get very difficult. And of course try it yourself. You'd think your stuff would just jump off the table at you, wouldn't you? For more fun, have everyone try to find your specific competitors—especially the ones that cause you the most grief—allowing thirty seconds.

The obvious problems make themselves known quickly: You're commoditized and your positioning is way off. If we—the people who live and breathe this stuff 24/7—struggle to find ourselves right away in a crowded, competitive market and see how obviously different we are from everyone else, how can we expect potential customers to find us and see us differently? The last thing you want is to be indistinguishable. Oh and by the way, I was being generous giving you fifteen and thirty seconds.

Now that you and your team are seeing just how similar you are to your competitors—and hopefully coming to the collective realization that you need to change the game—it's time to take the conversation outside and look at the bigger picture. What does it look like when every facet of a company's go-to-market strategy—not just marketing tools—mirrors its competitors? What do your potential customers see, experience, and remember when they encounter your business? Is it like our recent consumer electronics store and bank visits?

Here's a near- and dear-to-my-heart example, compliments of Harley-Davidson, about how easily lines between competitors can become blurred. Although what I'm about to describe happened during the company's darkest years, you'll notice that it's still standard operating procedure for most businesses you know. "Darkest years." That should tell you something right there.

Before Harley's reputation regained distinction and the company became dominant—and in the years when we were discovering better ways to position it—Harley salespeople, in dealerships around the world, were relying on product specs and "features and benefits" selling to convert prospects into buyers. In other words, product glorification above everything else. Let me be clear: For many prospective customers, this wasn't just their first time in our world, standing toe-to-toe with our people, it was their formal introduction to Harley-Davidson. And you remember what your mom told you about first impressions.

Obvious question: What could possibly be wrong with pushing excellent product using good old, tried-and-true features-and-benefits selling when you've got inventory to move? Not-so-obvious answer: plenty.

Let's all agree that pushing product right off the bat (think of car salespeople and how your shoulders always slumped on hearing "What's it gonna take to get you in a new car today?") directs a prospective customer's attention in the wrong direction.

Memorize this if you haven't already: We want a customer to remember and repeat what we say and talk about *us*—not just the product we sell. Which means our attention has to be focused on the prospect and creating an unexpected, and thus memorable, experience for him or her.

Further, I hope we can agree that features-and-benefits selling only works when the potential customer intimately *understands* what's being discussed and can personalize the information. In Harley's case, first-time buyers, to say nothing of long-term owners, typically didn't and couldn't. Harley reps relied heavily on product specs—you know, good old facts and figures—but presented much of them with "secret handshake" jargon that might have sounded cool but was working against us. For newbies, that stuff was as bad as that flatscreen lingo on the manufacturers' spec sheets.

I'll keep saying this until I'm blue in the face: If prospective customers can't *understand, remember, and repeat* what you've just told them, you told them nothing and likely blew your opportunity.

Worse still for Harley, though, was that features-and-benefits selling just happened to be the exact same selling technique that everyone else in the bike industry was using. So it just made us look like every other motorcycle company the potential customer had already visited—in dealerships whose only reason for existence was to push hardware—and more or less encouraged potential customers to make purchase decisions based solely on the hardware being sold. And when that happens, price becomes the dominant selling point. Sound familiar? Hello again, flatscreens.

Harleys are "premium-priced," which is a polite, uptown euphemism for "more expensive than everyone else," and of course reflect wonderful intangibles long associated with the company (that are now the widely promoted, discussed, and valued bread-and-butter noise of the business). Why would anyone wishing to maintain good or great sales margins want potential customers comparing their stuff feature by feature with competitors' stuff that performs similarly but costs less? Especially when a lot of those features aren't easily understood and used in everyday conversation? Isn't that creating a barrier to sales and working against yourself?

To be clear, there's a place and time for features-and-benefits selling and I'm not knocking it. What I'm knocking is *leading* with it, living and dying by it, and putting all of your emphasis and language behind pushing product and using language that prospects and customers don't speak. Doing this virtually guarantees that prospective customers will be forced to engage their brains instead of their hearts. And if the only thing a customer remembers about you is the product you sell, you'll quickly be forgotten when something new and better—or simply cheaper—comes along.

(You might want to reread that last sentence.)

Speaking of that, I'll tell you now—and more later—that when customers profess loyalty to a product, *instead of to the people behind the product*, that loyalty will become strained or ignored when something new and better comes along.

(You might want to reread that, too.)

But we still weren't done dampening Harley's competitiveness. If you went to an industry bike show somewhere—the equivalent of a trade show, only a helluva lot more fun—or into a Harley dealership, odds are you'd go home with spec sheets for each bike you were interested in. Harley's sheets would each feature a beautiful bike photo (you'd have to try pretty hard to make a Harley look ugly) on the top half of the page, and a list of product specs—accurate to the bazillionth of a micron—on the bottom half. Nearly all of this information would be detailing things you wouldn't likely understand, were of no importance to you, and used words that very few motorcyclists would ever use in their decision making, let alone in a conversation (gear ratios, bore and stroke, foot-pounds of torque, rake, trail . . . see what I mean?). *Hello again, flatscreens.* I've been around bikes forever and have *never* heard a human being utter the words "gear ratio" in a sentence. Not even mechanics, who I'm sure understand it. I have no idea what it means because I don't need to know.

Naturally, if you visited with any of Harley's competitors, you'd receive product spec sheets from them as well, with the requisite cool photo above a kitchen sink of information that's equally hard to understand and personalize.

By giving a potential customer that spec sheet, Harley and its competitors were saying, "Here's our one shot to tell you what we'd like you to know, remember, and repeat to others." And it was meaningless, confusing gobbledygook. That's not good positioning, is it?

While there are always going to be sophisticated, highly informed buyers who value highly technical data, the percentage of overall buyers who will actually use it as part of their purchase criteria is very small. It's a motorcycle, after all, not a robotic brain surgeon. But here's where this stuff hurt us most. When we gave a potential customer—especially a newbie with minimal experience and no brand preference—a ton of data and metrics they didn't understand, what did they do with that data? Just as with the flatscreens earlier, they'd compare it to the competition's equally indecipherable data. Given that scenario, of course, their eyes and minds would always lead them to the one piece of data that was equal parts understandable and memorable, and seemed to jump right off the page: the price. Harleys typically had the highest prices, which often became a critical bone of contention with prospects. So Harley was inadvertently making it easier for the other guys.

There's never a good time to give business away, of course, but Harley was giving it away at the worst possible time. Despite all of the brand's inherent marketability, we were assuming that nonowners viewed it and loved it the same way we did, while we unintentionally exhibited many of the go-to-market behaviors of our look-alike competitors. Acting like competitors does many things, all bad. Worst of all, it weakens your competitiveness by telling the market to view you and your competitors as equals. And I know you know the word for that: commoditization.

One reason Harley-Davidson does so well today is that it now looks and acts completely different—intentionally, to reflect the company's strategic positioning—than its competitors, who've long since continued to push look-alike product and price. This puts a lot of unnecessary margin and inventory pressure on those non-Harley dealers, many of whom have shuttered their doors in the wake of the inevitable market downturns wrought by the 2007 economic implosion. Even in today's fiercely competitive market, most motorcycle companies continue to render themselves indistinguishable, much to the advantage and delight of Harley dealers the world over.

So let's now dig into how and why commoditization and poor positioning have become so widespread, so we know what we need to fix.

How does it happen? There might be better words than mine, and more scientific explanations, for what makes businesses that compete against each other start to look, sound, and act like each other. I choose to simply call it the result of "marching in lockstep."

I'll illustrate: Let's say I gave a musician a band uniform and a trombone and shoved him into an established marching band, amid the other tromboners. What would he do? He'd look at the people around him and, without thinking, start mirroring them and moving precisely like they do. He'd play the same song they're playing—or at least fake it until he learned it—and stop, start, speed up, slow down, and cut left or right when they did. In no time at all, he'd blend right in and be hard to spot from a distance. It's perfectly natural. You can almost hear him thinking to himself, "This is how everyone else is doing it and now I'm doing it, too. This is how it's supposed to look."

Well, guess what? Businesses are like that tromboner and markets are like that band.

Look at any industry, even if it serves a highly specialized niche. *Any industry*. Here's what you'll see: As industries mature, every player within it, without realizing it, starts marching the same way its competitors are marching. When one player cuts left, the others all follow. Ditto when one lowers prices. Ditto when one player talks of its quality, value, commitment to customer satisfaction, and other such nonhelpful stuff. It doesn't take long before every player's products and/or services, if they weren't already similar, begin to look and perform identically and just like the current hot performer's. When one player gives prospects indecipherable product specs, others start doing it, too. See? Everyone's marching in lockstep, playing the same song and blending right in with the band.

Your business, right now, is marching in lockstep with your competitors. Otherwise you wouldn't be reading this.

I'm sure you get the gist of how this unfortunate phenomenon happens and the problems it causes. Now we can look at why it happens, being cognizant that this is something your business can control. So why does it happen?

First, there's comfort and less risk in walking the path that's already established. The language, visuals, and nuances are already there, as are marketplace expectations. So "it's always been done this way." It's why every retail or customer service person on the planet is trained to greet prospective customers with "Can I help you?" when there are dozens of better conversation starters. It's why every company's sales pitch—"Our quality and commitment to customer satisfaction are second to none"—comes off sounding like everyone else's. It's why every business proposal looks and reads like the others stacked on the potential client's desk and why the go-to-market stuff and bank websites we saw earlier are interchangeable. Nobody, obviously, is brave enough to be different. Or has even seriously entertained the idea.

The second cause is simple acquiescence. Unless we're trained and encouraged otherwise, we look, talk, and act—or, as you just watched, play and march—like our competitors without even thinking about it. It's as natural as breathing, yet most of us aren't aware it's happening.

"This is what people expect us to do," and its ugly cousin, "This is how it's always been done," have probably killed more businesses (and careers) than obsolescence, online discounters, and the Walmarts of the world combined.

But here's what you need to know: Comfort and acquiescence are cultural issues within a business. Meaning they reflect the attitudes of the business's leadership. They also tend to be deep-seated, since everyone who works for a living models the behavior of his or her "superiors." Leaders who inadvertently exhibit and tolerate behaviors that result in commoditization shouldn't be surprised when sales and margins wither. They're the only ones who can rally their troops to bust out of the marching band's formation. (I'll soon be sharing specifics on how to do this.)

This is why I say that commoditization can't be cured through marketing or rebranding alone. Or, more accurately, marketing or rebranding as most people know them. The tail can't wag the dog. Making noise to dominate competitors needs to be a priority powered by the full attention and enthusiastic involvement of company leadership. If it's not a key part of a business's strategic plans and day-to-day operations, it simply won't happen.

And you'd better believe it can be done, even in the oldest of old-line, predictable industries. Like, say, our old friends, banks. Just look up Umpqua Bank out in Northern California and the Pacific Northwest. It takes only a quick glance for you to get the feeling that they've decided to change the banking game. They have splendidly, and they're being widely applauded and rewarded for it. At nearly every bank meeting I attend—I've become quite popular with banks since the economic meltdown—I mention Umpqua and the gathered bankers nod in unison like "Boy. Ain't they something?"

Umpqua doesn't look, act, or feel like a run-of-the-mill bank. By design.

They call themselves a "lifestyle" bank. You read that correctly. And they live that positioning with a neighborly, customer-experience-focused feel you notice the first time you enter their turf. Unless your current bank happens to offer you coffee and chocolates and entertain you with local music when you're on-site, you're going to notice immediately that they're playing the game at a different level. The photos, newspaper clippings, and thank-you letters you'll see displayed speak highly of their well-promoted community volunteerism (as compared to every bank on the planet that claims to be "involved in the community" but you know nothing about it).

Here's something else they (note the pronoun) do that pleases me to no end: Umpqua employees are well trained to handle everything a client might need—versus traditional tellers who send clients needing anything beyond basic transactions to different staffers, causing delays and stranger danger. *"Please take a seat and someone will be with you shortly."* Employees with more responsibility and deeper personal relationships with clients tend to stay much longer in a field where high turnover has long been an issue. And don't we all appreciate doing business with people we've personally come to know? And who've made an effort to know us?

My small-town bank of nearly thirty years—a branch of a major player—still calls me "Next!" and treats me like they're meeting me for the first time every time I'm on their turf and slide my paperwork across the counter. "How can I help you today, Kenneth?" *Kenneth?!* I know you know what I'm talking about.

Huge bonus points: Umpqua's locations aren't called "branches," like they are at every other bank on the planet. They're "stores." (You'll see a little later how much I love it when businesses move away from expected vocabulary and replace it with stuff that's instantly seen as different and just as instantly memorized. And I'll show you how to do that yourself.) They're blazing a new trail and everything about them looks, sounds, and feels different. Because it is. And it's precisely what Umpqua leadership exhibits and demands.

I have no doubt that if I lived in an Umpqua-served market I'd choose them. *I live thousands of miles from them, yet I still know about them* based on a newspaper article I read and the buzz I hear at meetings. They aren't marching in lockstep with the rest of the band, they're in their own stadium, wearing cooler uniforms, and playing a more likable tune. And that kind of behavior tends to get noticed, please people, and pay great dividends.

Umpqua's proven it can be done. Other banks could certainly choose to carve out their own distinctive niches, too, and get a big leg up on their competitors. So who's stopping them?

If you were starting your own business right now, would you choose to look, sound, and feel like your competitors? Of course not. You'd want to be like Umpqua. Actually, you'd want to out-Umpqua Umpqua (say that five times fast). And I'm guessing the people at Umpqua would be the first to shout, "Amen, friend!" to that. And "How 'bout a chocolate?"

SEVEN

It's About to Get Loud; Your Journey to Domination Starts Here

This is one of those fork-in-the-road, which-way-should-I-go stories that I love to tell. It's only five paragraphs long, but it's meaty. Here's betting the moral won't be lost on you.

Warning: gratuitous celebrity name-dropping to follow.

Talk about being in the right place at the right time. After getting the first-class treatment at *The Tonight Show,* which was a gift I was fortunate enough to receive several times from the world's most beloved gearhead, Jay Leno, I was walking out the back door of the studio with the evening's special guest, country music legend Garth Brooks. Suffice to say his performance killed and the studio audience was thrilled to be in the presence of one of the brightest, fan-friendly, A-list stars in the universe. In addition to being a monster talent, he struck me as a supercool dude, the real deal.

We'd barely poked our head out the door before a mob of adoring fans, women mostly, many holding signs promoting their love, erupted in rapturous screams (this happens everywhere I go and it's annoying). Were it not for the chain-link fence and barbed wire, there would've been a stampede. Seriously, I'd never before seen nor heard anything like this in the flesh. And I still have no idea how they got back there.

I teased Garth about the walk he was about to make toward his tour bus, which was only about ten steps away. He made a little joke and said he could go one of two ways, toward the bus or toward the fence, but to him, there was only one option. Would his fans love him any less if he just went to his bus? I knew better and said, "I think it's about to get louder." He smiled and shook my hand, then turned toward his fans, tilted up the front of his cowboy hat, grinned like the happiest man in the world should, and made an exaggerated, slow-motion gesture that said, "Look out, 'cause here I come." And just like that the screams went Beatles-like.

At that moment, I could've approached the fence riding an orange elephant and banging a drum and I'd still be as invisible as a sand flea. So I just drank in the moment and watched as Garth answered questions from his swooning fans and signed everything shoved through or over the fence. Cameras flashed nonstop. He even climbed the fence and reached over to sign a few, uh, body parts. Respectfully, of course. It was great fun to watch.

Sure, he could've just hopped on the bus and been gone—after all, he'd completed what he came to do and, as everybody knows, big stars march past their fans all the time. But what would that do for his legend? Imagine the stories those screaming people told the next day and are probably still telling about meeting their hero and how great he made them feel. I've got to hand it to Garth: In addition to being an outstanding musician and performer, he sure knows how to make noise. From what I'd witnessed, I know there's no way his fan-friendly reputation is accidental or phony. He works at it and lives it like dominators are supposed to. Leno does, too.

Well, the good news is, what you just read is a showbiz way of saying you're going to make the right choice and take your first big step right now, so that it can get noisy for you, too. The bad news is Garth and Leno won't be involved and you'll not (likely) be hearing screams from would-be lovers or signing body parts.

You're already in pretty good shape. From what we've witnessed together so far, you've come to know what commoditization and lack of competitiveness look like and the damage this stuff causes. You've seen that businesses typically do whatever it is they do at a very high level, yet make no real effort to compete. You've seen how easy it was for your business—or for you personally—to inadvertently fall into monkey see/monkey do lockstep with your competitors and blend into the background. You've seen what makes businesses give in to low price as a default mechanism to attract customers. Best of all, you now know why all of that happens and that you want to leave all of that growth-killing stuff in your rearview mirrors.

So we're about to hit the road, bring Noise Cubed to life at your business—or in your personal life—and start your journey to dominance. Which means we've got some work to do. Prep work, to be precise.

If you must, you can think of what we're about to do as planning, but, oh man, that's a word I try to avoid. I put a lot of importance on words, as I hope you've noticed, so I try to stay away from those that carry a lot of deadweight and negative connotations. "Planning" is a prime example. I'm no more into mindless drudgery than you are.

I've learned through experience—and you probably have, too—that there are few things that will suck the life out of any business improvement initiatives faster than leaders who bow to the god of planning. You've likely spent time with such people. You know, those well-meaning leaders who make plans around planning and eventually begin the brain-numbing process of planning their plan, then actually working on their plan before re-working and refining their plan and then, finally, sharing it with others who believe the plan, years in the making, isn't going to amount to anything. Ah, yes. There are lots of fancy corporate-speak terms for this process and even more grumbled terms, nearly all of which are unfit for publication. Pick a winner.

In my early consulting days, I often found myself sucked into the vortex of way-too-intense corporate planning processes, wherein I'd be invited to join special "strategic task forces" (which is French for "run like hell," something I've long since learned to do) already deeply entrenched in cynicism and "data dumps," where everyone involved would've preferred to be somewhere else. *Anywhere else.* It paid well, but it was awful to endure. The bigger the business, the more confusing the planning objectives. The more confusing the planning objectives, the longer the process. The longer the process, the lower the task force's morale. The lower the morale, the worse the odds of the process amounting to anything. Then a new leader would take over, a new task force would start from scratch, and the whole shooting match would begin anew. If you've not endured this horribleness, believe me when I say it's standard operating procedure with most big businesses you know. You can reach your own conclusions for why this happens—"We're planning, so at least we're doing *something*"—and there are no wrong answers.

Conversely, there's no reason that the prep work we're about to do can't be as enjoyable as it is beneficial. We're not here to do the impossible, cure infectious diseases and end world hunger, we're here to chart a course to help your business grow by making it more human, likable, memorable, and story-worthy. Why should we allow that to become a mind-numbing drag?

So I'm going to expose you to a different kind of prep work than you're accustomed to and show you that you can, quite easily, forgo "this is how it's always been done" tradition, stop marching in lockstep with the rest of the band, and live without things you may think are essential. We're going to bring Noise Cubed to life for you with the same mind-set we'd use—believe it—to plan a long motorcycle journey. This journey we're about to start, you'll soon see, has next to nothing in common with traditional ways of doing things. And just as fast, you'll see why.

Time-honored ways of doing things can be beautiful. But we have to give them the old heave-ho when they keep us from focusing our attention where it needs to be—through the turns and farther down the road.

You know I like metaphors—like the one you just read—right? So again I challenge you, as you read this section, to see the direct parallels between what I'm about to share here and the specific things you'll be doing in your upcoming prep work. I'll point out any perhaps-not-so-obvious stuff, just to make sure we're all together.

And so we begin. Let's prep.

The most important consideration when prepping for a long motorcycle journey is being mindful that we're *prepping for a long motorcycle journey*. This means the only things our trip will have in common with the automotive road trips you're (un)comfortable with are internal combustion and motion. So you'll need to disregard everything you know about turn-by-turn directions and estimated times of arrival along with the punishment of freeways, overstuffed suitcases, eighteen-wheeler convoys, tollbooths, rest areas, five-dollar foot-longs, license plate bingo, and cookie-cutter hotels. That stuff, as you've probably just surmised, isn't welcome where we're going. And never will be.

Here's another one of those beautiful things about motorcycle trips that knock traditional travel on its rear and will improve your perspective: No matter what destination we choose and eventually reach, the ride there is going to be more fun, memorable, and educational than whatever's actually *there*, because we're going to make a point to ensure that. Ditto the ride back. You've never said that about a car trip. Say what you will about an overused office bulletin-board expression like "It's not the destination, it's the journey," but it couldn't be more appropriate here. And where you work.

Regardless of your desired destination—dominating competitors, building loyal followers, getting promoted—ride prep starts with map reading, and to me there are two ways to do this: The first, most logical and hands-down *worst* way is to strap on your internal Lean Six Sigma black belt and connect your journey's starting and ending points by focusing on your map's thickest, boldest lines in the time-honored, traditional, get-it-done, "planning" way. Sure those pool-table-smooth toll roads and interstates that we riders disdainfully call "superslabs" are efficient, easy to navigate, well lit, and offer the fastest, easiest passage between two points. But at what cost?

Superslabs, as you well know, are boring and unfulfilling as hell because, apparently, somebody somewhere back in time determined they have to be. Who needs scenery? Adding further insult to the visual injuries, those same somebodies pockmarked these slabs with rest stops serving up the world's worst chow. Seriously. You've never walked out of a rest stop patting your tummy and saying, "Damn! That was good!" Why?

Just think about your last rest stop meal: You knew before you ate that your food would be miles below average, yet you bought it anyway. Sure, you could have bailed out on an exit ramp somewhere, driven a few more miles into the closest town, and enjoyed a decent, memorable meal served by wonderful people—perhaps a family whose entire net worth is wrapped up in their business—who strived to earn your repeat business and seemed genuinely grateful to serve and delight you. But, God forbid, that would have added more time to the trip. And your time, apparently, is so valuable that on many road trips in your life you knowingly tortured yourself with bad food in bland, uncomfortable environments staffed by people who couldn't possibly care less if you ever come back again. Each time you drove away unhappy, even though what you experienced was *precisely what you'd expected and paid for.* How is that a good trade-off? Why be a slave to this grind? Don't you deserve better?

All of which is to say we'll be choosing our own path, sparing ourselves such unpleasantness and enjoying a much more civilized approach.

Here's how serious riders such as yours truly do it (all of which, remember, you'll see in another form when you begin your prep work): When scouring maps and prepping for a ride—especially a long one—we're not being scientific and exact; we're searching the fine-print areas between our Points A and B to find seldom-traveled areas we *suspect* will have roads too small to include on maps. These overlooked back roads are precisely what we want because we know they'll challenge our riding skills, supercharge our senses, and allow us to uncover hidden treasures. It's bonuses—value-adds, if you love business-speak—like these that, separately and combined, will provide us with sublime postride storytelling material and eventually land us where we're supposed to land. Emphasis on *eventually*. Nobody's timing us, so there are no deadlines to cause pressure. No matter what roads we ride, we know we may never ride them again, so we're going to take our time, savor the experience, and share the highlights.

Those green parts on maps indicate mountainous and undeveloped areas the superslabs were built to avoid. And they're precisely where we're going, using as many back roads as possible to get there. The first time you feel the temperature rise and plummet as your bike climbs and dips on a beautiful mountain road, or get a heady whiff of sea air or summer corn, you'll know why. No drug can possibly make you feel this great or be this instantly addicting. And it sure beats the grind of sucking diesel fumes, staring into "How Am I Driving?" stickers on the tractor-trailers off your front bumper, and having to admit to yourself that you're a follower.

Mountain and country roads tend to meander, just as the timbermen, farmers, and cattle that carved them around and through obstacles in the landscape did centuries ago. Cattle always find water, which is why downhill roads so often lead right to it, then—and this is the great part—follow it. When roads follow water, every bend in the stream, creek, or river means a corresponding bend in the road. Lots and lots and lots of them. Minor roads following water are almost always relaxing and challenging at the same time, the paradox we all love, and surrounded by beautiful scenery. Eventually (that word again) they'll lead to small villages with interesting places to talk with some of the most colorful people you'll ever meet and enjoy great, memorable meals that make the fast food served at those interstate rest stops look like prison slop.

It's these unexpected, intimately personal experiences, you'll see, that you'll never tire of. And that you'll intentionally seek out. Isn't that what we all want from life?

Studying maps in the days before a long ride never fails to recapture the same feeling of exquisite "it's about to get fun" anticipation I loved as a kid during the last week of school before summer vacation. Plus there's a discovery/reward element to it that always ramps up my excitement level. Here's how it plays out: A quick Internet search on rider websites of any geographic area that looks appealing on a map will almost always uncover posts from motorcyclists singing the praises of their treasured finds—the area's greatest roads, food joints, and "must-sees." Along with any "what to avoids." You'll be surprised how much amazing stuff is out there, even close to where you live, that you never knew existed. When sentences describing those treasured finds end with multiple exclamation points and four-star reviews, you know you're on to something too good to resist. These voices of experience tell no lies.

Using my map studies along with input from friends and those digital posts, I'll jot down a bunch of potential routes and stuff them into my bike atlas, knowing full well I can't possibly use all of them. The possibility always exists that I'll follow an unmarked road on my loosely "planned" route just to see where it leads, and end up someplace completely different and even better than expected (plug in your own metaphor for a good life here, if needed). This happens all the time. And it's what makes motorcyclists motorcyclists and motorcycle rides great. It really is the journey, amigo.

Let me tell you about how a recent jaunt, an easy one I've done more than a few times between the two cities where I live my life, Washington, DC, and my favorite city (in southeast Wisconsin), Milwaukee, played out. Any Internet map site will tell you these start and end points are about eight hundred miles apart, an easy, yawn-inducing, twelve-hour tollway jaunt when traveling its "recommended" route. Look, I love Ohio and Indiana, I truly do, but if you've ever slogged them border-to-border on Interstate 80, you know why I'd never waste perfectly good gas doing it on a motorcycle. Talk about boring.

By the time I reach Milwaukee—in two and a half eventful days—my trip odometer will have clicked at least 1,100 times, I'll have seen and enjoyed those aforementioned states and I'll have much to talk about and recommend. *That's how it's done!*

As you know, I always set out on long trips early in the morning (who can sleep before something like this anyway?) and ride days always find me up well before sunrise, loading my bike, checking her oil and tires, and sipping coffee. There isn't a rider alive who doesn't love this ritual and doesn't get excited just thinking about it. Jamming overstuffed suitcases into your car's trunk never seems to spark joy, does it? The first time you watch the sun rise while rolling across the Mackinac Bridge that takes you sky-high over Lake Superior from northern Michigan into Wisconsin will be the last time you complain about that early wake-up call. Early launches also come with the bonus of providing maximized riding in the light of day.

For this journey, I've selected a Harley-Davidson Street Glide from among my bikes, because it's my hands-down favorite for going long distances. It's a touring bike, meaning each feature from the stop light to the front-fender tip and everything in between is built for comfortable, long-haul riding. Touring bikes sharply contrast cruisers and sport bikes that, with their slimmer profiles and basic necessities, are better suited for short distances and/or aggressive, high-speed riding like you witnessed on my Swiss boondoggle.

It's got Tour-Paks, those fiberglass "saddlebags" (boxes, actually) that carry clothes and gear on each side of the rear wheel and another I've mounted over the rear fender that also doubles as a passenger backrest. When you hear someone refer to a bike as a "bagger" or a "dresser," this is the kind of bike they're talking about—a fully loaded, do-it-all-comfortably, long-distance warrior. The Street Glide is more nimble than Harley's fully-accessorized Ultra touring models and some of those massive Honda Gold Wings you've seen, but with many of the same features and, to my eyes, it's got way better lines. Style points are awarded in this game and the best way to get them is to be visually, pleasingly different than everyone else. Bottom line: I want people to see me and have immediate, positive reactions to my differences.

(You're thinking like a dominator now so you know precisely *why I just said that, right?)*

Up front there's a handsome console, called a fairing, that incorporates a windshield, headlight, and turn signals, instrument panel, and a stereo system with speakers powerful enough to cut through the wind at high speeds. There are wide footrests for long-haul comfort and a mount on my handlebars for securing my cell phone so I can stream music to the stereo or use its GPS, if necessary. I'll admit that there's also a cheap and painfully ugly cup holder mounted to my handlebars for hauling my equally ugly coffee mug. There's something decadent about sipping coffee while riding, especially on cool mornings, that more than makes up for the constant teasing I get about the ugly thing. And it's fun to see people curiously watching me going Juan Valdez in the last place they'd expect to see that happening. It's started many a conversation with strangers and I always love it when that happens.

My Street Glide is almost completely black and is heavily customized, but not in the ways you might think. Unlike a lot of riders, especially in the Harley family, I'm not into boatloads of shiny chrome, flashy painted parts, or bling. Dark black, where it's not expected, makes a very loud statement—Johnny Cash told you that and when was he ever wrong?—and suits my personality. It's the blackest bike you'll ever see. I've even removed the beautiful Harley-Davidson badge from the gas tank, which to some might seem sacrilege, but it starts a lot of conversations and I've yet to have someone look at my bike and ask who made it. You'd have to be blind to not know that. And deaf: Its engine also carries extensive custom work including larger pistons, race-tuned fuel injection, and high-flow exhaust pipes that, in addition to helping make my bike wicked fast, also produce a spectacular rumble that hits the ears right in the sweet spot (as compared to bikes that are irritatingly loud just to be irritatingly loud, or so wimpy they sound like sewing machines).

Let's talk packing. For a first-time long-distance rider, packing a week's—or even a weekend's—worth of clothing and gear onto a motorcycle is a daunting challenge. What would you bring? Just as important, what would you not have room for and need to leave behind? You can't hit the road on long trips without clothing to suit any weather extreme. Riding in snow, ninety-degree heat, and rain on the same day isn't unheard-of in some mountainous areas and being caught unprepared once is all it takes to ensure that it never happens again.

At the same time, overpacking's not an issue because every inch of storage space on a bike—and there isn't a lot of it—counts, so you've got to pack smart. Packing for two requires being doubly smart. Now imagine packing for several days when you'll be camping each night instead of staying in hotels. That means you'll need to find room for a tent and sleeping bags at the expense of your "essentials." Plus a coffeepot. But man, it's so much fun.

Hotel or campsite, your blow-dryer won't be making the trip. "But it's travel size!" just doesn't apply here. Ditto dressy shoes, magnum bottles of booze, bedtime books, pajamas, multiple "outfits," and any other personal grooming supplies beyond the barest of necessities. Shaving cream and razor? Hell no. Makeup? I've learned it's a no-win situation to make recommendations on that one.

It's not against the law to wear the same clothes, socks included, on consecutive days. Which is good because you'll be doing it all the time. And guess what? Nobody will notice, which means nobody cares. Hotel sinks clean undies just fine. If you must.

Here's an easy way I discovered to save space. Because I'm a sucker for buying Harley T-shirts on bike trips, a widely contagious disease among riders, I know I'll be able to wear a few of them on the return trip, so I only pack enough shirts to get me one-way. If you're like me, you have a drawer stuffed with old shirts that need to find new homes. On the front leg of the trip, I'll wear one oldie per day, then leave it in the hotel room or at the campsite when I check out. Great, no? I like to think that somewhere out there, a campground employee is wearing my 1999 Daytona Bike Week shirt. Or washing a car with it. Either way, it's being reused and I'm pleased.

Everything packed on a bike adds weight, of course, and managing that weight is vital to a bike's balance and your safety. So heavy stuff like emergency tools go low in the saddlebags. Lighter gear, like clean clothes and toilet kits, go on top, equally balanced on both sides. In the bike's rear Tour-Pak (or, if I'm rolling without one, a bungeed-down duffel bag) goes stuff I'm likely to need easy access to along the way—like a water bottle, sweatshirt, ball cap (the perfect antidote for helmet hair when off the bike), raingear, chaps, clear-framed goggles for eye protection when the sun's gone, road atlas, sunscreen, and a small towel for wiping rain or dew off the saddle, or to use as a neck-warmer if needed. Atop the Tour-Pak's contents sits the most important cargo, at least two jumbo boxes of Mike and Ike candy. Original green. I'll not ride without them (and you'll want to bum some from me later). The contents of an entire third box will be poured into the left pocket of my riding jacket, which I'll constantly raid throughout the day. Everyone's got a habit; that's mine. For all the Mike and Ike I've consumed and persuaded others to buy on rides, there should be a statue of me in front of their maker's headquarters.

Okay, so the bike's been looked over and packed, her contents have been double-checked and rebalanced, all latches are locked down, the coffee mug's been topped off, and Mike and Ike are at the ready. So it's time to roll. Woo-hoo! With safe-riding promises and goodbye hugs completed, I'll fire up the Street Glide and let the engine lope and warm up for a few minutes while I strap my boots, zip my jacket, adjust my goggles, and buckle my helmet. Just prior to pulling out of the garage, I'll reach down and do something very important: I'll flick the tiny "gremlin bell" hanging near my right footrest. Motorcyclists have long attached silver bells to their bikes, which, lore has it, keep us safe and ward off evil spirits rising up from the road. I'm not superstitious, but I'm not stupid, either. *Tink-tink* goes the bell and I'm off, imagining, as I always do, that my still-in-bed neighbors are hearing me leave, wondering where I'm heading, and wishing they were right behind me.

So I'm blasting away from the world I know best, free as a hippie and eager to uncover some of the road's secrets. My radio's on and, just before I hit the button to switch to my iPod and crank up some appropriate riding music, I hear the on-air person talking about, believe it or not, your business. What the? Amazing coincidence, wouldn't you say? I'm not even out of my subdivision yet.

Okay. That's an obvious lie. But that voice on the radio talking about you is my prompt to pull over, put the kickstand down for a while, and get you started on bringing life to Noise Cubed. To officially begin the journey in front of you, you're about to do my world-famous "Make Some Noise Radio Challenge" and start the process of determining the words that will fuel your journey and ultimately—if you play your cards right—become the basis of your marketplace narrative, the second tier of Noise Cubed: What do you want people to say about you?

So there's going to be work involved and you're the one who's going to do it. Actual. Work. And please, like checking your bike's air and oil before long trips, you absolutely *have* to take part in this. You have to own this. I once tried to learn how to play guitar by reading a book about it on a plane. Impossible! As with that, what we're about to learn here isn't done by reading, it's done by doing.

Here's how my "Make Some Noise Radio Challenge" works. I want you to imagine that I've given you an extraordinary, use-it-or-lose-it gift wherein I've arranged for you to have fifteen seconds of free airtime on the radio tonight to tell the world about your business and win them over. That might not sound so extraordinary, but this will: I've further arranged—believe it— for *every* human being that you've ever wanted to reach with your business to be listening. Yep. This means that 100 percent of your current and potential customers, even if you're a global enterprise, and every other person important to your business, such as partners, suppliers, potential employees, the investment community, legislators, and media, will be tuning in tonight with no other purpose than to hear what you have to say and decide whether they should be aligning themselves with you. How cool is that?

Like when the Beatles instantly gained millions of die-hard fans with their first American television appearance on *The Ed Sullivan Show,* this is your big chance to not only move the needle, but to bounce it against the limiter. With only fifteen seconds to tell your story and win your audience over, though, you know you'll have to choose your words wisely. And those words will need to address these four vital topics:

- Who you are,
- What you do,
- Who you do it for, and
- Why you should be preferred over any other option.

Presented in that order, these four topics create a natural flow, but there's no law that says your script needs to be bound by this structure. Besides, your days of staying between the lines and following others are over, so you can use any order you want, as long as each topic gets addressed. You can even throw in some music or sound if you want.

This is radio, so of course you'll have no visuals of any kind to support you. You'll have to rely on nothing but a voice—yours, a fellow employee's, or even a noncelebrity professional voice talent's—and your short script to connect with your listeners and convince them that they should be doing business with you and prefer you over your competitors.

Given this incredible one-shot opportunity to speak directly to the most important people in your business life and win them over, what are you going to say? Think of the journey prep process I just detailed. Are you going to stick to your map and jump on the freeway to get from Point A to B or are you going to explore more story-worthy, less traveled paths? We'll see soon enough.

If this opportunity was real, instead of make-believe, you and a team of your brightest cohorts would spend the rest of the day holed up in a quiet room, prepping intensely to create the best possible script. At least I sure as hell hope you would. It's not real, of course, and you have nobody to help you. You're riding solo today. To add more pressure, I'm giving you only five minutes max to think about this and write a script that addresses those four topics. A mere five minutes is all you're being given to shake up your world (so don't waste time thinking about music or sounds unless it's super-important to your business) and start making some serious noise.

Do I even need to remind you that you want people to *remember and repeat* what you'll be saying about your business or yourself? Please say no and that you take that as a given—meaning you're already thinking like a dominator. *Remember and repeat. Remember and repeat. R&R. Tattoo it below "Brains. Cause. Pain." on your forehead.*

I'm a tough taskmaster, but I'm also nice guy with a conveniently horrible sense of timing. I really want you to take that fifteen-second window seriously, but if your script goes a little longer—just a wee little bit—I'll look the other way because the words are what's most important here. You know you'll have to choose them wisely. And if you go a little over on the five-minute limit to write it, well, who's to know? But please try to keep it to five because I want you to think fast.

Hardball time: Look, I'm not standing in front of you right now, nor sitting next to you, nor peering over your shoulder, so there's no way for me to force you to create a script. And even though I'd love to, I can't send any of my thick-necked biker friends over to rough you up if you opt out of this. But let me please advise you that jumping ahead here without prepping a script will not only ruin the effectiveness of this exercise; you'll also miss out on the first step in learning how to effectively position your business. You might as well close the book now and give up. *You. Have. To. Do. This.* (Picture me trying to play guitar after reading some how-tos and how horrible it sounded.)

If you don't have something handy to write on, peck your script out on your phone, e-reader, or tablet. If you're on a plane, grab a barf bag. If it helps, let the *Jeopardy!* theme song bounce around in your head a few times while you concentrate. That never fails to get people focused.

Remember your make-believe experience at the trade show booth at the beginning of the book when you wished you'd had something memorable to say to a superimportant person? This is your chance to ensure that never happens again, reach all the superimportant people in your life, and bring what you've learned so far to light. And once again, your script has to address who you are, what you do, who you do it for, and why people should prefer you over any other option.

Set your watch. Ready? Go! I mean it! Start writing! We'll get back together in five. (Cue the *Jeopardy!* song.)

- - - - - - - - - - - - - - - - -

And . . . we're back. Well, I certainly hope you have something or, at bare minimum, a rough skeleton of something. Either way, thanks for playing along and congrats on taking your first big step toward dominance. Even though you know your business, or yourself, inside out and backward, it wasn't easy to describe so briefly, distinctly, and memorably, with such little prep time, was it?

More hardball: Let me tell you something before we go any further and without the benefit of having read your script. If what you wrote amounts to some semblance of an elevator speech, well, I have to say thanks for the effort, but I'm sorry that it's just not going to work for you. I've yet to hear one of those that in any way positioned a business or person competitively. The elevator speech idea, full credit to whoever came up with it, was a good one. Unfortunately, it's become oversimplified to the point that people believe if they can describe themselves or their business in just fifteen seconds—like an audible business card—they've accomplished something. That's not what I'm after here. Remember, we're here to make noise and position you to dominate. So I'm looking for words from you that get my attention, are distinct to you, and are memorable and repeatable, thus clearly separating you in a positive way from your competitors.

Does your first attempt pass that basic test? Are you feeling good about what you've written and ready to take advantage of this once-in-a-lifetime deal? Better, are you willing to risk your shot at glory by sharing it with the world?

Let's look at a random sample of a Radio Challenge script from a construction industry training session I led, which we can use for learning purposes (I've changed the business name, of course).

"We're Apex Home Builders, an award-winning construction company focused on the highest levels of quality and craftsmanship. We've been the number one dream home solutions providers for Our Town area families since 1975. Our commitment to customer satisfaction and passion for doing things right every time make us the best choice in the area."

What do you think? Did this guy nail it?

How does Apex's script compare to yours?

Let's see how you both did. Other than a bland elevator speech, the first thing that will derail your effort to make it to the big leagues is a script using any descriptive words—*any descriptive words*—that a competitor is using. If someone else is saying them, they certainly aren't distinct to you, are they? Remember to always think of it this way: Why would you, in an attempt to position yourself or your business as meaningfully different than your competitors, use any of the same words your competitors use to describe themselves? As you know, that's what got a lot of also-rans into trouble in the first place.

I have to lay down some serious law now and you'll see why. Your competitors are already using typical business descriptors like "quality," "award-winning," "number one," "solutions," some semblance of "customer satisfaction/customer driven," and others common to your specific industry, right? Well, if any of them are, from now on, you're not. You're officially done with those words—yes, for the millionth time, "quality" included. I hope alarms went off in your head when you saw that in Apex's script. If just one of your competitors is saying they've been "serving the community for X years," or (heaven forbid), "our people make the difference," you're no longer saying it. You can't. As tempting as it may be.

If someone else is saying it, you're not. Even if you said it first.

Quality, we all know, is superimportant, but remember what you've learned: You don't own it and it's a given, thus it's neither differentiating nor worth repeating. Kiss it goodbye. The same goes for the customer stuff. Oh, how business leaders all over the globe have tried to fight me on this! That is, until the errors of their well-intentioned ways became evident. And they always do.

Also remember: Saying what competitors say endorses them at your expense. It also sends a message to your important publics that says you don't see any difference between you and your competitors, so there's no reason anyone should prefer you. Pretty obvious, right? Yet it's such an easy trap to fall into, we've all done it.

Nobody, by the way, hates "solutions" and "solutions provider" claims more than I do. Did anyone using those horribly overused words to describe themselves or their business ever think about what they mean? Well, I did, and here's what I came up with: Every business ever invented in the history of the world provides a "solution" to something, otherwise it would have no reason to exist. Think about it. If you're hungry, KFC, Chef Boyardee, the makers of Pringles, and the world's finest restaurants are all solutions providers, aren't they? Car running low on oil? You know who has a solution.

See, those useless words aren't differentiating descriptors, they're demand killers. Remember earlier when you were in the supermarket and the guy from the dairy popped out and said all that worthless stuff? This is what everyone sounds like when they use those kinds of overused words, yet I hear them at most, if not all, meetings I attend, when folks describe their businesses or read their radio challenge scripts. Well here's the deal: Dominators don't use them. Which means from now on, you won't either. Monkey see, monkey don't.

Look at the construction company sample script again. It's a heckuva first effort, but the problems are now easy to spot, aren't they? Yet you wouldn't have been surprised to hear something like this on the radio or in a meeting somewhere, would you? You may even have thought, like most people do, that it "sounded" pretty good when you read it the first time.

You read that script only a minute or so ago. So ask yourself: How did it separate that business from its competitors? What's memorable and repeatable? What's distinct to them? Do you remember anything appealing about it? Or anything at all?

The reason I created this exercise—and why I only allow five minutes for your first draft—is so you can see what's on top of your mind. Not giving you lots of time to think means you likely used in your script the language you're comfortable using every day. The language you hear others using. The language you think others expect to hear from you.

It takes a lot of mental adjustment to accept the notion that the last thing any of us want to do is just jump on the freeway on a bike weighed down by a bunch of unnecessary stuff, ride the same route as competitors, and follow them. And to think about the importance of words and why choosing them carefully is so vital to your competitive positioning. These words are what you want people to remember about you and use when they describe you to others. R&R, baby. And, like with the Radio Challenge or that earlier trade show debacle, you often have just one chance to make that happen.

From this day forward, you're promoting you, which means you're no longer endorsing the folks you're battling against. You'll never again weaken your competitiveness and tell the market that you're a commodity by repeating what others are saying. To help ensure that, just remember this simple rule: If someone else is saying it, you're not. If a competitor can claim it, you can't. Fonzie was the coolest so Richie Cunningham couldn't be, remember? You're working to position yourself as a dominator, not an also-ran or copycat.

I've seen plenty of people looking dejected after discovering the Radio Challenge script they wrote and believed to be "not bad" might, if aired, actually hurt their business. I've seen those looks that say, "I guess I'm just not good at this." And "Please don't call on me." If that's you, fear not. Nobody nails this challenge on the first attempt. Who could in only five minutes? It doesn't matter if I'm working with executive leadership from massive conglomerates or owners of mom-and-pops, I have yet to do this exercise with any group where first-draft scripts—often from businesses competing against each other—weren't nearly interchangeable. And bland. You should take some comfort knowing that CEOs of household-name companies had the same "Oops!" moments with the challenge as small market pest exterminators.

As you'd (now) expect, I see lots of superpredictable stuff in first drafts, like all those overused words you'll no longer be using. That's okay. This is how learning happens and the lesson it teaches us is "If you're focusing more on getting the job done and sounding professional than making yourself different, you're simply marching in lockstep with the other guys and making the same noise they are." It ties back to when we were planning our long motorcycle journey and found that just looking at the map and coming up with the quickest, safest, surest, already-traveled route from Point A to Point B—the easy way out—isn't going to work for us. The scenery always sucks when you follow the brain-dead freeway drones.

Here's a scary thought. Can you imagine how the scripts would read if I asked every employee of your business to write one? The only place we'd see commonality would likely be the obvious "who we are" stuff. But on the "what we do, who we do it for, and why you should prefer us" parts, scripts would be all over the map. What do you think it says about a business when its leaders, to say nothing of its entire employee population, aren't describing their business the same way? The absolute least it should tell you is that a lot of great opportunities are being lost. How can we ever get our important publics to describe us the way we want to be described when we can't even do it ourselves? We'll fix that.

Later I'll ask you to take another pass at your fifteen-second script, only this time I'll be enforcing my "If someone else is saying it, you're not" rule. Trust me, when all the usual words have been taken, this short little script gets a lot harder—but more fun—to write. This tells you why positioning is so important and needs to be a leadership-driven business priority. And probably makes you wonder why most businesses completely overlook the simple yet undeniably vital task of defining themselves dominantly and staking their claim.

One of the best habits you can develop is to keep banging out scripts until you fall in love with one. Nobody nails the landing perfectly on the first or second (or fifth or tenth) attempt. It's a great group project—to say nothing of eye-opener—especially at smaller businesses. Anything that fosters creativity and gets people thinking boldly about competing is a good thing. You'll eventually find yourself writing scripts to position the products and services you sell, too. And even for internal workplace initiatives. No matter what it is, if it needs to be remembered and repeated, think of the Radio Challenge.

Before you start your next drafts, here's something familiar to you that might help you wrap your mind more snugly around this notion of getting off the freeway and not following the drones. You'll see both the cause and effect of not saying what's expected and what others are saying. The effect is the sexiest part. The simplicity underlying this, I'm positive, will stay with you.

Check this out: During a large business meeting at a cushy golf resort in Miami in 2015, I had the fun challenge of taking the stage after a billionaire you may have heard of spoke. Some guy named Donald Trump. His role there was to discuss his philosophy for developing and promoting resort properties and golf courses—both of which were mainstays of the audience's businesses. After speaking at length and in precise detail about those themes, he unexpectedly siderailed into a fifteen-minute political rant in which he pulled no punches (this was in the early days of the 2016 US presidential campaign, long before he became a front-runner) and made all of us in the audience lean forward in our chairs. About his political comments—and with no personal agenda whatsoever—I'll simply say he was "Trump-like."

When I took the stage after a break, I asked the group, "How many of you called your office or back home during the break and said you just watched Donald Trump speak?" No surprise, every hand went up. I then asked, "How many of you told the person you spoke to what Trump said about his business philosophy and practices?" Not a single hand was raised. Already knowing what was about to happen, I then asked, "How many of you quoted him *verbatim* on some of his way-out-of-left-field political commentary?" Every hand shot up amid laughter.

Now think of the televised 2016 US presidential debates (I know, I know, bear with me) for just a moment. Recall that every candidate, except one, answered each question in words you could have written yourself with minimal effort. Every candidate, except one, "marched in lockstep," said things you've heard said by people in their position a million times before—jobs, economy, education, defense—while repeating standard party lines. Tellingly, none of them gained any meaningful leverage.

That one candidate, you know who, never answered questions predictably, did he? In fact he never said much of anything you'd expect a candidate to say, in any forum. And in the days and weeks after each debate, who owned the lion's share of the media and office water cooler commentary?

Who was everyone quoting damn near 24/7? Who won? That guy. I'm wise enough to not offer my opinion of him as a president here, nor endorse or decry a single unexpected thing he's said or done, but as a candidate, I'd say he surely knew how to compete and steer narrative at a dominant level, wouldn't you?

Remember what I said back when I laid out my Schmidt-isms: When you say what others have already said, or what people expect to hear, nobody remembers or repeats what you've told them and you get lost among me-too competitors. *But when you intentionally say things that aren't expected, you get noticed and those things tend to get repeated.* Do you doubt it?

In that same vein, people almost always ask me why I never, in public, refer to Harley owners as "customers" and instead call them "disciples." I tell them, "Three reasons: One, I guarantee you'll remember and repeat the d-word; two, because nobody else in the bike industry—or any other—uses that word; and three, because I knew you'd ask me about it." That carefully chosen word, "disciples," immediately prompted a question that needs answering, didn't it? Knowing what you now know, I bet you could answer why I do this, but there's more below the surface.

See, anytime somebody asks me the why question, and somebody always does, it gives me the opportunity to tell stories about the extreme loyalty of Harley owners and the fact that we're the company's primary sales force, because we're always advocating for the company and encouraging friends, neighbors, and coworkers to buy a Harley and ride with us. The d-word imparts a biblical tone without being biblical (that would be the uppercase D-word), yet it conveys a lot of "this is what I believe in and you should, too" imagery, doesn't it? You didn't expect to hear it, you noticed it immediately, and it made you curious enough to ask me about it, which in turn gave me the opportunity to have more time with you and tell you stories.

But it doesn't stop there, because when you repeat those stories somewhere down the road, you'll also use the d-word, you'll raise your listeners' eyebrows, and be asked why. And the cycle will begin again. And on and on it goes. That's where positive narrative comes from. I could just call Harley owners "customers," which of course we are, but who'd bat an eye? (And Garth could've just walked to his bus.)

It's surprising how many opportunities we have to manipulate language about common subjects into positive noise. We'll be working on that shortly.

Now think of your radio script again. And why I address "Who you do it for" with disciple instead of customer. And think of all those tired, poison, overused words and "corporate-speak" that seem so natural to you and your industry. Then remind yourself that you'll not be using them again. Here's a short list I compiled in about ten seconds:

- Quality
- Solutions or solutions provider
- Customer satisfaction
- Customer-focused or customer-driven
- ISO-certified (manufacturers, you know what I'm talking about)
- Award-winning
- Certified
- Scalable
- Outside the box (by the way, claiming this proves you're not)
- Licensed/bonded
- We listen
- We care
- A leader in . . .

I'm sure you can come up with more.

Corporate-speak—like the overused words on that list—will always be a demand killer because the time spent using these words is time that could have been spent connecting with people in much more meaningful ways. So here's another Schmidt-ism I hope you'll remember and adhere to when it comes to describing your business and avoiding the corporate-speak trap, no matter who you're speaking with: "If you wouldn't say it at the Thanksgiving dinner table, don't say it in any discussions with important publics."

Nana wouldn't understand drivel about how your "scalable enterprise's paradigm shift modality is gaining traction in the C-suite," any more than she'd understand being told she's a "world-class viscous avian protein accompaniment solutions provider," when all she wanted was to learn how things are at your work and to hear some compliments about her gravy. R&R, baby. R&R.

When I'm leading groups through my Radio Challenge, I'll often have them take a stab or two at writing scripts for companies we all know and recognize, to get more comfortable with the concept and have a little fun. How would you describe Burger King in ways that would separate it from its other household name, similar-product-at-similar-price competitors, in just fifteen seconds, while making it sound more attractive than those other guys? Try it yourself sometime.

Because so many people believe their business to be dull and "nonsexy,"

I'll often foster creativity by challenging them to write scripts for an extremely tough to differentiate business like gasoline. Or for any of the major cell phone telecoms. It's far from easy, but what everyone will notice is that it doesn't take long—usually just one or two yawn-inducing, predictable drafts and some good laughs—before the notion of being noticeably different, memorable, and repeatable kicks in. R&R, baby! And that's the best time to turn the focus back to their own business.

> *Quick sidebar: This is a good and, hopefully, last time to shine a spotlight on those folks who believe their business to be dull or "nonsexy." That self-denigration has to stop. Now. Look, just because the product or service you sell isn't sexy, cool, awesome, and amazing doesn't mean that the people behind it aren't, either. You have to make a choice: Do we want to be known and discussed as fascinating, different, alluring, positive, fun, engaging, passionate, desirable, awesome, brilliant people? Or do we want to be known as people who sell something boring? This isn't a hard decision, folks. We, as humans, spend way less time talking about "what we buy" than we do talking about who we do business with, right? I don't care if you sell baby-casket lining, if your customers are saying "They rock" when they discuss you at trade conventions, you're doing things right. If you're speaking blandly or, God forbid, ill of your business, your fellow employees are, too. And, naturally, that kind of talk eventually seeps into discussions with important publics.*

The secret beauty of the Radio Challenge lies in the notion that it forces participants to confront the truth that even though they know more about their business than anyone else, they don't know about, and likely have given little thought to, how it's currently positioned. It's like looking at a map and realizing that if you don't know where you are, how can you possibly get where you want to go? When a group of people from the same business participate, it doesn't take long before everyone realizes, "We need to be riding and experiencing all of this great stuff together, rather than being scattered all over the place, heading in different directions."

It's also teaches participants that *every* business, whether by design or by default, is positioned. "Positioned by design" means leadership takes competing to dominate seriously and has chosen to put it at the top of its business process. "By default" means nobody within the business is paying attention to positioning and thus the business's important publics are left to reach their own conclusions. And without knowing what we want people to remember and repeat about us—the second tier of Noise Cubed—how can we adjust our behavior to bring life to those words and make them work for us? How does an organization know what it's working toward?

I'll never again ask you to crank out another Make Some Noise Radio Challenge script in just five minutes. Your understanding now how vital it is to not describe yourself as your competitors describe themselves, for the words you choose to be meaningfully, memorably different than your competitors' and to avoid obvious poison words makes it a much more difficult and time-intensive challenge. And as you've seen, the task on your journey isn't limited only to getting off the drone-choked freeway; it's also about determining the most memorable, story-worthy paths to getting where you want to be and eliminating the baggage that won't fit. You know, the stuff you can and need to live without. Like "award-winning quality." And that blow-dryer.

To help craft and fine-tune your desired positioning and the language you'll use to describe it, I have some more exercises coming right up, which, if we were approaching this within a traditional business philosophy of "let's get from Point A to Point B as fast as we can," I would have had you complete first, prior to attempting your Challenge script. We're not rolling that way, of course, and I much prefer the path we're on because it provides the teachable moments we've had. Keep reading. You're getting the hang of this.

EIGHT

More Road Work Ahead

This isn't the smoothest journey you've ever been on, is it? One minute you're cruising along, trying to describe the one thing you know best—your business—to the world in only fifteen seconds, the next you're hitting some potholes and discovering that the road to dominance isn't exactly a cake walk. I hope you can sense, though, that there are spectacular roads ahead and that things will smooth out beautifully. What kind of road captain would I be if I didn't get you to the great stuff?

I also hope you're taking some comfort in knowing that merely thinking about your journey to competitive dominance differently than you ever have before and starting to put some work into it are very positive things. This stuff's still new enough to be foreign to you, though, which means it's going to take a while for it all to sink in. I promise it will. Most people who've taken this road trip with me were disappointed that their first exercise, the Radio Challenge, showed they weren't quite ready for a shot at the big time and that they were in need of help. Many of those same people said they wished I'd stop messing around and just give them a road map to follow, with accompanying checklists and timelines, and send them on their way. Or at least something they could punch into their GPS to make this whole thing a lot simpler.

Sorry, I don't have an app for that.

But fret not and remind yourself that the best thing about starting this journey is knowing that the people and businesses you're competing against aren't thinking about any of this stuff, because they're too focused on figuring out how to do what they do more profitably than to worry about who's going to make them miserable. That would be you.

Right now you're at the starting point in the prepping stage of your journey, so—just as I do with my road trip prep process—you're about to start studying potential routes, looking for less traveled roads to explore, and gathering intelligence from those who've gone before you so that you can create your initial path. Then you're going to eliminate excess baggage and batten down the hatches. Once that's complete, we'll talk about how you're going to share your desired route with your entire organization so they can ride in formation along with you and take on the world.

All of which is a more fun way of saying you're about to uncover the best way to position your business and ultimately bring that positioning to life for competitive advantage.

This is going to take some effort on your part in the form of honest-to-God homework. But I promise it's not difficult. Like any road captain worthy of his postride beer, I'll do my best to keep you out of harm's way and make this fun for you. I should also mention that this first chunk of ride prep isn't time intensive and, for really small businesses, can be done in less than an afternoon. But you'll want to take as much time as you need and not rush. As you'll see, you'll know when you've done enough.

I've learned through years of experience doing this that leaders of small businesses and mom-and-pops can quite handily perform this part of my prep process solo. Large businesses often ask if it's okay to enlist help from an internal A-team to spread out the workload. While I would never discourage you from involving others from your workplace, realize that it's likely to be difficult to explain anything other than the most basic elements of this process to anyone who's not been with us on our journey thus far. Doing this solo now means you'll be able to understand and explain this process in detail later, should the size and scope of your business warrant a team approach. Plus, you're going to learn some valuable lessons here by doing it yourself.

To keep the language and instructions simple here, I'll present this assignment to you as if you're doing all of the work solo.

Remember how I described the "map study" process and that the right way to do that calls for avoiding the fastest, predictable, god-awful freeway route to connect Points A and B? You're about to do something similar, only instead of looking at maps, you're going to be studying your competitors' positioning. Think of this as identifying the boring freeway routes your competitors are currently traveling, so you'll know, specifically, what to avoid on your road to domination. You're going to find less traveled, more story-worthy routes.

To do this, you're going to need a computer with Internet access. Because you'll be doing some minor reporting, you'll need some paper (full sheets) and a pencil. You can do the reporting on your computer, but I've found it's typically easier to just jot your notes down on paper and then transfer your finished work to a word-processing or spreadsheet program. Toggling back and forth gets tedious quickly (at least for baby boomers like me).

A few chapters back I suggested an exercise—you're about to wish you'd actually done—that called for gathering as much of your and your competitors' go-to-market stuff as possible, covering all logos and identifiers, and mixing it all together in a confusing pile. Remember the Smackdown?

We're going to do something similar here, minus the logo cover-ups, that in a perfect, scientifically sound world, would call for a hunter-gatherer mission to obtain every one of those go-to-market materials (ads, website screenshots, business cards, brochures, sell sheets, premiums). We can get by without that level of specificity for this process and can achieve much the same results just by having access to your competitors' websites and any social media channels they may be using. The choice is yours to go all-in or just use the digital stuff. When we're through, larger businesses with lots of available hands—or the money to pay a marketing agency to do this—can and should have a team gather the physical materials, as they'll make for great show-and-tell with your employees and other important internal publics like dealers or distributors, later.

This exercise isn't at all complicated, but having said that, I guarantee it will make more sense to you and be easier to complete if you read the instructions completely before starting, rather than jumping right into the first step. If you get confused, I've included a sample document you can eyeball after you've read through these instructions.

Let's start.

On an empty page or screen, write "Competitive Noise." Under that you're going to add five sections in a top-to-bottom column. Title these sections: Competitor, Obvious Positioning Words, Solid Differentiators, What Are People Saying, and Exploitable Weaknesses.

Next, you're going to study, one at a time, each of your major competitors' websites and social media channels (and their go-to-market tools if you have them handy), plus any websites where you can see customer reviews (if any), then do a careful analysis and fill in a one-page chart for each of them. Some who've done this with me like to start with their biggest and most irritating competitors first, then work their way down by chronological rank. Others simply chart competitors randomly. Whatever works for you. Just make sure you hit everyone you battle against regularly.

Here's a step-by-step guide to how it works and what you'll be looking for:

Go to the home page of a competitor's website. Your chart's first column, "Competitor," needs no explanation. Write their name.

Under "Obvious Positioning Words," list those terms they're using to describe and define themselves and stake their claim, such as "a leader in," "quality," "committed to" etc., along with any taglines and slogans. These are often the headlines used on the home page of the website—the stuff that tells the world "This is what we want to be known for." If there's an "About Us" area, you'll want to click on that as well, as there's usually a longer business description in there. I know you know why I'm having you do this and how to find this stuff. Note that you don't have to list the obvious business identifier, like if you're a builder and your competitor's site says "Quality Builder," just record "quality."

Also scan any social media pages they use like Facebook, LinkedIn, Twitter, Instagram, and whatever new stuff has cropped up that I don't yet know about, with the same objective.

Be sure you only record words they're using frequently and for obvious self-promotional purposes.

Under "Solid Differentiators" list anything you see, read, or already know that is distinct to this competitor and that you know is *widely* recognized as theirs, such as a trademark color palette (the way IBM is famous for its use of blue), an instantly recognized logo, slogan, or jingle, a visible founder/leader or celebrity endorser, a well-recognized mascot (Michelin Man, etc.), easily recognized service or delivery vehicles (think Geek Squad Volkswagens), distinct work uniforms, etc. When I say *"widely* associated," I mean this is stuff that most people in your market instantly associate with this competitor—and only they can claim and use. And here's a hint: For some small business competitors there may not be a lot of these, or even any, for you to record.

Next, recall in my ride-prep process how, once I spy some possibly great areas to explore, I'll check on rider websites to see what other riders have said about them and that I'll take their recommendations seriously because these comments typically yield gold. You're going to do the same thing, only instead of looking for great "must-sees" you're going to sniff around online and see what others are saying—good and bad—about your competitors and record them under "What Are People Saying?"

Wise places to look for comments are on review websites like Yelp, Google, Better Business Bureau, and Angie's List, media like local newspapers (if you're a local business), and any trade publications that serve your industry. You're looking for frequency and patterns here. Meaning you can ignore any one-off comments like "They have the fastest service in town" but you can't ignore it—and should write it down—if you see this routinely. Also be on the lookout for frequency and patterns of negative comments, versus one-off complaints (one "they stink" comment amid ninety-nine positive comments means they don't stink). Customer testimonials on competitors' websites are always suspect since companies only post their glowing reviews, but sometimes patterns can emerge within them—"great phone reps!"—that are worth recording. Your sixth sense will kick in and tell you when what you're reading is genuine.

Finally, it's time to identify and record "Exploitable Weaknesses," which most participants—myself included—enjoy the most about this process. These are your competitors' shortcomings that will become evident in your online research. You also know some of their weaknesses from battling against them (if you don't, your salespeople surely do). If they're "indistinguishable and one of many," record that. Patterns like "bad service" or "overpriced" in the prior column are good examples. Others might include problems like poor return policies, short hours, difficult warranty processes, high employee turnover, overpromising, inconvenient location, language barriers, high-pressure salespeople, long waits on hold, ugly facilities, etc.

I've yet to find a company that has no known or invisible exploitable weaknesses. You won't find any, either.

You're not recording these weaknesses to attack them overtly ("Their service sucks but ours rocks!") but they can be of great help when you're crafting your positioning.

You'll need to create a separate Competitive Noise chart for each of your major competitors and as many lesser competitors as it takes until you see a continuous pattern where everyone is completely indistinguishable and saying the same things. Like I said earlier, it typically doesn't take long for these patterns to emerge, especially among your lesser competitors. The lion's share of your time on this will be spent with your majors.

Here are actual sample charts for two home construction companies—names changed, of course—serving the same community, created as homework at the conference where the sample Radio Challenge script you read earlier was created. Notice how simple they are. Then get to work.

COMPETITIVE NOISE

Competitor:
All-American Home Builders

Obvious Positioning Words:
Committed to quality
Award-winning
Build-to-order
Your vision is our passion
Custom
Leading since 1965
LEED-certified

Solid Differentiators:
Oldest in the area
American flag billboards
Stars & Stripes

What Are People Saying?
Involved in community
Stand behind their work

Arrogant
Overpromise/underdeliver
Oldest in the area
Bad communicators

Exploitable Weaknesses:
Arrogance/rest on laurels
Slow to respond
Scheduling problems
One size fits all
Always behind
Overpromising

COMPETITIVE NOISE

Competitor:
Super Bee Contractors

Obvious Positioning Words:
Quality
Award-winning
Family
Design excellence
We're not satisfied until you are

Solid Differentiators:
Bumblebee logo
Black and yellow

What Are People Saying?
Friendly crews
Always behind schedule
Too many shortcuts
Hands-on owners

Exploitable Weaknesses:
All show/no go
Cookie-cutter approach
Barely visible

Outdated imagery
Boring website
Outdated home show booth

See? Once you're created a chart for each competitor, it's not hard to see where everyone you do battle with is going. Or not. It's remarkable how similar they are, isn't it? And, when you study your charts, it's equally remarkable how they're essentially telling you what not to do if you want to stand out. As easy as this Competitive Noise exercise is, I've met very few business leaders who've ever done this kind of simple analysis. That's scary! It shows how little thought business leaders give to competing, versus relying on traditional marketing and sales functions to attract new blood.

Tellingly, many business leaders have told me that studying their competitors was routine for them, but only from the standpoint of what the other guys are selling and how much they're charging. In other words, "If I know what my competitors are charging, I can build demand for my business—or at least survive—by matching or undercutting them on price." Not much of a strategy, is it? You've come to learn that's no way to compete.

The owner of a large, heavy equipment dealership said something about his Competitive Noise charts that's stuck with me for years. He said the charts he'd completed reminded him of scouting reports sports teams create before playing against competitors. He got embarrassed nods from the room when he said, "Knowing what competitors charge and then countering is like knowing they're going to punt on fourth-and-long from their own end zone. Everyone knows that. What kind of coach goes into battle not knowing how to exploit his competitor's strategic blunders when they're right in front of him? Up until today, this one."

Before we move on to the next step and start strategizing your route, I need you to do one more chart. You guessed it: You're going to chart your own business using the same criteria. But instead of "Competitive Noise," title it "Our Noise" (or "My Noise"). It's very important to be honest in your assessment, especially with the "What Are People Saying?" and "Exploitable Weaknesses" categories, and not sugarcoat anything.

Be mindful of this easy misstep: Just because you're saying it doesn't mean others are, too (think Richie Cunningham saying he was cool like Fonzie, when nobody else was saying that). And also remember that no matter what others are saying about you, they're never wrong. If you need a little push to be frank in your self-assessment, look at your business the way a competitor, filling in this report, would.

Quick sidebar: Because I often get asked about this, I'll mention here that it doesn't cost much to have an outside researcher do intensive phone audits of customers and prospects and prepare these reports for you. Researchers do this type of work every day, work quickly, and have plenty of experience in getting even the most tight-lipped people to speak up, especially when it comes to your and your competitors' advantages and weaknesses. Ask any marketing firm you're working with to point you toward a firm or local freelancer. Or simply go online and search "market research" in your local area. Don't worry if there are no local researchers, though, because the audit work is done via phone and this work can be done anywhere. This can be surprisingly affordable—I know of many small businesses that paid around $5,000 and received excellent market intelligence. Is this vital? No. Is it beneficial? Always. In addition to being fast and thorough, researchers have no biases or preconceived notions about your competitors or you. They'll uncover things that you won't. I've yet to see an instance where their honest assessment wasn't worth the investment.

Here's an Our Noise sample.

OUR NOISE

Competitor:
    Us

Obvious Positioning Words:
    Quality
    Affordable luxury
    Green
    Craftsmen
    Customer-driven
    Second-generation
    No shortcuts ever

Solid Differentiators:
    Father & Sons
    Homes for Heroes
    Jobsite vets signage
    Architectural typeface

What Are People Saying?
Been around forever
Not as big as used to be
Storm-chasers
Friendly crews
Old school
Patriotic/vets support

Exploitable Weaknesses:
Minimal marketing
Quick to cut price
Trouble finding good subs
Not "techy"
Little hustle
Outdated website

With your reporting complete, it's time to summarize what you've learned about your competitors. This won't take long at all and will give you a focused, at-a-glance view of the superslab they're collectively traveling.

All you need to do is set up another page using the same format you used in your Competitive Noise reports. Then title this page "Competitive Noise Summary."

Under "Obvious Positioning Words" list everything you've collected from each of your competitors. Don't repeat anything here; once a word's been recorded ("quality") there's no need to record it again. There's no need to identify specific competitors by name here—just list the entire collection of words you've recorded. This will be your library of words to avoid using to position yourself. Again, I've included a sample at the end of my instructions. You'll notice I went back after the initial list was made and put these words in alphabetical order to make it easier for future use. You'll want to do the same.

Next up, do the same with "Solid Differentiators."

For "What Are People Saying?" the rules change a little. I want you to craft a simple descriptive phrase or sentence about each competitor that effectively summarizes them, based on your findings. The easiest way to do this is to describe first the most positive thing(s) they're known for, followed by a "but," after which you'll list their most prominent or important negative(s). You may not always have a "but" for each competitor, as some may have overwhelmingly positive or negative comments. Record each competitor's name, followed by your summarizing statement. This will make perfect sense when you see the sample.

For "Exploitable Weaknesses," list each competitor, then record their two or three most prominent weaknesses in order of their "exploitability." Said another way, record them starting with their most exploitable weakness, then any notable others, in descending order.

Do not include yourself in this report. I've got something bigger in store for you.

COMPETITIVE NOISE SUMMARY

Obvious Positioning Words:

Above-and-beyond service	Award-winning	Beautifully built
Building relationships	Build-to-order	Built to last
Collaborative	Custom	Customer-driven
Design excellence	Family	Family values
Green	Hands-on	Integrity
Leading since 1965	LEED-certified	Not satisfied until you are
Master builders	Premier quality	
Small-town values	Smarter	Stick-built
Stress-free	Unmatched craftsmanship	Your vision, our passion
Zero	Energy	Ready

Solid Differentiators:

Oldest in the area	American flag bill-boards	Stars & Stripes
Bumblebee	Black and yellow	Crossed hammers
Diamond	Red apple	Sponsor high school gym
Three generations	Woman-owned	Radio/sports sponsor
Lightbulb	Bluebird	

What Are People Saying?

All American Builders: Well known in community but don't live up to hype

B&B Builders: Friendly but never on time

Apex Builders: Likable owners but too new to be trusted

Rocco Construction: Great design talent but too expensive

Macorn & Sons: Very small, hard to reach

Gemstone Fine Homebuilders: High-end builders but salespeople too aggressive

Exploitable Weaknesses:

All American Builders: One-size-fits-all, over-promising, slow to respond

B&B Builders: Cookie-cutter approach, always behind, barely visible

Apex Builders: Owners look like kids, lack of experience

Rocco Construction: Expensive, snobby

Macorn & Sons: Very new, trouble keeping employees

Gemstone Fine Homebuilders: Expensive, pushy, impersonal

It always pumps me up when first-timers in this process tell me they feel their competitive energy spiking when they study their Competitive Noise Summaries, because they're seeing obvious positioning blunders and chinks in their competitors' armor that they didn't know existed. Yet there they are, in black and white, all on the same page. (These samples were done by a competitor in a small market with just a handful of players; for larger businesses, the lists for "Obvious Positioning Words" and "Solid Differentiators" will be much larger.)

Your summary is telling you where your competitors are going and, just as helpfully, telling you precisely where you don't want to go. Remember those superslabs I panned earlier? And how everybody's moving the same direction, following each other like drones through dull scenery that never changes? That's what you're looking at on your summary. And it's why you're no longer going that way.

Nope. You're not riding superslabs anymore. It's time to start creating your route and I have just the right tool to do it with.

NINE

Using Noise Cubed as Your New GPS

Show me a motorcyclist who doesn't get lost on a regular basis and I'll show you a motorcyclist who's spending too much time on the couch. For lots of riders, getting lost is the hallmark of a great day's journey. It means we were so caught up in the fun of exploring new roads and so intent on keeping off main drags that we ended up at one of those inevitable forks in the road and had to do a mental coin flip to choose which way to go. Sooner or later, we got our bearings—with or without help—and arrived where we needed to be, no worse for the wear and armed with at least one good story to tell.

Think of your life's many car trips, though, wherein the *last* thing you wanted was to be lost. I'm sure you can remember those not-so-long-ago days when you had to actually know where you were if you got off course somewhere on a road trip and needed to consult a map so you could reroute. That age-old conundrum that asks, "How can you get where you're going when you don't know where you are?" has slowed many a journey and ruined some altogether. All men—I pretty much guarantee this—can recall getting hollered at by women for refusing to pull over and look at a map or ask for directions just as surely as women can recall being exasperated that men lacked the genetic makeup necessary to complete such an obvious, simple task. Being lost meant you were in trouble. You've been there so you know.

Today, being lost means we just tap an icon on our phone or dashboard and our problem's instantly solved with accurate turn-by-turn directions offered from a voice way friendlier than your nagging backseat driver's. No more unfolding maps, trying in vain to find where you are, then taking nineteen attempts to refold the damned things. No more faking the urgent need for a rest stop (ladies, I'm looking at you) so we men would finally agree to pull off the road somewhere to seek help. Thanks to GPS technology that would have been unthinkable in our youth and is now standard equipment on our handheld devices and our vehicles, we get where we need to be and harmony reigns. I have to believe those maps we haven't unfolded in years would look like cave paintings to millennials, who've never given a second of thought to just how exactly a GPS works or what an amazing advancement it is. *My phone's telling me where to go by a satellite orbiting the Earth? Whatever. Yawn.*

But anyway. Here you are on your journey to competitive dominance, trying to get your mind around how you want to position your business—or yourself—to start making some beautiful noise. You've wrestled a bit with your Radio Challenge script, likely not really knowing what to say or not to say, and learned from that exercise what happens when you inadvertently march in lockstep with your competitors and say what they're saying. Meaning you're now thinking more and more about positioning and dominating instead of simply going where others have been. Then you studied your competitors and crafted a Competitive Noise Summary to identify the positioning blunders, commoditized behaviors, and exploitable opportunities within your market.

So you're feeling like you want to roll and you're ready to get on the gas. But there's a challenge in front of you: How can you decide which way to go without knowing exactly where you are? That should sound familiar.

After studying your competitive landscape, you've discovered that you've got so many options to choose from, it's like finding yourself staring at a five-way intersection of on-ramps littered with confusing signs and cloverleafs that look like spaghetti, as traffic's whizzing all around you. And, wouldn't you know it, you've got no GPS to bail you out and tell you which route to choose. Meanwhile, Johnny Roadrage behind you is offering encouragement by leaning on his horn and mouthing unpleasantries—something about getting off the pot.

Meaning it's time to move. Now.

As your faithful road captain, it wouldn't be wise to let you cross your fingers, pick a route, and see where it goes like motorcyclists with time to kill do. To say nothing of those stubborn non-map-reading men I just mentioned. Not this time. I'm all for exploring, but you're blocking hostile traffic and some of those on-ramps are heading right into stuff that's even worse. So I'm going to ask you to pull over and get some help, without having to fake the need for an urgent bathroom pit stop. When I find myself in situations like this, I determine it's time for one of those frozen ice-cream cones sold in gas station freezers. King Cones! Those suckers are awesome. You need one. So pull over.

While I don't have a map with designated routes to give you, or even a preprogrammed GPS—you know that's not how I roll—I do have an effective tool to help you see where you are and pick the most fulfilling route to continue your journey. I call it my N3PS, for, you guessed it, Noise Cubed Positioning System.

This—drumroll, please—is where the proverbial rubber hits the road and brings Noise Cubed to life for you.

To make this happen, you're once again going to need a paper and pencil, or your computer, because you're going to be making a chart similar to those you've already prepared. No Internet access is needed here, so you can do this anywhere. The first parts of the process are pretty easy. Fun, even. And can be done quickly. (Again, there's a sample for your reference following the instructions.) As with your prior efforts, this is being presented as if you're a sole proprietor. There will be plenty of time later to involve others.

Here's how N3PS works:

Start your document with the header "NOISE CUBED POSITIONING SYSTEM FOR (YOUR COMPANY NAME)." I know that title seems a tad silly, but humor me, please. If I gave it a more serious-sounding name, you'd forget it before you reach the next paragraph. And besides, once you complete this baby and fine-tune it, it's going to be the backbone of your effort to make noise and dominate. You'll notice that parts of it look very familiar to you.

Your first column on the left side should read "What Do We Say About Ourselves?" This is self-explanatory. Here you'll record how, in discussions with clients, on your website, in social media, and in any marketing materials, you describe your business, citing all obvious positioning words. You know more about yourself than you know about your competitors, so this should be easy for you.

Your next column entry will be "What Are People Saying?" There will be two subsections below, one titled "Positive Noise," the other, "Negative Noise." You'll then need to use much the same process you used in your Competitive Noise reports, only this time you'll be recording what's being said about you, and in a slightly different format.

Self-diagnosis is a big, big deal and it requires extreme care. For the most part, it was easy to sniff around and determine what's being said about your competitors, right? You may have even jumped to a conclusion or two while studying them, and pumped that intel into your Competitive Noise reports. That's not a problem. But when it comes to looking at ourselves, I've found, there can be a tendency to exaggerate the positive stuff and minimize the negatives. I'm sure you know what I mean.

This is one of those times in your business or personal life when absolute honesty and clarity are needed, even if it causes some discomfort. As Sergeant Joe Friday used to say on *Dragnet* when one of his witnesses started trying to put a spin on what she'd observed, this is one of those "Just the facts, ma'am," moments. It's not easy to confront the truth sometimes, but it's as vital as oxygen. So please don't gloss over any negative noise or record positive noise that isn't factual because that will just hold you back later. (A little while back when I mentioned that professional researchers' lack of preconceived notions and bias can make them a great investment, this is the kind of stuff I was talking about.)

In addition to sniffing around online to see what's being said, as you did for your competitors, there are other sources of intel you can use here. There are likely things you've heard consistently over the years about your business, often from comments shared by fellow employees, that won't show up in your Internet searching. Stuff you may have *repeatedly* heard from your salespeople, for example, should be included because this is likely coming straight from the mouths of customers and prospects. Same goes for media and investment reports, if such exist for you. And again, one-offs don't count here. If it's not said repeatedly, don't record it.

Simply add your noise commentary under the respective "Positive Noise" or "Negative Noise" subheads. When your list is complete, rank them by order of strength and frequency—your strongest, most frequently said stuff goes first, then the rest in descending order.

And bear in mind that any of the negative comments you've listed— your weaknesses—are things being used against you that you'll later be working to repair or, at least, minimize over time. Having this in writing and prioritized means you'll have a hard time ignoring it and be way more inclined to address it.

Look your list over carefully, then take a few moments to let it sink in. If something in your report doesn't feel right to you, for whatever reason, you may want to dig a little further. If something doesn't feel certain to you and you find yourself wrestling too much with it to make it work, use the "when in doubt, leave out" rule, delete it from your N3PS, but save it for later consideration and discussion. Before going further, you need to be comfortable saying and believing "this is an accurate reading of where we are."

With your present location squared away, it's now time to zero in on where you want to go, which is the best part of the prep process. Now the fun starts and you'll notice your energy level and commitment to the process starting to soar.

Under your "What Are People Saying?" findings, add a new column, "What Do We Want People to Say?" This is where you get to be a dreamer, stretch out, and be as creative as you want. Think of all the great stuff you want people to say about you, whatever it is, and write it all down here. There's going to be a lot, I promise. There's no point being bashful here, so crank away and don't slow down. Take as much time as you'd like; nobody finishes this in one sitting.

Go long and don't limit your scope. Think about what, specifically, you want your important publics saying not just about your business or you, but about your people, your approach, your amazingness, your products, your services, your facilities, your digital communications, your creativity, your community involvement, your leadership ability, your strength as a business partner, your growth prospects, the loyalty of those you serve, and the experiences you share with them. Nothing is off-limits. If it's important to you and your business—and you'd love to hear people talking about it and be able to stake your reputation on it—record it. If you think it'd sound more like a great tagline or slogan than something customers might actually say, write it down anyway. We'll whittle it all down to the most realistic and doable later.

Because it's been asked every single time I've lead a group through this process, I'll clarify something here before you have a chance to ask about it: No. The aspirational comments you're going to write don't have to reflect your business as it exists now. They don't need to be true. Hence the word "aspirational." Remember, you're working on what you want your business to become and what you want your important publics to say about it. How you'll make those aspirations and stories a reality comes later when we address the third tier of Noise Cubed, "What Are We Doing to Make Them Say It?"

A few more important considerations: If you'd love people to describe you the way they're currently describing a stronger competitor, write it down anyway. There will be opportunities to alter the language—think "disciples" instead of "customers"—later, if necessary. Also, try to avoid overgeneralizing or being vague. Meaning don't write that you want to be talked about as "The best construction company in town" when you'd much rather be talked about as "The friendliest, most recommended one-off custom home builders in town." It's those specifics that are going to make you story-worthy and dominant. What's a "one-off custom"? I'd want to know, wouldn't you?

Now just imagine how long and varied your list will get when others at your business join in later. Salespeople, in particular, and others on the front line will have tons of ideas. Most of them good. Most of them reflecting their desire to help them better perform their jobs. You'll see.

NOISE CUBED POSITIONING SYSTEM FOR FIRSTCALL BUILDERS

What Do We Say About Ourselves?
We want to be your first call

Family owned and always available

We always put quality above everything else

Whether it's a renovation or a new home, you get our very best

Every customer gets the VIP treatment

Small-town family values means we treat you the way we'd like to be treated

A reputation for doing things right and not taking shortcuts

You become part of our team and we work together

Our approach is modern but we take pride in our old-world standards

We're not storm-chasers

What Are People Saying?
Positive

High-end value for mid-price

Tech-savvy and modern approach

Superthorough sales process

Mike Smith is a great guy

Offer great recommendations and advice

Always do a nice job

Negative

Too much idle time waiting

Subs don't speak English

Takes forever to get started

Better at small jobs than homes

Too many change order surprises

What Do We Want People to Say?

If you're fine with shortcuts call someone else

They build like they're building it for themselves with the highest possible standards

Most professional, easy-to-work-with new home and renovation construction company serving Our Town

Most creative in-house design team

Experts at satisfying everyone's budget and vision

I'm happy to recommend them

FirstCall always exceeds client expectations

Done when you want it, how you want it, better than you imagined

No challenge is too difficult for them

Regardless of the job, every FirstCall customer gets the VIP treatment

They're just supernice people with small-town family attitudes and values

Working with FirstCall is like doing business with family

The best craftsmen working only with the best craftsmen

They're even more focused on details than their most demanding customers

They're more motivated by happy customers than winning awards

Management is available twenty-four hours a day to answer questions and concerns

A few notes about the sample you just eye-balled, and those seen previously, to help shape your thinking and, hopefully, inspire you:

Why did I pick minor market construction companies for my examples instead of something from supersexy and trendy industries? Easy. They're small businesses selling a service that isn't top-of-mind with most people, since what they're selling may only be needed once or twice in a customer's lifetime. They're not huge, sophisticated promoters with ample marketing budgets. They serve a fiercely competitive marketplace where most competitors are like-sized, indistinguishable, and price driven. They also happen to be damn good people who are proud of what they do and bust their humps every day to sustain what they've built. They're eager to grow their businesses and be more successful. Unless you're a household-name business in a top-of-mind industry, they probably share a lot in common with you.

Plus, it's way easier for leadership of large businesses to identify with samples created by small businesses than the other way around.

It's also worth noting that the owner of the "FirstCall" business scribbled more than three pages of "What Do We Want People to Say?" in one afternoon and said that the more he thought about it, the more "real" it started to become and the more he and his team needed to "own" the negative market noise and fix its causes. He also said he was fired up to discuss this with his business partners and get their input. Those partners, by the way, were his wife and daughter.

Looking at your own N3PS, I'm guessing you have a lot of great, wishful "What Do We Want People to Say?" entries and realize that the list would be much longer if more of your people were involved. You couldn't be more right. It's not time to do that, though, because we need to work together to complete the process so you'll know how to explain it to others in your business. For now, remember we're working on this as if you're taking this journey alone—as a sole proprietor.

I'm sure you realize that it's just not logical to expect all of those wonderful, desirable comments on your wish list to become reality. If I were to ask you to describe one of your favorite businesses, you'd likely have just a few distinct things to say, versus pages of stuff, right? Which means you're going to need to whittle down your list.

The easiest way to do that would be to simply eliminate those entries that lack punch while saving your best. Let's not go there. To do this right you'll need to give each item careful consideration because quite often you will have written the essence of something very powerful, yet worded it so weakly or simply that your first impulse would be to delete it. Sometimes changing a few words—think "disciples"—can make something common highly memorable.

Remember how, when I'm planning a long bike trip, I'm very cognizant about which potential roads might contain not just great scenery, but excellent storytelling material? You can't just tell someone that on your last ride you experienced "the best road in North Carolina" and automatically assume they'll be intrigued enough to ask for more details. But tell them you rode "the tail of the dragon" and they're immediately going to want to know more, right? It's like when I said a few pages back that you don't want to be talked about as the "best construction company in town" when you'd rather be talked about as "the most recommended one-off custom home builders in town."

That's what you're looking for now. Those aspirational, yet realistic, descriptors that not only say who you are in a way that memorably distinguishes you from competitors, but also prompts storytelling. Nobody bats an eye at hearing "custom builders" because every town's full of those. But one-off custom? What's that mean? A builder in my construction company group said he'd heard of a construction company that built the main room in a client's home in the shape of a grand piano and a massive rec room in the shape of an electric guitar. That's not just "custom" work, that's "one-off" work for clients who want something that perfectly suits their personalities and that nobody else has because the builder, as part of its go-to-market strategy, promises to never build the same stuff twice. See? One-off custom stuff is story-worthy. I bet you can think of a bunch of other descriptors for this, other than "one-off," without having to give it much thought. Like "never-before-seen customs." I came up with that in the time it took me to type this sentence. You can do this, too. Probably better. Scout's honor.

So look at your list and begin to eliminate those comments that are too close to something any of your competitors say, seem too unrealistic, aren't distinct to you, or don't lend themselves in any way to storytelling or further description. But pay close attention here: Before you eliminate anything you feel strongly about and that's important to you, but might not be distinct or story-worthy, think "disciples instead of customers" and explore ways to employ memorable language to bring it to life. Only when you can't make something work or aren't pleased with it should you delete it. You'll exhaust yourself if you keep pursuing something you know you can't catch.

Let's look at some ways to manipulate language a bit, compliments of our FirstCall Builders example, and see if we can find any ways to enhance what was created in their owner's first attempt.

First up: "If you're fine with shortcuts call someone else." The owner said his first inclination was to delete this message, believing it's not distinctive and memorable. I believe the point he's trying to make with the

message, though, could be a good one in that his business puts craftsmanship and doing the job right ahead of cutting corners to get the job done,
which I know is a frequent complaint in the construction market. Yes, it's
hard to imagine his competitors saying, "We take shortcuts," because they'd
all claim (even if it's not entirely true) that they're dedicated to completing
every job properly and beautifully and, geez, isn't everybody?

What do you think? Can this common message be changed to be more
effective? I remember saying to this business owner, "Wait. This was the
first thing that came to your mind when you created your list, so it's probably very important to you, yet you don't feel strong enough about it to keep
it?" Then I asked him to tell me about what he was trying to achieve.

He said that one of the first things potential customers say to him is that
they hate it when they look at new construction and see that the builder took
some obvious shortcuts like using cheap plastic trim instead of wood or
made some minor goofs, like uneven drywall, that weren't repaired, thinking nobody would notice. He also said his market is full of what he called
"rip and run" companies that put getting the job done quickly ahead of
doing it perfectly, even though these same companies would of course deny
that they take shortcuts.

Then he told me that his grandfather (ping! I smell something potentially story-worthy) who founded the business (ping!) used to take great
pains to teach him the differences between how "serious craftsmen" plied
their wares, built things to last (ping!), and put so much pride into their work
versus how cost-conscious shortcut takers do it these days. He also said he
was never more proud than when his grandfather studied his work and said
it lived up to his "old" standards, even if it took longer to complete that way.
(Ping! And ping!)

It certainly seems like his anti-shortcuts premise could go in a bunch of
different and memorable directions with a little care and feeding, couldn't
it? Maybe something about putting those prized "old" standards ahead of
speed? Or about how "FirstCall hasn't taken a shortcut in the three generations they've been around."

His second idea, "They build like they're building it for themselves with
the highest possible standards," tells me he's very serious about his anti-
shortcuts premise, even though he was prepared to drop it. What this tells me
is that he was giving up too soon, not thinking yet like a dominator and not
giving himself enough time to come up with better words to convey his idea.

I totally get that this doesn't come natural to most people and not all of
us have liberal arts degrees. That's why I want you to read and reread every

statement, and let it bounce around in your head and your imagination, before sending anything to the recycle bin. And remember: You're just one person. If and when you get others involved in this process, the brainpower and creativity will grow exponentially.

When I asked him why he opted to delete "Most creative in-house design team," he said because that was something any firm could say and that, frankly, he worked with a lot of the same outside designers and architects as other firms in the area and that this wasn't something he believed the business could easily uphold without looking dishonest. He said his "design team" was him, his wife, and outside architects. Do you agree with his deletion? I do. He said he "just liked the sound of 'most creative in-house design team'" but doesn't have the talent in-house and—most important—isn't planning to create a dedicated team in the future. Off it went. At least for now.

He said he also wanted to delete "FirstCall always exceeds customer expectations," because, again, he said everybody says that. When I asked him, "How do you know whether you exceed expectations or just meet them?" his answer was very telling. He said something to the tune of "You know how on those house remodeling shows on TV, the clients always looks like they're in shock when they see the finished product? That's how I like people to react when we show them something we've done that was particularly challenging or that they were worried or superexcited about. It's such a great feeling to see that 'wow.'" There are plenty of pings in there, wouldn't you say? So I challenged him to explore that "TV wow feeling" angle before retiring the idea. Was there something he could do with that to make it memorable? The gist of what he's trying to say here is also very easy to visualize, which could be a great bonus. What might you suggest he do with that?

Something else I saw in his document struck me as potentially powerful. Under "What Are People Saying?" is the comment "Mike Smith is a great guy." Yet there was no mention of his great-guyness in his aspirational comments, and before he could say that he was too modest to make the business about him, I said that competing to dominate means there's no time for modesty. Remember, there's no such thing as subtlety. The guy's known and liked in the town he's lived in forever and that his family has served for just as long. Personal reputation carries a *ton* of weight, but people in his town might know more about him and his family than his business. That warm familiarity could be leveraged for competitive advantage, especially given that two of his aspirational comments were about his company's "supernice people with small town family attitudes and values," and working with them is "like doing business with family."

Anybody who's into bikes or cars knows a mechanic nearby who does great work at a fair price, is friendly, explains things simply, and is super-liked and respected to the point of reverence. A guy we'd recommend to anybody. Maybe our FirstCall guy, Mike, is that guy, or could be that guy, when people in his area talk about construction companies or need work done. There's power in there that he shouldn't let his modesty upend.

I could go on all day with these small construction company examples, but I'm sure their points haven't been lost on you. The most important thing to keep reminding yourself of as you're looking at your N3PS is that this is about your aspirations—what you'd like your business or you to become and how you'd like to be known and talked about. So it requires a lot of thought, reflection, and forward-thinking, as you've noticed. It also requires creativity, which is something that every human with an imagination possesses. It's not possible to spend too much time thinking about your reputation, as that's something you should be thinking about every day.

If you're running a business, I know you've dreamt since day one about how successful your business could be and how great it would be to not only achieve that, but to have people extolling your praises. It doesn't require a special "gift" to put those dreams in writing. Just do it. And whatever you do, don't limit yourself. You're encouraged to keep at it and come up with as many great "What Do We Want People to Say?" ideas as you can, because the more you include in your N3PS, the more solid material you'll have to work with later.

When you've reached the point where you're comfortable with what you've written and deleted any you didn't feel strongly about, you've got one more task to complete before we fire up our machines and move on.

It's time to load your saddlebags for the journey ahead with your most valued stuff and leave the nonessential stuff behind. I bet you know what I mean. What you'll need to do is pare your list down to your top five (at most) favorite "What Do We Want People to Say?" aspirational statements, then rank them in descending order, starting with your most desired.

Here's what our friend at FirstCall came up with. And here's a heads-up: It ain't Shakespeare and it doesn't need to be.

What Do We Want People To Say?
> They put their reputation for old-school craftsmanship and family values ahead of everything else
> Mike Smith's family has been building people's dream homes for three generations

Every FirstCall customer gets the HGTV treatment whether it's a new home or a remodel

Their competitors go for speed but they go for wow moments

Mike Smith's your man—he's available twenty-four hours a day to answer questions and concerns

So what's wrong with Mike's list? Not a whole lot, really. This is one man's best effort, done under tight meeting deadlines. He wrote what he felt was best for his business. You can see where he's going with this, even if the words aren't perfect, right? You can imagine that with a few more days to mull this over, he could sharpen it a bit. Or perhaps do some more additions and deletions. And that's *before* he had the chance to share this with his business partners—his wife and daughter—and get their ideas and input. And maybe some of his crew, too.

Because you're still a bit wet behind the ears in learning about competitive dominance, you might not have noticed, as I did, that Mike's list doesn't include the expected "quality," "solutions provider" language. Bravo! But it does lean on "family values," which is a term at least one of his competitors is using. Oops. Remember our rule: If somebody else is saying it, we're not. That doesn't mean his top-of-the-list idea is a lost cause, though. It just means he's going to have come up with a different way to capture the essence of family values using different words, because this is something that's very important to him.

Because you may also have fallen into the trap of using a word or two from "Obvious Positioning Words" in your Competitive Noise report, you're going to need to reword a few things differently, too. And it's very possible that you've struggled a bit coming up with your top five and ranking them, given your many options and that your ranking seems to change and evolve with each review.

It sounds like a lot of work to pull this all together into a final working document, but it's not superdifficult. You just need to uncover some new ways of thinking to refine what you've done so far and make it more go-to-market ready.

And, wouldn't you know it? I just happen to have some great tools to help do that.

TEN

Tools to Lighten Your Load and Simplify Your Journey

There's a beautiful, unwritten rule among motorcyclists that's been around about as long as there've been motorcycles and that should be—but isn't—taken as a given by every human being: "Never leave a brother behind." It was doubtless co-opted from the battlefield ethos "Never leave a fallen comrade behind," and, reflecting the meteoric rise in the numbers of women riders of late, has been updated to say, "Never leave a brother or sister behind." Regardless of how it's spun, I'm sure you get the gist. If a rider's broken down by the side of the road, whether you know him (or her) or not, or ride the same brand of bike he's riding, no matter how much of a hurry you may be in or that it might be raining, you roar in like the cavalry, offer assistance, and bust out your tools. It's the right thing to do.

Don't you wish everyone on the road adopted such a humanistic approach? You probably know how awful it feels to be sitting by the side of the road when you've had a mechanical breakdown and how disheartening it feels when nobody comes to your rescue. You also know you've rolled past situations like this hundreds of times, intentionally avoiding eye contact with the stranded motorists and feeling twinges of guilt as you stepped on the gas and blasted past. It's sad. Even if you're not mechanically inclined, simply offering a friendly voice and keeping someone company until professionals arrive isn't the kind of gesture that goes unnoticed in the karmic, do-unto-others scheme of things. But if you come to the rescue with mechanical know-how and the right tools? You'll know the glorious feeling of being looked upon as an exemplary member of our species. And that's a beautiful thing.

Having the right tools at the right time is something to take pride in and I'll admit here that I have a beyond-healthy love for them. When I was working my way through college in the plumbing trade, my boss took me out to buy my first set, saying it was time for me to stop mooching off others and that "you've got to have your own tools and know how to use them." Truer words were never spoken. But being basically broke (and owning dual money pits in the form of a Honda CB350 and an old Buick, both of which were held together with duct tape and wishful thinking), the idea of spending a lot wasn't sitting well with me.

As we walked the racks of gleaming hardware, the boss man caught me eyeballing some cheap stuff, yanked it from my hands, then proceeded to teach me a lesson I've never forgotten and have repeated ever since: "Buy cheap tools and you'll be back to buy good ones. Get good ones and you'll use them forever." Again, truer words were never spoken and, forty-some years later, those same tools are still with me, along with a gazillion others, evidence of a treasured collection—and addiction—that started that very day.

I wouldn't dream of taking a long motorcycle trip, or even a short one, without bringing along a few tools, because I know that, sooner or later, I'm going to need them. In a small pouch on the bottom of my left saddlebag or in a bungeed-down duffel bag, I stow an adjustable wrench, fresh sparkplugs, a tire patching kit, a small flashlight, duct tape, a few clamps of varying sizes, and a multitool with built-in knife blades, screwdrivers, and pliers. My truck has much the same in its glove compartment. What have you got stowed for when the road gremlins surface?

More than once, I've stopped to help stranded motorcyclists by the side of the road and discovered they had no tools, but were sure delighted to see that I did. Each time this has happened, it's like I could see a light go on in their eyes that said, "I've gotta get me some of those." Yes. You do. Get good ones.

On the journey you're on, you've got to have tools and know how to use them. Because, well, here you are, miles from your starting point, yet misfiring a bit and needing some help when it comes to answering the second tier of Noise Cubed, "What Do You Want People to Say About You?" in ways that are memorable, repeatable, distinct to you, and position you to be dominant by being story-worthy. You've put in the legwork and have some good ideas framed in your mind, but finding the right words—especially when you can't use any your competitors are using—isn't as easy as you'd hoped. You're also wrestling a bit with determining your most important positioning statements by rank, because many of them seem equally strong. I see you there, by the side of the road.

And here I come, blasting in, tool kit at the ready, to get you on your way. I'm not just going to help you, though. I'm going to give you these tools and show you how to use them so that you can deploy them throughout your career, as I have, and share them with others. Trust me when I say they're good ones and trust me further when I say you've never used tools like this before. Sears doesn't sell them. Those rebranders don't carry them, either.

The first tool I'm going to show you is going to blow you away and expose a hidden talent you probably have no idea you possess. It's pure genius and works by giving you the amazing ability to expand your mind by forcing you to think minimally. No, that's not an oxymoron. With it, you're going to take those many ideas banging around in your cranium, reduce them to their essence, eliminate all but the most important words, and figure out the best way to say them. Yes, there's a tool for that. I didn't invent it, though. Someone in Japan did, centuries ago. What you'll be using it for certainly wasn't what that someone had in mind, though.

Here's a little foreshadowing, just for fun: On introducing this tool in classroom environments, a frequent first reaction, especially among high-ranking suits and rugged blue-collar types, has been an "Oh man, you gotta be kidding me" eye roll. Minutes later, when those same people see what they've done with it, their faces turn to "Well I'll be damned" astonishment. I live for moments like this. And, of course, shoving it back in the faces of judgmental types who minutes earlier thought they were too cool for school.

A quick demonstration, so I can show you how this baby works, is in order. To make it easy for everyone to follow, we're not going to focus on your N3PS entries yet; we're going to focus our attention on you personally. You'll need to grab something to write with and on. And please, for the umpteenth time, don't just read through this. Do it.

I want you to write down how you think of and describe yourself (cue those eye rolls). But here's the catch: You have to be completely honest and you must use exactly five syllables to do this. Five. No more, no less. If you haven't thought about syllables since your grade school days and forgot what they are, just think of them as the parts a word can be broken into. *Bike* is one syllable. *Bik-er* is two syllables. *Fan-tas-tic* is three. *Mo-tor-cy-cle* is four. *Un-be-liev-a-ble* is . . . you got it. It isn't childish to sound the words out and count the syllables on your fingers because, trust me, everyone does. Your challenge here is to write down how you describe yourself—and your most recognized qualities—then reduce it down to just five syllables. It's not easy and it's not hard. It just is.

To hot-wire your brain, here are a few samples taken from one of my classroom sessions of how some folks I've worked with described themselves:

"Nice family man." (Count the five syllables on your fingers: Nice fam-i-ly man.)

"Giant teddy bear."

"Overworked stress bomb."

"Kickass accountant."

"Fun guy to hang with."

"Good boss, better mom."

You get it, right? No sweat. Now it's your turn. It's challenging to get your personal description down to something so short and to the point, but I know you can do it. Just write down how you describe yourself—or think of yourself, if that helps—and edit it down to the five most potent syllables. Huge points will be taken off if you copy one of those examples (even if you are an overworked stress bomb). I'm giving you a deadline of only three minutes to do this, but I promise you'll be successful. Don't beat this thing to death, just describe yourself. Think. Write. Reduce. Count. Now go!

- - - - - - - - - - - - - - - - -

Your three minutes are . . . up. Finished? Congratulations on what I know is a job well done. Look what you did: You met my challenge and wrestled your personal description down to just five powerful syllables, even though you thought it would be difficult. Way to go! It may not be perfect, but I don't recall ever saying it needs to be.

Now I have a new challenge for you: Immediately beneath your personal description, write down how others describe you—or how you believe they do. Only for this, you get two extra syllables for a total of seven. And don't be overly modest with this because you either know definitively, or at least have a good hunch, what others say about you.

Here's how our "nice family man" sample guy did it:

"Drives himself crazy with work." (Count those seven syllables: Drives him-self cra-zy with work.)

Our "Giant teddy bear" came up with "Intimidating bully."

You know what to do. You have three minutes to produce those seven syllables. Now go do it!

- - - - - - - - - - - - - - -

Time's up. You're on a roll now and I know you have something good written down. Your ability to reduce a lot of wide-ranging, even complex thoughts into just a few simple words is amazing, isn't it? Imagine how much you'd think, rethink, and play with this if I didn't limit you to just three minutes and let you use all the words that immediately came into your mind.

You're doing an amazing job, but we're still not done. You need to bring this baby in for a landing. It's time for the final challenge and I wouldn't be surprised if you've already guessed what it is. Immediately beneath your two entries, please write how you *wish* people described you, in only five syllables and those same three minutes. Finish this thing so it looks like this:

> How I describe/think of myself (5 syllables)
> How others describe me (7 syllables)
> How I wish others described me (5 syllables)

Now go!

- - - - - - - - - - - - - - -

How'd you do? Here's what our nice guy's attempt looks like:

> Nice family man
> Good guy. Tries hard. Works too much.
> Hero to his kids

Next up:

> Giant teddy bear
> Intimidating bully
> Nicer than he looks

Pretty cool, no? Just three lines. But oh man! The power of those three lines! And those seventeen syllables! These brief samples provide a ton of insight into the lives of these people, don't they? You can sense the struggle of contrasts between how these folks believe they're seen and how they'd love to be seen because there's no excess stuff in there to confuse you. Each of these is a tight, crisp snapshot, with no further description necessary. Do you think our teddy bear would have admitted in a room full of people that he wishes people knew him for who he really is, instead of falsely judging him by his appearance? Or that he could have explained his situation so succinctly? His pain is now real to you; you know what this guy's about.

Your three lines, I'm assuming, surprised you a bit. Looking at what you just completed, you know that each of those lines, if I didn't limit you to just a few syllables, would have many more words and concepts. But you let all of that stuff bounce around in your head until you eventually eliminated unnecessary waste, then fed what was left into a funnel to capture the pure essence of what you wanted said. You were able to do it.

What you may not be aware of—unless you had a junior high school flashback while doing this—is that you just wrote a haiku, a Japanese poem of suggestive comparisons. You. Just wrote a haiku. As you can interpret from the samples, our first writer thinks of himself as a family guy, yet he knows that other people believe he works too much and that his work is keeping him from being seen the way he wishes he could be seen—as a guy who's adored by his kids. Our giant teddy bear scares people and wishes people saw him for who he really is (a common wish among bikers, I might add).

But whereas haikus, for centuries, have been written to describe nature, which, as you can imagine, is one of the hardest things to describe briefly, I've hijacked the art form as a reduction tool and made it a method for bringing clarity and simplicity to an abundance of thoughts and ideas about positioning.

I've seen some of the toughest people you can imagine—guys like metal benders and bridge builders—grinning like toddlers as they read what they created. Poets! Who'd have thunk it? And I'll never forget how enlightened I felt after leading a group of entry-level professionals in Lithuania through this process and seeing how tough it was for many of them to express something positive about themselves, as they were among the first generation to come of age after decades of Soviet occupation and oppression. Their haikus made them confront that it's okay to not limit themselves. Powerful stuff. Smiles all around.

So how do we use haiku to help with your N3PS? Simple. It's a flexible tool that can be utilized in countless ways. Here's what I recommend: Looking at your N3PS document, you'll see that it nearly mirrors the form you just used to write your personal haiku in that it follows the same pattern of how you currently describe your business, what others say about it, and what you want others to say about it.

Our construction company leader was struggling to prioritize his "What Do We Want Others to Say?" and how to say his favorites more succinctly. Here's how our new tool helped him: He was pleased with the comment "They build like they're building it for themselves with the highest possible standards," and felt it to be the most desirable, yet he realized there was nothing particularly memorable or distinct here. Could he condense this down into something more potent?

Rather than telling him to just try to rewrite that comment in just seven syllables, I instructed him to be more thorough by having him go to his N3PS and look under "What Do We Say About Ourselves?" to find a comment that "felt" similar to the desired comment you just read. He chose "Small town family values means we treat you the way we'd like to be treated." Before he could ask if he chose the right comment, I told him there are no wrong answers. Only the person drafting an N3PS document knows what he or she feels the most strong about or what feels right.

So having identified material to work with for the first and third lines of his haiku, he needed a line for the middle, "What Are People Saying?" I told him to go back to his N3PS, looking under "What Are People Saying?" and find a *negative* comment that seems most out of synch, or possibly even contradicts, what he's saying and what he hopes others will say. He chose "Too many change order surprises," explaining that costly change orders are the last thing customers want, are usually caused by poor communication between the contractor and the client, and that it's hard to say we "treat somebody like family" when everyone's upset.

What we have now is a lot of words that can be paired down and made easier to work with and remember. Written as they exist now, his three lines read:

> Small town family values means we treat you the way we'd like to be treated.
> Too many change order surprises.
> They build like they're building it for themselves with the highest possible standards.

Reducing this to haiku will help bring the third—and most important—line to life, while bringing more clarity to the others. So here's what our FirstCall owner came up with *in less than ten minutes*:

> We're small-town people.
> Change order surprises suck.
> FirstCall is painless.

Not bad. Not bad at all. Clearly, he wants to have superb relationships with his clients, make a stressful process much less so, and have that be a major positioning point of his business. And just look at the word "painless." Where'd that come from? It's a very a powerful word that doesn't appear among any of his competitors' Obvious Positioning Words and isn't something you think of when you think of construction companies, so it might just be a great differentiator for him. I'd say he's on to something. I told you this stuff works!

Please remember as you're reading this, that this is just one person's take. And a first pass. None of what he's written is being carved in stone. But I hope you can see what's happening and how it's not superdifficult to reduce a lot of complex thoughts into a few powerful words.

Look at your N3PS and follow the same procedure as our FirstCall leader. Do as many haikus as you can with the material you've already written. It doesn't take much time and, in fact, gets easier with each attempt. And please remind yourself that, other than the 5-7-5 syllables rule and the three-minutes-per-line limit, there are no strict rules for this. You can reuse any of the first two lines more than once, as long as your "What Do We Want People to Say?" entries are different. And be on the lookout at all times for those magic words that will appear from out of the ether—like

FirstCall's "painless"—that may prove golden for you. They're the greatest reward for doing this.

What you're looking to achieve is an N3PS made up of short, concise entries with the ultimate goal of a handful of great, memorable, repeatable, "What Do We Want People to Say?" statements. These can be worked, re-worked, edited, and revised countless times until you have something you love and that none of your competitors can lay claim to. And remember, you're going to need to rank them by strength, starting with your most powerful. Also remember not to throw any of your ideas away, because you might have a few hidden gems in there. After you've ranked your top four or five, keep your other ideas on the page for later consideration.

So I bet you never thought your fearless road captain would have you writing poetry, did you? And I'd also bet you never knew you were as creative as you've discovered yourself to be. My hope here is that you're gaining confidence in your ability to think differently and position your business to dominate and that you're enjoying the journey.

To ease your mind, your "final" N3PS entries before moving on don't need to adhere to the syllable limits of your haikus. Your poems are simply a tool to help you reduce and focus your thoughts. If, after editing, further noodling, and perfecting your document as your journey continues, you find a few more words and syllables are needed to say what needs to be said? Go for it.

Before we move, though, I'll ask that you please don't read beyond here until you're comfortable with what you've completed thus far on your N3PS, because you're going to need it for the next leg. Comfort doesn't come particularly easy at this point, I realize. You might even be a tad confused about what you've done and whether it's good enough to take you where you want to be. That's okay. Your N3PS doesn't have to be perfect—because it never will be—but it needs to be in good working shape with short, crisp entries. *"Working shape."* If magic words like "painless" don't appear, don't worry. They will. Eventually. To make sure of that, I have another tool in my saddlebag to help get you there, coming right up.

So don't get your undies in a bundle.

I'm sure you're curious what our FirstCall guy came up with for the rest of his N3PS after busting out his haiku chops, so here it is. Notice not only how haikus helped with his "What Do We Want People to Say?" entries, but how they helped him tighten the other entries in his document as well, which should make it easier for him to massage and for others at his company to understand and work with. Also notice that, again, this ain't Shakespeare, because it doesn't need to be.

NOISE CUBED POSITIONING SYSTEM FOR FIRSTCALL BUILDERS

What Do We Say About Ourselves?

Make us your first call
Craftsmanship tops all
We don't take shortcuts
You're a VIP
Small-town-values based

Unranked possibilities:

We treat you the way we'd like to be treated
Do unto others
You're part of our team
We're always open
Modern approach with old-world standards
Whether it's a renovation or a new home, you get our very best

What Are People Saying?

Positive

High-end value for midprice
Tech-savvy modern approach
Superthorough sales process
Mike Smith is an awesome guy
Always offer great viewpoints
Always do amazing work

Negative

Too much idle time waiting
Their subs don't speak good English
Takes too long to get started
Better at small jobs than homes
Change order surprises suck

What Do We Want People to Say?

FirstCall is painless

They don't take shortcuts
They treat you like kin
Good small-town people
On time, on budget

Unranked possibilities:
Creativity
They speak your language
They're the gold standard
Everyone loves them
Bring your dream to life
VIP treatment
A breeze to work with

CHAPTER

ELEVEN

Say What You Do.
Do What You Say. Start Here.

You're about to take on one of the most demanding and important challenges you'll encounter in your professional life and make monstrous progress on your journey to competitive dominance. The good news is, you've
already proven your chops, so I fully expect you to crush this the way you've
crushed every challenge I've thrown in front of you so far.

So get ready to begin the final section of your N3PS and to unleash
more creative energy than you knew you possessed. Here's the *Reader's
Digest* version of what lies ahead: First you're going to add texture to the
positioning language you want your important publics to remember and repeat, which is a superbig deal. Then you're going to determine the actions
and behaviors your business will need to exhibit at all times to bring your
desired positioning to life so you can make noise like a dominator. That's an
even bigger deal. This is where your journey gets very real, because when I
say "actions and behaviors," I'm referring to specific changes in operating
priorities and procedures you and everyone at your business will have to
embrace to make your N3PS work for you. (I just saw you shift in your seat.)

To use an overworked but completely appropriate cliché in this case,
this is where the rubber meets the road. Anytime you start digging into

changing how your business operates and what it's going to take to make that happen, it's going to be heady stuff, but stay with me because I've got a great way to smooth out the road before you and make your challenge more manageable. Before the work begins, though, I have a few quick stories to share that will provide some mental imagery and frames of reference for you as you get down to some serious business.

Remember that gremlin bell attached to my bike that fends off anything evil that could rise up from the road and wreak havoc? And how I nudge it a bit to make sure it's working before I hit the road? I long ago discovered these bells have a secondary purpose, the value of which dispels any potential suspicions one might have about their effectiveness. They're there to remind me, every moment I'm in the saddle, to be on the lookout for potential trouble. Texting drivers, drunks, wildlife, potholes, and God knows what else are out there, just waiting for that one brief moment when I lose focus to make themselves known and do me harm. I can live—literally—without that stuff.

You'd think it goes without saying that all of us would prefer to squelch threats and trouble before they can cause harm. That's a total no-brainer, right? Yet if that's true, why, in our business lives, do we so often sidestep dealing with trouble when it makes itself known, risking everything to "get to it later," when it's likely more difficult to defeat and perhaps even more widespread? Equally weak, why would we choose to ignore any real and present danger and hope it will go away when the downside for doing so is so apparent?

Leaders, if I may have a quick word with you: One of the most frequent complaints I hear from your people is that they spend way too much of their time fixing problems they're convinced you saw coming, or even caused, that could easily have been avoided. (If that sounds familiar it's probably because you voiced the same complaints before you were the one calling the shots.) More often than not, they'll say they saw the problems coming, too, but felt powerless or uncompelled to do anything about them. So, naturally, they're blaming you for the time and resources they're wasting fighting fires that never should have ignited. Stinks, doesn't it?

With that in mind, let's live a little and learn a lot about squashing trouble before it starts, killing the bad stuff that's already there and avoiding problems of our own making. You'll soon see, as you tear into the final phase of your N3PS, that there are plenty of places to inadvertently cause the kind of problems your people will be complaining about later. Like sidestepping the bad stuff you know about and see coming.

Join me as my mind drifts back to an incredible Harley Owners Group (H.O.G.) rally in Valencia, Spain, where thousands of motorcyclists gathered and three unforgettable lessons seared themselves into my hard drive. I think you'll find these teachable moments especially valuable, given what you're about to do. They'll also serve to remind you, as they always do me, that any journey worth reliving requires excellent food, free-flowing libations, and wonderful people. As if anyone needs to be reminded of such.

The first one's a doozy.

I'd just flown into Barcelona from Rotterdam with two giant crates of signage that I'd picked up at a shipping yard, where boat containers of Harleys bound for European dealerships were being offloaded. I intended to haul the stuff down to the Valencia H.O.G. rally site in a massive panel van. Other than the fact that I'd had plenty of experience with large trucks in my younger days, I've no idea why I volunteered for this task.

A tad nervous about driving a huge beast on unfamiliar roads, I forgot to grab a map and failed—this being the pre-GPS era and me being of the male persuasion—to ask anyone at the truck rental counter for some directions ("Uh. Dónde está el H.O.G. rally?"). I drove away from the airport confused and grinding gears like a rookie, then jumped on the first southbound freeway I saw, figuring I'd fake my way down to Valencia. I swear the truck must've had a giant gremlin bell hanging from its front bumper as, a half hour or so into my drive, I spotted about a dozen Harleys with Scottish plates and H.O.G. flags blasting past me. The Scottish cavalry! Those H.O.G. flags told me they were rally-bound, so I breathed a huge sigh of relief. But holy cow, those boys were carrying the mail, so my clunky truck struggled mightily to keep up with them.

My big break came when they pulled off to grab some fuel. I whipped in next to them, confirmed we were heading to the same place, and asked if I could be the tail end of their convoy. As I'd hoped, they were more than happy to help somebody from "the factory." That several of them were wearing tartan kilts and were built like linebackers wasn't lost on me. Anyone could see these guys would be fun to hang with and, one would suppose, dangerous as grizzlies to mess with. But I knew the real truth—more than likely they were giant teddy bears. We know the type, right? No haiku necessary.

Upon reaching the rally site in Valencia, some of the guys asked if I was camping on-site and invited me to join them at their campsite later that evening for some, let's say, festive merrymaking. I told them I was staying at a small nearby inn and, just to be cordial, said they should stop by later if they were out and about, so I could properly thank them for their help (cue foreboding Gaelic music).

After settling at the inn, I knew I had to whip over to the rally site, unload the crates, and help the crew get things dialed in. So I asked the innkeeper to keep his eyes peeled and, in the unlikely event a group of Scottish riders should show up looking for me, tell them to make themselves at home as I'd be back shortly. Uh-oh. Assuming they'd never show, "shortly" became, well, longly, and it wasn't until well past midnight that I made it back to the inn, where someone was waiting for me—my old pal the innkeeper. His face was red with anger.

Apparently, my new friends had indeed shown up and, having accepted my invitation to make themselves at home, had taken over my room and commenced to celebrate more robustly than the innkeeper and guests in adjoining rooms were comfortable with. So much more that he told me I needed to evict my noisy houseguests immediately. Gulp! With his stern face staring over my shoulder, I swallowed hard, pushed my room door open, and saw about a dozen guys and a few gals (lasses?) on the floor and on my bed, all sprawled out and happy, the TV blaring. They all looked up and said, "Allo Keen!" and thanked me for giving them such a nice place to hang out before we'd all head downstairs to do some serious partying. Awkward.

I explained that the inn was sold out, its tiny bar had shut down at midnight, their noise was bothering other guests who were trying to sleep, and they'd have to go. This, mind you, was the same thing the innkeeper had told them, but they made it clear to him how serious I was in extending my hospitality. And besides, nobody says talks smack to bikers in kilts and engineer boots who look like warriors in *Braveheart* battle scenes.

Thank God they understood our collective predicament, laughed a bit, and found their way to the door and back to their rally campsite, no worse for the wear. After all, as I'd later learn, their evening was just getting started.

The next day, I swung by their campsite to make amends and they invited me to have a seat under their party canopy, which I probably should have realized was a setup. The second I sat and got comfy, I was told, "Orright, Keen. Git ow-oot. You're scaring our guests." With lots of laughs, they made a giant production of telling everyone present how I'd invited them over, only to leave them waiting, then had them evicted. My embarrassment didn't wane until they presented me with some of their H.O.G. chapter swag—treasured keepsakes—and we raised a toast or three with something Scotch-y.

As a business leader and all-around good person, you'd of course never make a promise you couldn't keep, would you? Nobody would, right? You wish.

I'm asking about something this elementary now because it's something you'll soon be giving a great deal of consideration. Overpromising and underdelivering happen all the time in business and the results can be a helluva lot worse than embarrassment. I know, I know. Everyone knows that, right?

But look at your "What Do We Want People to Say?" aspirations for just a minute and I guarantee you'll see some areas where, even with the best of intentions, overpromising could easily come into play. Believe me, it's in there, like a gremlin, waiting to strike. I see it all the time when guiding folks through this process, especially when they're sharing any messaging relative to "customer service." It's almost too easy to overdo it here. Just think of the last time a business boasting about its great service let you down—which shouldn't tax your brain too much—and you'll see what I mean.

On your N3PS, as you begin to put actions and behaviors behind the words that will prompt your desired noise, you'll need to be on the lookout to ensure what you're promising is realistic and consistently doable. And to make it so. And then, of course, to make sure all of your important publics know about it. You'll see soon enough.

The second thing that really stands out about Valencia and has a direct N3PS connection happened that same Scotch whisky–scented Saturday afternoon on the rally grounds, when I saw a catering company prepping to make the "world's largest paella." Who knew people keep records of such things? Standing shoulder to shoulder in a fast-expanding crowd, I watched, agog, as into a pan the size of a swimming pool chefs dumped a truckload of rice, a ton—literally—of seafood, umpteen bushel baskets of vegetables, jugs of wine, bags of spice, and, of course, a few goats. Goats! Giant torches heated the pan as the chefs, on ladders, stirred the concoction with boat oars and tons of muscle. You know, just your average prep for an informal dinner to serve a few thousand motorcycle people who were loving the spectacle as much as I was. Cold sangria and hot paella were coming our way at sundown. Not bad, eh? I can still smell it and hear everyone speaking excitedly in all those beautiful languages most of us regret not having learned well in school.

What a joyous and unforgettable communal scene that night's dinner was, compliments of Harley Owners Group—a corporate-subsidized organization hell-bent on delivering just that to its members. Tellingly, throughout the evening, while bands played and rally attendees danced, H.O.G. members approached and thanked Harley and H.O.G. leadership and local Harley dealers for putting on such a great event. In turn, they were told, "No, thank *you* for coming and for supporting us. Have fun!" They also heard a chorus of frequent thank-yous coming from the stage. The gratefulness couldn't have been more obvious.

I shouldn't have to point out the obvious lessons in there, most of which will rise to the fore in your N3PS, but just to make sure: Memorable, story-prompting experiences. Customers and company reps sharing great times and conversation. Customers showered with warmth and genuine gratitude. Surprise. Delight. Community. Great visuals. And those are just for starters. I don't care what business you're in, you're capable of doing things for those you serve that create similar results, with or without massive pans and goats. Or even spending a lot. The question is, are you going to let one of your competitors beat you to it?

My third big recollection comes with a lesson even greater than the one I'd relearned with my new Scottish friends and certainly on par with the paella love-fest. At the Sunday afternoon close of the rally, while those same Harley and H.O.G. leaders, staffers, and dealers were wishing safe travels to the departing riders and basking in the glow of a successful event, a handful of H.O.G. chapter officers came over to voice some complaints. Uh-oh. Perhaps we hadn't done such a great job after all. While praising the rally and the effort, they said they were unhappy that alcohol sales after the prior evening's paella dinner had been cut off at ten p.m. and that the bandstand was shut down soon thereafter—time limits both then standard procedures for Harley rallies, based on guidelines for *American* rallies. ("It's how we've always done it." Ugh. The telltale sign of trouble.)

They proceeded to give us a polite primer on the differences between European and American cultures, telling us that while Americans start winding evenings down before ten p.m., Europeans are just getting started—which, of course, even the most neophyte tourist knows. The dinner wasn't served until eight p.m., so shutting the bar down "early" seemed, well, unthinkable to them. (I'd insert a joke here about how the Irish and German clubs had ample contingency beverage supplies, but it would be in bad taste to leave out the equally well stocked Brits, French, Swiss, Scots, Italians, Swedes, Portuguese, Spaniards, Scandinavians, Finns, Belgians, Dutch . . . you get the picture. It wasn't exactly Prohibition.)

They also pointed out the obvious fact that nearly all riders at the rally were camping on-site (which typically doesn't happen at American rallies), so the odds anyone would be riding after drinking, an evergreen concern at bike rallies, were slim. Given that situation, and the also-obvious fact that these folks were used to partying and dancing into the wee hours and then walking to their tents, careful but amenable adjustments were made for future events.

The market spoke: We hadn't done enough homework into local culture—or equally telling, ignored it—and, instead, opted to use a one-size-fits-all approach that didn't fit. We learned *a lot* from this and acted on it. The last thing anybody wanted was Harley disciples making negative noise by telling others not to attend rallies because the company was inflexible and not party-friendly. Harley's famously vocal customer base could've taken a huge bite out of the company's "people first" reputation in no time.

Let's look at this for a moment. From a Noise Cubed perspective, there are two ways to look at customer complaints: The first—the way you've seen businesses handle them forever—is to treat them as something to be swept aside or ignored or, equally weak, to be responded to with some tepid "We're sorry" script that's nothing more than a pathetic line of BS. We've all been burned by the slow boil of aggravation that comes from taking the time to voice a complaint and getting an insincere, form-letter-type response as our reward. Or calling an 800 number and having to explain our problem to someone who doesn't speak our language clearly (you know what I'm talking about) and who we know won't be doing anything to rectify our problem. Given a choice, why would any business want this to be the first thing a customer remembers and talks about? And why would customers, given lots of choices, ever want to do business with such losers again?

The second way to handle complaints is the smart way: to look at them—and stay with me here, because I'm serious as a heart attack—as compliments that pay dividends.

We have to be realistic. The last things any of us want to hear in our professional lives are complaints from those we serve, but I can't think of many instances where those complaints aren't actually improvement suggestions in disguise. When customers complain or point out our shortcomings, they're telling us what our friends and coworkers won't. They're telling us what we need to do better to avoid repeating our mistakes, losing customers, and battling the negative noise those problems create. From a competitive, dominance standpoint, could there possibly be a higher compliment?

Shouldn't we *want* to know when we've blown it and let someone down, so we can rectify the problem, commit to not letting it happen again, and—the bonus dividend—score some points for righting our wrong at the same time?

Better, shouldn't we want to convert known problem areas—customer turnoffs—into what Blue Ocean Strategy contributor and my great friend and occasional business partner Gabor George Burt calls "points of infatuation"? When the fix to a problem or a known turnoff (say, airlines charging you to check your bags) becomes an admired "wow" (Southwest Airlines, take a bow for your "bags fly free" strategy), people are going to remember it and talk about it while cash registers ring. That's guaranteed.

Now you see why your N3PS includes a section for negative comments under "What Are People Saying About Us?" These negative entries are there because you and everyone in your organization need to confront and remedy your known and talked-about shortcomings and misrepresentations. They're right there in front of you—you wrote them down yourself—like road gremlins waiting to rise up to ruin your journey. You should take some comfort in knowing that a big chunk of your upcoming work will be specifically focused on silencing your negative noise. You don't need me to remind you on whose shoulders the people working for you will place the blame for not dealing with this stuff.

If people are saying something bad, unflattering, or even untrue about any facet of your business, it has to be accepted as legitimate, because this stuff can spread like wildfire. And you know it. There's a restaurant in your town that you won't visit because somebody you know heard from somebody she knew that a friend of somebody else's cousin got a tough pork chop there. In 1982. And you've told everybody who's ever asked you about that place not to go there, despite having never been there yourself. The place has changed chefs twenty-six times since then, but you don't know or care about that, do you? Just think: You're spewing nasty noise about a business you've had zero personal experience with and nobody doubts a word you're saying. And thanks to you, they're probably spewing it now, too. Bad noise spreads fast.

You just can't move forward on your journey without addressing how you're going to quiet your known gremlins and turn down the bad noise. Do you think our FirstCall construction pal would be wise to ignore that people are saying his business takes too long to get started on jobs or that his subcontractors have language barriers with customers? Would you choose to ignore those voices if you were in his work boots?

Before answering those simple questions with an emphatic no, you should know that a common reaction from folks who go through the N3PS process with me is to display an immediate aversion to accepting and discussing the negative comments in their documents and to start defending their businesses. I hear a lot of dismissive comments like "Oh, this problem only happened one time." Or "That doesn't happen anymore." Or "These people don't know what they're talking about." I'm sure that's not hard for you to imagine.

While I respect anyone's immediate instincts to be defensive, here's the blunt truth I use to confront deniers and defenders: "If you can't accept negative comments as legitimate, then you can't accept the positive ones, either." When their eyebrows lift, I say, "So you're telling me that only the people saying good things about you know what they're talking about? Come on!" That's always greeted with bowed heads and silence. When it comes to negative noise about your business, like it or not, the market has spoken. And as you know, the market tells no lies because the market is people just like you and me.

And get this: Protesting with "That only happened one time" or "That doesn't happen anymore" at the same time voices in the market are repeating this nasty stuff means *this stuff is still happening, even if it isn't.* Get it? The fire might be out, but the stinky smoke still lingers (Exhibit A: tough pork chop from 1982) and it's got to be dealt with. Lucky for you, you've got an N3PS to help you squelch the negative voices and better control your marketplace narrative, which we're about to dive back into.

With those thoughts in mind, let's combine a quick pep talk with a level-set before we move ahead. What you have right now with your N3PS, in the parlance of our long-distance motorcycle ride, is a pretty solid idea of where you want to go. The fact that you've come this far with it, intentionally ditching the competitor-choked superslab, and have begun finding more memorable and distinctive roads—and have a document that proves it—says you're embracing the challenge and thinking like a dominator.

(By the way, if it seems like I've been complimenting you more frequently than perhaps you'd expect, well, thanks for noticing. You'll be doing the same with your people as you lead them through this process. Journeys often veer off course or end abruptly when positive enforcement disappears. You know that. Never underestimate the power of positive stroking. Or the damage its absence can cause.)

Just look at what you've done. You've crushed something that, in the early stages of the process, you couldn't picture yourself doing. You've studied your business and how you present it to the world and how it impacts the people you serve or wish to serve. You've done the same with the competitors blocking your path to dominance and viewed them through a lens you'd never peered through before. You've created a stellar list of things you'd love to hear your important publics say about you to distance you from those competitors. You've even written poetry and made it *work* for you. Whoever said being innovative requires a power cord, microchips, and an advanced degree? I'll never stop reminding you about the poetry thing, by the way. You're a regular Longfellow.

What you'll do next is an even bigger deal than everything you've accomplished so far and I'm not overselling it. This is going to require your strongest effort yet. Your rubber-meets-road time is now, and if you've already forgotten what that means, it means you're about to tighten up your positioning language, then lock down the specific actions and behaviors your business will need to exhibit at all times to bring those words to life and make them memorable and repeatable.

When you've completed your first pass on this, you'll go on the offensive against your previously identified road gremlins, otherwise known as your negative noise, and identify specific actions your business needs to take to quiet them before they have a chance to rise up and cause further harm. This is big stuff. It's where you'll determine what you're packing for your journey and what you're leaving behind.

Now let's make like dominators and get back to work. Even though your upcoming challenges will be considerable and tax both sides of your brain, have no fear. You're up to it.

Here we go.

What you're going to do now is take each of the ranked, top five desired comments under "What Do We Want People to Say?" in your N3PS and brainstorm specific language you and your people will need to use in all conversations with important publics, as well as in all of your go-to-market tools, to separate you from competitors and serve as repeatable language for your customers. This will become your bedrock language—the stuff that becomes engrained in your business's DNA.

So start a new N3PS page and title it "N3PS Positioning Directives." A little show-and-tell is in order here, as it will be much easier for me to describe what you'll need to do—and for you to understand it. I'll show you how our FirstCall pal, Mike, completed this process and you can use his work as your template.

Recall the comment he'd most like his business to be known by is "FirstCall is painless." So he created two columns: the first to record what he and his people must always say in conversations and in all go-to-market materials to make "painless" top of mind with their important publics; the second to specifically detail what he and his people must do to bring this "painless" language to life and spur his important publics to repeat it. So the top of his page reads:

N3PS Positioning Directives

Because We Want People to Say "FirstCall Is Painless"

We Must Always Say: **We Must Always Do:**

Then he imagined himself or any of his employees or subcontractors having a conversation with a current or potential customer. He asked himself— because dominators make a point to do this before *any and all* conversations with important publics—"What do I have to say and do in front of this person, or over the phone, or via email or text, to make him or her remember and repeat that FirstCall is painless?"

Under "We Must Always Say" he wrote the specific conversational phrases he felt were needed to increase the probability that his important publics will recognize and recall FirstCall's philosophy of being "painless." As he told me, painless to someone having a home built includes not having any nasty surprises, always knowing what's happening, not being overwhelmed by complexity, and having fun. It's important to note that none of the words or phrases he chose to support "painless" appear in the Competitive Noise section of his N3PS. As you know, that's a mandatory, no exceptions rule. Also, note that his entries may not always be complete phrases or sentences because there may be times when just a single word, or a few, are all that's needed (like Harley-Davidson's "lifestyle" or Cracker Barrel's "homestyle").

Under the "We Must Always Do" column he listed the actions and behaviors he and his teams must make standard operating procedure at First-Call to bring that desired language to life. Both columns combined, then, are the stuff people will see, hear, experience, remember, and talk about. They'll become the engine powering his business.

Again, I'll remind you that the sample you're about to review is the work of just one person. And don't forget it's also a first draft. Involving others at his company will eventually lead to alterations and improvements in FirstCall's N3PS. Recognize, too, that no document like this is ever "final." Your N3PS will evolve with time, just like the route on our long motorcycle trip. We're in it for the journey, not the destination.

Let's see how he did before you start your own.

N3PS Positioning Directives

Because We Want People to Say "FirstCall Is Painless"

We Must Always Say:	We Must Always Do:
We're painless	Use "painless" in every conversation/promo to explain how and why we do things
We hate surprises too	Make no changes without prior notice/approval
	Develop/use change order template w/customer signature required
	Explain big changes face-to-face and minor changes via phone. No texts/emails for changes!
We want this to be fun for you	At least one big customer surprise per month—always say "We want this to be fun for you"
	Friday night happy hour on-site with crew and customers at halfway point
	Present thank-you book at completion with progress photos and signed photos from crew
	Laugh and use humor—show our fun side!

You'll always know what's happening	Develop/use weekly Friday status report—include progress photos
	Return customer calls within thirty minutes
We keep things simple	Avoid trade talk, use photos for support
	Show, don't tell, so customer understands and can tell spouse

Nice work, isn't it? Just looking at this, I can imagine his fellow leaders and employees shouting out more ideas when he shares this with them, especially on the "we want this to be fun" stuff. Being a construction company customer myself on more than a few occasions, I can certainly say I don't remember any overt efforts by any of the companies I've worked with to be "fun." Nor did any give me printed progress reports, or photos to log that progress. I would've loved that, remembered it, talked about it, and even showed it to others.

Take a look at the second of FirstCall's "What We Want People to Say" work and you'll gain further inspiration. And I bet you'll agree with what I said when I first read it: "Hey, that 'correctly versus quickly' thing is pretty cool and supereasy to remember." Again, as somebody who's done business with a few construction companies, I can vividly recall being very upset at having to wait for mistakes to be repaired, so I fully understand what's being said here and why.

You'll also see that his "zero tolerance for sloppy work" policy is going to require constant communication and enforcement among his employees and work teams or it isn't going to work. I wouldn't be surprised to hear team members suggesting the idea of creating an incentive for crew workers to ensure adherence to the rule, as well as ideas on how to manage those instances when someone falls short. Remember: If we can't live up to it, we can't say it.

After that, you'll see the rest of his top five desired customer comments, which should serve to make you more comfortable with the process.

N3PS Positioning Directives

Because We Want People to Say "They Don't Take Shortcuts"

We Must Always Say:	We Must Always Do:
We don't take shortcuts	Always explain our philosophy of doing the job correctly versus quickly like competitors
Correctly versus quickly	Show customers specific areas where we could take shortcuts but don't
	Always say when describing issues on job site
	Describe problems caused by shortcuts when selling
Zero tolerance for sloppy work	Crews need to bring sloppy work to attention of manager/owner and to team members
	Never let customer see something that should have been done better
	Immediate discussion with site manager

N3PS Positioning Directives

Because We Want People to Say "They Treat You Like Kin"

We Must Always Say:	We Must Always Do:
We treat you like kin	Tell grandfather story
	Display customer family photos in sales office
	Ask questions like "how are your kids today?" so customers know we care about them

	Make random phone calls at least every two weeks to check in and ask "how are we doing?" and "how are you feeling?"
Bring your kids	Engage customer kids at job site. Give them FirstCall caps and let them hold tools and shake hands with workers
	Take pictures of kids with equipment and crew
Call me any day anytime	Tell about late-night customer calls and Sunday job-site walk-throughs

N3PS Positioning Directives

Because We Want People to Say "Good Small-Town People"

We Must Always Say:	We Must Always Do:
We're just good small-town people	Mention our local roots and that we know everybody
	Recommend local businesses—we know owners
	Have some customer meetings at Dairy Queen or Smoky's BBQ
Mike has been on the school board for sixteen years	Put photos of school board in office
	Talk about involvement in the new middle school
	Ask what schools customer's kids go to or will go to—make recommendations
We're active in kids sports	Show photos of teams we sponsor and ask parents if their kids play or want to play

We're active in kids sports *(cont.)*	Point out team photos and thank-you letters in our conference room—put on website
	Buy ads in high school sports programs
Family very active in our church	Invite to Knights of Columbus carnival
	Recommend churches if new to area
	Put KofC carnival booth photos on website
We're active with Girl Scouts	Show photos, connect customer's kids with troop leader—put photos on website

N3PS Positioning Directives

Because We Want People to Say "On Time and on Budget"

We Must Always Say:	We Must Always Do:
We take great pride in finishing on time and on budget	No customer surprises! Be upfront about all timing and budget issues as soon as they're known
	Err on the side of longer timeline on estimates to finish job ahead of schedule
	Confirm supplier availability and communicate any back-order issues to client as soon as they're known
	Remind customer in all progress discussions about our effort to stay on time and on budget

We take great pride in finishing on time and on budget (*cont.*)	Increase pool of subs to ensure availability and reduce/eliminate downtime
	Always inform customer at job completion that we came in on time and on budget

Well, what do you think of FirstCall's effort, so far? I'm impressed, as I typically am, when I see what I call, "perfectly average people doing extraordinary things." And when I consider that all of this work was done in an afternoon, I'm all the more impressed.

So now it's your turn. Start fleshing out the words and actions of Positioning Directives and I promise you'll be amazed not only by how quickly the time will fly by without you being aware of it, but also by the quality of your ideas. That's what happens when your brain and your heart are working together, you're envisioning a better future for yourself and your business, and you know that what you're working toward is completely achievable. And as you review your progress, you'll take great comfort in knowing that the document you're creating is guaranteed to get even better with more time and more of your people involved.

Allow me to offer a few pieces of advice before you start, gleaned from years of watching people just like you plow through this: Remember, just as you did in your earlier work when you studied your Competitive Noise—and, as I'll never stop reminding you—when you're crafting your "We Must Say" words and phrases, obey my rule that states that if somebody else is saying it, you're not. Avoid falling into that trap that others before you have fallen into with their N3PS documents. Don't be like them.

Also, please relax. You're not writing the Declaration of Independence, by candlelight, with others looking over your shoulder and the fate of a nation at stake. This is just a first draft. So don't let it overwhelm you. Just think positive, think fun, think doable, think "memorably different," and whatever you do, don't think too much. If you find yourself getting bogged down in minutiae or wrestling with whether some of your ideas are realistic and doable, that's telling you something. It's saying that the last thing you want here is complexity. Think simple. You can, and surely will, add more layers, color, and detail later.

Think, too, of those kilt-clad Scottish bikers partying in my room after I made a promise I failed to keep, and what an embarrassing debacle that turned into for me. As you're crafting your words and actions, keep a sharp eye out for anything that looks unrealistic and undoable, or, equally bad, like well-intentioned overpromising. That just feeds the gremlins.

Draw "Must Do" inspiration from my story about the paella dinner at the H.O.G. rally and FirstCall's idea to hold occasional customer meetings at the local Dairy Queen. (Isn't that great? It just screams "small town" and I've got to believe the meager cost of a few chocolate shakes is going to pay huge dividends.) It doesn't matter what business you're in—and I'll accept no arguments here, because nobody's ever given me a good one—there are ways for you to create memorable experiences with and for the people you serve. Think surprise, delight, community, memorable visuals, storytelling material. This stuff is always top of mind with dominators.

Finally, if you find yourself lost and bewildered, just reread FirstCall's document. It's nice and simple and everything in it seems doable. And take some comfort from knowing—and this is the umpteenth time I'll tell you—that what you're about to create is a first draft.

I know you're ready to get started and dive into this thing. So please do. Take as much time as you need, whether that's a few hours or even a day or two. It's just like our long motorcycle trip—nobody's timing you and you absolutely should explore any side roads you stumble upon to see if they lead somewhere amazing. Should some of your exploratory runs lead you down a path your competitors are already choking or even to a dead end, well, so what? You had the guts to dig deeper into your ideas, make the effort, and learn what *not* to say and do. More often than not, discoveries like those invariably lead to something better. Now go be a dominator. Let it rip and we'll get back together when you're done. Please don't read on until you've finished your work.

I'm assuming you've completed your first pass at your Positioning Directives or have at least reached a point where you're somewhat comfortable with what you've created. Once again, I congratulate you. You've just picked up a lot of speed on your road to competitive dominance. It feels good to think like a dominator and to see—in black and white—what it's going to take to *be* that dominator. Enjoy the buzz.

But, much as I know you'd love to, you can't pull up your kickstand and start rolling yet. Not while you know there are gremlins out there waiting to spoil your journey. It's time to address your negative noise head-on and determine how best to make it disappear, because you're not going to do what bazillions of other businesses around the world do and pretend this demand-killing negativity doesn't exist or hope it will go away on its own while competitors steal your thunder. You want to silence the bad noise while ramping up the volume of the good noise, right? So let's get started on that.

What you're going to do next is very similar to the N3PS Positioning Directives work you just completed, only you'll be looking at your challenge from the opposite perspective. Now, instead of focusing on the words and actions you'll be deploying to get others to say about you what you want said, you'll be focusing on what you want people to *stop* saying and the words and actions you'll need to deploy to make that happen.

Look to the "Negative Noise" listing under "What People Are Saying?" in your N3PS and you'll know the specific gremlins you need to address. And just like with the post-paella complaining session I told you about, you know that only bad things happen when negative market voices aren't silenced. This is the time to make lingering negatives fade out or turn them into positives—like those points of infatuation I mentioned earlier.

So let's get after those gremlins. All it's going to take to get you started on this is a slight change in your Positioning Directives template. Using FirstCall's document as our example, your header for the next section of your N3PS will read:

N3PS Positioning Directives

Because We Don't Want People to Say "Too Much Idle Time Waiting"

We Must Always Say:	We Must Always Do:

I know you see the difference here. So now you'll need to dive back into your document and, as you did previously, craft the words and actions you'll need to squelch the negativity and, if you're really on your game, turn it into something positive.

Some strong words of advice here, before you start. When thinking about what you must say to silence negative noise, it's imperative that you never repeat any of that negative noise. In other words, you'd never want to say, using the FirstCall examples, "There's no idle time waiting." Or, equally dangerous, say something defensive like, "Some people say there's too much idle time waiting, and that's just not true." In communication strategy circles, that's what's known as "repeating the negative."

When you repeat a negative, what you're really doing is exposing it to more people. You're spreading the exact words you never want to hear again. If Mike from FirstCall talks about "too much idle time waiting," when he knows people in his market have said that about his business, he's inadvertently endorsing that negative noise and sowing new seeds of doubt about his business. If an NFL quarterback said on TV, "Some people say I collapse under pressure, but I don't," what would you remember about that QB? I'll say it again: Never repeat a negative.

In nearly all incidences and in every industry, there are ways to overcome negativity. The odds of doing that will forever be in your favor if you make silencing bad noise a priority, versus taking a wait-and-see position. Before you get back to work, take a look at how FirstCall handled this. That way you'll get a feel for what you need to do. Then dig in, get it done and we'll regroup when you've finished.

N3PS Positioning Directives

Because We Don't Want People to Say "Too Much Idle Time Waiting"

We Must Always Say:	We Must Always Do:
We take great pride in finishing on time and on budget	Show examples of previous customer build schedules, completion dates, and budgets
You will always be told if we run into any delays	Be 100 percent up-front and realistic with schedules
	Immediate communication of delays or schedule changes
We hate delays even more than you	Work closely with all subs/suppliers to control what we can control. We have to be more aggressive with them and tell them we can't tolerate delays.

We hate delays even more than you (*cont.*)	Explain job process, that supplier backups are normal and unavoidable and that we make every effort to stay ahead of them

N3PS Positioning Directives

Because We Don't Want People to Say "Subs Don't Speak English"

We Must Always Say:	We Must Always Do:
We only hire the best. Period.	Require there to be least one English-speaking person on-site at all times
	Make sure English-speaking person knows he is first point of contact when no job manager on-site
	This person to greet any job site visitor first
	Make sure all subs know to direct customers, etc. to English-speaking person

N3PS Positioning Directives

Because We Don't Want People to Say "Takes Forever to Get Started"

We Must Always Say:	We Must Always Do:
We take great pride in finishing on time and on budget	Fully explain every step of the start-up process
	Manage expectations. Explain schedules.
We're as excited to get started as you	Give start-by estimate and immediately inform of any changes

| We're as excited to get started as you *(cont.)* | Control what we can control and explain this to customer up front |
| | Invite customer to job site first day of work and have memorable activity like groundbreaking photo or champagne toast |

N3PS Positioning Directives

Because We Don't Want People to Say "Better at Small Jobs than Homes"

We Must Always Say:	We Must Always Do:
We've been building homes for generations	Show customers photos of our homes
	Give customers addresses of homes we've built and tell them to have a look or take them for a ride and show them
We do it all, but homes are our focus	Put more home photos on website and less remodels and constantly update
	Stop being modest about our work
	Show older homes we built and photos of updates on those homes on website
	Only show remodel photos after customer has seen new home builds
	Keep emphasis on home construction as bread and butter

N3PS Positioning Directives

Because We Don't Want People to Say "Too Many Change Order Surprises"

We Must Always Say:	We Must Always Do:
We hate surprises	No customer surprises. Mike or site leader to personally speak with customer about all changes or delays and cost implications before they happen.
	Fully communicate job process to customers to make sure they understand how and why change orders happen
Change orders are a normal part of all construction jobs	Make sure customers know that all jobs have change orders and that they are often driven by customers
	Make sure customer signs off on any change orders and include in status reports

Finished? Raise your right arm over your head, bend it past ninety degrees, and pat yourself on the back. With the completion of your N3PS's negative noise entries, what you have in front of you, in black and white, is a quantum leap forward in your quest to be a competitive dominator. Your first N3PS attempt is complete. Likening it to our long motorcycle ride, you've now got a great list of suggested routes and the story-worthy Must Dos to experience along the way. You've got your bags packed and balanced. And no part of where you're prepping to go bears any resemblance to the routes your competitors are riding, which should make you very proud.

The only thing left to do is your preride ritual to make sure your machinery's in place and in fine working order to get your journey started. Before we get to that, though, let's talk a bit about the FirstCall N3PS to provide a frame of reference for yours.

Overall, I'm quite impressed with it from front to back, as I was the first time I saw it. Is it better than most I've seen? Absolutely not. In a word, it's typical, which is why I shared it with you. And "typical" is an appropriate word here because I'm typically impressed with every N3PS document I read. I see very few that don't reflect levels of creativity and forward-thinking their authors didn't believe they were capable of. Any time I read one, I can sense profound improvements about to be made and can envision these first-draft documents evolving and improving further as their creators invite others at their businesses to participate. Can't you just see sales, marketing, and communications people having a field day with these things?

The real beauty of N3PS documents like FirstCall's, of course, lies in the fact that they're created by or with the full involvement of business leaders. Remember that the *only* way a business can position itself to be a competitive dominator is if making that a reality is at the top of that business's list of priorities and is driven by visibly active, constantly encouraging leaders. Employees and other team members embrace what their leaders visibly and passionately embrace, and support what they feel they've helped create and will ultimately benefit from. Losing sight of that would be tragic.

There's some amazing stuff in FirstCall's effort that everyone can learn from. It's obvious that FirstCall's owner is thinking about creating customer experiences that will provoke positive noise and eventually drown out any lingering negatives that are holding his business back. I'm particularly taken with his idea to do groundbreaking ceremonies or champagne toasts at job sites when work begins. That looks like a game-winning home run. None of the construction companies I've hired have done anything like that and I'd bet my eyesight none of yours have, either. Who wouldn't remember that? Can't you just see that photo of mom, dad, their kids, and FirstCall's owners, all holding shovels on a job site, with the FirstCall sign in the background, breaking ground for their new house? And who wouldn't show that photo to friends, post it on social media, and tell stories about it? Or react positively to seeing shots like that on FirstCall's website? And what would it cost FirstCall to hold mini customer events like that? Peanuts! The rewards would far exceed the nickel-and-dime investment. And you already know how much I liked his idea to hold a few status meetings at the Dairy Queen. Little by little, the positive noise will build as the negative stuff fades. Assuming, that is, that FirstCall proactively manages customer expectations about when jobs will start and adheres to its Must Dos.

Remember the small water softener company I mentioned earlier that's taking on the big-box giants and their lower prices? And how well adherence to their small town positioning was paying off for them? It strikes me that FirstCall's going to be pulling some different levers to achieve similar results. Being real, genuine, likable, and tugging those Mayberry strings just has to work for community-based businesses, doesn't it? But I can't think of any instance where those same descriptors wouldn't work for any business of any size. And that includes online-only and narrow niche businesses.

FirstCall's "correctly versus quickly" language flat out strikes me as a winner because it's got great R&R—remember and repeat—appeal going for it and it offers lots of opportunities for story-worthy show-and-tell. Like many construction company customers, I've been angered a time or two by shoddy work—poor drywall, trim that wasn't square, sloppy painting—in the name of speed. Uncomfortable discussions always followed (it's also worth noting that I remember the names of the companies that did that unsatisfactory work, all these years later).

FirstCall showing me photos, before a job starts, of the kind of work they don't tolerate while explaining their philosophy of correctly versus quickly will resonate with me and I'll be more patient to get my job done at the highest professional standards instead of having to wait to have it redone because it wasn't done properly the first time. The challenge for FirstCall is obvious: They damn sure have to ensure that the work crews they hire do the job correctly every time and that the crews self-police themselves. If customers discover sloppy work, they're going to squawk about FirstCall not keeping their promises.

I hope you noticed when reading FirstCall's ideas to stop people from spreading negative noise, that every Must Say is a positive expression. You know why this is important because I tipped you to this earlier: Repeating negatives is a huge no-no. It's like that bad, old joke about a politician trying to dispel negative press by saying, "At least I don't beat my wife anymore." Positive messaging and positive actions create positive results.

Before we move forward, please read and reread your N3PS front to back a few times and make any tweaks, edits, or wholesale changes you feel are appropriate. The more you read it, the more tweaks you'll make and the more comfortable you'll grow with it. Anything that doesn't feel right or that just doesn't seem doable or realistic or overpromises, should jump off the pages. Don't let this cause you grief, though, since there's plenty of time ahead to refine your work and even to make changes on the fly as you move forward. It's the journey, not the destination, that's important here. I know you know that. Making occasional turns onto new roads, to see where they lead, is part of what makes these journeys great. And it's never a big deal if you head down a road that turns out to be a dud. Just pull a quick U-turn and get back to the good stuff. Even the greatest hitters strike out more often than they hit home runs.

To quiet any lingering voices in your head about your N3PS or what you read in FirstCall's first draft, let me address some comments and questions I've heard from others about their documents. I've never led people through this process where these questions weren't asked. It's always wise to clear the air on this before we move on.

Nearly all the initial questions I get from business leaders at this point in their journey prep process include the words "How long?" As in, "How long after starting this will I begin to see results?" And "Assuming a business adheres to their N3PS, how long will it take for negative noise to disappear and for the positive noise to spread?" Or "How long will it take for my employees to change their behavior?" I'm sure you're having the same thoughts.

Man, I wish there were easy answers for these, but the truth is they're impossible to answer as there are tons of variables at play with every business and every document. It's important to recognize that in most instances, it's going to take time for negative noise to simmer down or disappear—just as it likely took time for it to build. Severely negative noise, like, say, Harley's "outlaw biker" halo, took a few years to wane and still lingers in some locales (a great reminder that it's the journey, not the destination). Bad noise about Harley's product reliability and unfriendly dealers faded much faster and soon was drowned out by glorious, positive noise as the company's positioning changed and dealers became more "people focused" and "lifestyle" oriented.

As a rule, the smaller the market and/or the more frequent the contact with important publics, the faster people respond to noticeably different behavior and begin talking about it. Any mom-and-pop owner will tell you: Word spreads fast in small towns. And any business owner will tell you: The larger the business, the longer it takes for work cultures to evolve.

Let's say FirstCall's employees and work crews adhere to their Must Say and Must Do lists and their next few customers hear those Must Says several times, don't experience any waits to get started, change order surprises, or language barriers and love those DQ shakes. That's great, but it doesn't mean the local community will instantaneously be abuzz with positive stories. That's obvious, right? This business doesn't have thousands of customers in its community (yet). We need to recognize that positive noise about these great attributes will spread, though. It always does when great and thoughtful things are happening for customers. A few good Yelp reviews, for instance, can start a chain reaction of more positive reviews. A delighted customer showing pics and telling stories at a book club meeting about her home-building experience with FirstCall is going to pay big dividends. Same goes for that customer in her working environment. People talk. When positive noise shared by one delighted customer brings FirstCall a new customer, the results will speak for themselves.

The larger point that addresses those "How Long?" questions: You're now going to be saying and doing things specifically to make positive noise and quiet your negative noise. This is stuff you weren't saying or doing before. You're going to win. Addressing your negatives haphazardly or randomly or, worse, by doing nothing, was working against you. Tackling this stuff head-on means you and everyone working for you knows you're taking this seriously and waging war against it. Your important publics are going to notice it and talk about it.

Bottom line: You've got to start somewhere. And your N3PS proves you already did. If a company with a disjointed work culture and as much ugly noise surrounding it as Harley-Davidson once had ("Harley riders kidnap teenage girls!"), can become respected, beloved, talked about, and in demand, while at the same time building legions of fiercely loyal followers, well, friend, who's stopping you from achieving even greater results?

But there's something larger than timing bothering you and I know what it is. The stuff that makes even quiet business leaders become vocal when they read a sample document like FirstCall's is the same stuff that's making you a tad uneasy right now: It's those damned new and required changes in standard procedures under "We Must Always Do." FirstCall's requirements for an English-speaking person at every job site, for a top leader to explain and get sign off on change orders, and those weekly customer progress meetings are clear examples. Yikes! This stuff doesn't fall under the "snap your fingers and it happens" category. You learned as a child that words without action are meaningless and that you'll be way better known for what you do than for what you say.

What you're feeling is the precise reason so many "rebranding" efforts fail to generate positive momentum and why I'm so adamant that competing to dominate isn't a marketing function. Noticeable improvements and enhancements in your business require change in how your business operates and it's your job as a leader to ensure that your "We Must Always Do" actions become standard procedure. Big stuff to be sure. Nobody I've met gets excited by the prospect of making sweeping changes in their business processes. Who would? It won't surprise you to learn that many leaders I've guided through this journey have pulled on their skeptic caps saying, "Yeah, this stuff looks good on paper, but I don't know if I can make it all work because . . . blah, blah, blah, excuse, excuse, excuse."

What leaders like this need—hell, what everyone needs—is some secret weaponry that's powerful enough to knock down the real and imaginary obstacles and challenges in front of them. Weaponry that will change the way their people see them. And make their people more inclined to embrace leadership and their new workplace expectations—those Must Say and Must Do directives—while reducing workplace turnover. And, since I'm on a roll now, weaponry that will make their business more attractive, likable, and loyally supported by customers.

Ah, the stuff of dreams, right? Come on, man, you know me better than that. I've got what you need. Just flip the page.

TWELVE

Behold the Indefensible Weapons of Mass Attraction

I'm about to drop a bomb on you. Several, actually. The good kind.

This stuff you're about to read is what I live for. It's also what paid for at least half of my house and my adult playthings, so I'm forever energized by it, grateful for it, and excited to pass it along. You're going to feel the same way about it and what it's going to do for you.

Look, everyone in business knows that we tend to make things more complex than we need to. If you've ever tried to flowchart a workplace initiative or make an org chart—for no larger reason than to flowchart a workplace initiative or make an org chart—you know what I mean. So let's simplify things.

From my viewpoint, when you strip away all the intricacies and complexities of day-to-day operations, the overall responsibility of any dominance-minded business leader can be condensed into two simply stated challenges: The first is to attract more customers than competitors. The second is to rally the troops to make the first one happen indefinitely. I know you get that.

Your N3PS is a mighty powerful tool for helping you meet those challenges, but it's going to benefit greatly from the addition of some high-caliber weaponry. The stuff I just tipped you to that will make it easier for you to attract customers, make them fiercely loyal advocates for you, and, of course, scare the pants off of your competitors. "Easier" is the operative word.

This same weaponry is equally potent for helping leaders achieve that second prong of their overall responsibilities. Getting your people to enthusiastically buy into, improve, and participate in the N3PS process and loyally support and follow leadership is also about to get way easier for you. There's that word again. And yes, I mean it when I say "enthusiastically" and "loyally."

The weaponry I speak of is effortless to deploy, never misfires, always hits its target, keeps you protected from incoming assaults, and is available in abundance. Nobody sees it coming, ever, even though it's clearly visible.

And better than all of that? It doesn't cost anything. I know it's hard, but please resist your natural inclination to be cynical about anything promising great rewards at no cost and with zero complexity.

This stuff's going to make you rethink what you know about how the world works and a million other things you take for granted every day. Best of all, it's going to usher you onto an incredibly smooth new road that will not only accelerate your journey to competitive dominance, but also make you a better leader. I kid you not.

I can promise five things here: First, you've never in your life given a second of thought to what you're about to read. Second, you'll understand every element of it immediately. Third, you'll find ways to incorporate your newfound knowledge into your N3PS. Fourth, you'll recognize opportunities in your daily personal and business lives where deploying it will improve your effectiveness as a leader and boost your likability. And fifth, you'll wonder why the hell nobody ever told you this stuff before.

Above everything else I do, this is the stuff that ushers me into executive offices far and wide and keeps me out on the road burning gas and racking up frequent flier miles. Behold, then, as I reveal my Weapons of Mass Attraction. And for the love of all that's sacred, load up. Your arsenal can never be too full of this stuff.

Once again, it pleases me greatly to inform you that in order to show you where your new weaponry is hiding in plain sight and to serve up examples you'll use when you deploy them and share them with your people, motorcycles and motorcyclists will serve as my primary visual and aural aids. I just can't help myself.

So let's roll.

Everyone with at least one working ear knows that Harley owners—even Harley-riding cops—like our bikes loud. Nothing shocking there, right? But contrary to what you might think, the bikes aren't made that way. Pencil-pushers in Washington insist that Harleys leave the factory with muted, heavily muffled exhaust systems, and Harley-Davidson is happy to comply. And not just because they're an outstanding corporate citizen.

When buying new Harleys, most owners, yours truly very much included, buy specialized exhaust pipes to give them that throaty signature roar before we take our first ride. And then, anytime we're sitting motionless at a red light or stop sign—or if we're in a parking garage, the temple of great acoustics—we rev our engines. Hard. We're not moving, yet we're revving anyway. You've witnessed us doing this, but if by chance you haven't, you'll surely notice it now. Either way I'm sure you've never had the desire to, say, rev the family car's motor at a red light, because you know how goofy you'd look.

I'd long assumed our engine revving was a cultural thing—something we Harley riders learned from watching other Harley riders—to separate us from the rest of the bike-riding community. That's partly true, I suppose. And many is the Harley rider who'll tell you that loud pipes make a bike safer, presuming that their roar will alert nearby motorists to their presence. There's probably some truth in that, too. But one day while watching a rider *watch others watching him* at an intersection, I discovered the whole, nondebatable truth about all of this and it woke me up like a knuckle sandwich to the jaw. There, right in front of me and everyone else on the street, an uber-powerful secret weapon, long hiding in plain sight, had been revealed. And with it, my calling.

See, just as my world revolves around me, yours revolves around you. You see yourself as the center of the universe and the most important person in it. Because, to you, you are. You can't see yourself any other way. Every thought or feeling you experience in a day—even if it's specifically about another person, the loves of your life, or the problems of the world—is processed by how it impacts the center of everything, *you*. Everyone else feels the exact same way. It's who we are, it's how we've rolled since day one, and it's perfectly healthy.

Let's add some junior high–level science to back this up. One hundred percent of the human race—including every customer, potential customer, employee, and anyone else important to your business—has an ego. And because of that, we all share something in common: Just as we need food, water, and shelter to survive, we also need others to react to us and make us feel good about ourselves. Like we're important and worthy of attention. Ego boosts aren't something we want, they're something we *need*. They improve our self-esteem and are the sweet elixir of our existence. When do ego boosts not feel good? And who among us isn't hungry for more of them?

If only.

You see, most of us, especially in our increasingly digitalized, run-faster-than-you-ran-yesterday world, don't get anywhere near the ego fulfillment we need. Compounding this, the concept of a living, breathing "community," where everybody knows, speaks to, and looks out for each other, is fast disappearing and taking humanity along with it. Today, people not only fail to light up when they see us, they flat-out ignore us because we're just faces in the crowd. We're the friendly people next door that our neighbors don't know by name and the hardworking but easily replaceable employees our coworkers pass in the hall every day. We're creatures of habit who buy the exact same groceries in the same stores week after week, then use the (always screwed up) self-checkout. We're the no-status passengers shoehorned into the plane's middle seats and the noninterested targets of limitless spam. Life has rendered us nearly invisible while the business world, with its relentless drive to get us what we want, where we want it, faster than we need it—accompanied by predictably insincere "Can I help you?" and "Customer satisfaction is our goal!" drivel—renders us even more so.

(Wondering where this is going? Please stay on the line. A customer service representative will be with you momentarily.)

We're seldom more joyful than in those rare moments when someone reacts to us as if we are important, special, and worthy of being the center of attention—even if it's only for a few seconds. And it's the simple joyful feelings in those personal experiences that bring my first weapon out of hiding and into the light. Its power is revealed in the form of a question: What do we do to any source of joy in our lives?

My billion-dollar answer—which will soon be richly enhancing your business, leadership skills, and personal competitiveness—is, we return to it, *loyally*, until it fails to give us joy. Guaranteed.

We're instinctively a joy-seeking species, meaning we'll always be attracted to things and people that give it to us. Always. Give us a boost to our esteem—Ah! Joy!—then watch as we come back for more. Mark my words: We will always return to the sources of our joy. Boom! You're going to weaponize that.

Ever wonder why Facebook is so popular? I just told you. Bluntly, Facebook proves that humanity is failing. Just think about it. We're so desperate as a species for validation—to have people react to us, listen to what we have to say, give us a thumbs-up, and make us feel good about ourselves—that we're willing to get it from the false, digital world. For billions (billions!) of people, this is the *only* outlet they have in their lives to say something about their favorite subject in the world, themselves, and have others react to it in ways that boost their self-esteem. This is their community. That little dopamine rush in their brains every time somebody gives their (completely lame, "Look what I just ate!") posting a thumbs-up is precisely what they came for and why they'll habitually come back for more. "Somebody just reacted to the single most important person in the universe! Me! That feels good! I better post something again right away! Like maybe a shot of my dog doing something cute!" Don't pretend you don't know what I'm talking about.

When we Harley owners rev our engines and make some noise, it's the same thing, but in the real, analog world: We're talking to you. And what we're saying couldn't possibly be easier to understand. As we're cranking our throttles, we're yelling, in all caps, LOOK AT ME! If you don't look, we just rev louder. LOOK AT ME! Eventually you look. Everybody does. Bingo! You just gave us a thumbs-up. Dopamine squirts in our brains, we love we how that feels, and we're hungry for more. And what do we do to any source of joy in our lives? You know it. Which means we're going to rev again at the next intersection. And the one after that. All. Day. Long.

We see you checking us out from the sidewalk or out of the corners of your eyes from your awesome minivan. And we feast on this. We're proud of our bikes, but we're even more proud of ourselves for owning them—which, given their steep prices, is a worthy achievement—and helping create them. Our pride soars when you look at us on them, *because that's precisely what we want you to do.*

We don't even care if you misjudge us when you look at us—trust me, plenty of nerds and dentists on Harleys *hope* you're misjudging them as badasses—because just seeing you seeing us is giving us such a great reward. It feels glorious to be noticed and to get that ego boost, and we'll never tire of it. And guess what? Somebody is making a ton of money from this beautiful quirk of human behavior. Lots of somebodies, actually.

Harley-Davidson and its dealers around the world are making boat-loads off all those gorgeous replacement exhaust systems and the not-even-remotely-cheap engine modifications required to make them roar. They're profiting from the simple truth that nearly every one of us Harley owners wants our bike to stand out from the pack so that we can stand out from the pack—look at me! So we'll gladly pony up not just for pipes, but also for shiny parts, custom wheels, and exotic paint jobs to make that happen.

(Do you doubt the underlying thesis of what I'm saying here? If so, try this simple little experiment: The next time one of those rough, ornery-looking Harley riders who looks like one of the Sons of Anarchy *returning from a gang fight is revving next to you at a light, look him in the eye and mouth two words, "Nice bike." Then watch him light up like a Christmas tree. See? Boosts to self-esteem work for everybody, every time. Plus you get the added life lesson of feeling guilty for falsely judging someone based only on his physical appearance.)*

Oh, and speaking of standing out from the pack, have you seen any Harley-branded shirts or leather jackets lately? Of course you have. They look a little, well, garish, don't they? There's a good reason for that. If they were subtle and modest, we'd blend in, you wouldn't notice us, and we'd notice that you didn't notice us, so we'd stop buying them. *Capisce?* (More on this, later.) And when we Harley riders see others dressed in similar garb, we'll always nod our hello. Just as you do to members of your community, if you're lucky enough to know any. Ah, yes. Belonging. Boom! Another Weapon of Mass Attraction. (More on this later, too.)

When you enter a great Harley dealership and the employees seem thrilled to be there and more interested in making you feel welcome, wanted, and part of something special than overtly trying to sell you something—well, now you'll know why they're doing it. They're not just looking to sell you a new bike, *they're looking through the turns, man!* They know there's way more money to be made in helping people feel good about themselves and part of something special than in simply selling products or services.

Harley and its dealers learned that lesson the hard way, which is why they don't play to simply move product and win, they play to dominate. They know delighted people will return to the source of their joy. Just look how crowded Harley shops are on Saturdays—even in winter—as riders routinely pull in to hang out a while, inhale some coffee and donuts, catch up with the folks working there, and sniff out whatever's new. That, ladies and gentlemen of the jury, is the best illustration of the cause-and-effect power of loyalty I can imagine. It also proves my long-held belief that we're more loyal to people than we are to hardware.

Read those last ten words out loud a few times so you never forget them. Replace "hardware" with whatever you happen to sell or provide, if that makes it more appropriate for your business.

The rewards of loyalty, great as they are, don't stop there, though. Smart Harley dealership people know another secret weapon that's unleashed by giving others joy: When we're pleased by something, or someone, it's such a rare event in our daily lives that we not only return to it, we tell others about it and who's responsible for it, so they can go to that source of our joy and experience it, too. Just think about all those social media sites that cater to the people you serve or want to serve. Or a trade show crowd. And how much you'd benefit from some of those folks raving about you. And that's just for starters.

When those dealership people are delighting us and heavily peppering our discussions with Harley's differentiating language—as you will with your Must Say language—they know we'll spread the company's distinct messages of freedom, passion, rebellion, community, and lifestyle far and wide, thus bringing new customers over the threshold. It doesn't stop there, either. We'll further reward a dealership's efforts to please us by buying (expensive) T-shirts bearing their name and becoming walking billboards for them.

Boom! You're witnessing the power of Noise Cubed and Weapons of Mass Attraction in plain view and if this stuff isn't beautiful, I don't know what is. It's going to be hard to not think about this when you further refine your Must Say and Must Do directives, which is precisely why I'm sharing this with you.

So dig it: Any business—even if it's in the dullest industry imaginable—that emphasizes humanity over its products and/or services and helps its customers and employees meet needs for fulfillment and validation is going to outcompete businesses that don't. Even if those competitors are selling the exact same stuff at lower prices. Believe it. Understanding and leveraging basic drivers of human behavior—those Weapons of Mass Attraction—for competitive advantage is what can transform any me-too, also-ran into a leader or, better, a dominator. Which is precisely why you're going to incorporate this stuff into your N3PS and make it a big part of your journey to dominance.

Uh-oh. What's that rumble I hear again? The one that follows me everywhere I go, despite my best efforts to squelch it? "Sob. Sniff. We don't make and sell cool stuff like Harleys that make people happy." "Boo-hoo. Our business is boring." "Wheeze, whine. Our industry's highly regulated so we're not allowed to give away free donuts." "Pout. Fuss. Our customers only care about price!" No. Please. Stop. Going. There.

Always remember: It isn't the product or service being sold that makes the business a dominator or an also-ran. It's the people—the "they"!—behind it.

Sure, Harley-Davidson builds and markets awesome motorcycles. But so what? That's the very least they should do, right? You've already learned that every one of their major competitors is a household-named, well-capitalized behemoth that also builds and markets awesome motorcycles— many of which look similar to Harleys yet are priced way lower. But while the Hondas and Yamahas of the world tout low price and the product-first "features and benefits" of their spectacular hardware, Harley-Davidson has carved out a hugely profitable segment of the global market by focusing their most visible efforts on catering to their people. This people-first approach allows them to glean and act on very intimate knowledge about how we wish to be served, which in turn further delights us and creates legions of fiercely loyal, passionately vocal advocates for them. The same stuff would work if they were selling tax software, copy paper, or portable toilets.

So, then, my question to you isn't "Can you build a more successful business by helping everyone your business touches—employees, customers and potential customers, suppliers, resellers, investors, and the communities where you do business—feel better about themselves and meet their needs for attention and validation so that they'll become fiercely loyal, passionately vocal advocates for you?"

And my question isn't "Can you become a more successful leader—the kind of person others are drawn to, loyally follow, and come back to—by doing those same things?"

My question is "What the hell are you waiting for?"

Don't bother answering. Let's go deeper with these ever-present forces of human nature that can be leveraged, with stunning effectiveness, for competitive dominance and heightened leadership ability. There are plenty more weapons at our disposal that will find their way into your N3PS and it's helpful to learn why they're so potent.

I'm sure we can agree that no two businesses (appearances to the contrary) are exactly alike. The same, of course, goes for people. Yet despite the wide-ranging ages, ethnicities, socioeconomic backgrounds, collective complexities, life experiences, idiosyncrasies, and desires of the people you work with and the customers and other important publics you hope to please, there's one thing they all have in common with you and me: They're human. And be glad for this superobvious, hiding-in-plain-sight blast of reality because you're about to discover more about how to use it to your advantage.

The simple fact that we're all human means that we all have the same basic needs—the stuff we can't live without. You may recall these from your school days where they undoubtedly were presented as "Maslow's hierarchy of needs," named for the psychologist who fathered the creation of a simple framework to help us understand each other.

You may also recall thinking, as I always did when being taught scientific theories back in the schoolrooms of my youth, "When the hell will I ever need to use this stuff?" Well, that would be now. Abraham Maslow's about to become your pal. It would take five hundred pages here to spell out and substantiate the intricacies of his work, but for our purposes, I'll cut it down to a few paragraphs and oversimplify it (and appeal to the psychological community for kind indulgences).

Hopefully, you recall Maslow's pyramid chart that broke human needs into five distinct categories, with the most-vital-to-our-existence needs making up the largest layers at the pyramid's bottom. Even if you weren't taught this, or skipped class that day, it's simple to visualize because everyone knows what a pyramid looks like. The base layer of his pyramid holds our physiological needs for the absolute necessities of life: air, food, water, and sex. The layer above that holds our needs for shelter and safety. Generally speaking, those two bottom layers are the easiest stuff—in first-world economies, mind you—for us to attain. And the easiest things (sex, ahem, notwithstanding) for people and businesses to provide. When those basic needs that make up our foundation are met, our attention turns to the three categories above them that focus on our emotional well-being.

It's those top three categories—specifically our needs for belonging/love, esteem, and self-actualization—that are way more difficult for us to attain. Self-actualization, the pointy peak at the top of the pyramid, defines our quest for fulfillment in all facets of life and understanding of the meaning of life, making it an elusive, ever-evolving lifetime pursuit. So we're

going to leave that one alone. You and your organization are going to weaponize the other two.

Here's my rationale for their deployment: Because we all have the same
needs, we're an easy species to attract and lead, which means we can be
swayed by others. Sell cool water under a shady canopy in the desert and
parched people will be attracted to your business. Or say "Follow me to
water and shade" to those parched people and they'll follow your lead. Simple, right? You have what they need and they'll come for it or follow you to
it. And that's precisely how most businesses operate; sell people what they
need (or want) and move on. "Next!"

What nearly all of those businesses overlook, though, are those other
needs hiding in plain sight—otherwise known as my Weapons of Mass
Attraction. In and of themselves, these weapons, when deployed, will be
complete game-changers for you. They'll give you the firepower to be a
competitive dominator and to convert customers into fiercely loyal friends.
Better still, when combined with a superpowerful contagion you'll soon
know more about, they're all but indefensible and unbeatable.

I'll remind you again that no matter what you're producing, selling,
or trying to sell, no matter how and where it's sold, and no matter how
necessary—or not—what you're selling is to human existence, the basic
underlying equation never changes: Business always comes down to people buying from people. Or people being served by people. It's never more
complicated than that and it can't be. So no matter what business you're in,
there's nothing stopping you from leveraging basic human needs for competitive leverage.

Compliments of Harley riders, you've already seen what our common
need for esteem looks (and sounds) like, what we're willing to do to get it,
and the rewards that come from meeting it: joy, pride, fulfillment, and even
a sense of belonging for the rider, ringing cash registers and loyalty for
the business behind it. Great as these are, though, we're just scratching the
surface.

As we've learned together, it's tough to differentiate your business with
just your product or service in a commoditized market with me-too competitors. But you've already made great progress toward dominating those
other guys with your first stabs at your N3PS. Adding the "human" element
to your weaponry, you'll see, will hit your competitors where they least expect it. You're going to succeed with this because they know nothing about
this. Yet. Yes, they're going to buy this book eventually (he said, wistfully).

Which means you need to get a head start on them. And you're going to succeed because you'll be first to unleash the power of the world's most potent contagion. And woe to anyone who gets in on this one too late.

Before I give you the download on this weapons-grade contagion, with some virtual show-and-tell for illustration, there's something we need to be completely clear on first to ensure it doesn't get misused and turn into a massive dud for you.

Let me ask you a question: What do you think of when you hear a businessperson use the word "passion"? I bet it's not what I think of. To me, passion—what I call "the P-word"—has become one of the most improperly overused words in modern vocabulary. Hence that eye roll you just performed when you read it. As is so often the case, the business world has corrupted what can and should be something wonderful and positive into something meaningless and cliché. You don't have to look far to see what I mean: "We have a passion for ceiling tiles!" "We're passionate about medical forms processing software!" "Our passion is serving you!" Right? You see and hear this every day and it begs an obvious question each time: Do you believe it?

Passion has become such a throwaway word that people use it without giving a second of thought to how it's being received. It's the new "quality," in that everybody claims to have it and wants to tell you about it. Here's what I mean: I heard a well-known American CEO say, from the stage in front of a thousand people and in a dull voice, "We're so passionate about what we do that our employees don't say, 'Thank God it's Friday!' they say 'Thank God it's Monday so we can get back to work!'" Those thousand people simultaneously reacted the same way you just did (assuming you threw up in your mouth a little). We all know BS when we hear it.

"Oh, come on, man," I hear you saying. "What's the big deal?" The big deal is there's a problem with this well-intentioned, seemingly innocent stuff and it's an ugly one: It's wasted breath that should have been spent on something more valuable to take advantage of what may well be a one-time-only opportunity. That kind of drivel isn't weaponized passion, it's poorly used cliché. Remember what I said earlier: Nobody believes what you say about yourself, but we put a lot of weight behind what others tell us. Meaning you're not passionate about what you do unless the people you serve say you are.

That last sentence is worth repeating.

From now on, you're going to look at passion as weapons-grade artillery, as powerful as nitroglycerine. So you've got to start taking it seriously. Passion, as you're about to witness, is the contagion that makes the Weapons of Mass Attraction so instantly potent. Nothing is more easily deployed or spreads faster. Nothing in the universe is more magnetic. And there's nothing like it for smoothing the road to fulfilling human needs and making you a dominator with loyal followers. But you can't just talk about it and expect it to have impact.

As with any big-time weapon, if you're going to use it effectively, you have to commit fully to it so people can see it, hear it, believe it, remember it, and talk about it. Here, let me show you.

Let's turn the calendar back a few years and relive two noteworthy business anniversaries that showcase the unstoppable, contagious power of passion. Not forced, marketing-spin nonsense, but feel-good stuff we all long for and can spot from a mile away. Then we'll see how it enhances the impact of our Weapons of Mass Attraction. The first example you'll recognize instantly.

For the National Football League's fiftieth Super Bowl in February 2016, some seventy-one thousand rabid fans, clothed in the jerseys of their favorite teams, jammed into Levi's Stadium near San Francisco. For most, it was the fulfillment of a life's dream, so they spent obscene amounts of money on airfare, hotel rooms, game tickets, souvenirs, food, and bar tabs. They partied like rock stars and enjoyed not only American football's main event, but one of the sporting world's most aspirational experiences. Their collective roar was earsplitting (even though my beloved Packers got gypped and weren't playing). The passion of those gathered couldn't be more obvious.

An impressive gathering, yes, but peanuts when compared to motorcycling's main event, the Sturgis Motorcycle Rally, or as it's known more simply throughout the bike world, Sturgis. The rally's held the first week of August every year in the Black Hills of South Dakota, headquartered in the tiny town it's named for. And talk about aspirational experiences. You'll look a long time before finding a motorcyclist who hasn't been to Sturgis or doesn't have it on his or her bucket list.

Sturgis draws multiple hundreds of thousands of riders from around the world every year, but its recent seventy-fifth anniversary drew more than 1.15 *million* for a weeklong celebration of all things motorcycling. As with the Super Bowl, most attendees were also clothed in the jerseys of their favorite team (see: black Harley T-shirts). As amazing as Super Bowl 50 was,

Sturgis 75 made it look and sound like a chess tournament. When's the last time you were at an event that drew more than a million people?

For the uninitiated, Sturgis has grown from its humble beginnings as a weekend of motorcycle races, into motorcycling's premier event, a week-long blowout with demonstrations, seminars, historic and custom bike displays, massive vendor areas, races and stunt shows, concerts from some of the biggest names in music, photo ops at Mount Rushmore, and, of course, spectacular riding through the mythical Black Hills.

It's the kind of "Must Do" thing good friends were made for. Nights in some of the larger campgrounds, after the bikes are safely retired and the beer is flowing, are the stuff of bacchanalian legend. Think Mardi Gras or Vegas at two a.m. and you're almost in the ballpark. Some of these campground parties just don't stop. (And if that's too rowdy for you, there are plenty of other campgrounds that cater to more, shall we say, reserved crowds. No Alice Cooper or Lynyrd Skynyrd concerts. No pole dancing. You get the picture.) I've long described Sturgis as a celebration of freedom where you can pretty much do anything you want, or be anyone you want, with no fear of being judged by your neighbors. Adult Disneyland. Fun covered in fun.

For someone like me who attended his first Sturgis more than thirty years ago, the look, feel, and tone of the rally has changed, despite the fact that it's stayed pretty much the same. Back then, if one hundred thousand people showed up, it was considered a *massive* success. That's still a lot of people, but nowadays it takes more than half a million people on-site to turn heads or make the evening news.

And back then, when Harley's resurgence was just starting to gain momentum, the vast majority of the attendees were men, most of them riding the Harleys that were most popular at that time, old "hardtails" (think "chopper-esque" bikes, devoid of rear suspension—ouch—windshields, and luggage carriers, with riders' sleeping bags and gear bungeed to any part of the bike that would hold them down) or newer "softails" (bikes that maintained the beloved hardtail look, with hidden rear suspension to soften the ride). Generalizing, these were noncushy, brutishly powerful bikes ridden by hard-core guys whose bodies could tolerate the beatings that thousand-mile rides on bikes with minimal suspension could dish out. Most attendees back then, if I can pigeonhole them, would have been considered either blue-collar or the next level above, gray-collar, as Harleys had yet to gain favor beyond that niche. Probably because the company wasn't doing anything successful to make that happen.

Man, how Sturgis attendees have changed over the years. And I bet you're starting to figure out that this isn't accidental. The social spectrum couldn't possibly be any wider now, as white-collar "professionals" and even uber-rich socialites blend in, or at least try to, with the more we shall say *traditional* crowd. And women, once vastly outnumbered, are every-where. Sturgis is a spectacular, welcoming community of people who share a common passion for motorcycling. And world-class partying.

The bikes have changed, too. Massive touring models—like my Street Glide described earlier—and extensively (spelled expensively) customized bikes are the order of the day, crowding jammed streets like salmon swimming against the current. They now outnumber cruisers by a wide margin. Once comfort and luxury entered the equation at no cost to style points, the migration to touring bikes was inevitable.

And guess what? More comfortable bikes with more room to store luggage also meant more women riding to the rally as passengers each year. Many thousands of them fell in love with riding, eventually "moved up front," and bought their own bikes. Or soon will. There are so many women riding now that the novelty of it is disappearing. Women didn't just break the Harley world's glass ceiling, they blasted right through it and brought their friends with them. This, too, isn't accidental. I love it.

The influx of riders with fat wallets I just mentioned is a huge reason why Sturgis streets are thronged with one beautiful custom bike after another. There's long been an unspoken competition among Harley riders to ensure the uniqueness of their hardware (look at me!), which is why so few bikes are identical. Compared to the old days when black was the predominant bike color and there simply weren't a ton of options available to customize bikes, it's a new world now where riders are limited only by their imaginations and wallet thickness. Riders spy a million new ideas on every street and find countless reasons to upgrade to a different bike. Creativity abounds.

Think about this purely from a business sense: Hundreds of thousands of Harley disciples in the same place at the same time, socializing and having a ball. At the same time, they're being exposed to all these beautiful bikes on the street, Harley's newest models, the latest and greatest parts and accessories, along with the thousands of other gizmos the company produces and sells. And of course, enough leather clothing to cover an army. Coincidence that Harley has massive display areas to showcase its new product offerings—and offer test rides of its new bikes—and plenty of enthusiastic employees and leaders standing by to offer encouragement and know-how? Coincidence that Harley dealers in the area are open twenty-four hours during the rally, their cash registers straining to keep up?

If I'm you right now, I'm thinking, "Yeah, good for them. Whoop-dee-do. But what's this got to do with me?"

Well, plenty, actually. Let's look first at what's obvious. Reduced to its most simple terms, what you're looking at here is a group of like-minded people, in the same place at the same time, with lots of stuff to buy. That's the same description you'd use to describe a retail environment, a trade show, Internet shopping, or even most sales opportunities, right? Military types would call this a target-rich environment. Let's go deeper.

I say it's high time we pull out my good old Reality Goggles again and see how this business opportunity has been weaponized in ways you and your business can begin deploying immediately. During my virtual show-and-tell, I hope you'll be mindful to compare what you're seeing to the many opportunities you and your business have every day wherein, with some simple adjustments to your approach, you can turn common, predictable moments into memorable, pleasing experiences that fulfill basic human needs for the people you serve and hope to serve. Including, of course, your fellow employees.

Okay, then. Pull those Goggles on. Let's jump straight to an area of the rally that has the most similarity—from a commerce standpoint—to your business: The new bike demonstration area. Again, we'll take a quick look at the obvious go-to-market stuff, then zoom in a bit for a better view of the weaponry in use.

The new bike demonstration area is a vibrant, loud scene. A few huge tents cover static product displays, product literature kiosks, and refreshment areas while brand-new, sparkling-clean motorcycles are lined up outside in rows on the asphalt, fueled and waiting for interested would-be owners to take them for twelve-mile test rides through the surrounding Black Hills. The potential owners of these newest models are milling about, checking out the displays, looking for just the right hardware to fall in love with, filling out some paperwork to take test rides, and mingling with company reps. Music's cranked—think classic rock, country, maybe some old-school hip-hop thrown in—that appeals to a broad spectrum of people. There's a nice, friendly, communal vibe.

Distilled to its essence, then, it's the best-of-all-worlds scenario of company reps, new products, and potential customers in the same place at the same time and it's nothing you've not routinely witnessed in one format or another over the course of your business life. With or without the Lynyrd Skynyrd soundtrack.

Keep your Goggles snug and your mind open, because when we're taking in close-up views of what's happening, you're going to need to visualize for yourself the beyond-obvious stuff. Don't worry, I'll point it out to you and the Goggles will do the rest.

The first group of riders, their paperwork completed, are seated on the new bikes, lined up in single file, helmets cinched, and ready to be released out of the parking lot and onto the well-marked roadway for their demo rides. The *easiest* thing to do right now would be to simply give the "start your engines" command and wave riders out the exit gates one at a time and onto the road. After all, demo rides on the newest stuff is really what this is about, isn't it? That's what these folks came for.

Not so fast. Let's hit the reverse button on our Goggles and go back in time a few decades, not for nostalgia's sake but to learn a big lesson. The scene looks nearly identical to today, with new bikes lined up and ready to go, lots of people, and, more than likely, Lynyrd Skynyrd blasting from the PA (I promise that'll be the last Skynyrd reference in this chapter). A man astride a gorgeous new Electra Glide touring bike is waiting his turn to head out for his ride, soaking in the gauges, and getting a feel for the handlebars, when a company rep—who volunteered to work at the rally for the week—calls out to him from where he's standing, about six feet away, under the shade of an awning. Our rep could perform virtually any function at Harley. Let's call him an accountant.

The company rep/accountant smiles and asks our rider if he's ready to rock and roll, then slides into heavy product promotion mode—that's what he's there for—and says, "Check out that new motor, man. Torque's up almost seven percent over last year, so you'll be pushing ninety pounds to your rear wheel at 3500 rpm. You'll see! You're gonna love the new seat height, too. The bike's been lowered to twenty-eight inches to get you closer to the ground and make it easier to keep that 890-pound beast standing straight up." Our rider flashes a huge grin, says, "Cool! Thanks man!" then, once given the order to let fly, opens the throttle and disappears.

That sound blaring in your ears right now is warning bells. You're hearing them, right?

What do you suppose our rider's going to remember about the time he spent with that rep? Think he's going to tell his friends back home that finally—*finally!*—Harley's building a bike that can generate ninety pounds of torque at 3500 rpm, a 7 percent bump over previous models? Think he'll remember that seat height?

No way, José. And you know, partially at least, why: You know "Brains. Cause. Pain." Hitting this guy up with data he quite possibly couldn't understand and process, let alone remember and repeat, means our well-intentioned rep, who did precisely what he was trained to do and did it well, completely wasted his time and quite possibly blew a great opportunity to create some demand for the home team. Without even being aware of it. Hopefully our rider dug the bike and how he felt riding it—and being seen riding it—enough to buy one when he got home.

Here's something you couldn't have known. I intentionally left out an important detail. The demo rider you just watched happened to be one of many who rode to Sturgis on a competitive product. He's a happy, longtime Kawasaki owner. So not only does this mean the rep's recitation of product specs was tough for the rider to process, but this may well have been the rider's first-ever conversation with someone from Harley-Davidson. I'll say the obvious: First impressions carry a ton of weight. Not so obvious: For that brief moment when they spoke, our rep/accountant was "Mr. Harley-Davidson"—the face, voice, attitude, and mannerisms the rider will recall if and when he tells a story about his experience. Or even thinks about it.

Meanwhile, the next rider in the queue moves his or her demo bike forward a few feet and is now in front of our rep's shady spot. The scene repeats itself as it will for the rest of the day and for the duration of the rally, a nonstop parade of people on new bikes, waiting their turn to head out on the road and make some noise, listening to a litany of friendly product-speak and secret-handshake lingo. At an event as big as Sturgis this might happen thousands of times over the course of the week. Like a trade show.

Let's return to the present and see how a different kind of effort can make a huge impact. We're in roughly the same setting, with another Kawasaki-owning customer matching the same description as our demo rider of yesteryear. You and I know what he rode in on but nobody else does yet. He's sitting on a new Road Glide Ultra, soaking in the gauges, playing with the Infotainment center's touch screen, and getting a feel for the handlebars, when a company rep/accountant, barely able to conceal his excitement, bounds up to him. No shady awning for this guy.

He's standing right next to the demo rider and as close inside his personal space as a person can get without being what Jerry Seinfeld would call a "close talker." He's giving him a "bro" handshake and even some light slaps on the back, the way good friends do when they see each other. You can't miss the huge grin on his face and the excitement in his voice. So far, so good. Again, I don't believe anyone would argue that this isn't an ideal selling situation: A potential customer, brand-new product, and a company rep all within inches of each other at the same time.

With only a few seconds to work with before the rider blasts off, our rep announces, "Woo-hoo! Looking good, bro!" to the rider's obvious delight. Then he says, "Quick, give me your phone!" As our man's walking around the bike, snapping photos of the wide-grinned rider posing on what might be his next big purchase, he asks, "What are you riding now, bro?" When the rider lowers his eyes a bit and says he's on a Kawasaki Vulcan, our man says, "Oh, those are great bikes, but this one's gonna feel totally different to you, man. Hey, what's the most fun thing you've done so far this week?" As the rider is answering his question, the rep is responding excitedly, then says, "Quick! Let's get a selfie!" and the two crowd into the lens, flashing thumbs-ups and grinning like goofy kids. The phone gets shoved back into the rider's pocket and he revs his motor, then roars off as the rep hollers, "Ride safe and have fun!"

A similar scene is playing out with the next riders in line, with other reps showering them with attention and enthusiasm.

Crank your Goggles to the highest setting because you're going to see everything that just happened in a different light. And what you're going to see is Weapons of Mass Attraction. A lot of them, working separately and in tandem with each other. You're also going to see the effects of their deployment and the power of the contagion that fuels them. I'll start at the top and work down.

What happened first is superimportant even though, as you were first observing it, it may have seemed inconsequential. Remember back in the earlier example how the company rep was staying under the shade of an awning, several feet away from the rider? Seems understandable, given the monotony of the work and the sun's rays, to say nothing of the heat reflecting off the asphalt and emanating from all those revving engines. It's the same comfortable way salespeople stand behind counters and reps at trade shows stand or, even worse, sit behind booths. It might be understandable, but it's not good. In fact, it's criminally bad.

In the present-day example, the rep excitedly bounded up next to the rider, got close enough to touch him—which he did—and stayed close. This is very good, as you'll see, for lots of reasons.

Remember what we've already learned: Humans are a joy-seeking species. We're instantly drawn to things—and people—that give us some happiness. When the earlier rep didn't venture out from his shady spot toward the rider, the rider picked up on this immediately. Without thinking about it, he knew that the rep wanted to keep his distance from him and that he, therefore, wasn't worth approaching. This happens so often in our lives, we rarely notice or process it. Any passion that rep possessed likely wasn't shared by the rider. We've all seen a million fake smiles. And let's not forget the "Brains. Cause. Pain." effect of the technical lingo. That left only the hardware to impress a rider who already owns some exceptional hardware.

As will become habit with you and your employees on your road to domination, you've got to think about what you want people you come into contact with to remember and repeat. And, of course, you need to look through the turns. Think of our Kawasaki rider of yesteryear, back home at his job in Springfield, Missouri, a week after the rally. Sure he told his pals that he raised all kinds of hell out in Sturgis, had a blast, and took some new Harleys out for test rides, but did he have a "they" story to tell about his experience with Harley-Davidson? Did he have things to talk about that folks who've never been to Sturgis, let alone a Harley dealership, and even nonriders could understand? And did that rep do anything to impact that? Did our Kawasaki rider tell others about the lowered seat height and improved torque on the Harley he rode? Fat chance. Who'd give a rip? ("Oooh, tell me more about that seven percent torque improvement!" Said nobody, ever.)

Let's get back to present day: When the exuberant rep/accountant bounded up to the rider, several very powerful things happened. First and most obvious, our rider felt validated, along with a boost to his self-esteem. "This guy (Mr. Harley-Davidson) is treating me like I'm special and import- ant, so I must be." Plus, "He's slapping me on the back and we're laughing like I'm a good guy and we're pals on the same team. He's asking questions about me," and "I've even got a photo of me on the bike with this guy." The rider's wide grin is matching the rep's tooth for tooth and says he's feeling good about himself and his situation. Every element of his experience, thus far, has been good for him and for Harley-Davidson.

Look through the turns again, to another workplace somewhere in America, where our modern-day Kawasaki rider is regaling coworkers with stories of his vacation trip to Sturgis. Not only did he take demo rides on Harley's newest stuff and have a blast while doing it, but he also feels compelled to talk about it. He's even got photos to show others while telling his tales. "Here's me taking a demo ride with some dude from Harley. They're really cool." What's that worth? He printed one of the photos of himself on his dream bike, snapped by the rep, and posted it on the bulletin board in his workspace so he can be reminded of it every day. How many people will see that and ask about it, thus prompting more storytelling? That's. Just. Smart.

Those are obviously great benefits for everyone involved. What's not so obvious, though, is what I feel to be the most valuable takeaway from this and the most potent of all Weapons of Mass Attraction.

In the modern-day example, basic drivers of human behavior leap to the fore as the company rep makes the demo rider—the human being—the star of the thirty-second show. "Looking good, bro!" He's been given and gives him precedence over the product being sold, makes him feel welcome and wanted, and that's not something he's used to experiencing. The rep's not there to talk tech and product features and benefits (unless the rider speaks that language and asks for them); he's there to delight the rider and get him talking about himself. And here comes the clincher: His primary objective isn't to get the rider to buy the bike, it's to get the person to *like Harley-Davidson*. Even if he's already a customer.

Think about this, because it's huge: In a marketplace where product differentiation is difficult and it's hard to tell players apart, whom do we choose to buy from? Whom do we choose to talk about? Whom do we recommend to others? The answer is we prefer to do business with people we like. Period.

This is yet another time when you should reread those last ten words aloud a few times. Yes, it's obvious. But maybe so much so that you and the others who work with you haven't given it a second of thought. So let's do that now.

As potential customers we can all compare product specs and prices, and probably will at some point, but our comfort level and inclination to buy from a specific competitor are driven foremost by likability. "I like them." Or "They're friendly." Or "They're cool." Boom! If I like you, it greatly increases the probability that I'll want to learn more about you and dig into the specifics of what you're selling. Put it this way: If the only thing separating you from your competitors is the fact that customers and potential customers like you more than the other guys, even if it's just a tiny bit more, you win. If they don't like you? You'd better start chopping prices.

And if you're already using price as a competitive weapon? What does that tell you?

Okay, then. You want to get people to like you and your business and prefer you to look-alike competitors and you're not exactly sure how to do this, specifically. Well, thankfully there's no need for specificity when you have that incredible contagion I spoke of earlier at your disposal. You just saw it in action and watched it spread. Let's study it.

Do you know what the most magnetically attractive human trait is? I don't mean "magnetically attractive" in the Victoria's Secret model or Cary Grant sense, I mean it in the literal sense, as in a "force that pulls your body forward." The answer isn't, as most guess it to be, a smile. As you've witnessed countless times, anybody can fake a smile, just as the rep/accountant under the awning did while he was laundry-listing those product specs. Nope. The hands-down most magnetically attractive human trait is also the most potent force in the universe: It's Visible (with a capital *V*) Passion (with a capital *P*). It's fully fail-proof. And it's going to become the contagion that fuels your N3PS and your Weapons of Mass Attraction.

Visible Passion isn't easy to define in words everyone can understand, but that's okay because no definition is needed. (It's like what the Supreme Court said decades ago about pornography: We know it when we see it.) We instantly know when someone is clearly enjoying himself or herself and happily in the moment. We see it, hear it, and feel it. Because we're a joy-seeking species, we're instinctively drawn closer to this person, and the reason is simple: We want some of that joy—that passion—to rub off on us. As in, give me some of that! It's useless to resist its power, so we don't even try. The last time you were turned off by a Visibly Passionate person was never.

Like all forces of nature, there's a yin-and-yang equation with Visible Passion that you need to know about. Just as surely as you can't resist being drawn toward Visible Passion, you can't help but be repelled by an obvious lack thereof. You know you've had countless situations of the latter in your life and every time it happened, your first instinct was to distance yourself from it. The last time you responded favorably and memorably to a fake-smiling employee's "Can I help you?" question was when? The last time you approached a sales or information counter where the employee was frumpy and staring at the ground was when?

Put simply, you don't want an unhappy or uninterested person's vibe to invade you, so you'll reflexively make an evasive maneuver to escape it. You don't think about it, you just react and move away. Given a choice, nobody in the universe wants to be around unpleasant, disinterested people. We heartily and instinctively dislike people like that, don't we? But here's something that makes this situation even worse: When we see or talk to an unlikable person in a working environment, we associate that behavior with *everyone working at that person's organization*, which should tell you something. That person just became a they.

Need proof? Go to Sears (better hurry) and watch a once-great retailer, in one of the worst business declines in history, dying right in front of you. What do you think is killing Sears? Most people want to knee-jerk-blame "the Internet." Nope. Are the products Sears sells substandard? They can't be; they sell much the same stuff you can get from other sources in the same malls. Are their prices too high or is their stuff too cheap? I'm guessing it's been so long since you've been to a Sears, you don't even know. Or worse, even care. Sears has become that place in the mall where everyone turns around instead of entering. For a guy like me who grew up on Sears and was loyal to them for eons, this is sad stuff. And while I very much hate picking on them, I know what's got them in a death spiral and don't want it to happen to your business. I'm of the strong belief that their pain is self-inflicted. Learn from this.

If I asked you to visualize a Sears employee, what would you see? I see an appliance salesman, leaning against a dishwasher, staring at the floor. We've all seen this guy, haven't we? Well intentioned. An expert on appliances. Bored out of his skull. Counting the minutes until break time.

Let's say you have to go to Sears today to buy some Craftsman tools— fine products worthy of their stellar reputation. As you're bounding through the store heading toward the tool department, you walk past the appliance area where my aforementioned salesman is quietly dying. As you walk by, he sneezes or you sneeze and, for a split second, the two of you make eye contact. He takes that eye contact as "permission to approach" and begins to take a few steps toward you.

Quick! What are you thinking at this exact moment?

The answer is you're not thinking anything. Because faster than your brain can process the input it's receiving, and in about the time it takes your eyes to blink, human avoidance behavior kicks in and you step away from him instantly. You have to. Human avoidance behavior's been programmed into our species since day one and it dictates that we will instinctively and reflexively move away from anyone or anything that has the potential to give us harm or displeasure. A miserable-looking person is coming toward you and bringing his disease of unhappiness and boredom with him (along with, no doubt, a binder full of dishwasher specs with impossible-to-decipher technical language and data). You can't allow his bad vibe to infect you so you make an abrupt evasive maneuver to get away from him without a millisecond of thought. You move away from people like this all the time. We all do. Every day.

Retail, everyone recognizes, is a high-turnover business. So plenty of new Sears employees on any given day can see Mr. I Hate My Job Dishwasher Salesman absent-mindedly leaning against his wares, willing his watch to move faster. And they hear what he and his body language are saying loud and clear: "It's okay to slouch and look disinterested. If I can do it, so can you." You'd better believe this is contagious, easy-to-model behavior. So the new people start doing it, too. And so on. Which is why so many of us have chosen to not like Sears.

It's not the products or prices turning you away, it's the work culture; the "they" behind them. If they look like they don't care, it's because they don't. *Even if they do.* Who wants to be around people like that when we have other options? This demand-destroying behavior, somehow, is tolerated and permitted to spread by the same management who could make their business rock again if they chose to. Instead, they keep closing stores and reducing their footprint. In other words, they're grasping at one costly mathematical "solution" after another to improve their bottom line when they should be fixing their behavioral problem. Jobs lost. Lives ruined.

You can probably think of other businesses in your local area suffering from those same self-inflicted wounds. Been to a Kmart lately?

In sharp contrast to the dishwasher salesperson example, our programmed behavior is exactly the opposite in the presence of a person with Visible Passion: We're drawn to him or her. We want that person's happiness to become ours, even if it's just for a few seconds. So Visible Passion, then, is clearly a business rep's best opening salvo. It says, "Come to me, friend, and stay close. I'll make you feel good about yourself." That's a person you'll be drawn to, remember, and, best of all, return to. From a workplace point of view, you'd best believe that this, too, is contagious, easy-to-model behavior.

Let this sink in for a second: In a blink of an eye, less than one-third of a second, you determine whether the person in front of you is worthy of sharing your space. It sounds really unfair and judgmental, I know. But hey, that's life. If you're walking down the sidewalk and see a stranger coming toward you with his or her head down, looking unhappy or complaining on the phone, you'll immediately and without thinking create more space between the two of you (don't forget they're reacting to you, as well). And you know what? You'll never approach a person you don't know who has his or her back turned to you, unless you absolutely have to. We're human, after all. What if that person is in a lousy mood?

Need more proof? At your next trade show or trip to the mall, do this little experiment. Look at all the trade show booths, or mall kiosks, that have absolutely no energy around them. No potential customers milling about, no conversations taking place, nobody waiting in line, and nothing being sold. What's the common denominator between them? Reps in the booth who look disinterested or, worse, are staring at their phones, seated facing each other (as in, "Don't bother us, we're talking to each other"), or simply have their backs turned to you. They could be selling cures for infectious diseases but you, and everyone else, will simply walk right past them without a second thought. Now think of who's renting those spaces and paying those reps. And how unhappy they must be when they total up their receipts and ask themselves, "Why isn't this working?"

Knowing what you now know, what would you tell them?

It's important to recognize that vision isn't our only sense for determining whether someone's passion is real, forced, or nonexistent. You're probably ahead of me on this one. I bet I can predict your immediate reaction when you call a business and hear a hurried voice grunt nothing but "Please hold!" Or a memorized spiel rattled off so quickly and unenthusiastically that you can't understand it.

Yes, that person's obviously under the gun and yes, that's not a pleasant predicament. But just look through the turns, baby. That brief encounter ruined your mood, didn't it? And painted a nonflattering picture of that business in your mind. It took only a few seconds for you to decide you don't like that business. I know I'm not alone when I say that anytime I get a hurried "Please hold!" or an otherwise bored, disinterested voice when I call a business I've had no previous relationship with, my initial instinct is to hang up and move on. ("They suck!") Bad vibes we'll gladly live without and there's never a shortage of competitive businesses that may be more eager to hear from us. Who's answering your phone?

I've had people in administrative positions tell me their job, or a big part of it, is to "answer phones." That immediately tells me that whoever's managing these folks is shortsighted and sure as heck isn't looking through the turns. I'd like to suggest that answering the phone is not the job or even part of the job. Being the voice of the company—trite as that may sound—is the job. Remember what you just read a few pages back: We associate that person's behavior with everyone's behavior working at that business. And if the company wants to be liked by its customers and other important publics, it had better make darn sure that voice is always enthusiastic and pleasant. Which means your phone people have to be enthusiastic and pleasant. And you know whose job it is to make sure they feel that way. And to demand nothing less than Visible Passion from them when they're on the phone. Even if they have to fake it once in a while.

It's not hard to make Visible Passion come through and paint that picture in the minds of whoever's hearing it. You've heard it before. You know what it sounds like and the image it projects. Dominators surely know. (Just call Disney or L.L.Bean if you need a reminder.)

As great as it is, though, and as much as I get excited about it, there's something even bigger and more valuable than Visible Passion's magnetically attractive pull that you need to know about. Visible Passion is like money in the bank because it pays an invaluable dividend. You know how much I love to use the word "contagion" to describe Visible Passion and you're about to find out why.

Just watch and you'll see this. Whenever you're getting attention from a Visibly Passionate person you will, again instinctively and reflexively, start to *mimic that person*. You can't resist this; it's another thing that's been programmed into our species since day one. The happier he or she looks, the happier you'll look. Our Kawasaki-owning demo rider broke into an immediate grin upon seeing the superenthusiastic rep approaching him. He had to. We all do this and you know why: It's that joy-seeking thing we do. "He loves what he's doing and he's happy I'm here! I like the way that feels!" The grin never left the (presumably now former) Kawasaki guy the entire time they were together. It's the same grin he'll wear—and I'll bet my eyesight on it—when telling stories about his experiences with Harley people.

Objective number one for any would-be dominator is to be the most-liked business serving its market, right? That's you. When your Visible Passion is being imitated by the people you serve, you're drawing them closer to you while building a tremendous gap between you and your competitors.

If my business is selling the nozzles that squirt oil into the hundred-year-old machines that put the little plastic nibs on the ends of shoelaces—otherwise known as (forgive me) an unsexy, uncool business—you'd best believe my business is going to be the most liked, Visibly Passionate company selling those nozzles and I'm going to be crushing my competitors. Shoelace manufacturers are going to like us and how we make them feel, they're going to come back to us and they're going to talk us up at industry meetings and seek out our trade show booths. Our client contacts are going to tell their coworkers about us and make introductions to ensure continuity of our relationships with their businesses. I can't imagine tolerating anything less than this.

Here's something I bet crossed your mind. As you'd expect, investors and financial media people on-site at Sturgis would always ask me about Harley's return on investment from offering demo rides. I suppose I could've given them the ROI but, seriously, what would they do with that? Suffice to say Harley wouldn't make the investment in demos if they didn't pay off. But thinking like a dominator means you need to remember: Any conversation with people important to your business has to focus on what you want those people to remember and repeat. I'd much prefer these folks focus more on positive messaging and passion than data that doesn't tell a story without tons of supporting backup.

They'd still persist, though, as I suppose all left-brained people must do. Surely, they assumed, data must be shared with prospective customers and that data, if unfavorable, would trump the emotion being displayed. They'd say, "But Harleys cost more than most other bikes. Shouldn't this be the time and place where potential new owners learn about the differences between products and what justifies your higher prices?" That's a good question. And it deserves an equally good answer. "Nope."

I'd then explain. "Price and value aren't the same thing. The value of a Harley (just like the value of whatever you're bringing to market) doesn't lie solely in the physical hardware and on the price tag, as most people tend to believe. The value lies in what Harley owners, and those who aspire to be owners, believe and say about them and the people—the 'brand' if you will—behind them. What's the dollar value of the incredible experiences people are having here? The positive vibes they're feeling? The collective, inclusive passion? The spirit of camaraderie, fun, and being part of something truly different and special? As the experiences and stories unfold, the value of the product—the conduit to everything I just mentioned—increases.

Should product-speak, specs, and data be our priority when we're together with potential and existing customers? The kind of talk that can suck the life out of what's supposed to be a great time? Or should we just be focusing on making this a memorable, rewarding experience for them?

Of course, if potential owners want to discuss price to the penny, or product features down to the thousandth of an inch, they're going to get their answers immediately. Nobody's hiding from that. But making that stuff the thrust of the discussion or encouraging conversations about it, as most businesses do because they feel it's "expected," only leads to brain pain. That stuff's not personal, it's transactional. Sitting in the saddle of a gleaming bike, or standing next to it, while its mirrors shimmer in unison with that thumping motor, is no time for such hooey.

Yes, to answer the question you're naturally thinking, I understand that price is always on the minds of people considering buying something. Please just try to remember: Above all else, dominators want the people they serve and hope to serve to like them more than they like competitors, because they'll have to work a lot longer and harder to win them over if they don't. Harley wants demo riders to make it a priority to visit their local Harley dealers intent on joining the brotherhood and sisterhood—or "family." And you'd better believe those Harley dealers are going to be hell-bent on making these folks feel special, welcome, and wanted with a full-on display of their Visible Passion and eagerness to please when they arrive. That's got to make any discussions about price a bit easier to manage, don't you think?

And here's one more thing about Visible Passion you should know, using our present-day rep/accountant as our example. I'll again remind you that because that rep is unleashing those Weapons of Mass Attraction and rewarding potential customers—many of whom are having their first interactions with a Harley employee—and those potential customers are mimicking his Visible Passion, all of those positive feelings those people are having are being attributed to *all* Harley employees. This is where "they" memories and stories come from. The stories these potential customers will tell, and the positive beliefs they have about Harley, may be based entirely on their brief encounter with just one person. (Who's answering your phone?)

To ignore that is to ignore the reality behind what makes people tick.

We're covering a lot of ground here, but before we move on, let me ask you to personalize our exploration into Weapons of Mass Attraction and their powerful contagion, Visible Passion, as this stuff should make you—and, certainly all leaders—pause a bit for self-reflection. And, at the very least, ask yourself obvious questions like "How do my important people react when they see me? How do I carry myself? What do my people say about me? Or simply hear my name?" I hope you're thinking about this right now because it's going to play a huge role in determining how successful your journey to domination will become. Take this stuff as personal, because it is.

A quick story to illustrate my point: I was once called in to provide consultation to the newly minted CEO of a recreational equipment company we all know that was suffering from underperformance, poorly executed reorgs, and bad morale. He sought my advice on how he could communicate his vision as the new leader to his troops and gain their buy-in for improvement initiatives. Our work together started earlier than planned.

As we rode up the elevator from the lobby to his office, I couldn't help but notice how, as more employees got on at each floor, the new CEO just stood at the back and stared at the ground—the typical elevator posture you've seen a million times. (Remember, we judge and react instinctively and in the blink of an eye.) When we got off and walked to his office, I had to tell him the truth: "I hate to say this, but in the minute or so it took to ride up six floors, you turned some of your people off and gave them unpleasant first impressions of their new leader." And the gut punch: "They're going to remember this and talk about it with others."

As I explained why, he understood immediately that he was going to need to change his personal style and be a lot more attentive to it. He understood that if he simply made it a habit to greet everyone with Visible Passion and friendly hellos, they'd get a positive read on the new guy that they'd remember and, of course, tell others about. And they'd mimic his behavior. Who would you rather have as your new leader? Some dullard who can't be bothered by your presence or someone who's happy to see you, chat you up a bit, and invite you to stop by and say hello? Whose meeting would you rather attend? Whose behavior would you want your fellow employees to emulate?

The new CEO said, "Wow, I never would've thought about any of this if you hadn't pointed it out." Would you? It's so simple and obvious that it's easy to overlook. To this day, it troubles me how so many leaders, without thinking about it or intending to, stride the hallways and shop floors of their companies as if they're lords or kings, then eat their lunch alone or only with others from top brass, sending out a signal to nonleaders that says, "You're not important enough to sit here, let alone speak to me." They then wonder why they're having a hard time connecting with their people and why their people aren't comfortable enough to bring forward ideas and concerns. How sad. It goes back to what I said before about leaders who wish to be known as "Mister" instead of their first name.

I know you can see how these negatives can quickly be turned around, with next to no effort, and yield lasting benefits. "Hey! You'll never guess who I had lunch with today," said a grinning junior-level employee to others in her work group. "What a great guy." Boom!

Here's something else leaders need to know: Remember how our rep/ accountant excitedly bounded from one rider to the next instead of positioning himself in the shade to avoid the sun? Well, he's passionately sharing space with customers and potential customers for another huge reason that goes beyond the benefits I've already explained and, quite possibly, answers a question bouncing around in your brain. He's doing it for the same reason the counter staff at Chick-fil-A beams as you approach the counter: It's required by his employer. Meaning it's also the behavior enthusiastically modeled by leaders, as in "This is what we do here." Otherwise known as the stuff of dominators' Must Do lists. If you're going to be a dominator, you have to hold yourself and your people accountable. "If you're not willing to do what the rest of us are doing, you're not going to work here." This. Isn't. Difficult.

Which means, leaders, it's important to recognize that you can't ask people to do what you're not doing, or willing to do, yourself. Because it won't get done to your liking. I've learned over time that it's belittling and dehumanizing to simply tell people what to do—"Come on, gang! Be Visibly Passionate!"—and expect them to do it with any measure of pride. You really hate being told what to do and so does everyone else. The net result of this, I've also learned, is we do what the boss tells us to do *only when the boss is looking*. Otherwise we do what the boss *does* and model his or her behavior. Simple. So don't just demand adherence to marching orders, because it won't work. Be Visibly Passionate, model the behavior you want imitated, and give boosts to your people's self-esteem and sense of belonging along the way. They'll follow.

Beyond your soon-to-be ever-evident Visible Passion, here are a few more pointers anyone can put to immediate use, like, say, in your N3PS Must Dos and Must Says, and in your daily interactions with your people, to unleash the power of Weapons of Mass Attraction in and outside your business.

This one comes compliments of a great, instantly remembered line I heard from a terrific consultant/speaker I had the pleasure to meet, Christopher Barrat, from the United Kingdom. He said that when it comes to making a great first impression and quickly establishing lasting impact with someone, "Be interested, not interesting." Meaning: Foremost, be inquisitive and attentive to the person you're with, rather than talking about yourself, your business, and your products. You'll never fall out of favor if you ask people questions about their very favorite person in the world, themselves, and react enthusiastically to their responses. "Oh man, that's awesome! Tell me more!" This will also save you a lot of discomfort when you're at functions, don't know anybody, and need to make small talk. Or when you're meeting employees for the first time in the elevator or company lunchroom.

A simple rule: The faster you get a person talking about himself or herself, the faster that person will start to like you. So it's important in one-on-one or small-group situations, especially with people you're meeting for the first time, to avoid asking "closed" questions that can be answered with just one word and will kill a conversation. Your objective is to make them feel your attentiveness and start talking.

You'll find that the easiest way to do that is to ask what are called "open" questions, which force the responder to offer details. A closed question would be "Do you own a motorcycle?" An open question would be "What are your favorite things to do on weekends?" Or, my personal favorite for establishing solid rapport with those working under you, "If you were made boss (or CEO, president, etc.) for the day and you had a magic wand that would instantly fix any problem we're having here at work, what would you point it at and why?" Not only do open questions get people talking, but they're also an easy way for you to uncover what people are really thinking but may not feel comfortable enough to share. You'll be amazed by what you hear and they'll be delighted you asked, listened, and reacted.

There are few questions you can ask someone that will make them feel more important than one that sounds like this: "What could we do better?" Or "What would you like to see us improve on for next time?" This can be asked at almost any time during a conversation with a customer, employee, or other valued public—like when she's finished a product demo, attended an event, or finished placing a phone order—and always results in making the person feel important, while at the same time adding validity to your messages that says, "We care." "We listen." "You're important to us." You'll also notice that people who are naturally soft-spoken or hesitant to complain, point out problems, or offer feedback will be way more likely to speak up if asked to do so in a personal, inquisitive way.

Any opportunity to boost the self-esteem of someone who's important to you should be seized upon. How easy, to say nothing of valuable, is it for any Harley rep in the demo area to greet returning riders with a little boost to their egos? "You looked great out there, bro!" Any genuine compliment, delivered with Visible Passion, is going to be well received and remembered. "I overheard you talking to that customer and could tell she was really impressed with your enthusiasm. Well I am, too! Awesome job!" said the boss who's now seen as a "great guy" by the junior-level person he said it to.

Want a gut punch? Ask your fellow employees or folks working under you, "When was the last time somebody here offered you an unexpected compliment or praised you for your performance?" When's the last time somebody did that for you?

And here's a white-hot tip: In any face-to-face situation, always make sure to have a pen and notepad handy so you can write down responses to the questions you ask. See it in your mind: If someone asked you a question, then, as you started to answer, whipped out a notebook, and enthusiastically (key word) started writing your responses down, there's no way you wouldn't notice that: "She's clearly listening and what I'm saying is so good, she has to write it down. Yay me!"

Write stuff down even if you're writing it for the ninety-first time and just watch: The more you keep writing, the more your important publics will keep talking. That's an old trick anyone with a journalism degree knows by heart, because it works every time. Can you think of an easier way to get market intel and delight people at the same time? Think back to my dealings with Mr. Hotel and how I felt when I got a survey in the mail after I stayed at one of his properties. Any of his staffers could have simply asked me a few questions, given me a little joy, and created a positive, memorable moment.

Here's something I always say to sales organizations, especially in the B2B arena, where folks tend to believe that the stuff I've been sharing here—at first blush—doesn't apply to them, is somehow below them, or their customer contacts aren't going to notice or care about it: "If you don't know your clients' hobbies, favorite teams, what they love and hate about their jobs, and what their families are up to, you don't know them, and you don't have a personal relationship with them. So they're poachable." Then I say, "You don't want them to think of you as someone they have a business relationship with, you want them to think of you as a friend, so treat them like one."

And if that doesn't convince them, I simply tell them an absolute truism of business that perhaps they've forgotten: If you have to compete on price, it's because you don't know your customers and they don't know you.

Easy way to get a B2B client to love you? Write a letter to her boss, complimenting her and saying how much you've enjoyed working with her, how much you've come to respect her, what a rare treat it is to work for such a thoughtful, committed person, and what a great asset she is to the boss's company. When a copy of the letter shows up on your client's desk bearing an "Atta girl!" over the boss's signature, you're golden. Sure, it's an obvious ploy to get your client a pat on the back, a self-esteem boost, and some joy. You'll not hear any complaints about it.

Remember way back in our earliest Reality Goggles examples, the guy who fixed the machines that bend coat hangers and how he shopped around for replacement parts? Just think how he'd react if, upon calling a supplier, the voice on the phone said, "Great to hear from you, Phil! Shouldn't you be out fishing with your grandkids today?" You know darn well he's going to enjoy a brief conversation about that because it feels good for him to be remembered, thus important, and talk about himself.

How did the customer service rep on the phone know that Phil has six grandkids he loves to take fishing, is a die-hard Dodgers fan, worked at the same business for twenty-three years, and rebuilds classic cars in his spare time? It came up on her screen as soon as she typed in his name at the start of their conversation. Because the leader of the company insisted that any and all customer intel gleaned by field sales staff finds its way to the company's database and is instantly available so there's plenty of stuff available to start personalized discussions with customers and delight them. You see why.

While I'm on the subject, customer intel—like what we know about Phil—can be extremely useful in the "surprise and delight" category. A fishing lure with a hand-signed note packed on top of the parts he just ordered isn't something he'd likely forget. Or a Hot Wheels model of a '57 Chevy. Do this a few times each year and customers aren't going to forget you. Or send a memento randomly, without attaching it to an order, along with a note saying, "Saw this and thought of you." That's what friends do. Boom!

Think of all the money wasted on ads you've seen from financial services firms, banks, and other businesses that routinely say "We care" or "We listen" but completely failed to connect with you. Now think of how memorable and valuable it is to actually know somebody is listening to you and cares about you. It'd be tough to not notice the effort. The same goes for a business sending you something personalized—not some tacky holiday card with the company name rubber-stamped where a written note should be—that made it clear that they know a lot about what's important to you and appreciate doing business with you. And if that's all it takes to get that person to like you a little more than your competitors? Boom!

Let's shift gears again and turn our attention to meeting your important public's mutual needs for belonging, as this presents some obvious and not-so-obvious benefits to those who weaponize it. Belonging is another need we all share, yet we typically don't think about it. For most of us, close personal connections—family, friends, faith community—are taken for granted. But don't let that fool you into thinking you can overlook our human need for belonging at your business, where, properly managed and executed, it can pay extraordinary rewards. Emphasis on "properly managed and executed."

As with everything involved in meeting needs, you've seen plenty of misfires in this area, such as businesses creating "loyalty programs" and "membership clubs" as ways to stay close with their customers and reward their buying behavior. While it's hard to find fault with rewarding frequent buyers with discounts—anything that successfully promotes repeat purchasing is a good thing—I'd be hesitant to say programs like this, in any way, meet anyone's needs for belonging. Nor do they reflect true loyalty.

For example, I participate in several of my local grocery stores' rewards programs and I bet you do, too. But I don't consider myself a member of anything, or feel like I belong to anything, as a result. That's way too much of a stretch. And I'm not loyal to any of them in particular, since I usually just pick the most convenient choice when needed. I'm also a Sam's Club member, but I haven't been invited to any club meetings, if you know what I mean, and I don't feel a sense of belonging. They wouldn't miss me if I went AWOL and I wouldn't miss them if they disappeared. Ditto those grocery store programs.

To find businesses successfully weaponizing belonging, we have to look pretty far, because there aren't as many as there should be. That's too bad. But good for you, from a competitive standpoint. Some businesses— like REI, The Chive, and my favorite motorcycle company—have fostered a great sense of belonging for their customers and members through social activities and owners' clubs, and they've done it masterfully. Which means they continuously put effort into bringing people together in ways that are desirable, aspirational, exclusive, and distinct to their brands.

REI, the outfitter, doesn't just sell outdoor adventure merchandise. It regularly puts on how-to clinics to train people how to get involved in new adventure sports, and they sponsor outings and even global excursions to keep people climbing, biking, paddling, hiking, skiing, snowboarding, fly fishing, and camping. Their stores are always the gathering points. And that's just for starters. Think of all the new friendships they've created over the years by bringing like-minded people together. If they simply sold product, as most sporting equipment businesses do, they'd likely enjoy nowhere near the success they have now. They might not even exist.

Yes, REI is a member-owned co-op. Yes, you can buy a lifetime membership (twenty dollars) that entitles you to a yearly dividend—a rebate based on how much you spent over the year. But no, they're not an impersonal "loyalty" club. They know the value of emphasizing the human side of their business by bringing people together. The sense of belonging they provide to those who want and need it is a tremendous differentiator for them. It's smart business, especially in the digital age, when we can just buy whatever outdoor equipment we need from whoever's willing to sell it to us at the lowest price.

Ditto Harley with its Harley Owners Group. While global in scope, with well over a million dues-paying members, H.O.G. is a hometown organization for owners of Harley-Davidson motorcycles, sponsored by local dealerships. Oversimplified, H.O.G. members are welcome to attend member-organized club functions, activities, parties, and rides—and any combination thereof—as often as weekly. There's always something planned and the sponsoring dealership is typically the gathering place where it all happens.

It's not hard to imagine the monetary benefits of customers returning to their dealership a few times each month and dealers giving their customers more excuses to get out and ride. But H.O.G. does so much more than that. Because of the gatherings, dealership employees develop even stronger personal relationships—friendships—with those they serve while local riders meet tons of new people to ride, socialize, and, best of all, becomes friends with. Taking it further, H.O.G. members proudly identify themselves with H.O.G.-branded clothing and patches bearing the name of their local chapter. You've seen this. It's a win-win for everyone involved. How could it not be? Anything that gets people out of the digital world and into the real world is a good thing indeed.

Speaking of which, I always mention The Chive when I speak with businesses that are entirely Web-based and don't believe there's a way for them to have real, physical, meaningful relationships with those they serve and to fulfill basic human needs to engender loyalty. The folks at The Chive have successfully lifted the digital veil and made a virtual business a human business. Bravo.

The Chive, if you're unfamiliar, is a global, Web-based social community. Their site and app are continuously updated throughout the day with humor, offbeat news items, hundreds of member-submitted photos, and, oddly enough, opportunities for members to get involved in or donate to very personalized charitable causes. My description's not doing them justice, so the best way to describe them, actually, is to just refer you to their website, theCHIVE.com.

Yes, there's no shortage of websites offering humorous videos, photos of pretty girls, and cats being cats, along with offbeat takes on current events. But most stop there. There's no relationship or sense of belonging when the content is available to anyone and everyone. Which is why The Chive stands out. They make their virtual community a living, breathing life force by bringing people together. They've weaponized "belonging" and pulled it off beautifully.

Chive gatherings, extensively promoted on their site and app, are essentially cocktail parties and meet-ups that most Chive members will never attend. That's not the point. We see coverage of their events on their website and there's an aspirational, even vicarious, quality to them. We know we can attend if there's one held near us, meet the people behind the site, hang out with other fans, and party our brains out. And, of course, buy tons of Chive merchandise and even drink Chive beer while we're there.

Next time you're stuck in freeway traffic, do what I do and look for KCCO bumper stickers on cars. Chive followers know that stands for "Keep Calm and Chive On." I see them all the time, just like I see people, mostly young professionals and members of the military, wearing Chive shirts or shirts bearing images of The Chive's trademark muse, Bill Murray (yes, that Bill Murray). The stuff just works. They make money—I have to believe tons of it—not just by giving people the kinds of reliably good "product" via their constant website/app updates that attract eyeballs and national advertisers, but through their popular, branded merchandise. The site always features photos of deployed military people holding Chive flags while on duty—like in fighter jets or on battleships. Ditto firefighters and first responders. That's just cool. Anyone wearing Chive gear has to feel a sense of belonging to something pretty special when they see that.

Among all the amusement it provides every day and the millions of dollars it raises for people in need, The Chive gives its members a sense of belonging to something. When two strangers in Chive shirts pass on the street, there's that "'Sup man?" nod or hello of acknowledgment, like the Harley wave. Same goes for whenever two cars with KCCO stickers pass on the freeway. Or when Chive celebrates the success stories behind the piles of money they've raised from members—often in less than a day—to help an injured vet or a child with special needs. That, too, is just cool. "I'm part of that. I helped that person. Nobody else is doing this."

There's no reason why your business can't do something similar, regardless of your size or scale. Any time you bring people together—your employees and your customers—you're all bound to benefit. But it's important to recognize that this stuff that businesses like REI, The Chive, and Harley do so well doesn't just happen. It's also important to recognize that weaponizing "belonging" (or its sisters "community" and "family") for competitive advantage this way can get expensive. The reason for this isn't just the costs inherent in running clubs and hosting activities. It lies more in the fact that if you're using them as a cornerstone of your positioning and having success with it, you have to not only continue to do this stuff well, but you have to constantly improve upon it. And you absolutely can't back out once you start because the tide can turn on you in a hurry. Here's a hero-to-zero story to prove it.

You may recall that Saturn Corporation did an excellent job of creating a sense of belonging among their customers when they first launched, positioning themselves as a "different kind of car company," running ads that encouraged their customers to wave to each other, à la motorcyclists, hosting enormous "homecoming" events at their factory, and offering free car washes along with coffee and donut socials in dealerships Saturday mornings. I loved this, the buzz and sense of community it created, and, most of all, the shock wave it sent through the car industry. I spoke with and shared ideas with Saturn's CEO and his leadership team on several occasions in their formative years and their Visible Passion was genuine and refreshing.

Owners of a specific car brand waving to each other on the street? Score! Those same owners driving thousands of miles to party at the factory where their cars were built and meet the folks who built them? *Olé!* Those same owners making those Saturday morning car washes and donut socials part of their weekly routine and choosing to hang out with car salespeople? That's just unbelievable. Imagine hanging out at your car dealership this Saturday just for fun. Saturn was just plain fascinating to watch.

Too bad it didn't last. Because when parent company General Motors (and its old-school culture that seemed to resent the new upstart) put the heat on Saturn to generate more profit by reducing costs, Saturn elected to rein in its subsidizing of dealer expenses for those weekly events and socials. Many dealers naturally assumed that if headquarters didn't see these social events as worthy of investment, they shouldn't, either. And just like that, the social side of Saturn, and the fun sense of belonging and community it had nurtured—to say nothing of the great intel the company and dealership salespeople gained from customers and those wonderful company/ customer friendships—started fading fast. When it disappeared, Saturn was another car company competing against other car companies. They'd lost their wow factor and their humanity and, with those, their reason to exist. And now they're gone. How could something that started so well go so horribly wrong? You know why.

I told this story to a Harley dealer in Indiana who, during the economic implosion of 2008, said he was dialing back on his customer events because people weren't spending money. At first blush, his thinking made perfect sense. But he got religion and came to understand that if he stopped giving people reasons to come to his dealership, even if they weren't in an immediate position to buy, they might not ever show up when the market improved. And what kind of message would he send his loyal customers by denying them the fun they'd come to expect from him and his team at his shop? And the friendships they'd built? You have to stay the course and remember my mantra: Never underestimate the power of a free donut.

All of this is not to say that fostering a sense of belonging requires sponsoring expensive clubs and social events, effective as they can be and fun as they can be to create. Far from it. The simple act of reacting positively to repeat customers—like Phil the parts-buying fisherman/Dodgers fan—over time and lavishing them with attention should do the trick. As would calling them on their birthdays or out of the blue for "How can we serve you better?" checkups. You get the point. Giving people what others aren't, consistently and over time, simple as it sounds, is always going to be the difference maker between also-rans and dominators. I know you and your people can create some memorable ways to do this.

Three quick small business examples to inspire you: I know of an equipment rental company whose shops have lounge areas with large-screen TVs, free snacks and drinks, and comfortable places for construction workers to hang out on their way to or from work. It's like a clubhouse. They also haul massive grills out to construction sites and cook up surprise lunches for the workers there. Everybody gets to know everybody. And we do business with people we like. That's just smart business.

I know of a real estate firm that rents out a local movie theater at least once per quarter, and every month during summer, and hosts family movie nights for clients and friends of clients. Families get to enjoy a movie with snacks completely free of charge and, of course, there's plenty of schmooze time with agents. This is nowhere near as expensive as I'd thought it would be, based on what it costs to see a movie these days. That's also smart business.

I know of a parts machining company that has photos of its customers posing with employees on the shop floor, lining the main hallway of its headquarters building. Under each photo is a brief description of what the customer's company does and how the machining company helps them do it. The best part? Each photo is autographed by the customer. Each time customers are on-site, they get a kick out of seeing themselves on the "wall of fame" while those descriptions not only remind company employees that what they do every day is important, but also help them better understand their customers' businesses. And, of course, recognize them when they're on-site. These things are simple to create. And how much do eight-by-ten photo frames cost? A few bucks each. Smart.

The best part of these three examples, to me, is knowing that each was an employee idea.

Speaking of employees, I'd like to focus now on how beneficial it's going to be for your business's adoption of your N3PS initiatives when you do a better job of meeting your people's collective need for belonging. I know you're already thinking of how you'll be offering them boosts to their esteem and constant exposure to your contagious Visible Passion, but meeting your people's needs for belonging becomes paramount when you think about how tough it's become not only to energize employees, but to attract and retain them.

Nearly every business I've worked with has cited turnover as one of their most pressing, time-consuming, and expensive problems and the song is nearly always the same: "We have a hard time attracting good people. We train them. We invest in them. They leave. We start over. The cycle begins again." Ka-ching!

This should get your attention and, hopefully, make you scratch your head a bit: Almost every time I ask a company leader who's battling turnover problems, "Why do your employees leave?" I am told, "Same reason as always—to get more money." No surprise there. But do you know what that is? It's a BS excuse and a shield to hide behind. I don't buy it and you shouldn't, either. In the majority of instances, the accountability for voluntary turnover shouldn't reside with departing employees. Business leaders need to step up, take responsibility for this, and change the way they look at their people.

Based on my discussions with workers at every level, in companies of every size and scope, I've developed a theory about turnover that I'll not back down from: People who leave their employer typically do so because they have no compelling reasons to stay.

I'm not talking about higher-ups who get lured away by massive pay bumps, I'm talking about average workers. They leave because nobody makes them feel important, valuable, special, part of something good. Nobody's looking out for them, advocating for them, helping them grow. They certainly don't feel like they're part of a family, or community, or even wanted. And even though they have no idea where their working lives will ultimately lead them, or if there's a clear path to promotions and higher positions, they're sure that nobody at their current place of employment is doing anything positive to help them find out. So they keep switching employers, jumping from job to job, hoping fatter paychecks will act as salve on their wounds as they wait for someone to make them feel important and give them the comfort and security that comes from belonging. Honk if you know what I'm talking about.

Here's an obvious workplace problem that presents an equally obvious solution: As members of the working class, one of the most disappointing discoveries we've all made—or will make this very minute—is the fact that nobody in our places of employment is looking out for us. This is a particularly painful discovery for young employees, as they're used to having someone (spelled "parents" and "teachers") looking out for them, advocating for them, cheering them on, and brushing off their boo-boos.

It always hurts to discover that nobody—like some mythical HR staffer—is secretly planning your career for you, creating your path to scheduled promotions and raises, and wondering what they can do to make your work life run more smoothly for you. No wonder, then, so many good employees bail out and look for this stuff somewhere else. Quite possibly over and over for the rest of their career. You've seen the "millennials will change employers seven times before they're forty" stories on this. It's nightmarish.

If I'm you, I'm all over this. First things first, we have to identify the real problem. So here it is: Knowing what you now know about our never-ending needs for esteem and the rewards that come when we encourage our most important publics to talk about their favorite subject, themselves, how often do you think the vast majority of working people have an opportunity to discuss themselves, their plans, challenges, and dreams with the people they view as the greatest influencers in their work lives, their bosses? In large businesses, this may never happen. Ever.

It's senseless but the only time most employed people will actually have a personal discussion (if you can call it that) with their boss is during an annual performance review. And reviews are almost always done in an atmosphere of nervousness, anxiety, and a strong sense of "let's get this over with as quickly as we can." Who doesn't know how uncomfortable this can be? I've run into plenty of business leaders who consider the time and expenses required to maintain their facilities and equipment as standard costs of doing business, yet bristle at the thought of investing time in their people. That's just wrong.

I have to believe it's near impossible to foster workplace loyalty among people who don't have personal discussions with their bosses and who don't feel necessary and important. How willing would you be to follow someone you felt didn't know you and made little if any effort to? How much extra work, or different work—like, say, getting involved with repositioning and N3PS efforts—would you be willing to take on in that environment?

I know what you're thinking and, yes, you can mandate that personal discussions with employees are part of your leadership's responsibilities, regardless of how many employees you have and how busy everyone is. And, yes, you can mandate that your leaders make obvious efforts to meet their people's needs for esteem and belonging. This can only happen, of course, when you're having those kinds of discussions with your fellow leaders. They won't do this stuff if you're not.

Here. Try this. It's an easy way to take advantage of something you're probably already doing. Instead of asking obvious performance review questions like "Where do you see yourself in five years?" (ugh) and "What were your major accomplishments this year?" (ditto; you're the boss, dammit, you should already know that) make it more personal and ask the kinds of questions your people want to be asked, such as, "Which of your accomplishments here are you most proud of? Where do you want to go with your life? What's your dream? What's it going to take to make that happen? And how can I/we help make that happen for you here?"

Now you're going to find out exactly what your people are made of and you're going to be surprised by what you hear. And for the love of all that's holy and righteous, you're going to react very positively to what they're saying and write their answers down. And keep on writing. Say, "Let's create a plan to make that happen. What do you think it's going to take and what's our first move?" They'll tell you what they want—promotions, raises, more responsibility, more say in initiatives, more freedom—and you can, based on their work performance, tell them what you expect from them—additional training, more vocal participation in meetings, more volunteering, more mentoring—to increase the likelihood that they'll get it. One hand washes the other. And that's the key element here: "We're going to do this together."

Then schedule brief updates and progress reports with your people so you can continue these conversations and watch how they don't run for the exits. Always make it a point to ask about family, home life, and outside interests. You can't know too much. Show them you're listening and reacting. When they see you taking a serious interest in them, and helping them devise plans to get ahead and improve their lives, you're golden. And when they feel the sonic blasts of your Visible Passion, and experience the accompanying ego boosts and validation from your Weapons of Mass Attraction, you're bulletproof. Your employees will encourage their friends to work for you, and your company will become known as a great place to work.

I believe that convincing employees to focus their energy on bringing your N3PS to life and meeting unfulfilled human needs for those you collectively serve becomes a much easier task if your employees feel that their needs are being met and that you want them to be with you for the long haul. You don't want hired hands, you want hired hearts and brains. Sounds corny, I know, but who'd want it any other way?

As I've said before, every association people have with a business is a direct reflection of that business's culture. Think how hard it can get for a business to delight its customers and other important publics by meeting their unmet human needs if it's not doing the same for its employees. Employees who feel wanted and part of something special and share a sense of belonging are naturally going to be more inclined to adhere to N3PS directives and follow their leaders.

That's the best segue I can imagine to lead into the next chapter, where you're going to learn how to get your fellow leaders and employees involved in enhancing your N3PS and gain their support and active involvement in bringing it to life. And here's hoping you'll tell them what you know about Weapons of Mass Attraction so that, together, you can discuss specific ways to deploy them, inside and outside of your business. Nothing shakes things up more on the road to competitive dominance and fierce loyalty than dropping some bombs.

THIRTEEN

Grab Your Helmet (and Cape) and Rally the Troops. It's Time to Fly.

"Anybody can jump a motorcycle. The trouble begins when you try to land it."

—Evel Knievel

I'm sure you remember the guy with that impossibly great name from back in the late 1960s and early '70s, when he was one of the most beloved super-stars in the galaxy. He's been name-dropped a couple of times already on these pages and I'm sure the name at least rings a bell with you (then again, I know fifty-year-olds who can't name all four Beatles, so maybe not). I quoted him here because I can't imagine more appropriate words to launch the next—and most critical—phase of your journey.

If you're too young or can barely place the name, well, man, I feel sorry for you because you really missed something. So let me attempt to explain who Evel was, why he's so important to millions like me, and what made him so extraordinary. I say "attempt," because Evel was comparable to no one and what he did to earn his glory was startling in ways that had never been seen before. It's a bummer that in our always-on digital world, those four words, *"never been seen before,"* don't carry as much currency as they once did. But back then? I hate to say it, but you really had to be there.

Humor me and my fond reminiscence, though. In a nutshell, Evel was the bravest—I guess that's the right word; mothers everywhere used other ones—showman who ever lived. He was the embodiment of the word "daredevil" and a camera-attracting fireball with a supernatural talent for making us feel ecstatic, nervous, and horrified in the same breath. Aboard a red-white-and-blue, star-spangled Harley-Davidson, with matching helmet, jumpsuit, and superhero cape (why not?), he did unthinkably dangerous stunts that remain among history's most hyped and widely seen. Should jumping a motorcycle over, say, fourteen end-to-end Greyhound buses, with nothing other than that caped jumpsuit and helmet for protection, seem thinkable to you, let me assure you that in the days before computers, let alone YouTube, it was anything but.

Back when most of us had only six or seven TV channels to choose from, if you can remember or imagine such horror, Evel plied his insane trade and built his legend in heavily promoted prime-time network specials, with the world watching. My pals and I were swallowed so deeply by the rapid-fire hype surrounding each special that nuns at our grade school would threaten to tell our parents to bar us from watching them as a means to keep us in line. It worked.

Picture this: During the rise of his career, live and barely in color, Evel would pull a packed stadium audience and millions of others in our living rooms to our feet doing hundred-yard wheelies (never mind that most people had never seen anyone casually riding a motorcycle with its front wheel in the air before). As if that feat weren't eye-popping enough, he'd grab an American flag, hold it high over his head with his left hand, and do a one-armed, hundred-yard wheelie with his right while the flag snapped in the wind. Unbelievable! Difficulty on a scale of 1–10? Somewhere around 60.

All the while and amid all this pomp, our eyes couldn't avoid the other stars of the show: the trucks, buses, or other crazy obstacles he was about to jump and the launch and landing ramps bookending them. I know I'm not alone when I say those ramps remain seared in my memory bank as the most dangerously cobbled-together-looking things I could possibly imagine. They reeked of disaster. They were supposed to.

After the wheelies and some painfully long commercials, it would be time for the main event. Everyone's pulse would elevate as Evel raced up to his runway's starting line, pointed his bike toward the launch ramp and those body-maiming obstacles, killed his motor, bowed his head, and . . . wait. Is he scared? The silence was beyond torture. And, more to the point, great showbiz. A breathless (they were always breathless) TV announcer would run up and ask him if he was having second thoughts and Evel would just shrug him off, grinning and nodding at the camera, oozing bravery in those carefully orchestrated extreme close-ups. Then he'd kick-start his bike, slam it into gear, and roar at full speed toward the launch ramp with the announcer screaming, "Here he goes!" And at the exact point of no return where your eyes couldn't widen any further . . . he'd make a sharp detour around the ramp like he'd chickened out. Argh! A classic showman's tease that made our already swarming stomach butterflies start double-timing it.

Finally, when we'd had all the anxious moments we could stand, he'd wheelie back to his starting point (who wouldn't?), turn around, blast down the straightaway, hit the ramp, and launch himself into glory as the world collectively gulped and flashbulbs lit up the sky. He was flying. Fly-ing. On a motorcycle. We were going crazy.

Kids like me couldn't get enough of this stuff. We built makeshift ramps to jump our "customized" bicycles on the sidewalks in front of our homes, daring each other to fly higher and farther and, often enough, straight to emergency rooms. Because so many of us wanted to be like him, he did for sales of minibikes and entry-level motorcycles what the Beatles did for guitars and bad haircuts. My Evel lunchbox? Should've held onto it.

But let's be honest. The thing made Evel Evel, gave him household-name status, and caused the world to stop so we could jam around our TVs with nervous tummies was the uncomfortable truth that after launching himself sky-high and flying great distances over dangerous, nonforgiving obstacles, he, uh, well, didn't always land his jumps safely. Or at all. And when that happened, he didn't just lose control, slide into some hay bales, pop up, and wave, red-faced, to polite applause. No, Evel bounced off his landing ramps—or missed them completely—and slammed onto the unforgiving asphalt, mangling himself so horrifically that the world simultaneously went slack-jawed, wondering the same thing: "My God, is he dead?"

As ambulances screamed to his rescue and his broken body was scooped up and hauled away—accompanied by the announcers' whispered concern—the failed jump would be shown over and over so you could see him bounce his helmeted head off the ground, flip, contort, and, eventually, grind to a gruesome halt. It was entirely possible that a man had just killed himself for our entertainment and we wouldn't know until the next day if he'd survived. There was nothing phony or special effects about it.

Then the routine would start anew. After a few months of surgery and rehab for his (always) head-to-toe broken bones, Evel would announce an even more outrageous jump—over the fountains at Caesar's Palace in Vegas or the width of Snake River Canyon in a rocket-powered cycle—and, again, the promo machine would run full bore so we'd go batty with anticipation and tune in. Sometimes he made it and landed perfectly, to huge sighs of relief, rapturous delight, and more sidewalk bicycle imitation. But it's the times he blew his landings that folks like me remember just as much if not more vividly all these years later, long after his passing, and that ensure that his legend will endure. In spite of his frequent setbacks, that dude would always come back and try something else.

Why, you're wondering, am I telling you this?

Other than that I owe Evel a huge debt for single-handedly getting a generation of kids—me and scads of the others you see riding Harleys right now—jazzed about bikes, it's because I admire what he did. And it's not just the death-defying stuff I'm talking about. See, Evel didn't just talk about doing this never-before-seen stuff, he actually did it. He didn't, as we're all used to seeing, announce big plans, endlessly strategize, mull over ideas in his head, then table them for later discussion because the thought of pulling the trigger was too unsettling.

He didn't—in the spirit of the present-day corporate world—announce projects that would come to fruition so far into the future that we'd forget about them long before they missed their due dates. Or sandbag his goals to make them seem harder to reach, then meet them "before expected" to look heroic. Nor did he disengage from the process, turn over to underlings responsibility for making his plans happen, then ask, "Why isn't this working and why doesn't anybody know who I am?"

No, Evel flat-out did the work to position himself, rallied his team to create new and better Must Dos to bring his positioning to life, lived those Must Dos, generated a sonic boom's worth of positive noise, and was richly rewarded for it. Danger aside, doesn't everyone respect people who have the courage to *loudly* turn left to make themselves more successful when everyone around them is turning right and marching in lockstep?

Okay. So then why am I telling this to you now?

Because you're at that point where you've got to decide if you're going to rally your troops, hit the gas, and go for it or if you're going to, as some undoubtedly will, swerve around the launch ramp, take the easy way out, and bail on repositioning your business.

It pains me to say this, but in any room full of business leaders I've guided through the N3PS process, I know there will be a few who, after we part company, have second thoughts and bail out, believing it's too much for them or their organizations to absorb. Or they'll bust out that old chestnut of an excuse that the timing, somehow, isn't right. As the Evel quote that started this chapter implies, courage and enthusiasm can wane for some when the time comes to move beyond prep work and actually finish what they set out to do.

I don't want that to be you, especially after you've plowed so much effort into this thing. It's time to thumb the "start" button, hit that launch ramp, and fly, amigo. And I've got a feeling you're going to look good doing it and land this thing. Timing and second thoughts be damned. If not now, when?

Let's do this.

What you're about to read—the nuts and bolts of how you'll share your N3PS with others and gain their buy-in, then refine it further and put it to work for you—may seem, at first blush, to be simple to implement. While there's some truth in that, please don't allow its lack of complexity to fool you into a false sense of ease, as if you can just call a meeting, share your N3PS, bang a gavel, and bring this stuff to life.

Your intention to improve your competitiveness is a huge deal—certainly among the biggest initiatives you've undertaken since your business started—and you need to ensure that the people working with and for you see you treating it as such. Because if your team's not taking this seriously, you could easily blow your takeoff and miss your landing ramp. And that could tingle a little.

A big part of your daily work life going forward will be building your team and making sure everyone in your organization knows that you're collectively making some big adjustments in day-to-day operations. And that their participation isn't just expected, it's required. *Required.* What a scary workplace word. See? Positioning your business to be a dominator is serious stuff. Good thing you know of a few secret weapons to keep your people enthused and engaged.

In the smallest of small businesses, the leadership team, by default, will be the N3PS implementation team. Larger businesses have more options for whom to include, as you'll see in a moment. Regardless, your first task is to share your intentions and your N3PS with top leadership, as their early buy-in and enthusiastic participation will make the journey forward smoother for everyone else.

First, what do you know about adding people to any major workplace initiative? Right. You know this often creates two opposing dynamics. On the plus side, it means more ideas, more positive influencers, and faster implementation. On the minus side, it means more opportunities for enthusiasm killers like second-guessing and the whining that comes with it to surface, needless complexity, and momentum loss. You know what I'm talking about.

Those potential minuses are what scare some leaders away from the launch ramp, because they've seen them seep into and weaken other company initiatives. The pluses, along with that N3PS road map you've labored over, are what give dominance-minded leaders like you the confidence to blast toward glory. You just have to be like Evel and ensure that your people have your back.

With input received over the years from leaders who've started this journey before you, I've created and fine-tuned a set of requirements for taking your N3PS from document stage to real life. I advise you to read this listing slowly and give yourself some time to personalize and envision the actions behind the words. In your mind, see yourself doing this stuff—the way pro athletes visualize making big plays—so it will become more real to you. That will make you more comfortable when sharing this with your leadership team and fellow employees. If you're comfortable, they will be, too. You'll look like Evel in those extreme close-ups, showing no fear.

Here are your N3PS implementation requirements:

1. Full, Visibly Passionate involvement from every member of top leadership is mandatory for N3PS adoption and implementation to succeed. *Remember that everyone working at your business models the behavior of their leader(s). Your enthusiasm becomes their enthusiasm.*

2. N3PS implementation must be the top priority of your business, superseding all current go-to-market and/or workplace initiatives. *Any current initiative that doesn't specifically support your N3PS should be viewed thusly: If it's not going to improve our competitiveness by serving our "What Do We Want People to Say?" goals, why are we doing it now?*

3. Unless you're a one-person business, a team must be built to oversee the N3PS process and serve as process leaders. At minimum, the team is to be composed of senior leaders responsible for all go-to-market and customer-facing initiatives, plus HR/culture functions. The primary requirement for team

membership is enthusiasm. *You (and your first lieutenants) know who your positive influencers are as surely as you know who the naysayers and buzzkillers are.*

4. N3PS implementation team members must understand that their roles require them to participate in further refinement of your N3PS document, then gain employee buy-in, oversee implementation, and encourage/demand adherence to Must Dos and Must Says. *Remember the "Do as I do, say as I say," influence of Chick-fil-A's on-site managers on individual, team, and store performance.*

5. There can be no N3PS implementation team without full buy-in, active participation, and accountability. It is the top leader's responsibility to encourage or demand such. Weak or nonenthusiastic team members must be removed from the team before they can have a negative influence. *Remember the rewards that come from meeting your people's needs for esteem and belonging. And that accountability is seen as a positive in dominance-minded organizations.*

6. By formal launch time, all employees must be comfortable with your N3PS Must Say and Must Do directives, be able to communicate the meaning and intent behind them, and understand that adherence to them is a requirement of employment. *If you're not for us, you're against us. This is what we do here!*

7. Leaders must continuously seek feedback and input from their people by asking, "Are you experiencing any challenges with your Must Says and Must Dos that I can help you with?" "How can I help you do your job better?" "How can I be a better leader for you?" and "How can we work better together?" *People support their leaders and workplace initiatives when they feel they're being supported, heard, and valued.*

8. N3PS status, including individual and team successes, must be shared on a regular basis with all employees. Team setbacks or unanticipated challenges must also be shared and discussed so solutions or route changes can be made. *See number 7. And never miss an opportunity to boost your employees' esteem.*

9. Don't just communicate to employees; connect with them and continuously offer gratitude for their involvement and effort. Emphasize face-to-face contact over electronic or print channels when feasible. *Unleash Weapons of Mass Attraction. Talk*

to employees like you'd talk to customers—get in front of them frequently, be Visibly Passionate, emphasize gratitude, and ask how you can better serve them. They'll model you.

10. Never underestimate the power of a free donut. *The golden rule for attracting people to meetings—or just about anything— and getting them to come back. Compliments and pats on the back are like calorie-free donuts. Small rewards often lead to large rewards.*

All right, then. It would be great if I had a simple, one-size-fits-all set of instructions for making N3PS directives standard operating procedure that would apply to every business. But there are way too many variables for that—as many as there are businesses on the globe—as I'm sure you can imagine. However, I've got the next best thing, a three-phase road map that provides the basic directions and requirements to get any business moving in the right direction on its journey. You can tweak these any way you want to make them work for you.

PHASE ONE: ALL-HANDS LEADERSHIP MEETING

No matter if you're a mom-and-pop or a massive conglomerate, your first move is to share with every member of top leadership your intention to reposition your business, along with the details of the N3PS you've started. You know you'll need their full buy-in and participation before you share this with your workforce. But this takes tact and some preparation because what you'll be sharing is going to be a bit of a stunner, especially for folks who aren't expecting anything like this. And who is? As you've seen, this isn't the kind of stuff that people often think about, so botching your launch can make it difficult to land in one piece. The last thing any leader wants to see at a time like this is eye-rolling. That's the equivalent of a wobbly landing ramp.

When presenting to your leadership team, the best way to minimize the risk of misinterpretation and conflicts is to hold a mandatory, all-hands meeting, to ensure everyone is getting the same information and hearing everyone else's questions, comments, and ideas. As you're thinking about what you'll share with them, please ask yourself (because you'll want your fellow leaders to get into this habit), "What do I want these people to remember and repeat from what I'm about to say?"

Given the weight of the information you'll be sharing, I recommend scheduling at least three hours for your leadership discussion, to avoid any possibility of rushing and to have time to address concerns and build comfort. I'm a huge believer in morning meetings, followed by relaxed lunch conversations.

I also recommend treating your leadership discussion as you would any major discussion with your most important publics. In other words, you'll need to do some scripting (or at least outlining) and make some visual aids to have maximum impact. I've included recommendations for both here.

Do yourself and everyone who works with you a huge favor and practice your presentation until you're comfortable and conversant with the information. I can't stress this enough: You want your fellow leaders and, eventually, all of your people, to see that you're committed to this, so professionalism and confidence are paramount. You wouldn't risk making a major presentation to your most important customers or investors without rehearsing, right? Think of your fellow leaders the same way. Even famous CEOs of massive businesses rehearse before speaking to their people (and pay people like me to help with their presentation skills; just sayin').

When it comes to business meetings, I've found that there are three solid ways to hold any audience's attention, gain their buy-in, and relieve the pressure of being the only person talking:

1. Make it easy for your people to visualize what you're saying by telling stories that use common examples from everyday life or aspirations..
2. Encourage audience members to share personal experiences or memories that expand the stories you've told.
3. Use visuals to boost memorability of key messages.

As you're eyeballing my suggestions to help you frame your discussion, including key messages and some storytelling cues to get you running and up to speed, please know that "suggestions" should be taken literally. You should massage and personalize these any way you'd like, so that they sound like *you* talking, not some ridiculously cool guy from a book you just read. Whatever you do, don't read this stuff I'm giving you word for word. Instead, make some cheat sheets or note cards with the key points you'll use to support your presentation.

Along with key messages, I'm providing you with suggestions for your supporting visuals, too. Know this: Nobody hates seeing "word slides" in presentations more than me, but sometimes—and this is one of them—you have to use a few. The important thing is to put only your *key* words on your slides so your people can follow along and see what's most important. You never want to put so much on a slide that people are reading when they should be listening. That's torture for everyone and the sign of a presenter not comfortable with his or her content. Think R&R: What do I want these folks to remember and repeat? Because you'll be sharing the entirety of your N3PS, I've also included recommendations for breaking it into smaller, easier-to-digest pieces.

As you're getting input and ideas from your group during your presentation, be sure to record what's being said—you can write on an easel or ask someone to be designated note taker. You now know how important it is to make sure whoever's speaking can see that someone's writing down whatever they're saying. (Here's a tip: When you're writing someone's comments, be sure to record their name, too. That way you can always reference who said what and let people know that their input, specifically, was remembered, should you bring it up later. "Katie had a great idea about . . ." or "Dan was concerned with . . ." You get the picture.)

A final note: I'll caution that as you're reading my suggested messages, you may think I'm pushing the opening discussion on competition and commoditization harder than necessary. I'm not. You're much more comfortable now with these topics than people hearing and seeing them for the first time. So lead your people into this gradually and use as many examples up front as possible to open minds to the notion that your intent here is to improve competitiveness, ensure that everyone knows what the reasons are, and gain their buy-in to make it happen. (At the risk of sounding self-promotional, you might consider sharing copies of this book with your fellow leaders prior to the meeting, or having copies available for them to read afterward.)

Starting from the top, then.

Message: "Effective immediately, our top priority is to improve our competitiveness. And we're going to do that by strengthening our most important asset, our reputation." (Header: "Improve Competitiveness, Strengthen Reputation.")

- Remember, competitiveness isn't a subject that people, leaders included, pay much attention to. Most take it as a given, as in

"We're in business, so of course we're competing." But as I've visited with businesses over the years, I've learned the universal truth that everyone understands "reputation," its importance and how it impacts competitiveness.

- Ask the group, "What do you think it means when a business is described the same as its competitors or when customers can't see differences between one competitor and another?" (If nobody speaks up, ask a few individuals directly.)

- "Being described in our market the same way as a competitor is no way to compete. It means customers and potential customers believe we and our competitors are interchangeable equals. It's what forces businesses to compete only on price. I don't want us to live in that world any longer."

- Bring your audience into the discussion by saying something akin to "Think back to your younger days. Would you want somebody to describe you to the others at your school as 'the same as everybody else'? No way. You'd want to stand out. You'd want to be described as amazing and really cool, awesome, superfriendly, and fun. So you'd make sure that people saw you doing things that lived up to that, right? That way, the people you were hoping to attract and associate with would know you're different and more desirable than everyone else. The same goes for our business."

Message: "Starting now, we're going to reposition our business to change how the people we serve and want to serve see us and what they say about us by changing how we treat them and what we say to them." (Visual: Grab an online image of a highway sign showing gas stations available at the next exit—there are plenty to choose from. Add header: "Commoditized Market.")

- "We're in a commoditized market (or industry). Which means we and our competitors look interchangeable, do the same things, and get described the same way. There's nothing good about that."

- Ask the group about choosing from multiple gas stations at an intersection they'd encounter on a road trip. Which will they choose and why?

- Do they have a preference or do they assume they're all selling the same thing?
- Now ask them to view this from a business leader's standpoint: "If you owned one of those gas stations, would you want potential customers to assume there's no difference between players and choose whoever's cheapest or closest?"
- "What would you do differently to make your gas station stand out more and be more competitive?"
- "What do you think happens to businesses that do only what potential customers expect them to do?"
- Ask the group if they can think of other businesses and industries where there's little, if any, known differences between players. As your people offer answers, ask them why they feel there are no differences between those businesses and what, if they worked at those businesses, they might recommend as "quick" changes to create differentiation.

Message: "To stop blending in with our competitors and break out of the commodity mind-set, we're going to stand for something bigger than what we sell (or make, do, etc.)" (Visual: Grab an online image of a flatscreen TV retail display. Add header: "No More Blending In.")

- Compare someone shopping in your business category to a person shopping for a flatscreen TV, as you read earlier. Which one is best? Nobody knows. Everything's good, but you don't know who's better or worse than anyone else because they all look the same, do the same things, and are described the same way. So manufacturers and retailers lower prices to generate sales, knowing you'll be happy with what you get because it will perform exactly the way you expect it to, no matter whose name is on the front.
- Ask the group, "Why do you think all flatscreens look the same, perform the same, and are priced so similarly?"
- Remind them that as industries mature, all players within the industry march in lockstep with each other, until everyone is indistinguishable. Everyone talks the same way about "quality" and "customer satisfaction." And tries to sell their products by touting confusing features and benefits. And that's bad for business.

Message: "Even in markets like ours, where there's not a great deal of difference between us and our competitors, where everyone's good at what they do and working just as hard as we are, there's something we can do that will separate us from everyone else and position us to be a dominator. It starts when we and everyone working here can answer three questions. (Visual: Noise Cubed questions.)

What do the people we serve say about us?
What do we want them to say?
What are we doing to make them say it?

- "You can see that what's being addressed here is a business's most important asset in its marketplace, its reputation."
- "These questions are based on repositioning methods Harley-Davidson used during its successful turnaround back in the 1980s and '90s to improve their reputation and to foster the fierce loyalty and customer advocacy they're famous for today. It's worked for lots of other businesses and it's going to work for us, too."
- "These questions are called 'Noise Cubed.' Here's the reason: Harleys are famous for their signature roar, while nearly all of their competitors' motorcycles make an indistinguishable hum. You can always tell when a Harley's coming, right? (Ask somebody to imitate the sound—always good for a laugh.) But everything else just sounds like a motorcycle. You have no idea who built it."
- "We can equate the noise Harley's bikes make to the noise their customers and other important publics make when they talk about the company. Good noise is when people are saying great stuff that the company wants said. Bad noise is the opposite."
- Ask, "What do you think it means when a company makes no noise at all?"
- "Harley wants to ensure that their noise stands out and separates their business from competitors who are selling look-alike products and essentially copying each other. Like those flatscreens."
- "As you'll see, we'll be working to develop specific answers for those Noise Cubed questions, and the actions we'll need to take as an organization to bring our desired positioning to life."
- Ask your people to imagine a customer served last week having

a conversation with somehow who potentially could be your dream customer.

- "What kind of noise would that customer be making on our behalf?" In other words, "How do you think that current customer would describe us?" Follow up with "Do you think that description would convince this potential customer to do business with us?"

- (Be on the lookout for great intel here. When somebody offers a suggestion, ask a follow-up question like "Why do you say that?" or "What made you think of that?" to help them provide specifics to their answers. You'll also likely hear some predictable "quality" and "customer service" responses, which will set the stage for your N3PS discussion.)

- Turn the dialogue: "Assuming we could have direct input on this conversation—or that we could plant a chip in our customers' brains that would control what they say about us—what would you *want* that person who just did business with us to say about us to make that potential customer choose us?" And don't forget to ask those follow-up questions.

- As suggestions are made, ask the final Noise Cubed question: "What would we have to do—*that we're not doing now*—to make that happen?"

- "What great dominators like the Harleys and L.L.Beans of the world do well is make loyal, vocal advocates out of their customers by not only providing great products and services, but delighting them in ways no other business does, so they'll tell their friends and coworkers. It's awesome. We can do that, too."

Message: "We can't compete at a dominant level until we're making some distinctive noise in our marketplace and our customers are advocating for us and bringing us new customers." (Visual: Grab an online image showing people who look like your current customers talking to each other. Easy to find. Add header: "Time to Make Some Noise.")

- Ask the group if anyone can think of a recent instance where any business they're familiar with did something so memorably different or special for them that they actually told somebody else. (You'll hear little, if any, responses.)

- "It's tough, isn't it?" The intent here is to show that it's rare for someone to have positive stories to tell about businesses, because most businesses focus on delivering only what customers expect.

- "Our business is going to be a rare exception."
- "I want us to start making some awesome noise and become the most talked about and successful company in our market. We have the ability to do that."
- "Bottom line: We need people to start making noise on our behalf, right?"

Message: "There's a simple formula we all need to know: When no positive story gets told, no demand gets built." (Visual: Screenshot of Las Vegas. Add header: "When no positive story is told, no demand is built.")

- "We have to think like they do in Vegas. You know the famous saying, 'What happens in Vegas stays in Vegas,' right? The people working in Vegas know that what happens in Vegas *doesn't* stay in Vegas and they know that if it did, there wouldn't be a Vegas anymore. They know the great benefits that come from delighted Vegas visitors going home and telling others about their trips, so those new people will vacation there, too. They know a simple equation: When no positive stories are told, no demand is built."
- "You've never in your life told somebody about a business that met your expectations and gave you what you paid for—because *all* businesses do that now. That's what happens in commoditized markets."
- "Vegas workers know their job is to ensure that people go home with stories to tell about the experiences they had there. So people hearing these stories will come and not spend their vacation time and money somewhere else."
- "We just talked about what a customer we've served might say to a potential customer. If he or she has no story to tell, no demand is being created for us. Which means we blew a great opportunity."
- "We've got to give our customers experiences that they'll remember and talk about, and make them feel special, so they'll refer us and bring us new customers. It's easier than it sounds and it's precisely what we're going to do."

Message: "We can't compete at a dominant level by simply doing what we do at a higher level, because customers are used to getting great products and services from everybody these days. We need to say and do things they don't expect and we have to exceed their expectations in ways they don't expect." (Visual: Photo of your product(s) or service(s). Add header: "Quality Isn't Enough" or "Great Isn't Enough.")

- "We have to look at things like quality and customer service through a different lens because our customers don't see these things as differentiators anymore. Everything we buy is great today—quality is expected. And everybody claims to back up what they sell."
- "Look at your own buying behavior. You buy things online from businesses you might never have heard of, because they're willing to sell you what you want at the lowest price. You know it will show up at your door when it's supposed to. You know the stuff will be good and do what it's supposed to do. But you won't think about who you're buying from, remember them, or recommend them to someone else because you're getting what you paid for and expected. We can't operate like that anymore."
- "Why can't we be like Chick-fil-A? They're selling the same stuff others are selling, but they're easily the friendliest people, they're always focused on proactively delighting customers—instead of waiting to be asked—and generating the most buzz, so they're always busy. They pay their people the same as other fast-food places, but their people do a great job of exceeding expectations, exuding enthusiasm for what they do, and creating a very positive environment, because their leadership and work culture demand it. They've created an atmosphere where doing so is as natural to them as breathing. We can do this, too."

Message: "We can't easily change our products (and/or services, offerings, etc.), but we can change what we emphasize. Rather than being product (or service) first—and making what we sell the thrust of business—we're going to put people first." (Visual: Photo of employees. Add header: "They.")

- "Think about this: Whenever you discuss a business, positive or negative, you humanize the business by using the pronoun 'they.'

You're not talking about the products the company makes or sells, you're talking about the people—the culture—behind it."

- Ask the group to describe any local business or one of your competitors; when you hear "they rock," "they're awesome," or "they stink," you've proven your point.
- "We're going to become the 'they' our customers tell others great things about. Which means we need to change the way we view our work culture here and the way we view the people we serve and, most important, what we do for them."
- Ask: "What do you think causes somebody to be loyal to a business?" (Your people will likely say some combination of great products, great prices, and solid relationships.)
- "Everyone needs to know this: We're way more loyal to people than we are to products—just ask companies with fierce loyalty like Harley, Chick-fil-A, and L.L.Bean. We're going to use this to our benefit as we change what we're doing here."
- "It's going to be our job, every day here, to delight customers in ways they don't expect, so they'll remember us and return to us for more."
- "A big part of our road map going forward addresses how we're going to do this. And you're a big part of the how."

Message: "We have some weapons at our disposal that we can and will start unleashing to build loyalty among our customers, attract more customers, and create a working culture here that will make that happen." (Visual: Photo of employees in work environment. Add header: "Drivers of Behavior.")

- "There are two very basic drivers of daily life that we're going to start weaponizing for competitive advantage and to create a more people-focused working culture here. We've got to do this before someone else does."
- "The first: When all things are equal, we always choose to do business with, or associate with, and talk about businesses— people—that we like. Period. Even in a market like ours where it's hard to differentiate ourselves with products, price, or services, if we can get the people we serve to like us just a little more than our competitors, we win."
- "Just providing/selling/making great products and services will never make us likable. That stuff just gets us in the game. Being

likable means focusing more on the human side of what we do, by putting people first. You'll see in a few minutes how we might start to do that. And there will be plenty of opportunities for you to offer suggestions."

- "The second driver reflects a fact of life that most people aren't aware of: We always loyally return to any source of joy in our lives. That's guaranteed. If someone makes us feel good about ourselves, or surprises us just a little, or makes us feel special, wanted, and valued, they're helping us meet basic human needs that typically go unfulfilled in the business world. So we'll keep coming back to that person for as long as they're delighting us. The same goes with businesses. That's what real loyalty is and where it comes from."

- Ask the group to think about restaurants or other local businesses they frequent and are loyal to. "The common denominator of businesses you return to loyally is the fact that you happen to like them more than their competitors. Which means you like the people who work there more than the people working at their competitors. It also means those people consistently put forth effort to make you feel welcome, wanted, and special. That makes you feel good and that's why you go back."

- "We're going to become the business our customers prefer, refer to others, and return to."

Message: "The key ingredient for making our business more attractive, preferred by our market, and the kind of business customers return to loyally and talk about is Visible Passion." (Visual: Photo of passionate worker. Or split screen with photos of happy phone rep on one side, bored rep on other. Add header: "Visible Passion Makes People Magnetic.")

- "At the end of the day, no matter what's being sold, how exciting it is or isn't, or how it's brought to market, all business comes down to people buying from people. We're going to be the people our market prefers by unleashing our passion in ways the market can't miss."

- "Visible Passion is the most attractive of all human traits. We instantly know it when we see and hear it and are drawn to it. This is basic human behavior we see every day. It gives us some joy—and remember what I just said about that. We always loyally return for more."

- "You know how it feels when you're talking with someone who's fully engaged, happily living in the moment, and wanting you to be part of it. Like talking with someone from Zappos or Harley or Chick-fil-A. These businesses make Visible Passion a huge part of their competitive strategy because they know it attracts people and makes them feel good, even if it's just for a few seconds."
- "You also know how the opposite feels."
- Ask the group to share some examples of bored-sounding phone reps, retail salespeople leaning against counters, using dull and predictable business-speak like "Can I help you?" or "Please hold," and how they reacted to these businesses. Are these the kinds of businesses they'd reward by returning to and recommending?
- "We're going to be the most liked, most Visibly Passionate business in our market. These are things we can directly influence and control and we'd be foolish not to."
- "Why can't we be the Harley-Davidson of our market, treat our customers like gold, and benefit from their great loyalty? Harley didn't become great by just selling motorcycles; its dealers built a reputation for being awesome, for taking unbelievable care of their customers and always working to delight them so they have good stories to tell, loyally come back for more, and recommend them to new customers. They're a family-owned business in control of their own destiny. We can do what they do, too, so our customers are always bringing us new ones. Our market is every bit as competitive as theirs. Even though what they're selling is supercool, the real reason their customers are loyal is how the people working in those dealerships treat them and make them feel."

Message: "Making people feel welcome, wanted, important, and special won't only be an outward-looking initiative here, it's going to benefit us internally by helping us attract and retain people." (Visual: Photo of some of your company employees. Add header: "Our Culture—Welcome. Important. Special.")

- "The way people view a business is a direct reflection of its culture. So if we want to be seen as a Visibly Passionate, people-focused business, that's what we have to be."
- Ask the group, "What businesses can you think of that have a Visibly Passionate work culture?" (If no responses, cue to Chick-fil-A, Disney, etc.)
- "As our Visible Passion and efforts to give people some great experiences and some joy become engrained in our culture, it will help us do a much better job of understanding and meeting the needs of the people who work here. People who feel like they're important, special, and being looked after tend to stay loyal and rise to new challenges. We can make that happen as you'll soon see."

Message: "Our journey to competitive dominance calls for us to reposition our business, create new go-to-market strategies, and take advantage of the unmet human needs of the people we as a business, and as leaders of this company, serve. We're going to need a road map to get us there." (Visual: Shot of an open road. Thousands of choices online. Add header: "N3PS—Reposition to Dominate.")

- Because you're about to share your N3PS, it's always a good idea to take a level-set with your people, to make sure everyone's getting it so far and to address any questions or concerns.
- Be extra prepared to handle anyone who gets defensive and lapses into self-doubt because "Our product isn't cool," or "We just sell ball bearings and our customers don't care about that stuff, they just want the best price." This is the time to remind them, "Competing to dominate isn't about what we sell, because there are others who do what we do. It's about people and how we treat them, how we make them feel about themselves and about us. If they like us more than our competitors because they like what we're doing for them beyond simply giving them what they paid for, or because we surprise them once in a while, they're going to continue to do business with us. We win."
- "I recently completed a document called a Noise Cubed Positioning System—or N3PS for short—which helps businesses like ours chart a course to dominance. It involves studying competitors

to determine how they're positioned and how the market makes noise on their behalf, then doing the same for our business. This is a really big deal."

- "I can't wait to get your input and ideas before we share this with everyone."

- "The idea is twofold: First, we're going to use our competitors' predictable, commoditized behavior against them by finding holes in their armor that we can take advantage of, while finding areas of overlap and commonality that we need to avoid."

- "Second, we'll identify new, specific actions we must take—along with supporting language we must use in all of our dealings with important publics—to create separation from our competitors, attract and retain more customers, and improve our reputation. This is where your ideas and input will be invaluable."

- "From now on, we'll be looking at competing through a different lens than before. While the competition is saying and doing the same things, we'll intentionally be creating distance from them."

Message: "The first leg of the N3PS journey requires us to look at how competitors position themselves, their greatest points of differentiation, and what customers and prospects say about them. It's called Competitive Noise. This is what we're up against every day." (Visual: Logos of the competitors studied in your N3PS. Add header: "Competitive Noise.")

- "By studying how our competitors position themselves through their websites (and marketing materials), then looking at what people say about them on social media, and what we hear about them over the course of the year, we not only get a clean snapshot of our competitive environment, but we can also quickly find areas of overlap that we need to avoid, as well as opportunities for us to stand out." (Visual: Competitive Noise page from your N3PS, titles only.)

- "Each of our competitors is analyzed in four categories, Obvious Positioning Words—the way they describe themselves and what they do; Solid Differentiators—the things they do or say that stand out and that they're known for; What Are People Saying?—which are the most frequently heard comments about their business taken from social media and what customers have told us about them; and, finally, Exploitable Weaknesses—which speaks for itself."

- "Let's look at each competitor, one at a time."
- "This is the work of just one person, me. So it will get better with your input and ideas." (Visual: Show completed page of Competitive Noise from your N3PS for each competitor.)
- Review each category for each competitor. Before you switch to the next competitor, be sure to seek input and buy-in by asking questions like "Am I missing anything here?" "Are you with me so far?" "Is this making sense to you?"
- "It's amazing how we can size up our competitive environment this way. What's even more amazing is the fact that we've never done anything like this before."
- "The best part is, our competitors probably haven't done anything like this, either, so we're going to take advantage of that."
- As you're progressing through competitors, ask the group if they're seeing areas of commonality and overlap so they'll gain a better understanding of how your competitive environment is commoditized and the opportunity that presents for your business.
- After your final Competitive Noise page, ask the group what they felt the most commonly overused positioning words were and how they feel about this.

Message: "We need to look at ourselves using the same criteria. Let's look at our noise." (Visual: "Our Noise" page from your N3PS.)

- "Looking at ourselves can be tricky, because we always have to remember that just because we say something about ourselves, it doesn't mean our customers are saying it, too. Or that they're even aware of the things we think we're great at. We have to look at ourselves the way our competitors would if they were doing this exercise."
- Ask open questions, like, "Based on what I've shared so far, what are your immediate takeaways?" "How would you describe our overall competitive environment?"
- "What surprised you?" "Is anything missing?"

Message: "Our Competitive Noise Summary gives us a snapshot of every-thing we've looked at so far and a great overview of our market." (Visual: Competitive Noise Summary page from your N3PS.)

- "This Obvious Positioning Words listing is like a dictionary of words that we'll never use again with customers because if we ever find ourselves describing our business the same way any of our competitors do, we're sending a message that says we're the same as them. That hurts us."
- "The Solid Differentiators are things we can't own, ever. But they should always be present in our minds as we discuss how we're going to position our business to ensure we don't acciden-tally use any of these."
- Before moving on, ask if there are any other competitors you may have overlooked. If you get one or two suggestions and have the time and an Internet connection, have the group participate in a Competitive Noise assessment of those businesses. Other-wise, complete the work yourself after the meeting, or assign the task to a fellow leader.

Message: "To create separation from our competitors, we need to look closely at how we describe ourselves and what we do." (Visual: Noise Cubed Positioning System, page one.)

- "Let's look at how we describe ourselves when we're talking to people, on our website, and through any of our marketing mate-rials."
- "What am I missing here?"
- Ask individuals, "How do you describe us to others?"
- "How much of what we say when we describe ourselves did you see customers repeating when we looked at what people say about us? Anything?"
- Ask the group what it means if customers aren't repeating the words your people use to describe your business.

Message: "If the people we serve don't describe us the way we describe our-selves, that means there's a disconnect that's causing confusion and working against us." (Visual: "What Are People Saying?" page from your N3PS.)

- "A big part of being a dominant competitor is controlling narrative—what people in our market say about us. If they don't say the same things about us that we say ourselves, that means we need to sharpen our approach and change our go-to-market vocabulary."
- Look at the positive comments first and ask if everyone agrees with them and if anyone has any additions or clarifications they'd like to make. Be sure there's agreement on your draft as well as any new changes or additions.
- Now focus on the negative comments. "We have to take negative marketplace comments as serious and as completely truthful, because whoever says this stuff absolutely means it. And people hearing it and reading it have no reason to doubt it."
- "The good news is, this tells us what we need to be working on."
- Ask the group—or specific individuals—how they reacted to the negative noise comments when they first read them.
- Note that people may become defensive about negative comments and say things like "That only happened once," or "That doesn't happen anymore." Use this as an opportunity to remind the group that voices in the market are never wrong, even if they are wrong. Meaning: Accurate or not, if this is what people are saying, it's true to them and whoever they're saying it to, so it needs to be addressed.

Message: "Remember our Noise Cubed questions that will guide our journey going forward: What are people saying? What do we want them to say? And, what are we doing to make them say it? We now know what they're saying. So let's talk about what we *want* them to say when they talk about us." (Visual: "What Do We Want People to Say?" page from your N3PS.)

- Remind the group that what they're reading is the work of just one person, you.
- Read them one at a time and ask for reactions or improvement suggestions for each.
- Don't forget to ask follow-ups like "Why do you say that or feel that way?"
- Ask the group for their suggested additions to the list and why they feel their additions would be helpful in your journey to

dominance. And remind them that "if someone else is saying it, we're not." There can't be too many suggestions, as the list will be culled in the next phase.

- Ask an individual: "If you had just one chance to describe who we are, what we do, and who we do it for, what would you say? Can you say this without using any Competitive Noise words?"
- "That's our challenge."

Message: "Now we need to reduce our list of ideas down to what seems most powerful, doable, and ownable—and what's easy for our customers to remember and repeat." (Visual: "What Do We Want People to Say?" condensed page from your N3PS.)

- "Here's what I came up with."
- "What we're looking for now are aspirational descriptors that we want customers and our other important publics to use when they're talking about us and telling stories about us. This is what we want to be known for."
- "And we need to remove anything that looks like something a competitor can claim or that isn't realistic."
- "We also need to be on the lookout for any words we can use that are completely unique to our business and our approach, the way major brands do. Harley doesn't say they sell bikes or transportation like their competitors do, they say they sell freedom and a lifestyle. They don't have "customers," they have "disciples." Levis doesn't say they sell jeans, they say they sell American style. Those are memorable, repeatable words that make for great differentiation, memorability, and storytelling."
- "Can you think of any ways we can change how we describe something common that we do using this kind of thinking?"

Message: "Once we have solid ideas on what we want people to say, we need to reduce those ideas down further, to be able to communicate these ideas with the fewest possible words." (Visual: "Less Is More.")

- Tell the group you have a quick challenge to determine their ability to describe something complex in very few words. And to have some fun at the same time.

- Tell them they have only five syllables to describe themselves. Be sure the group remembers what syllables are and give examples if needed (a fan-tas-tic guy). Give them three minutes to write their responses. (Header: How I describe myself in five syllables.)
- When complete, ask a few volunteers—or select a few volunteers—to read their work.
- Then tell them they have only seven syllables to write how others describe them. (Visual: How others describe me in seven syllables.)
- Give them three minutes. Ask for volunteers to share their work.
- Then tell them they have only five syllables to write how they wish others described them. Three minutes. (Visual: How I wish others described me in five syllables.)
- Ask for volunteers to read all three lines.
- Ask the group if they recognize what they've created. Tell them it's a haiku—a poem of just three lines—and that it's a great tool for taking a lot of complex thoughts and ideas and reducing them to their most bare essence. Congratulate them on their previously hidden poetic talent.
- Now do the same for your business; give them three minutes to answer each question: How do you describe our business? How do others describe our business? How do you want others to describe our business? (Visual: How I describe our business [five syllables]. How others describe our business [seven]. How I want others to describe it [five].)
- Ask for a few volunteers to read their haikus. (Depending on the size of your group, you might ask everyone to vote for their favorite and award a small prize to the winner.)
- Explain that you used that same exercise to reduce your N3PS entries into more concise, distinctive language, and then ranked them in order of preference. (Visual: "What Do We Say About Ourselves" page from your N3PS, final draft.)
- "This is how one person—me—reduced everything I believe we say about ourselves into simple five-syllable phrases and ranked them by preference."
- Ask how the group might suggest any changes in your wording, as well as in the order of preference (and ask follow-up "why?" questions).

- Remind the group that the number of syllables isn't as important as the idea.
- If no one makes suggestions, ask specific people how they might reword some of your entries.
- "What's missing? Are there concerns here? If any of this doesn't seem correct or realistic, please explain what and why because we want to be comfortable before moving to the next phase."
- Next, I've reduced "What Are People Saying?" into seven syllables each and ranked them by weight, both positively and negatively. (Visual: "What Are People Saying?" page from your N3PS, final draft.)
- Ask for input, suggested improvements, and any questions, concerns, or ideas.

Message: "Before we discuss how we'll bring our N3PS to life, we need to discuss the most important part of the process: our role as leaders." (Visual: Photo of employees or something that captures the essence of your working culture. Add header: "Bringing Our N3PS to Life.")

- "These major changes we're talking about here—once we finalize them—aren't suggestions or wishful thinking. To build our reputation to the point where people are describing us the way we want to be and referring us to others, we need to put specific, consistent actions behind these words. This will require changes in how we do things."
- "These changes will be required of me, you, and everyone working here. None of this will work without our active involvement and encouragement. None of this will be optional for any of us."
- "Employees won't simply adopt new methods of doing things and speaking with our customers and important customers because we tell them to. They'll follow our lead. They'll do what we do and say what we say. Everyone needs to realize that employees model the behavior of their leaders. If we ignore this stuff, so will they. If we embrace it, they will, too."
- "We and our people need to be united on this. They'll need to become conversant on our messaging, know the behaviors we expect of them, and understand that their involvement is a requirement for working here."

- "We'll need to continuously seek input from our people, provide encouragement, and give them status updates."
- "Building the kind of working culture that our marketplace sees value in, appreciates, and relies upon, while giving our people a greater sense of pride and loyalty, will be the biggest challenge of our work here. I can't wait to get started."

Message: "Let's look at the specific directives we'll follow to bring our N3PS to life." (Visual: First page, Must Say/Must Do directives from your N3PS.)

- "If we want to have direct influence on how the marketplace sees us and talks about us, we have to put specific actions behind our desired positioning language. You'll see how detailed this is, what our priorities will be going forward, and what will be expected of you, me, and everyone working here."
- "Here's my current draft of Must Say and Must Do directives required to bring our desired messaging to life and make us a dominator."
- "There's a separate document for each element of the 'What Do We Want People to Say?' goals we just discussed. Once we've refined it, this will be our road map going forward."
- Starting at the top, work your way through your N3PS, constantly seeking input and suggestions.
- Ask specific leaders, "What's your first reaction to this?"
- "What would you add to this?"
- "How do you think our important publics will react to this?"
- "What specific challenges might we encounter within our culture as we try to make this happen?"
- "If anything's troubling you, now's the time to discuss it. Nothing's carved in stone at this point. You'll have more time to think this over."

Before ending discussion on the "Because we want people to say . . ." section of your N3PS, ensure the group is ready to proceed.

Message: "As important as it is for us to start making this positive noise in our market, we also need to strategically confront the negative or inaccurate things being said about us." (Visual: First page of "Because We Don't Want People to Say . . ." from your N3PS.)

- Project and discuss each page of the final section of your N3PS. Ask the same questions as in the prior section, ensuring that you're constantly seeking input by asking open-ended questions that encourage them to speak.

Message: "We've got a decision to make. Do we want to keep riding the same road we're on, doing the same things we always have that got us to this point, moving in the same direction as our competitors, and blending in or do we want to chart a different course to stand out, differentiate our business in ways people notice and talk about, and become a dominator? You know where I stand. (Visual: Two photos. On top, a shot of a traffic jam on a straight highway. On bottom, open-road shot. There are thousands of each online to choose from.)

- "Nothing's going to get easier for us in our market. Our competitors aren't going away. The longer we wait, the harder it will become for us to gain momentum and the more likely it will be that one or more of our competitors start to reposition themselves, too."
- "I'm sure you've noticed that none of this is meant to be superficial window dressing. This is going to require the active participation of everyone in the organization. It's going to be a challenging adjustment for everyone, but it's absolutely doable."
- "I have complete confidence in you and the rest of our organization to bring this to life and make us the dominator I know we're capable of becoming."
- "This is going to be an all-hands effort."

Ask individuals for their overall impressions of the entire N3PS, what they feel most strongly about, and what specific concerns they may have.

Message: "Sharing this with you and getting your input is just the first leg of the journey. So let's review what happens next and what each of us will need to do." (Visual: Open-road shot. Add header: "Next Steps.")

- "I'm going to send each of you a copy of our N3PS that will include the suggestions you made today, for you to review. This isn't something I want you to give a quick once-over because it's ultimately going to impact everything we do here. So please take your time with it and be prepared to make suggested improvements and voice any concerns when we reconvene in a week."

(For small business where company leadership will be the N3PS Implementation Team):

- "At our next meeting, we'll work together to complete a working draft that we'll eventually share with all employees. Because people support what they help create, we'll be giving everyone an opportunity to offer input and suggestions before we create our final N3PS."
- "We'll also discuss how to best roll this out and bring it to life."

(For larger businesses that will have a multifunctional N3PS Implementation Team):

- "I'll be creating a cross-functional N3PS Implementation Team to work with me and lead the process for the entire organization. I may be asking some of you to join the team or make suggestions on who you believe would be ideal candidates. I'll share with them the N3PS that we've created together, then seek their input as well as their suggestions on how to best communicate our intentions to reposition our business to our people."
- "It's important that everyone here know they have a voice in what we'll be doing and it's up to all of us to ensure their voices are heard. Who knows better about what's going on in the trenches every day than the people doing the work? And who knows better how to make our Must Says and Must Dos easier to implement? If they feel their ideas and input aren't valued, they'll be much less enthused about supporting our efforts. We're not going to let that happen."
- "The N3PS Implementation Team is the driving force of our repositioning journey. Once we're up and running, we'll be the leaders, coaches, managers, communicators, and cheerleaders

every step of the way. I'm hoping every member of the team will
see their involvement as an honor."
- "Thanks for your participation today and thanks in advance for
  everything you'll do to make our new journey successful. You
  guys are the best."

So there it is. Your journey is officially under way. Now open the floor
to questions, comments, and concerns.

Assume you'll get a lot of questions as you wrap up—and during each
phase of your rollout. I've listed the most frequently asked here, along with
some suggested responses. Remember, you want your people to see that
you're confident and comfortable with what you're presenting, so be sure to
be conversant on these. That's French for "rehearse your answers."

Frequently Asked Questions and Suggested Answers

Why are we doing this now? (We have so much other stuff going on . . .)

- "This can't wait. Commoditization cripples markets, crushes
  loyalty, and causes negative pricing pressure. We can't participate in that anymore if we want to grow our business and find
  new opportunities."
- "We need to do this before our competitors do. And sooner or
  later they will."

How long is this going to take before we start to see progress?

- "That depends on a lot of factors. This isn't a short journey with
  a defined destination. What's important is the fact that the journey starts, that our people recognize why we're doing this and
  know what's expected of them. We'll all begin to notice changes
  here before the market does, of course, but eventually they're
  going to notice. Small victories will lead to larger ones as these
  changes take hold and are recognized in the market."

How will we know if it's working?

- "We'll know. Any changes in how we've always done things here
  are going to be easy to spot."

- "We'll sense it in our discussions with our people. We'll know it when we hear our people using our desired Must Say language and when they hear us using it."
- "We'll hear it from our customers and we'll notice our negative noise starting to fade."
- "You'll see me smiling more. And when our numbers improve and continue to improve, we'll all be smiling more."

How do we make this happen? (Or: How do we enforce required behaviors?)

- "With a great implementation team leading the way."
- "We'll be ramping up the frequency of our communication with our people and we'll be continuously discussing our Must Say language and Must Do actions."
- "Everyone working here—leaders included—will come to realize that when we say 'Must Say' and 'Must Do,' we mean it, without exceptions. Adherence to these will be a requirement for working here."
- "Managers/team leaders will be required to set the right examples every day and ensure that their people know what's expected of them and are participating in our efforts. Our Visible Passion will become theirs."
- "We, as leaders, will also need to continuously monitor and encourage one another."
- "As we move forward, we'll be discussing more ways we can create a more positive working culture and reduce turnover by helping our people feel a sense of belonging here."
- Discuss how Weapons of Mass Attraction will improve your working culture.

How can we expect our people to be passionate about our dull industry?

- "Remember, at the end of the day, everything in business comes down to people doing business with people. Given a choice, we all prefer to do business with people we like."
- "As simple as it sounds, the bottom line is that if customers just happen to like us more than anyone else, we win."

- "Just look at Chick-fil-A. All they're selling is a fried chicken sandwich, and if there was something exciting about that, everyone would be selling them."
- "If we're Visibly Passionate and our customers sense we're awesome people to do business with, they're going to prefer us. If we delight customers in ways our competitors can't or won't, they'll reward us."
- "It's up to us to maintain an atmosphere here where Visible Passion becomes engrained in our DNA. This is very doable."

How will we handle naysayers?

- (It almost goes without saying—almost—that it's important to be prepared for naysayers among your fellow leaders, or those intent on raising obstacles or voicing major concerns about our N3PS journey. In a family business, this stuff's almost guaranteed. It's best to be aware that many of these comments will be coming from a place of discomfort. As in, "I like the way things are now, so why do we have to do this and why do we have to do this now?" Or, "I just don't see our people supporting something like this.")
- "When we raise the bar and our people see us striving to make our N3PS real, they're going to model our behavior. As long as we continuously communicate what we expect from our people and show them support and encouragement, they'll put forth the extra effort in tandem with ours."
- "Combined with a few bombs of Mass Attraction, a raised bar is a welcome sight. It pushes people forward."
- "Our people will support our N3PS efforts if they see us living up to them. They'll model our behavior and feel good about it. And they'll also know that this is the bare minimum requirement for maintaining employment."
- "It's best to remind naysayers that people working at any organization, regardless of size, naturally perform to the level of what's expected of them. Meaning, they do what their leaders do and what their leaders expect or tolerate."

What about employees who never have contact with customers? How involved with the N3PS will they need to be?

- "Everyone in the organization, regardless of their responsibilities, will be fully involved. At minimum, people will need to be conversant on our Must Says and understand their meaning. The same goes for our Must Dos. Even people who never speak with customers have opportunities to be ambassadors for our business."

- "Remember that the way customers see us is a direct reflection of our culture, so we need to ensure that everyone's working together, understanding what we're doing, and knowing why we're doing it."

Approximately one week after the initial presentation to leadership and after their input has been reviewed, you and your leadership team will reconvene to create a "final" document, incorporating the best and most appropriate improvements over prior documents, as determined by the team. This is the document that will be shared with all employees in small businesses, or shared with the N3PS Implementation Team in larger businesses.

Remember: Don't move ahead until everyone on your leadership or Implementation Team is in agreement with your N3PS.

PHASE TWO: ROLLOUT TO EMPLOYEES

All-hands meetings and new programs/initiatives rollouts are standard fare with most businesses and some of what you're about to read—especially if you're at a big corporation—might seem obvious. But sharing with employees your intention to reposition your business along with the directives within your N3PS is far from standard fare. This isn't the time to go business as usual. And it's an even worse time to go half-fast.

I once attended an N3PS rollout at a four-hundred-employee manufacturing business that I was promised would be exciting and well done. It was anything but. Put simply, the top leaders hadn't practiced their presentations with each other and everything came off sloppy, disorganized, and amateurish (though they each told me before showtime, "Yeah, yeah. I've got it covered"). The audience was clearly bored and disinterested, a presenter's worst nightmare. For every positive step company leadership had made in developing their N3PS, their presentation was taking them two steps backward.

I wangled my way to the front of the room and did my best to resuscitate the crowd, then—because I wasn't intimately familiar with what leadership had prepared for their presentation—engaged the presenters in some Q&A that allowed us to collectively discuss the elements of their N3PS, while incorporating lots of examples their people could identify with. We saved the day and the embarrassed leadership team learned some hard lessons about the need to be sharp, prepared, and on-point with their people.

This isn't going to happen with you. Here are some recommendations to make your N3PS rollout a smash hit right out of the gate.

To the extent it's possible, make your rollout a mandatory, all-hands meeting. The word "mandatory" sends a clear message that something big is about to happen. But you don't want employees to think your meeting is going to be in any way typical or communicate some bad news. Because this is a very big deal for your business, a celebratory tone should be used in every facet of the meeting, from the invite right through to adjournment. You're not simply inviting your people to an all-hands meeting, you're inviting them to the start of something that's going to change every facet of your business in a positive way.

While it's not a necessity, I'd never dissuade you from creating (or, more likely, having someone else create) a slogan or logo to support your N3PS communication efforts. Something like "Our new journey begins now." Again, anything that says this isn't business as usual is likely to be noticed and remembered.

Plan on having snacks and beverages available because they instantly lift spirits and get people talking and relaxed (plus you never know when I'm going to show up). Have walk-in music playing as people enter the meeting room as this, too, sends a signal that something out of the ordinary is happening. Speaking of out of the ordinary, I've attended a few rollout meetings where leaders rode into their meeting rooms on their Harleys. You'd better believe the audiences roared their approval. That's not something you see every day. I also attended one where the leaders rode in on little foot-powered scooters. Same reaction.

I know you're getting it. This is a big day for your business. Years from now, you'll want your employees to be able to look back and remember when they first learned about how they were going to stop following the crowd and start dominating. Make sure to have someone take a few photos to memorialize the meeting because later on, I promise, you'll be glad you have them.

Depending on the size of your leadership team, consider having several members serving as presenters so your people see that you've made this a priority and that leadership is an allied front on this. You might have a separate leader present each section of your N3PS, for example. Anyone with poor speaking skills—and you know who they are—should have minimal, if any, podium time. I can't stress this one enough. For leaders fitting that description who would be conspicuous in their absence, I always advise hiring a speaker training professional because the benefits far outweigh the investment. (Just think, the cost for a day of speaker training for the ill-prepared leadership team I spoke of a minute ago would have been far less than the costs associated with shutting their manufacturing lines down for a few hours so employees could be bored half to death. I train when it fits my schedule, go to my website for info. I'm always happy to refer other trainers, too.)

The bottom line on this is, you want your very best presenter(s) doing the lion's share of the speaking. There's no shame in the top exec opening the meeting then turning the floor over to more dynamic speakers.

You've already got an outline and some visuals in the can from your all-hands leadership meeting, so fine-tune your existing language and sharpen up your visuals as necessary. Plus you have the benefit of knowing what went over well and where you may have stumbled a bit with your explanations and visuals, thus making course adjustments easier.

No matter if the presentation will be a solo gig or a group effort, consider it mandatory to practice until it's seamless and to the point where, if you had to, you could present without any notes or cheat sheets. You know how I feel about practice. And every speaker training pro on the planet feels the same way. Carson, Leno, Letterman—some of the best speakers ever—never gave a monologue without rehearsing it.

As you're preparing your outline/scripts for your rollout, take into account the questions asked by your leadership team when you first shared this with them, as questions after a presentation are often about items that weren't presented clearly or where details were lacking. So be sure to cover those questioned items carefully in your all-hands meetings. Also, you and your leadership team should think of tough questions your people may ask, agree on how they should be answered, and rehearse your answers. Nothing breeds employee confidence faster than leaders who confidently chew through questions.

If a question comes up that completely stumps the presenters, it's appropriate to say, "Wow. That's a tough question. We're still in the early stages with this, so we'll find the answer to your question and share it with you as soon as we have it."

Remember: Everybody at every level of every business understands "competition." The Competitive Noise section of your rollout will likely generate the most audience interest and attention because they're confronting—most likely for the first time—precisely what they're up against. This also makes the "why" behind your initiatives more memorable. Make sure to have visuals of your competitors' home pages along with any other visuals—photos of marketing materials, ads, signage, delivery trucks—to drive your messages home as you're discussing this section.

Also remember: It's always a good idea to manage expectations and remind your people from time to time that everything you'll be doing together as you go forward is going to be completely new to your business and, quite possibly, new to your industry and/or market. As with our long motorcycle journey, you're going to be on side roads all the way, checking them out to see where they lead. Some roads will be great, but occasionally you'll try one that requires some rerouting. This isn't a bad thing at all, as long as people know they'll have the opportunity to be involved in the rerouting and as long as everyone in the organization is informed when changes are made.

Whether you're presenting to a dozen people or a cast of thousands, ask the same kind of questions you asked in your leadership rollout, so they'll remain engaged and thoughtful. "What do you think happens when every business we compete against describes what they do the same way?" "If you were starting your own business today, would you want potential customers to believe you're the same as your already-established competitors? Of course not!"

For businesses with multiple locations and a cross-functional N3PS Implementation Team, where meetings are common and typically well done, most of the recommendations you just read will apply. Whenever possible, it's best that employees get their first exposure to the N3PS process through the top leader and in person. If that's not possible, I suggest having him or her speak in a short, high-energy video to introduce the initiative, before an N3PS Implementation Team member takes over. Emphasis on "high energy," as it's important to not only set the tone for what's about to be shared, but also to make clear that this is the top priority of the business, being directed by the top leader. If you're going the video route, please make it brief and make it powerful. Use a professional video crew. I'm asking that on behalf of your audience.

To further deepen understanding and buy-in, be sure, as you're presenting your Must Say and Must Do directives, not just to explain the why behind each directive, but to offer examples of how and when they'll be used and who, specifically (person, department, etc.), will be using them. Recalling our FirstCall construction pals, their leadership would make sure to share with employees that it's the job site foreman's responsibility to ensure that everyone working on the site knows who the English-speaking reps are and that any customers or vendors on the site are personally walked over to that rep and introduced. "If we want our customers to tell others that we treated them like family, we have to live up to that, with no exceptions."

Lest anyone forget: It's the expectation of leadership that all employees, regardless of their position and responsibilities, will be conversant on the company's Must Say and Must Do directives, even if they're never in contact with customers or prospects. And that adherence to these directives is a condition of employment. Why? "You never know when that person standing behind you in line at the grocery store and asking about where you work might be our next big customer or a great new employee. So we've all got to be saying the same things about our business. This isn't hard at all."

Before closing the meeting, open it to Q&A and be sure everyone knows that their suggestions or concerns are always welcome, wanted, and valued. If you're doing multiple meetings and if any employees in previous meetings made suggestions you've incorporated into your N3PS, be sure to mention that. It'll add further weight to your requests for input.

Close the meeting by saying you'll be gathering with all company leaders—area supervisors, team leaders, department heads, anyone with responsibility for managing people—to further discuss how to make N3PS directives a reality in their respective work areas. And let everyone know there will be regular communication to discuss progress and implementation in the days, weeks, and months ahead, and opportunities for everyone to offer input and make their voices heard.

This is paramount: Because the vibe people are feeling when the meeting ends is what they're going to remember most, do everything in your power to close on a high note, with lots of Visible Passion, as much excitement as you can muster, warm gratitude for the world's greatest employees, and promises of more information to come. Then send them off to the snack table so you can all enjoy some social time together.

PHASE THREE: MAKE SOME NOISE

Okay, Evel. You did it. You just cleared the launch ramp and you're flying. It's been a long time coming, so enjoy the moment. Your people know that change is afoot and they're going to be participating in it. They just don't know what that all means, exactly. What do you say we land this thing?

Given that every business is different and that size and scale impact every aspect of a business's culture, I'd need a thousand more chapters to route a course that every business could follow to make adherence to N3PS initiatives in their organization as natural as breathing. Instead, I'll give you some absolutes that apply to all businesses. Besides, this isn't rocket science. Your business most likely has rolled out plans and initiatives in the past, offered training and retraining to make them standard operating procedures, and maintained standards for what is and isn't acceptable.

Your N3PS initiatives can pretty much follow your established norms for rolling out new programming, only with more enthusiasm and—key to success—accountability. These absolutes will help.

1. People Support What They Help Create

Within days of your rollout to your employees, all leaders within the organization should hold meetings with their teams to discuss specifically how your N3PS impacts their work areas, their individual work responsibilities, and what's going to be expected of them going forward. Leaders must take advantage of this opportunity—and all subsequent meetings with their people—to seek input and ideas from their people and allow them to voice any concerns.

It's very common for employees, especially those who are customer-facing and speak with customers every day, to have superb suggestions for tweaking Must Say language so it flows more naturally in their conversations. That goes quadruple for marketing and sales people. Leaders who wish to see team input continue over time won't miss these great opportunities to offer positive acknowledgment to all employees who offer ideas and suggestions (Weapons of Mass Attraction).

Employees who aren't customer-facing are often the first to ask—trust me, you'll hear this—"Why do I need to know this?" or "What's this got to do with me?" This is the time to reinforce the importance of everyone in the organization pulling in the same direction, saying the same things, and being able to describe what others are doing.

"We can't dominate competitors unless we're all speaking the same language and able to describe what we do here and why." Emphasize that, sooner or later, every employee will talk to customers or potential customers, to say nothing of potential employees. It's also the time to reinforce the notion that none of your N3PS directives are optional. And, of course, "I'd love to hear your ideas."

I'll mention here that over my years at Harley-Davidson, I'd often receive hand-drawn ideas for ads or marketing campaigns from manufacturing workers that showed a lot of insight and imagination. They understood, "We're all in this together and I can contribute."

As soon as is feasible after these discussions have taken place, an all-hands leadership meeting should be held to discuss the best and most actionable of employee suggestions with the goal of having a "final" N3PS by the close of the meeting. "Final" is in quotes because, remember, nothing's ever final and revisions may be made at any point when they're deemed necessary. In instances where leaders disagree on suggestions or what should be considered "final," the buck always stops with the top leader. Please don't overanalyze this and bog down. Make the decision and bang the gavel.

Leaders will then present the final N3PS Must Say and Must Do directives to their work teams with the expectation that the directives are effective immediately and the understanding that they are responsible for their implementation. If changes to the document are the result of employee suggestions, be sure leaders communicate that to their charges so employees know their input is being taken seriously by everyone in leadership.

2. Expect Some Rerouting

There are going to be some missteps and stumbles as directives begin to roll out and take hold. Count on it. If trying something new worked as desired every time (see: New Coke, Pepsi Clear, McDonald's Arch Deluxe, Microsoft Zune) leaders wouldn't be needed and life would get boring in a hurry. That's why nothing's ever "final."

Remember what I said about long motorcycle trips and how it's great to explore some side roads, just to see where they lead? Well, remind yourself—and constantly remind your people—that your N3PS journey is composed *entirely* of side roads, many of which will be great. So it's wise to assume you'll experience some rough patches and the need for some tweaking or a reroute or two along the way. No biggie. That stuff's just part of the experience. As long as lessons learned from mistakes are shared with others in your organization who have the potential to repeat them, those trials are invaluable. And if the folks involved in the mistakes are involved in rerouting to better options, then you're running like a well-oiled machine.

3. Thoroughness Counts More than Speed

The two most frequent words I use when leaders express challenges with bringing their N3PS to life? "Slow down." When it comes to full-scale workplace initiatives, I always say it's better to think in terms of "rolling thunder" rather than "big bangs." Aggressively pushing for immediate buy-in and participation—big bangs—too often causes resistance because no two people, leaders included, adapt to change at the same rate.

If some of your people aren't embracing new responsibilities and leadership's expectations as quickly as you'd like, this likely means they don't fully understand what's expected of them (as opposed to intentionally not playing along, which rarely happens). Emphasizing thoroughness when educating your people, encouraging them, and modeling your Must Say and Must Do directives, allows the changes to take hold organically. So take your time and offer tons of encouragement. As your early adopters grasp the changes and receive praise and boosts to their self-esteem for doing so, others will begin to follow their lead. That's a certainty. Like rolling thunder, momentum will build across your workplace as everyone begins to model your desired behaviors.

4. Enforce Accountability at All Levels—Especially with Leaders

Having once owned a business with four others years ago, I saw how we collectively learned the hard way what happens if anyone in leadership believes he or she doesn't need to participate in improvement initiatives ("I'm just too busy!"). The bottom line in this dynamic is confusion in the work culture and the resentment that builds when people wonder why they have to participate while others feel they don't. I know that's not hard to imagine.

Therefore it's incumbent on the top leader to act quickly at any sign of leaders not enthusiastically participating and modeling your N3PS desired behaviors. Often, participation that doesn't meet top leadership's expectations is simply a matter of individual leaders not fully grasping their roles and responsibilities, which can be addressed in one-on-one sessions with those people. Beyond that, leaders who intentionally aren't participating need to be treated in accordance with your standard procedures for disciplining employees not performing at levels required for employment.

This needs to be said: One way or another, and no matter the size of the business, word spreads far and wide anytime an employee at any level has been disciplined. Or, way worse, "separated" from the business. People talk and everyone gets the message that accountability is being taken seriously. Nobody wants to be the next person gossiped about.

Here's something else everyone talks about: If we're putting in the effort to take on new workplace challenges, yet see no negative ramifications for someone who isn't, we complain among ourselves. Worse, we may start to revert to our old behavior. This is why I always say accountability is seen as a positive among dominance-seeking businesses. Absent accountability, you're hampering your ability to improve competitiveness and setting your entire organization up for disappointment.

Encourage often. Act swiftly to squelch personnel problems. It's as simple (on paper) as that.

I'll not delve into it here, but you might want to consider creating incentives such as gifts, cash bonuses, or some other form of variable compensation to create that perfect balance of an organization whose members know they can be rewarded for generating improvements and know what they're risking by not doing that. And to be sure, those incentives partially help answer the ever-popular employee refrain, "What's in it for me?"

5. Don't Hit the Street Until You're Running Right

Resist the temptation to take your new messaging to your external publics until you're confident that your organization can consistently deliver on your Must Say and Must Do directives. As everyone knows, overpromising and underdelivering is hazardous to your health, yet easy to do.

While leaders are working with their people to bring your directives to life throughout your organization, the folks charged with marketing and external communication should be crafting their strategies to bring your new messaging to market via all of your go-to-market channels (website, social media, brochures, newsletters, ads, etc.) when there is consensus among leadership that the organization is in fighting shape to back up your new claims and promises. Again, think rolling thunder instead of expensive big bangs, so you can make course corrections along the way if needed.

Your leaders (or Implementation Team) will know when your organization is external launch-ready.

6. Promote. Repeat. Promote. Repeat.

Why does McDonald's bother advertising? Or Budweiser? Do they think there's someone out there who doesn't know about them? Of course not. They're smarter than that and aren't spending hundreds of millions of dollars each year for kicks. They're working to stay top of mind with their target markets and keep everyone thinking about them, so they're continuously sharing and resharing their messaging to do that.

You have the same challenge, only right now, your target market is your organization. Use every channel of communication you have to ensure your Must Say, Must Do directives are always in sight of your people, supported with words of encouragement and success stories. Take full advantage of bulletin boards, electronic signs in manufacturing plants, employee intranet, paycheck stuffers, and newsletters. If you've got employee communications pros on staff, harness their talent. Encourage leaders to open any of their department or team meetings with quick N3PS updates and success stories, so their people know this is a vital part of your business and their jobs.

I remember Rich Teerlink (great human being), who was the CEO of Harley-Davidson during the most dramatic turnaround years, opening every employee or leadership meeting with an overhead that listed the company's values and a quick pep talk about them. Every meeting. He understood that if he wasn't a Visibly Passionate cheerleader for one of the major building blocks of the company's improvement strategy, nobody else would be, either. That carries a lot of weight.

When leaders stop talking about something, employees do, too. When top brass stops supporting something, everyone else assumes they can too (Saturn, anybody?). Which leads me to . . .

7. Feedback Is Your Fuel

Part of the beauty of your N3PS is that it feeds on input. Look how far it's taken you already. Regularly scheduled leadership meetings for discussing status, success stories, and any stumbling blocks, based on feedback they're encouraging from their people, are a must. If N3PS discussions are going to be included as part of your customary weekly or biweekly leadership meetings, ensure they're always at the top of the agenda so they're always seen as top priority.

If an organization's top leader frequently asks first lieutenants for "What can I be doing better?" input and feedback, those leaders, in turn, will seek the same input from their own people. Never stop encouraging this.

And customers should be queried on what they like, what kinds of changes and improvements they've noticed in your business, and what they'd like to see you doing better (complaints are compliments, remember?) as a common element of your relationships with them. Please don't blow your opportunities to let customers know your value, and act on their input until after your service has been rendered or your product's been paid for. Ask and you shall receive. Acknowledge their input with praise and gratitude and they'll keep sharing. Sending them a survey later puts you back on the freeway, stuck in traffic.

But feedback isn't limited just to employees and customers. No way. Solicit feedback from suppliers, partners, your bank—anyone who knows you well. They've got eyes and ears, too, and perhaps some suggestions on what your business can be doing better. They also often learn of new business opportunities before you do, so it's best to be on uber-friendly, conversational terms with them instead of transactional terms.

The customer hasn't been invented yet who isn't pleased to hear that changes and improvements in your business resulted from customer-provided input. Substitute any of your stakeholders for "customer" in that sentence and the meaning is the same. "We did this because you asked us to" carries a ton of weight.

In most organizations, customer and other stakeholder feedback never moves beyond the employees' ears that first heard it. That's just wrong. The reasons are known to everyone who's ever been a leader: Employees typically have nobody to tell and no incentive to speak up because they've never seen such feedback acted on before. Dominators have zero tolerance for such nonsense.

The onus is on leaders at all levels to get input from their people, encourage them (with Weapons of Mass Attraction) to speak up and share what they're seeing and hearing, and, for the love of all that's good and sacred in the world, make sure this input reaches the ears of people who need to hear and act on it. Close the loop and further encourage employee feedback by sharing the results of any corrective actions taken as a result of this.

Imagine the look of surprise on the face of a customer who voiced a concern or a suggestion to an employee on a Monday and got a personal call from a company leader on Tuesday saying, "Thanks so much for bringing this to our attention. I can't tell you how valuable your comments are to us. What can I do for you in return?"

8. Continuously Deploy Weapons of Mass Attraction

No human in history ever said, "Please stop praising me." Encourage leaders in your organization to make a habit of giving their people what they need: Boosts to their self-esteem, blasts to their egos, and that glorious feeling of belonging and being wanted. And do it everywhere. Inside the walls of your business, on factory floors, in the warehouse, in the hallways, loading docks, lobbies, cafeterias, and (remember the leisure company CEO) in the elevator. Remember that the way people see your business is a direct reflection of your culture and that your culture is a reflection of your leadership.

Remember, too, that the primary objective of your repositioning efforts is to get people to like you more than your competitors. So deploy those weapons with abandon as you go to market. Let your Visible Passion shine in front of customers, at trade shows, on retail floors, and at job sites. Let it light up your website, where photos of delighted customers using your products, or employees rubbing elbows with customers, say a lot more than photos of products. And use it in your social media posts that read like friends talking to friends, rather than a business trying to drum up more business. And over the phone, where every voice heard is the official voice of your business.

Need a one-word reminder? "They."

A two-word reminder? "Surprise. Delight."

9. Teach Those Following You to Look Through the Turns

This is the essence of Noise Cubed and something that becomes habit quickly. When you and your people are asking, "What do I want to be remembered and repeated (R&R)?" before every encounter with important publics, you're thinking and acting like a dominator. One of the biggest challenges for leaders is to guide their people away from viewing the sale— the transaction—as their desired result. Businesses that post sales quotas and targets on their bulletin boards are doing themselves a disservice by promoting the idea, "This is what's most important to us. This is why we're here." Take that stuff down.

(True story: I was in a franchise store recently and saw a bulletin board posting urging employees to "Push hard for the sale so we can end our month with a record." Of course, there was no excuse for that being posted where a customer could see and be disgusted by it. Bigger picture: What employee, after reading that note, would react positively and feel encouraged to work harder? Would you?)

Sales are great, of course. But sales that result in customers loyally returning to you and referring you to other customers are greater. By far. When that's being measured and rewarded—a bulletin board posting we'd all like to see—the lessons take hold and the organization is thinking and working like a dominator.

10. Never Stop Pushing

What else is there to say? Like our old pal, Evel, with every safe landing, celebrate your achievement, then push the ramp back a little further and try something a little harder. With every not-so-great landing, learn from what went wrong, then move on. The challenge of being challenged is its own reward and an organization that grows accustomed to being pushed thrives on each new challenge.

You've got this thing. You're flying.

FOURTEEN

You'll Know Noise Cubed
Is Working for You When...

Before I venture off alone onto a side road and leave you and your team to continue this amazing journey we've shared and take it to places we haven't thought of yet, I need to answer the question you've wanted to ask since we first fired up our motors: "How will I know when Noise Cubed is working?"

First let me get the easiest and most obvious answer to that question out of the way. You'll know it's working when the metrics that are most important to you compare favorably to where you were prior to starting your journey. Like when: You're making more money; your profit margin improves; your market share improves; you're serving more people; existing customers are buying from you more frequently; more business comes your way via customer referrals; floor traffic, phone, and/or online inquiries increase; and your employee turnover decreases and the number of people seeking to work with you increases. You're probably tracking several of these already.

I get asked all the time about so-called Net Promoter Score metrics, because these things have become an accepted part of doing business and seem to mesh neatly with Noise Cubed initiatives. The questions always end with "This stuff's expensive. Should we be doing this?"

So I'll answer that right now: It depends.

Net Promoter Score programming is everywhere and I see it discussed at a lot of meetings I'm invited to attend. If you're unfamiliar, but travel a bit, you know what it looks like because airlines and hotels are heavy users. The underlying premise of promoter scores, gained primarily by online surveys, is "Based on your recent experience with our business, how likely would you be to recommend us to someone?" Given that, I can see why so many folks naturally assume I'm a fan, given that it seems to be in synch with creating and monitoring Noise. Actually, I'm not.

Used as originally designed, I believe such scores can be quite valuable assuming—and this is huge—that their sponsors actually do something meaningful with their collected data. As in share it with all employees and identify areas for improvement that can be further monitored.

Too bad that doesn't seem to be happening very much anymore.

Most of the time now, when I'm with clients and they're showing me their score data, I feel the sudden urge to retch. My God! The wasted resources! So many of the companies using these metrics have learned how to water down or sandbag the questions to lead respondents to click a favorable response, which renders the data meaningless. Unless—ahem—it's being used to determine variable compensation for company leadership.

I've watched employees roll their eyes as the information is presented, as if to say, "Yeah, great. What's this got to do with me?" Because it *has* nothing to do with them, since leadership hasn't created an environment where customer responses impact individual workers and their responsibilities. And they've collectively seen what started as a means to gain valuable customer feedback reduced to "data that we can share at meetings to show we're serious about tracking customer satisfaction."

So it's becoming an increasingly rare day when someone reporting findings can answer an obvious question: How does the data become actionable? If I fill in my office products supplier's promoter score survey and report that, based on my recent experience with their website, there's only a fifty-fifty chance I'd recommend them, what, exactly, are they going to do with that? If they don't reach out later to ask why—and I've never received a query from any business I've given less than positive marks asking what they'd have to do better to please me and earn a higher score—well, was that data worth paying for?

That's why I say "It depends" when asked about these things. Tell me you're going to use the data consistently, as a means to identify areas in need of improvement—and immediately take steps to rally your troops to improve them—and I'm all in. Tell me you're going to use the data to praise and reward the people behind your stellar feedback scores, then rally them to push those positive scores even higher, and I'm doubly all in. Tell me otherwise and you've lost me.

To tell you the truth, here's how I answer the "How will I know Noise Cubed is working?" question. It never fails to connect.

At least once per year, I do something I'd like to see more people do, leaders especially: I get completely off the grid and disappear. I don't know about you, but I treasure any opportunity I have to take myself, quite literally, away from it all. So I make it a point to find someplace to go where I'll see no signs of my "real" world of work-related stuff like metrics, calendars, to-do lists, balance sheets, people who think they're important, meetings, deadlines, responsibility, stress, and missed dinners. The kind of place where I won't have access to newspapers, TV, or even radio and, above all, my digital, email-driven life. A place where I can feel completely human, yet responsible to no one other than myself.

My favorite escape is to get lost and stay that way for as long as I can by vanishing deep into the natural world, where nobody can find me without some real effort. Not only does this clear my head, but it also serves the dual purpose of making it way easier for me to focus on work when I return.

Wallowing in nature allows me to turn off my internal clocks, decompress from daily anxiety, halt my brain's constant need to worry about numbers, and, best of all, remind myself just how insignificant I am in the grand scheme of things. I might lose myself on a remote Canadian lake or somewhere off the coast of New Zealand with nothing but fishing gear and a cooler of beer, or chasing elk with my bow up and down the steep, wooded mountains of Colorado, or lazily snorkeling off some desolate South American beach that hasn't been developed and commercialized. My grandest dream is to ride a motorcycle up, over, and under the western shore of Norway until the road runs out, then snowmobile the rest of the way to the North Pole. Soon. (Find me if you're up for this.)

We've reached the point in our evolution—if you can call it that—where a person has to search long and hard to find a place that doesn't have Wi-Fi, let alone TV, but please believe me when I tell you it's worth the effort and that you'll return from any off-grid adventure a better person than you were previously.

Every adventure I've enjoyed has enriched my life and left me with a surplus of great memories and stories. I'd like to share one of those stories with you now and not just because it's my all-time favorite. As you're about to see, it also has a direct parallel to the power of Noise Cubed and answers, quite beautifully, "How will I know if it's working?"

It goes like this.

When you get a minute, look up a tiny band of specks in the Indian Ocean about 250 miles off the southern tip of India called the Maldives (and begin planning a trip there as a reward for all you're doing to become a dominator). You'll have to look hard. Since you're probably unfamiliar, the Maldives comprise roughly one thousand miniature coral islands amid a few dozen atolls—ring-shaped reefs of varying shades of blue that your eyes have likely never seen before and that are so stunningly beautiful your mind will tell you they can't be real.

Very few of those tiny islands are developed or inhabited by humans and those that are tend to be home to intimate beach resorts reachable only by floatplanes or small boats from the Maldives' main island of Male. As luck would have it, I'd been invited to stay at just such a resort and there was no way I was going to pass it up. This, to me, represented the best possible type of escape and the kind of place where I could completely disappear into the unknown. The timing, you're about to see, couldn't have been more perfect.

After an exhausting three-day ride home in scorching August heat from an even more exhausting Sturgis rally, my wife and I boarded a plane that would carry us some nine thousand miles in a little more than thirty-six hours of travel time, including a long layover in Doha, Qatar, to Male. Once there, we boarded a small floatplane for the final stretch to our tiny coral island home for the next week. The views from the floatplane were so spectacular we quickly forgot our long hours wedged into seats on those long-distance flights. I've never seen anything so dictionary-level awesome.

Our floatplane skittered atop the water before dropping us off at the pier serving an island so small a person could swim around its perimeter in less than twenty minutes. I know this is true because I watched a pale-skinned man in a too-small Speedo—a chain-smoking boozehound no less—do it with ease. There might have been twenty-five guests in total at the resort, being served by twenty-five employees working there. So figure no more than fifty human beings on this little rock in the middle of the Indian Ocean.

We settled into our beach hut and washed away our jet lag in our own private pool (oh, did I forget to mention this was royalty-level luxury?) then we sat under a cabana, enjoying a never-ending happy hour and looking at water so clear it was invisible. Seriously, the water was so clear that when fish and rays swam past, they looked like they were floating on air because you couldn't see the water. It didn't seem possible. And relaxing? Dear God, yes. Nothing but nature at her absolute finest, complete silence, minimal clothing, and fine food and drink. (Who's in?)

Suddenly, things got weird.

While watching the sky change colors as the sun set and losing myself in the calm and the visual treats, something caught my eye that, literally, made me choke on my beer. My wife and I shot instant, shocked looks at each other and said, "Oh my God" in unison as there, walking toward us on the beach, came a man who couldn't possibly be real. Not here. And most certainly, not now. He appeared to be Indian—judging by his black beard and turban—which, for reasons you'll soon read, was half of what was knocking me backward. The other half was the black T-shirt the dude was wearing. It read "Sturgis 2012."

As in Sturgis 2012, the motorcycle rally I'd just left less than a week earlier from the middle of nowhere in South Dakota. Let's quickly review those numbers again. To get away from anything that reminded me of my work life—and after three days in my bike saddle—I traveled more than nine thousand miles to the other side of the world, in thirty-six-plus hours of travel time, to reach an island smaller than a football field that hosted, at best, twenty-five visitors. *Only to run into someone who just came from the exact same tiny spot I'd just left.* The odds of this have to be one in billions, don't they?

Making the calculus more impossible for me was the fact that the T-shirt-wearing beach bum was Indian. Impossible because, up until 2010, Harley-Davidson was not permitted to sell motorcycles in India and, as such, was just beginning to establish a toehold there. So at the time when I saw him approaching, there were but four Harley dealerships serving a country five times larger than Texas and home to more than 1.3 billion people. Maybe one hundred bikes had been purchased in India so far and this guy, quite possibly, had one of them.

Now the booze started talking—or in this case, yelling—and I hollered out, "There's no way you were at Sturgis!" and the guy slammed to a halt before jogging up, offering his hand, and excitedly introducing himself as Kochar. Like my wife and me, he was beyond shocked to learn we'd both just come from the same place. He gladly accepted our offer of a chair and a cocktail, then began telling a story that will delight me until my last breath.

He told us that he and a bunch of his lifelong pals had always had bikes growing up in Bangalore, then through college and into their professional lives. They were mostly small Indian bikes, like Royal Enfields and Heros, and Japanese makes, which they'd used as their primary source of transportation, just as billions of people in India and Asia do every day. He said they loved to tinker with their bikes to make them go faster so they could race them, go on long-distance group rides, and have even more fun.

"We'd all heard about Harleys over the years, of course, and read about them in bikes magazines," he said. "And we'd always say, 'One day, we're going to go to America, ride Harleys through the West like cowboys, and end up at the massive rally in Sturgis.' "

I should mention here, only because it's good fun, that mythical cowboy imagery—think longhorn steers, horses, cactus, tumbleweeds, and wide-open spaces—has long been an attractant to motorcyclists living outside the United States, especially those from densely populated areas. You can understand that, right?

Kochar then explained how he and seven pals searched online and found a Harley dealer in Boise, Idaho, with eight bikes to rent, so they convinced each other "it's now or never," somehow sold their wives on the idea that they'd be going on a long vacation trip without them (that's not easy, trust me), bought their tickets, and flew to America. I still find it amusing that, of all the places in my country where they could have started their journey, they wound up in Boise, Idaho. I love Boise, mind you, but let's just say it's probably not top-of-mind for America-bound visitors the way Vegas, Los Angeles, New York, and Chicago are. You know what I mean.

His story kept getting progressively better. He said the local Boise Harley dealer picked him and his pals up at the airport and brought them back to his shop to get them set up on bikes and ready for their two-wheeled adventure. "We were getting the rock star treatment, which was really cool," he said, smiling over the top of his beer. "They weren't used to having brown-skinned Indians in their store, so they rolled out the red carpet and had snacks and stuff for us. We took lots of pictures and answered a ton of questions about riding in India. And the people in the shop gave us lots of suggestions on routes and places to see."

More color followed. "Everywhere we went as we headed north out of Idaho, into Oregon, Washington, Montana, and Wyoming, people would wave to us. Everyone in that part of the country is used to seeing thousands of Harley riders heading toward Sturgis, but not riders who look like us. They'd approach us at gas stations and food stops, ask where we were from, where we were headed, and if we were enjoying our time in America. We met so many cool people, went to so many amazing places, and explored one great road after another. People just love to talk to guys riding Harleys and there's no better way to see America. It's the ultimate freedom, man."

It's important to note that he had absolutely no idea of my background.

To him I was just a fellow Harley rider who'd also gone to Sturgis. It's also worth noting that the entire time he was talking, he was animated, with an enormous ear-to-ear grin. Like me, he was clearly loving our exchange.

By the time he and his posse reached the Sturgis rally, he said, it was running about a half-million people strong. "It was a twenty-four-hour party, just insane," he said with a laugh. "We were so tired after days of long-distance riding, we needed to rest, but we just couldn't wait to check out the scene. So sleep had to wait. You could tell everyone else there felt the same way. Harley people just have so much passion for riding and living the lifestyle. Nobody wanted to miss out on anything."

That's fantastic stuff, but fine-tune your radar a bit and check this out: "On our first day there, we got to meet a bunch of people from Harley and even got autographs from some of the Davidsons," he continued. "Everyone was so friendly and made us feel like we were part of their family. When I told them I'm in the metal-bending business, they invited me to tour their factories and see how they transform metal into bikes. Some of my riding buddies are engineers, so they got introduced to some Harley engineers and they talked shop and compared jobs. It was really cool that we could find common ground so easily with them."

He said he and his posse went to see Mount Rushmore, did photo ops all over the place, took demo rides on a bunch of different models, bought tons of souvenirs, went to massive parties with thousands of people at outdoor saloons, and basically just "rode and partied our brains out." I asked if they experienced any nastiness and he swept that notion aside, saying, "Everyone made us feel welcome everywhere we went, nobody made us feel like outsiders, and not a single bad thing happened."

I was considering bragging about my long days and my long rides to and from Sturgis, until he explained that, after the rally, he and his posse wanted to see even more of America, so they made a game-day decision and hightailed it more than a thousand miles to Las Vegas—for just a few hours of partying—before blasting the final seven-hundred-plus miles to Boise. Even the most hard-core biker would say 1,700-plus miles in a day and a half is some superaggressive road work. Damn, these dudes ran hard! I'm sure they slept the entire flight home.

I was shaking my head in disbelief and thinking his story couldn't possibly get any better. Then he dropped an inadvertent showstopper: When I asked, "Of all the things you did in Sturgis and on your ride, what's the one thing that stands out as your best memory?" His response remains among the greatest things I've ever heard. "Oh, that's easy," he said. "We got to see

Lynyrd Skynyrd sing 'Sweet Home Alabama.' " I choked again on my beer and said, "What?!" He said, "We love Skynyrd, man!" (Who knew?)

I was laughing so hard I was drooling. Then he said, "But that's not the best part. The boys in Skynyrd saw us in the audience—I guess we were pretty easy to spot—and invited us back to meet them and get some pics and autographs after the show! It was unbelievable!" By the time I could say, "Oh come on man! No way!" he pulled out his camera and showed me the photos. Yep. There he and his pals were, hanging with the band and grinning like idiots who'd just won the lottery. I was in hysterics. Only in America, baby!

"Yeah," he said laughing, in the understatement of the century, "that was one hell of a night."

Please tell me your radar was pinging and that you noticed—as I most surely did—that his story was peppered with exactly the kinds of passion, energy, and Harley language that the folks who depend on Harley-Davidson to make a living, well, live for. He spoke of his extraordinary experiences. Of getting rock star treatment. Of family and belonging. Of passion, life-style, and freedom. Of being invited to tour factories (by Davidsons, no less). Of how he and his friends felt welcome everywhere they went. Of how great it is to see America on a Harley. Of how riding Harleys opens doors and encourages people to approach and talk to you. I couldn't have scripted his story any better than he'd told it.

Now here's something I bet you didn't notice that I couldn't miss: Never once during his story did Kochar speak specifically about "product." He didn't talk about the particular model of Harley he rented until I asked. Nor did he ever cite the specs of its motor, seat height, torque, horsepower, handlebar width, acceleration time, or stopping distance. And he never mentioned quality or reliability. Rather, his story contained what *all* stories contain: people, experiences, and how those people and experiences made him feel. And that kind of storytelling, as you know, is what separates dominators from also-rans.

But wait, as cool as this stuff is, as powerful as Kochar's stories were that night, and as glorious as the noise was, this story isn't over. We're about to look through the turns and watch this thing evolve into something even more extraordinary.

I'd had such a great time talking with Kochar and partying with him, his family, and his friends on the beach for the week—smoking hookahs, Bollywood dancing with them in traditional Indian garb into the wee hours, and learning about family life in Bangalore—I wanted to stay in touch with him. So four months after returning from the Maldives, he and I spoke over

Skype. While it was fun to see him again and enjoy a blast of his contagious enthusiasm, there's just no way I could've expected to hear what he'd tell me.

When I asked what he'd been up to since we went our separate ways home, he said he and his pals had started a riding club in Bangalore, the Pandhis (which is southern Indian dialect for "Hogs," a term you probably recognize as the generations-old affectionate nickname Harley riders give their machines) and that the requirement for membership in the Pandhis is ownership of a Harley. Bear in mind that, at the time, new Harleys were priced at more than twice what they'd cost in America, meaning they could easily exceed the equivalent of $40,000 or even $50,000 in India.

When I asked, "How many members do you have?" He said, "About one hundred fifty-five." Given that Harley's presence in India was still in its infancy—and considering those high prices—I was shocked this club was formed so quickly and had so many members. So I asked, "About how many of those hundred and fifty-five bikes do you believe you personally sold?" He didn't bat an eye and said, "All of them!" I laughed and said, "No, really, how many do you think you sold?" And then he laughed again and told me he wasn't kidding.

So, if you had to guess, what's Kochar worth to Harley-Davidson? What are his stories and passionate advocacy worth? Of course he likely didn't personally convince 154 people to travel a great distance to go to a dealership and buy an expensive bike. But, come on, even if he convinced only ten of them to make the move, what's he worth? How much influence does he—just one person—have in Bangalore? Just. One. Person. What did he start?

Can we not assume Kochar's riding pals from the Sturgis adventure are also telling similar stories? And ditto the new Pandhis?

And how do people in the crowded city of Bangalore react when they witness something they've never before seen nor heard: large groups of riders rumbling by on shiny new Harleys?

And how many of them, after witnessing this and noticing that everyone else on the street was watching and listening, too, will dream tonight of riding a Harley of their own?

The next time I heard from Kochar, he and some pals were riding rental Harleys in Europe and conquering some of my favorite roads through the Alps (I love this guy!). I and hundreds of others followed their adventures and lived the experience vicariously through Kochar's frequent Facebook photos and updates. Comments shared by his friends were priceless: "Take me next time!" "Jealous!" "That's so cool!" "Harleys!" Once again, his stories were inspiring others and creating demand. And I'm sure his riding friends' stories were, too. The math gets compelling, doesn't it? Such is the power and beauty of noise.

Let's bust out a simple scoresheet and, based only on Kochar's stories, see how Harley-Davidson might answer the "How do you know when Noise Cubed is working?" question:

Is the business clearly differentiated from competitors? *Check.*

Was there clear evidence of Must Do and Must Say directives? *Check.*

Did customers/important publics enjoy story-worthy experiences? *Check.*

Was contagious Visible Passion on display? *Check.*

Did company leadership model desired employee behavior? *Check.*

Did employees model leadership behavior? *Check.*

Did leaders and employees make people (not products) their main focus? *Check.*

Were customers/important publics made to feel welcome and special? *Check.*

Did customers/important publics enjoy boosts to their self-esteem? *Check.*

Did they feel a sense of belonging? *Check.*

Are customers/important publics loyally returning to source of their joy? *Check.*

Are they telling others about the source of their joy? *Check and double check.*

Back, then, to your nagging question, "How will I know when Noise Cubed is working?" My answer, even if you're not using metrics or a simple scoresheet like the one I just showed you, will always be "Just listen for the echo. You'll know. Believe me, you'll know."

More specifically and with no math required, you'll know your Noise Cubed efforts are working when:

People you serve say they've noticed positive changes in how your business operates.

Your fellow employees routinely discuss your business's competitiveness and reputation and how they can be further improved.

You routinely see and hear your fellow employees emphasizing humanity—putting people first and visibly striving to meet their needs—over whatever your business produces and/or sells.

Customers you historically served are doing business with you more frequently than in the past.

Your fellow employees are more comfortable speaking up and offering improvement suggestions than they were before.

You feel a swell of positive attitudes, hustle, and momentum among your fellow employees that you hadn't felt before.

Customer/important public social media commentary and media coverage increases and includes your Must Say language, meaning you're controlling your narrative.

You're doing more business with new customers referred by existing customers.

You're focused more on how your business can create more distance from competitors than wondering what they'll do next.

You're worried less about *everything*.

That's all pretty simple stuff, isn't it? Why complicate it? Remember, you're not looking to put a spacecraft on Uranus or cure all infectious diseases. What you're doing is making your business more competitive so you can dominate those who choose to march in lockstep with one another. And you're well on your way.

Let me lay something else on you.

At a recent meeting in Nashville, I caught up with a business owner I'd worked with two years earlier and asked him to describe his job. How he answered should tell you everything you need to know about what great leaders do, how Noise Cubed becomes engrained in a business's DNA, and, bottom line, why we work.

He didn't say, as most do, something to the tune of "My job is to drive revenue growth, create demand for our products, ensure a great working environment for our people, provide excellent after-sale service, and continuously improve all facets of our operation." I can virtually guarantee he'd have spewed predictably bland corporate-speak like that a few years ago when we'd first met. But not anymore.

What he said was so much better, it's how I'll close our time together.

"I'm one hundred percent responsible for what people living in my community say, think, and believe to be true about my business, the people who work there, the people we serve, and the products we sell," he said. "Which means we can't run our business the way our competitors run theirs or describe what we do the same way they do. We have to be seen as way different than they are, and it's my job to make sure that we *are* different than they are. We need to maintain a great atmosphere where everyone we come in contact with can sense our passion and energy so they'll feel good when they're with us, come back often, and refer us to their friends."

He wasn't done. "This means I have to model the behavior and attitudes our people need to exhibit every day or none of this will happen. And we need to actively encourage more frequent use of what we sell, to keep our customers engaged and coming back, which means we need to continuously share our expertise and passion with them and be their primary source of information." Then, the clincher: "I'm not running this business to win. I want to dominate our market. Otherwise, what's the point?"

You're probably thinking this guy's helming a famous-name business like Tesla or Rolex. Or maybe a Harley dealership. Something really trendy and cool? Nope. He's an audiologist. His business sells an expensive brand of hearing aids. He competes against big-box stores, multiple local franchises, and hundreds of online, low-priced players. He has four employees and doesn't have an advertising budget. It's not a coincidence that he and his business are making some beautiful noise and that—there's no other way to say it—he's killing it.

He also said something that brought a huge smile to my face. When I asked how he knows his efforts to make noise are working, he said he asks a simple question to all first-time visitors to his operation: "Who told you about us?" Note the "who." That's a heckuva lot different than the more traditional "How'd you hear about us?" Increasingly, he said, his new clients give him the name of a client who referred them. And the referring client? Within days, he or she receives in the mail a coffee shop gift certificate along with a thank-you note signed by everyone working at the business. That's a lot cheaper than buying ads, he said.

So on that note, my friend, this is where our ride together ends and we go our separate ways. You're going to continue your journey to dominance and I'm going to take the long way to my next adventure. In case nobody's told you, the road work you've done so far is stellar, your confidence is showing, and you're looking good. So keep it up. Get on the gas and stay on it, but leave the racing to the pros. Don't go so fast that you out-run your riding partners, risk a sloppy pileup, or miss those twisty side roads and the treasures they hold. You'll never know where they'll lead you if you don't take a look. Savor every mile.

I'll keep an eye out for you, but please don't be a stranger. Drop by my website or find me on LinkedIn and let me know how you're doing. The same goes if you need some inspiration or route recommendations. Or if you just want to meet up somewhere and do some riding. I'm always up for that.

Keep your helmet on and your head clear. Ride safe and demand that of everyone you're leading. Be noticeably different so people can see you. Be sure you always check your mirrors and look through the turns. Finally, have a lot more fun than you're supposed to and wave to riders coming from the opposite direction because, sooner or later, one of them will be me.

Later, gator.

Index

About the Author

KEN SCHMIDT is widely known as one of the business world's most outspoken and provocative thought leaders. As the former director of communications for Harley-Davidson Motor Company, he played an active role in one of the most celebrated corporate turnarounds in history—and got paid to ride motorcycles. Since 1999, he has delivered more than one thousand keynote presentations at industry meetings and has provided nontraditional consultation on improving competitiveness to more than one thousand businesses, from household-name giants to start-ups. He cowrote *100 Years of Harley-Davidson* with Willie G. Davidson, released in 2003. He lives in Washington, DC.